AUTHENTIC FAITH

AUTHENTIC FAITH

Bonhoeffer's Theological Ethics in Context

Heinz Eduard Tödt

Edited by
Ernst-Albert Scharffenorth

Translated by
David Stassen and Ilse Tödt

English edition edited by
Glen Harold Stassen

WILLIAM B. EERDMANS PUBLISHING COMPANY
GRAND RAPIDS, MICHIGAN / CAMBRIDGE, U.K.

First published 1993 as *Theologische Perspektiven nach Dietrich Bonhoeffer*
© Christian Kaiser/Gütersloher Verlagshaus

English translation © 2007 Wm. B. Eerdmans Publishing Co.

Published 2007 by
Wm. B. Eerdmans Publishing Co.
2140 Oak Industrial Drive N.E., Grand Rapids, Michigan 49505 /
P.O. Box 163, Cambridge CB3 9PU U.K.

Printed in the United States of America

12 11 10 09 08 07   7 6 5 4 3 2 1

Library of Congress Cataloging-in-Publication Data

Tödt, Heinz Eduard.
    [Theologische Perspektiven nach Dietrich Bonhoeffer. English]
    Authentic faith: Bonhoeffer's theological ethics in context / Heinz Eduard Tödt;
    edited by Ernst-Albert Scharffenorth; translated by David Stassen and Ilse Tödt.
        p.   cm.
    Includes bibliographical references.
    ISBN 978-0-8028-0382-5 (pbk.: alk. paper)
    1. Bonhoeffer, Dietrich, 1906-1945.
    I. Scharffenorth, Ernst-Albert.   II. Title.

BX4827.B57T6313   2007
230'.044092 — dc22

                                                          2007003411

www.eerdmans.com

Contents

Foreword from the Editors

Heinz Eduard Tödt was chair of the editorial board of the new critical edition of Dietrich Bonhoeffer's works in German and highly respected internationally for his Bonhoeffer scholarship. He was professor of theology and ethics at the University of Heidelberg, and lived through and personally experienced the times of Adolf Hitler's rule of Germany, the Holocaust, and World War II. He interprets Bonhoeffer in his context of struggle as no one else can now do.

I went to study under Heinz Eduard Tödt at the University of Heidelberg in 1981-82 because I believed he was the best theological ethicist in Germany, and what I learned from him solidly confirmed that judgment. Tödt's publications have an analytical sharpness, an ethical incisiveness, and a genuine truthfulness that is rare even among the best. His study of Dietrich Bonhoeffer is the climax of his career.

He unearths major dimensions of Bonhoeffer's ethics, and enables us to enter personally into the political, ecclesiastical, and family context in which Bonhoeffer wrote. As I read, I find myself drawn deeply into analysis of my own ethics, tested by Tödt's careful and incisive digging into Bonhoeffer's ethics and his context in ways that no one who did not participate in those struggles could duplicate. Tödt's own personal wrestle with guilt and forgiveness, and for an ethic that can guide us with the wisdom we deeply need in our own time of manipulation of faith for ideological ends, draws me into the struggle with deep personal identification. If you are raising questions as I am, this book will draw you into the struggle with a depth of feeling and insight as it has me.

Tödt achieves a precision in understanding key dimensions of Bonhoeffer's theological ethics that is hard to match elsewhere. He shows the meaning and importance of Bonhoeffer's diagnosis that our time needs a "religionless Christianity" — a Christianity not confined to ideals for private life or to gaps where we cannot solve problems — a Christian faith that gives concrete guidance in the center of life. He gives insightful depth of analysis of the context and meaning of Bonhoeffer's participation in an attempted coup to remove Adolf Hitler from power. In times that are not as totalitarian as the Third Reich, Bonhoeffer's ethic of resistance calls us to participation by means of law, justice, human rights, and group action in checking and balancing concentrations of power and the ideological and interest-based misuse of power.

But Tödt also focuses our attention on a more important question, less often studied: what was it about Bonhoeffer's ethics that enabled him to see more clearly and speak out more decisively than other theologians and church leaders — for all Jews and against war — from the very start of Hitler's rule? At that early time, when Hitler had not yet taken control of all parts of the society and had not yet made organized resistance impossible, checks and balances by church and group action could have made a difference. Tödt shows how Bonhoeffer passes the test in the laboratory of history — the test that so many failed. And he asks why.

Tödt shows Bonhoeffer's profundity in naming the sources of evil and self-deception as any realistic ethic must do, and in seeking societal and ecclesiastical checks and balances against authoritarianism. He clarifies the vocation of churches in *speaking* concretely, and the vocation of groups in *acting* concretely. He articulates the underlying theology and the specific peacemaking practices in Bonhoeffer's ecumenical ethic of peacemaking — in ways that motivate my own ethic. He shows that Bonhoeffer develops an understanding of human rights as based on human solidarity rather than individualism, and contends that Bonhoeffer's is "the only systematic Protestant attempt to conceive of human rights" before the end of the Second World War. He shows the problems of self-deception and relativism in an ethic of conscience, and analyzes the implications of Bonhoeffer's assessment of the kinds of ethics that failed to give the clarity and wisdom needed for guidance in the time of testing.

Tödt's extensive analysis of the social, theological, and ethical characteristics of the Bonhoeffer-Dohnanyi Circle of resistance, based on an extensive research project that he led at the University of Heidelberg, goes well beyond what can be read elsewhere in English. In the concluding chapters, he gives a sense of the personal struggle of those times, and a sense of the desperateness of the context, that cannot be matched. I come out admiring not only Bonhoeffer, but also Tödt himself.

I am warmly grateful for Heinz Eduard Tödt's hospitality and encouragement, and for his arranging for me to be a visiting researcher in *FEST* in Heidelberg. I am especially grateful to Frau Dr. Ilse Tödt for meticulously editing David Stassen's translation of the book, and to Clifford Green for conceiving the idea of this publication and arranging it with Eerdmans. I should also like to thank Magda König for editing work on the translation of chapter 6; and Maria Doerfler on chapters 11 and 13.

Frau Dr. Tödt and I have agreed to omit one chapter of the German original, which focuses on euthanasia and human rights during the Third Reich. We have also updated Ernst-Albert Scharffenorth's foreword slightly.

Professor Tödt told me also what Scharffenorth reports — that the farther he went, the closer he got to Bonhoeffer. I identify personally with that witness myself as well, and I am so grateful that we now have Tödt's incisive analysis of Bonhoeffer available in English.

Heinz Eduard Tödt was born in 1918 in Wester Bordelum, North Friesland. Because of his compulsory "Arbeitsdienst" and military service, including five years' service at the front throughout the Second World War, and then five years of detention in prisoner-of-war camp in Russia, he could not begin his studies until 1950. He earned his Doctor of Theology degree in 1957 at the University of Heidelberg. He became a member of the Heidelberg research institute — Forschungsstätte der Evangelischen Studiengemeinschaft (FEST) — in 1961, and university professor of systematic theology, ethics, and social ethics in 1963. He was a leader in ecumenical discussions, especially in the Lutheran World Council, and has published extensively on the responsibility of churches in a world of technology, revolution, and the struggle for human rights. He chaired the editorial board of the German edition of *The Dietrich Bonhoeffer Works,* and is held in high respect in Germany, Japan, and the United States. In addition, he thought and wrote with enormous and admirable integrity about his own experience of the German context during the Third Reich. He died of cancer May 25, 1991.

He published *The Son of Man in the Synoptic Tradition* (London and Philadelphia; 1965), and books on themes of peace in a technological world, theology of revolution, human rights, Rudolf Bultmann's ethics, theological orientation in a technological world in crisis, perspectives in theological ethics, Bonhoeffer's theological ethics, and victims and perpetrators in Hitler's regime.

Their German titles are: *Der Menschensohn in der synoptischen Überlieferung* (Gütersloh: 1959, fifth edition 1984); *Frieden im wissenschaftlich-technischen Zeitalter: Oekumenische Theologie und Zivilisation,* with Günther Howe (Stuttgart: 1966); *Theologie der Revolution: Analysen und Materialien,* with Trutz Rendtorff (Frankfurt: 1968); *Menschenrechte: Perspektiven einer menschlichen Welt,* with Wolfgang Huber (Stuttgart: 1977; third edition, München: 1988; Japanese 1980, third edition 1984); *Rudolf Bultmanns Ethik der Existenztheologie* (Gütersloh: 1978); *Das Angebot des Lebens* (Gütersloh: 1978); *Der Spielraum des Menschen* (Gütersloh: 1979); *Perspektiven theologischer Ethik* (München: 1988); *Theologische Perspektiven nach Dietrich Bonhoeffer* (Gütersloh: 1993); *Komplizen, Opfer und Täter des Hitlerregimes: Zur "inneren Geschichte" von protestantischer Theologie und Kirche im Dritten Reich,* ed. Jörg Dinger and Dirk Schulz (Gütersloh: 1997; Japanese 2005).

Several of H. E. Tödt's essays on Bonhoeffer, peacemaking, ethical method, and especially human rights, have been translated and published in English. More deserve to be translated. A bibliography of his publications and an interpretation of his theological ethics can be found in the dissertation by Randall Lloyd Harvey, Jr., *The Ethics of Heinz Eduard Tödt* (Louisville: Southern Baptist Theological Seminary, 1993), in Wolfgang Schuhmacher, *Theologische Ethik als Verantwortungsethik: Leben und Werk Heinz Eduard Tödts in ökumenischer Perspektive* (Gütersloh: Gütersloher Verlagshaus, 2006); in Tödt's own *Perspektiven theologischer Ethic* (München: Christian Kaiser, 1988), and in the *Festschrift* for Tödt, *Schöpferische Nachfolge,* ed. Christian Frey and Wolfgang Huber (Heidelberg: FEST, 1978). More recently, "Dietrich Bonhoeffer's Decisions in the Crisis Years 1929-33," trans. David Stassen, has been published in *Studies in Christian Ethics* 18/3 (2005), 107-24.

GLEN HAROLD STASSEN
Pasadena, February 4, 2007

This volume brings together Heinz Eduard Tödt's essays, which are fruits of his decades-long pursuit of Dietrich Bonhoeffer's work. The first eleven chapters analyze themes in Bonhoeffer's theology and ethics. The concluding three chapters deal with contemporary history, in which Tödt's thoughts revolve around questions of the guilt and responsibility of Christendom in Germany. These essays have been included because they concern a theme that is central for Tödt, deeply anchored in his own life history, and connecting him most closely with Bonhoeffer. Tödt's insights here, where Bonhoeffer is not cited, are also recognizably stamped with Bonhoeffer's spirit. So this volume makes clear that *Theologische Perspektiven nach Dietrich Bonhoeffer* will not be devoted to interpretations of past positions, but primarily to present tasks in theology and in the church, and also for understanding our own way of life. Tödt has clearly expressed this in a note from January 12, 1985:

> Dietrich Bonhoeffer has come nearer and nearer and become more and more important for me — not merely with one single flash of light — but in a continuing process over twenty years. Of his many remarkable character traits and abilities, the concentration with which he exposed his faith in Christ to the tests that life brought, all the way to the extreme situations of resistance, and then thought through theologically what happened to him and those involved, occupies me most of all. I perceive this theology as deeply authentic and as showing the way for me as a theological teacher. Here, inspirations of a personal faith enter into a dramatic life-reality, to be thoroughly turned into lucid discoveries of faith. It pains me again and again when I see how all those who cannot follow the whole way of Bonhoeffer tear out individual elements of life and thought and progressively instrumentalize them or conservatively distort them, and then believe that the guilt for deficits of the modern churches lies in Bonhoeffer's guidance. Bonhoeffer is not right in all things, but from no theologian am I now learning so much as from him, and, to be sure, with my intellect and with my heart.

The plan for this publication goes back to Tödt's own intentions. He himself composed a handwritten summary of a table of contents for *Bonhoeffer Studies: Theology — Ethics — Resistance* from May 7, 1987, and it has guided the present publication. I have supplemented this with later important works on this complex of themes that set the context for understanding Dietrich Bonhoeffer's theological ethics — including the contribution about the Bonhoeffer-Dohnanyi circle. Although this work, first published in 1987, was only to have been "the interim report of a research project," it summarizes Tödt's research on the German resistance, beginning with work on Bonhoeffer since the early eighties, but remaining unfinished at his death. After the completion of research by younger scholars led by him, he wanted to describe the profile of this resistance circle. This "central study" was planned as the final volume of the *Heidelberg Examinations of Resistance, Persecution of the Jews, and the Church Struggle.* It seemed sensible to me once again to put this self-contained "interim report" in print. I have worked remarks on the progress of this work, initiated by Tödt, and now led by me and Heide-Marie Lauterer-Pirner, into the notes of this essay.

Next to the selection of the essays, my work as editor included their uniform formation and light stylistic revision. I have verified quotations from literature. In some places, I have inserted references that substantiate Tödt's statements and make them verifiable. Bonhoeffer's writings have been cited according to the *Dietrich Bonhoeffer Werke* (DBW) or, if already available, *Dietrich Bonhoeffer Works English* (DBWE).

I should like to thank my colleagues who have supported me in my work with advice and suggestions, and, above all, Claudia Stichel, who prepared the manuscript for this volume.

ERNST-ALBERT SCHARFFENORTH
Heidelberg, January, 1993

1 The Disquieting Legacy: Characteristics of Dietrich Bonhoeffer's Theology

1985

Today, no German-speaking theologian attracts more attention among Christians around the world than Dietrich Bonhoeffer. This is especially true in certain nations where people suffer under difficult political and social conditions, such as in South Korea, South Africa, and Latin America. Bonhoeffer's writings have long transcended confessional boundaries, and they have long been available in translation in many languages. This is understandable, for here is a theology not separated from personal life. Rather, the theology and biography of Bonhoeffer constitute a unity, full of tension but clear. What makes Bonhoeffer's legacy so attractive is that, here, faith finds expression in life, and, here, the harsh reality is dealt with in faith. It is true, however, that in the established churches of the Federal Republic of Germany considerable reservations concerning Bonhoeffer can be perceived. There certainly exist many Bonhoeffer communities, schools, and the like. He has been the basis for countless conferences. But this influence is countered by voices that represent church leadership. Academic theology keeps distance as well, and widely ignores Bonhoeffer research. The memorial for Bonhoeffer's seventieth birthday in 1976 was celebrated by the World Council of Churches in Geneva and not, as one would expect, by the German Protestant Church. I will name and then treat in more detail three problem areas in which disquiet about Bonhoeffer and caused by Bonhoeffer is manifest.

First, the way in which Bonhoeffer spoke of a coming religionless world and the worldly interpretation of the Bible in his *Letters and Papers from Prison* is disturbing. In view of a newly revived interest in religion, some find Bonhoeffer to be a false prophet in this matter.

Then, it is irritating that Bonhoeffer, pastor of the Confessing Church, belonged to the core of the resistance group that planned the violent elimination of the Führer and Reich Chancellor Adolf Hitler. May a man of the church participate in such a deed?

Finally, there are the consequences of the fact that Bonhoeffer, when he was hanged in the concentration camp of Flossenbürg at the age of thirty-nine, did not leave behind a completed major work that would make evident the overall consistency of his theology. Thus it is quite easy to tear individual fragments out of context and thereby gain a one-sided view.

These three problem areas will be treated in reverse order: the consistency of his work, resistance, and the concept of religionless Christianity.

I. A Consistent Theological Perspective in Bonhoeffer's Works

1. When Karl Barth had read Eberhard Bethge's great Bonhoeffer biography in 1967, he showed his surprise. In a letter dated May 22, 1967, he described the new insights that the book had communicated to him. It should be remembered that Bonhoeffer had sided staunchly with Barth during the entire church struggle, even when the Confessing Church, frightened, distanced itself from Barth in 1938, and that Barth and Bonhoeffer had kept up a dialogue equally friendly and full of tension. In 1967 Barth praises, first of all, the fact that Bonhoeffer had already in 1933, as the first and even almost the only person to do so, vigorously addressed the Jewish question, both in its theological focus and in its consequences, which Barth himself had done only later. In the second place, Barth remarks that Bonhoeffer from the outset had concisely elaborated a row of connected themes that he, Barth, himself had only much later declared publicly but had always silently assumed. This line is, paraphrased in Barth's words, "ethics — co-humanity [*Mitmenschlichkeit*] — serving church — discipleship — socialism — peace movement."[1] There were, however, two crucial matters that Barth could not understand. Firstly,

---

1. Karl Barth, *Gesamtausgabe* V, Briefe 1961-1968, Zürich 1975, 404-5 (403-7).

Bonhoeffer's reproaching him for "revelation-positivism" [*Offenbarungs-positivismus*]. Secondly, the concepts of "a world come of age" and of "non-religious interpretation." He was irritated and angry that these concepts of Bonhoeffer's were turned into fashionable slogans attacking Barth's theology — which indeed happened amply enough in the sixties. Under this impression, Barth harbored doubts in 1967 as to the systematic consistency of Bonhoeffer's theological work. Did Bonhoeffer perhaps coin such formulations on the spur of the moment, without fully considering the theological consequences and implications?

We must clarify, then, whether there is a clear and strict consistency in Bonhoeffer's thought, that is, whether a systematic-theological outline can be found. For this clarification, Ernst Feil's *The Theology of Dietrich Bonhoeffer* must be referred to in the first place.[2]

2. On December 17, 1927, the theological faculty of the Friedrich Wilhelm University in Berlin graduated the twenty-one-year-old Dietrich Bonhoeffer with a licentiate's (doctor's) degree in theology, summa cum laude. Bonhoeffer had ventured on a topic the intellectual level of which can hardly be surpassed, *Sanctorum Communio: A Theological Study of the Sociology of the Church*.[3] The community of the saints, that is, the church, was this young person's topic. An urgent topic. At that time, among both the Berlin working class and the intellectuals, the Protestant church was thought to be of minor importance. People were, as a rule, still Protestant, but at a considerable distance from the church. Karl Bonhoeffer, Dietrich's father, was a psychiatrist, holding the professional chair of his field with the highest reputation. Karl, like his physicist son Karl-Friedrich — Dietrich's brother — adhered strictly to natural science, and was otherwise a characteristic representative of that time's educated citizenry [*Bildungsbürgertum*] at its best. Dietrich, when he was thirteen years old, decided to study theology, which certainly made his brothers and sisters and his friends, the majority of whom were jurists, wonder greatly.

In his Berlin semesters, Dietrich Bonhoeffer had renowned teachers: first, Karl Holl, the great Luther scholar, then, Adolf von Harnack, and, finally, Reinhold Seeberg, whom Bonhoeffer assessed ambivalently. From

2. (Philadelphia: 1985); *Die Theologie Dietrich Bonhoeffers. Hermeneutik, Christologie, Weltverständnis* (München: 1971/1991).

3. First printed in 1930. English: *Dietrich Bonhoeffer Works* (= DBWE), volume 1 (Minneapolis: Fortress, 1998), based on the German edition, *Dietrich Bonhoeffer Werke* (= DBW) 1, 1986.

this time on, Martin Luther's theology decisively influenced Bonhoeffer. In consequence of this loyalty to Luther, Bonhoeffer, in all reverence for and solidarity with Karl Barth, never came to be spell-bound by Barth.

The difference between them is implied in the question of how God enters the reality and world of humankind in becoming human in Jesus Christ. Barth, in the preface to his 1922 book on Paul's letter to the Romans, had pointed Christianity in a way that could not be ignored to the "eternal qualitative difference between time and eternity." God is in heaven, but you, human being, live on earth, and therefore you should not imagine yourself capable of knowing on your own about God in the right way. So be on guard against religious transfiguration of anything from human reality, for such religious elevation means idolizing earthly things, whether natural orders such as family, people [*Volk*], race, blood and soil [*Blut und Boden*], or even the church as a given formation established by human beings. In Barth, an old Reformed principle regains its brightness: *finitum non capax infiniti,* that is, the bounded, the earthly, is not in and of itself capable of receiving the unbounded, God's being. But then, doesn't God's being move completely into imperceptibility?

Bonhoeffer saw this as a danger. He now endeavored to hold on to Barth's experience of the difference between God and human being, and yet to expound strongly, with Luther, God's entering the reality of human life, even its bodily stratum. Referring to the Lutheran *finitum capax infiniti* — the bounded is, through God's deed, made capable of receiving the unbounded — he praises how Christ is truly present in the bread and wine of the Lord's Supper. Therefore he emphasizes that God is not only free from, but free for, the human being. And: Revelation does not merely touch the world in the way a tangent touches the arc of a circle, but really enters time. Such theses appear to stand in direct opposition to Barth's theology of that time. But only now does Bonhoeffer come to his actual point of concern. Revelation not only enters time, the finite, but deeply changes the finite and explodes the form of time.[4] This dogmatic statement has immediate consequences for ethics. Namely, the Word of God and faith do not simply leave the earthly orders as they are, but urge them on to open up to the coming of Christ, to be transformed so as not to hin-

---

4. Dietrich Bonhoeffer, *Act and Being. Transcendental Philosophy and Ontology in Systematic Theologie,* DBWE 2, 1996, 90-91, 99-100, 113-14 (first printed in 1931; DBW 2, 1988, 2002).

der the coming of the gospel.[5] Here Bonhoeffer unites again with Barth and anticipates much that Barth expounded in full clarity only after the end of the war. No actually given order is to be religiously transfigured. But, since neo-Lutheranism did hold the orders — family, nation, race — in their given form to be holy, and thus was prepared to pay homage to the National Socialist political order in 1933, Bonhoeffer terms it, disappointedly and embitteredly, "pseudo-Lutheranism." A drastic example of this "pseudo" is the Ansbach Advice [*Ansbacher Ratschlag*] of June, 1934, signed by the Lutheran theologians Werner Elert and Paul Althaus, opposing the Barmen Theological Declaration of May, 1934, that became the charter of the Confessing Church.

3. For Bonhoeffer's eightieth birthday on February 4, 1986, Bonhoeffer's first book, *Sanctorum Communio*, was republished. It is the first volume of the new edition of Bonhoeffer's works.[6] The editor of this volume, Joachim von Soosten, proposes in his afterword that the theme of vicarious representation [*Stellvertretung*] runs through Bonhoeffer's theology as a leitmotif.[7] We will examine this proposition. It should be clear, however, that this is in no way the only theme, but one among other important basic lines of thought in Bonhoeffer's theology. The notion of vicarious representation arouses some refusal in us modern people. We want to come forward and stand up for ourselves. This is likewise proclaimed in a shallow democratic exuberance. But the practice of democracy cannot do without representation, without persons standing up for others, for example, congress people and government officials. All of our life is pervaded by vicarious representative action, in which the father or the mother step in for the children, the free for the imprisoned, the gifted for the ungifted. We prefer to speak of solidarity — but solidarity is offered by those who, at least in principle, are equal, and stand on the same level. Vicarious representative action, however, happens when one person stands in for another person in a place where this other person cannot stand.

The theme of vicarious representation does not reach its full meaning as an ethical principle demanding that human beings stand up for each other. Rather, it comes to fulfillment in the authoritative acting, the suffer-

---

5. Dietrich Bonhoeffer, *Ethics* (Minneapolis: Augsburg Fortress, 2005), (hereafter DBWE 6), 2005, 161-63 (DBW 6, 1991, 1998).

6. DBW, 17 volumes (first printings München: 1986-1991, Gütersloh: 1994-1999).

7. DBWE 1:303. The following page numbers also refer to DBWE 1.

ing, the dying, and the resurrection of Christ. While the human being evades the holy God, realizing that entanglement in guilt and sin makes standing before God impossible, Christ stands in for the human being. For it is God's will in the love of God revealed in Christ that the human being should be freed from the bondage of sin and guilt, and, freed for the human being's true destiny, should come to true fulfillment of life. In the bondage of guilt, the human being is an isolated individual in the chains of self-love, unable to turn toward the fellow human being in true love. Christ frees the human being from this predicament through taking upon himself, in vicarious representation, the human being's guilt, and atoning for it by his own death. Where human beings accept that their guilt is thus taken from them, where they trust that Christ has really stepped in in their stead, there a new humankind comes into existence, beginning in the church of Jesus Christ. The consequences of sin, which drive the human being out of the community and into an isolation where the isolated individual is nevertheless chained to others in an evil way, become ineffective. No one should still say they are supposed to stand up for their own guilt on their own and alone. Community in the new humanity means community with God and community with the sisters and brothers, with all of God's children.

Bonhoeffer here appears to be in complete agreement with traditional Lutheran dogmatics. One should notice, however, that the energy of the dogmatic argument usually ends at this point, content with stating that the individual is torn away from the power of the individual's sin through Christ's vicarious representative action. Bonhoeffer argues differently. Namely, according to him, vicarious representation, as it characterizes Christ's being, proceeds into the community where it becomes the fundamental principle of life (146-47), the specific content of relationships between Christians, and thus of the new humanity (156-57). This happens because Christ, resurrected, now exists as church-community (189), his life being present in the community. Therefore there arises among human beings in the communities not only a new way of being with each other, but also a new way of being for each other, in the sense of vicarious representative action. Just as it was no concern of Jesus' to achieve his own perfection, just so can no one in the community merely seek after their own salvation. Rather, each one is being referred to others to whom their own needs, tribulations, and joys are communicated, and each one stands in for the others where their burdens, mistakes, and deficiencies are concerned. Bonhoeffer cites here Luther's magnificent communion sermon of 1519,[8] in which it is shown how, through the sacrament of the Lord's Supper, innermost intercourse with each other is brought about among Christians (178-80).

From his dissertation to his latest manuscript for an ethics, Bonhoeffer lives with the theme of vicarious representation.[9] This shows the strong continuity in his theology. But this theme also joins dogmatic, ecclesiological, and ethical teachings of his together. Vicarious representation is grounded in Christology, and it determines, from this grounding, the teaching on the church: "vicarious representative action is the life-principle of the new humanity."[10] Therefore Bonhoeffer can say in his papers from prison, "The church is a church only when it is there for others."[11] The church for others — this is no plea for moral or diaconal behavior; it is the description of the essence of the church. But vicarious representation immediately proceeds from the church to ethics. Bonhoeffer's famous ethics of responsibility has its basis in the theme of vicarious representative action. The responsible person must step in in other persons' stead *(an die Stelle treten),* must act for them, and yet may only do so without patronizing and depriving them of their maturity.[12]

4. So I must contradict my teacher, Karl Barth, as far as his judgment on Bonhoeffer's theology is concerned. Bonhoeffer's theological outline does have a strong continuity in it, from its beginnings to the end. In Bonhoeffer's theology there does exist a stringent connection between Christology, ecclesiology, and ethics. Like no other theologian in his time, Bonhoeffer struggled for the proper understanding of the church.

II. The Resistance Against Hitler as Commission and Guilt

1. In the German churches there is still, to this day, an uneasiness about Bonhoeffer's participation in active resistance against Hitler. In 1978, the

---

8. "The Blessed Sacrament of the Holy and True Body of Christ, and the Brotherhoods" (*Luther's Works,* American edition, volume 35; Weimar edition, volume 2).

9. DBWE 6:404, and more often in *Ethics.*

10. DBWE 1:147.

11. "Outline for a Book," August 8, 1944; Dietrich Bonhoeffer, *Widerstand und Ergebung* (DBW 8, 1998), 560. Bonhoeffer, *Letters and Papers from Prison,* new enlarged edition (hereafter, LPP) (New York: Touchstone, 1997), 382.

12. *Ethics,* DBWE 6:257-59.

theological vice-president of the Chancellory of the Protestant Church of Germany, Wilkens, held the opinion that this participation had arisen from a contingent decision of conscience of Bonhoeffer's. Contingent means casual. A casual decision is not the outcome of faith, but rather an underivable and, thus, non-binding and by no means exemplary act. Obviously, Wilkens' attitude toward Bonhoeffer's resistance is so defensive because we are torn by this resistance into the fundamental problems of the relation between faith and politics, that is, into unresolved questions that are a heavier burden on the Protestant churches today than any other problem area. What is the matter, then, with Bonhoeffer and the resistance?

2. We know today that as early as 1930 the vast majority of the Protestant theologians and pastors were astonishingly uncritical and often sympathetic toward the rising National Socialism and anti-Semitism. The national revolution beginning in 1933 thrilled many and carried them along, and it prevented, through psychological pressure and physical terror, the rise or the public expression of doubts about the infringements of the law perpetrated by the new regime. A large majority believed that they could stand for the cause of the church, and yet remain unpolitical but affirmative to the state. They lived in an enormous delusion as to the true character of National Socialism, because they did not want to interfere in politics and did not look for realistic information.

Bonhoeffer the theologian did not give in to such delusions. He saw through the false messianism that aimed at a thousand-year Reich and thus linked up with chiliastic ideas, and he criticized the Führer cult that made the followers live in bondage. As a preacher, he declared on June 19, 1932, in the memorial church for the Emperor William [*Kaiser-Wilhelm-Gedächtniskirche*] in Berlin, "We must not wonder when times will come for our church as well, where the blood of martyrs will be demanded. But this blood, in case we really would still be courageous and faithful enough to shed it, will not be as innocent and shining as that of the first witnesses. Our blood would be overlaid by guilt, the guilt of the useless servant."[13] So Christianity's sins of omission stood alarmingly in Bonhoeffer's view already in 1932. Simultaneously, his theology compelled him to grasp concrete problems clearly, which includes political problems. Precise and responsible knowledge of reality is needed when the empowerment of the

---

13. DBW 11, 1994, 446, alluding to Matthew 25:30.

church and of Christians to vicarious representative action in all dimensions of life follows from Christ's vicarious representation.

In this regard, Bonhoeffer's continuous discussion with the public, international, and constitutional lawyers in the family, with his brother Klaus and his brothers-in-law Hans von Dohnanyi, Gerhard Leibholz, and Rüdiger Schleicher, is of great importance. Dohnanyi, who from 1928 to 1938 was a personal advisor to four successive Reich ministers of justice, assembled since 1934, at the latest, a chronicle of criminal actions of the National Socialists. Leibholz had already in the twenties inquired into Italian fascism and the constitutional aspects of National Socialism. When Hitler came to power in 1933, the Bonhoeffer family judged unanimously: This means war! And: This means, for Germany, the end of the modern rule of law in a constitutional state, the end of the freedom legacy of the past centuries that had largely been the achievement of liberalism.

Dietrich Bonhoeffer thus was outstandingly well informed regarding the theological ethics of political affairs. This prepared him to write, already in April of 1933, his essay on "The Church Before the Jewish Question,"[14] much praised today and admired also by Karl Barth in 1967. Bonhoeffer expected the church to protest against the state's outlawing of the Jews, to render charitable help, and to convene an evangelical council in order to deliberate whether immediate political action by the church was necessary, itself to grab the spokes of the wheel that was grinding up human beings.[15] So already in April of 1933 Bonhoeffer considers active resistance on theological and ecclesiastical grounds, a resistance that certainly has to be offered by wholly legitimate means of the church, but that can also reach people who bear responsibility in the state, so that these, prompted by their Christianly determined consciences, would defend rights and the law by the means at their disposal. How this proposal to proceed was founded — theologically — will be discussed a little bit later on.

3. From 1935 to 1938, Bonhoeffer especially dedicated himself to the task of strengthening the spiritual power of resistance in the Confessing Church. In the preachers' seminary in Finkenwalde, he provided theological education for those pastors-in-training who had not submitted to church authorities that collaborated with the National Socialist regime, young pas-

---

14. DBW 12, 1997, 349-58; 359-61; in English: "The Jewish-Christian Question as *Status Confessionis*."

15. DBW 12, 353.

tors who because of this refusal had little hope of ever taking over a regular ministry. All such endeavors to provide theological education were suppressed into illegality by the Gestapo, the state's secret police; many young theologians got to know the prisons from the inside. In 1938, the resolutely confessing minority of the Confessing Church had arrived at a low point. In a situation of being constricted through power wielded by the police and the state, and pressed hard by the National Socialist Party everywhere, discouragement and internal strife spread out in the Confessing Church. By the spring of 1939 people sensed that war was close at hand. Bonhoeffer was decided on conscientious objection when the call to arms would come, knowing full well that this decision could have the penalty of death as its consequence. His brethren in the Confessing Church were horrified, because the case of Bonhoeffer's conscientious objection to military service — after the case of Karl Barth who in 1938 had vehemently warned against swearing an oath of loyalty to Hitler — would give the National Socialist Party a new occasion to deny the patriotic dependability of the church. At this moment, an invitation to New York came. Bonhoeffer was offered the position of a pastor to refugees there, and the opportunity to teach at the famous Union Theological Seminary. He traveled to the United States, but after grave inner struggles returned to his homeland. He felt that he would not have the right and authority to participate in the reconstruction which the church would have to tackle after the war if he did not share the lot of the brothers and sisters in the war. The decision to return made his conscience free and joyful. It was a decision that was bound to lead him into active resistance, since Bonhoeffer was convinced of the criminal nature of the regime. His brother-in-law Dohnanyi arranged that Bonhoeffer finally was conscripted to serve in Admiral Canaris' military intelligence office [*Abwehr*]. Here Bonhoeffer especially made use of his ecumenical connections by assisting in the attempt to bring about an understanding between German resistance groups and the English government.

But does a Protestant pastor have the right to travel such a path? When Bonhoeffer was arrested on April 5, 1943, the Confessing Church did not put him on its intercessory prayer list. Even after 1945, his church paid little attention to Bonhoeffer and his friends. Many church members recognized as genuine martyrs for Christ only those who had lost their lives for the cause of the church, but not those who had endangered themselves and perished in the struggle against a regime of notorious injustice for the sake of justice and human rights.

4. So the earlier mentioned judgment by Wilkens — that Bonhoeffer's resistance was due to a contingent decision of conscience — is significant of a widespread manner of thinking in the Protestant church, but it is also astonishing. The Reformers, whether Luther or Calvin, taught that resistance is commanded where authorities are so badly perverted that they destroy the rights and basic ordering of human life in society, thus counteracting notoriously their own — political — mandate. However, such statements by Luther had long been forgotten, and had to be rediscovered in Luther's writings, which happened in Hitler's Third Reich and in the time after its end. If the directives of the Reformers would be followed, much would depend on the recognition that the Hitler regime, amid all of its great political successes, would in the long run have the effect of exterminating life, reliquishing law, destroying itself, and annihilating the free proclamation of the gospel. Bonhoeffer, together with his friends, had already recognized this in 1933; he had recognized it without a doubt, thanks to Dohnanyi's information from the Reich ministry of justice. The increasing persecution of the Jewish co-citizens confirmed this persuasion ever anew.

For a person who knew of the crimes perpetrated by the regime, the alternative was clear: either to let all of this happen and to become, through passivity, an involuntary accomplice to the regime of injustice, or to plan effective resistance. Complicity — what does that mean? I can say from personal experience in World War II: Since 1942, we officers and soldiers held the eastern front to the utmost of our power — but, protected by the front, and mostly without our knowledge, the task forces of the SS and the extermination camps, such as Auschwitz, Birkenau, and Treblinka, accomplished their murderous labor on Jews, Poles, Russians, so-called gypsies (Sinti and Roma), and opposition members from all over Europe. The same holds true for the railroad workers who reliably, as duty-bound, provided the means of transportation with which the Jewish co-citizens where shipped to the extermination camps. The doctors in the hospitals and nursing institutions supplied diagnoses that actually served the selection of sick people for the purpose of extermination of "worthless life." The parish registry offices assisted in genealogical research without which the selection of non-Aryans would not have been possible. Preachers and professors of theology strengthened the Christian's "nationalistic desire for military defense," as Werner Elert phrased it in the title of his 1937 book *Der Christ und der völkische Wehrwille*. In short, in an unjust state that is simultaneously a modern and total state, it is very difficult, even for persons who are subjectively distanced from the regime and its ideology, to withdraw from complicity, that is, from indirectly aiding and abetting injustice. This fact was constantly repressed both in the Third Reich and in the postwar era. Bonhoeffer, however, concerns himself with this subject matter, as is impressively evident in the text "Ten Years Later," an account rendered at the end of the year 1942 for the group of his friends. The text is published as a prelude to the book *Letters and Papers from Prison*.[16] Once again the theological notion of vicarious representative action appears in the background. Whoever steps in for others, for the defenseless, must venture to take over free responsibility. There is no official professional directive for such action. Rather, free responsibility, so Bonhoeffer writes, "is grounded in a God who demands the responsible deed freely ventured in faith, and who promises forgiveness and consolation to the human being who in doing so becomes a sinner."[17] This means that not only in complicity with the unjust state does a person become guilty, but also in resistance. For resistance cannot be done without violence, without cunning, lying, or deceit, and demands action that, for the time being, is not legitimized by any law and order. This is indeed the tragic aspect of the illegal resistance; it must act within the sphere of lawlessness where the lives of many people are jeopardized, in order that law and order be reestablished at all. What conflicts of conscience, what inner struggles, doubts, and depression accompanied such risky behavior, and what meaning the gospel had in these predicaments, can be gathered from Bonhoeffer's writings. After the failure of the July 20, 1944, attempt on Hitler's life, when there was nothing left that needed to be concealed, members of the Bonhoeffer-Dohnanyi group, face to face with the jackals of the Nazi justice, laid open their motives for resistance. They named as reasons for their opposition the persecution of the Jews, the abolition of the rule of law in the constitutional state, the concentration camps, the persecution of the churches, while a further reason was still kept secret in this situation, namely, the destruction of Germany through waging a maniacal war of aggression.

Their action was directed not against "the state" but against a totally perverted and lawless reign that, in its time, managed to make the deepest evil appear in the form of light and of success.

---

16. *Widerstand und Ergebung*, DBW 8, 19-39. LPP, 1-17.
17. DBW 8, 1998, 24. LPP, 6.

III. The Rise of a Religionless World

1. Many voices today proclaim triumphantly: We are experiencing at present a renascence of religion, a boom in religious emotion! Bonhoeffer, however, wrote in 1944 while in prison, "We are heading for a completely religionless time; the people, such as they happen to be, simply cannot any longer be religious."[18] At the beginning of 1985, a retired bishop of a western German regional church, Wölber, accused Bonhoeffer of having set a wrong course for church and theology when he turned against religion. The reproach is somewhat queer, for — unlike the churches and theology in the eastern German Democratic Republic — the churches of the Federal Republic had up to 1985 not been under any determining influence by Bonhoeffer. Only in the 1960s had some groups torn out of context Bonhoeffer's statement that the world's coming of age must be taken into account, and had made it into an irritating fashionable slogan. In all brevity, we will place Bonhoeffer's fragmentary formulations and visions from prison on the theme of religion and religionlessness into the context of his life and theology.

2. Bonhoeffer describes precisely how he experiences the religiosity of the people in the Third Reich and in the war. He observes that they somehow manage to cope, quite unconcerned about God, with the common questions of all humankind like death, suffering, and guilt. This is also true for the anxieties during the terrible air raid nights of the bombing of Berlin. The ages-old wise adage "emergency teaches you to pray" [*Not lehrt beten*] appears to be no longer valid. How does that come to pass? Bonhoeffer answers: The world of today has arrived at an awareness of its own laws of life, wants to take its lot in its own hands, and refuses to be talked into believing that it is underage and thus needs God and God's guardianship. Even developments that run astray and endeavors that fail do not bewilder this world come of age; "they are taken into the bargain with the sober valor of a mature person, and even an event like the war is not an exception to that."[19]

Was this diagnosis correct? I do think so. The German population did not respond with religious revivals to all the shocks that the Hitler regime and the terrible war had provoked, but rather exerted themselves for a completely profane postwar reconstruction, and, in the course of these efforts, work and success turned out to be an effective substitute for religion. It is a

18. Letter of April 30, 1944, DBW 8, 403. LPP, 279.
19. Letter of June 8, 1944, DBW 8, 477. LPP, 326.

different matter altogether that at present, decades later, a new awareness of crises and the call for new religion arises in the world. The orientation toward this-worldly things and the progressive secularization that characterized the German postwar generation may hardly be denied. This fact was only barely hidden by Christian vocabulary; most of the people expected, and still expect, nothing from the Bible when, for example, the elemental questions of peace and security, of armament and survival were, and still are, at stake. The history of the Federal Republic bears testimony to this.

But Bonhoeffer's interest is, lastly, not focused on the diagnosis. He first of all asks the question, "who, actually, is Christ for us today?" Is he the founder of a religion of redemption that looks to the beyond; does he point all our pondering and striving to the other-worldly side of the boundary of death? Does he concern each of us only as individual beings in our private inwardness, in our feelings of guilt, and where we sense our weakness, our failure, and our helplessness? Is Christ, is God the "God of the gaps" who must help out where we are at a loss?[20] Traditional Christian religion answers all of these questions with a yes. It leads the human being to inwardness, to an aspiration for the salvation of the individual's very own soul, which, often enough, makes the human being flee from the world and thus into irresponsibility. Such religiousness was incapable of preventing the evil complicity of Germans with those who wield power in the world, as in Hitler's regime of injustice. Because of such religiousness Hitler, with his feigned Christian and his actual nationalistic [*völkisch*] religion, was able to awaken much naïve belief even among the people of the church, a belief that, after the collapse of the Nazi regime, was bound to end up as its opposite, namely, unreligiousness.

In view of his analysis Bonhoeffer then asked the question, "How can Christ become the Lord also of those who are religionless?" Is there a "worldly interpretation of the biblical concepts" that avoids what is wrong with the religion of inwardness?[21] I can only hint at Bonhoeffer's answers to this basic question of his.

It is crucial to take seriously the human being who is willing to come of age, and not find fault with the courage to master life on one's own, nor with the resolution to accept responsibility. It is not necessary to speak re-

---

20. Letters of April 30, June 27, and May 29, 1944, DBW 8, 402 and 407, 500, and 455. LPP, 279, 281, 336, 311-12.

21. Letters of July 8 and July 16, 1944, DBW 8, 512 and 535. LPP, 346, 359-60.

ligiously of the boundaries of the human being only in order that God might still have some room in the world. Bonhoeffer declares, "I want to speak of God not at the boundaries, but in the middle [of life], not in the weaknesses, but in the strength [of humankind], that is, not where death and guilt, but where human life and goodness are found."[22] The human being who thus is claimed is one who is strong, capable of taking over responsibility in vicarious representative action, rather than being primarily interested in one's own sufferings. Then, faith means in the first place taking seriously God's sufferings in the world. This is faith, this is following Christ as his disciple in full this-worldliness, namely, living as a human being in the fullness of tasks and questions, of successes and failures.[23] Then, hope grounded on resurrection makes the human being enjoy the earthly life to the full, endure its sufferings to the full, and recognize therein God's claim and blessing, as it happens so clearly in the Old Testament. Christ who became human does not alienate us from life, but leads us deeper into life, and does so in a way that the place where our sufferings predominantly originate is not we ourselves, but our being for others. For Jesus was the human being for others par excellence. Transcendence, that is, something not of this world, is experienced by those who experience this as coming from Jesus, and suffer him to work on their own life.

Bonhoeffer was no prophet of secularization, for secular thinking believes erroneously it can understand the world through itself. It is characteristic of him that he finds his basic orientation in following Christ as his disciple, and starts from there when contemplating the power and powerlessness of the human being. In faith in Christ he finds the authority and freedom to address human beings, respecting their maturity, so that they take over responsibility and find the strength to bear responsibility in faith. He traveled that path himself. In this way he has testified with his blood and has become a martyr for Jesus Christ, one who surrendered all possibilities of religion in order to live by Christ's vicarious representation, and to become responsible in vicarious representative action himself. Such a life in faith is always lived between two poles, which he indicates precisely in the short formula, "praying and righteous doing among humankind."[24]

22. Letter of April 30, 1944, DBW 8, 407. LPP, 281-82.
23. Letter of July 21, 1944, DBW 8, 542. LPP, 370.
24. "Thoughts on the Day of the Baptism of Dietrich W. R. Bethge," May, 1944, DBW 8, 435. LPP, 300.

2 Meaning and Promise:
Considerations Regarding
Dietrich Bonhoeffer's Late Theology

1983

1. "The unbiblical concept of 'meaning' [*Sinn*] is simply a translation of what the Bible calls 'promise' [*Verheissung*]." Dietrich Bonhoeffer wrote this in a letter to his friend Eberhard Bethge, one month after the failure of the July 20, 1944, attempt to overthrow the Hitler regime. We can read it in Bonhoeffer's letters and papers from prison, first published by Bethge in 1951 under the German title *Resistance and Submission* [*Widerstand und Ergebung*].[1] Indeed, meaning — in the sense that something makes sense — is not a concept for which a biblical equivalent could be found. The term, in its various current usages, has its origin in the modern history of Western secularization, and is connected with existentialist philosophy and nihilism without being exhaustively determined by their influence. It is surprising that Bonhoeffer uncovers a connection with the fundamental biblical concept of promise. This term points out that something, brought from God by the gospel, comes to meet the human being, whereas meaning is something that the human being looks for in human life and its surroundings, in the past, the present, and the future — often enough in vain. Promise does not depend on human beings. It is a message spoken to and received by the human being, if only they as recipients are capable of hearing and trusting in what they heard. Seeking after meaning, however, the human being hazards all that one's own self is, or

---

1. DBW 8, 573. Bonhoeffer, *Letters and Papers from Prison*, new enlarged edition (hereafter, LPP) (New York: Touchstone, 1997), 391.

hopefully is; for if no meaning is found, one's own life sinks into meaninglessness, haphazardness, bleakness, and nothingness, and is threatened by resignation or fear.

Generally, or mostly, people do not instantly grab for the whole, but are, for the time being, content with what lies near at hand and supposedly contains an evident meaning — to mean something to others, to be there for others, to accept responsibility and tackle tasks, to experience happiness, to persevere in sorrow, and to unfold one's own gifts. All this appears to be meaningful. But even such familiar areas of meaningful behavior are, in various ways, undermined and destroyed by what happens in the surroundings and entangles them, whether or not the person concerned is willing to be aware of that. Whoever seeks meaning, then, cannot finally isolate the familiar areas of meaningfulness as if they had lasting existence in and of themselves. These areas must be seen in their relation to the whole of what is happening, even if the person defends them, whether defiantly or most heroically, against meaninglessness that is pressing in on all sides. Even despite being crowded by an overwhelming void of meaning, or indeed by absurdities, a person can still say: For me, in any case, this or that makes sense, even when I am not able to relate this sense with the whole of what is happening. But behind this self-willed and, simultaneously, desperate setting up of meaning there lurks the danger of arbitrariness and self-deception, and also the danger of violating others, in so far as they are forced to orient themselves toward an arbitrarily posited meaning.

No generation in this twentieth century has experienced the public and notorious loss of meaning more dramatically, fatefully, and stiflingly than the generation that was exposed to the violent dictations of meaning by Hitler — and by his contemporary, Stalin. Bonhoeffer wrote in an account rendered by him to his friends in the resistance and to himself, shortly before the year of 1943 began, that is, almost exactly after ten years of National Socialist arbitrary rule had passed, and immediately before the defeat of the German troops in Stalingrad which was the turning point of World War II, "Have there ever in history been people who had so little ground under their feet in the present — for whom all the alternatives within the realm of possibility in the present appeared to be equally unbearable, adverse to life, and meaningless — . . . like us?"[2]

2. "After Ten Years," DBW 8, 20. LPP, 3.

People who in this time were thinking philosophically were made aware through existentialism and nihilism, through Nietzsche, Heidegger, and Sartre, of the bottomlessness of their lives, of the crumbling or intentional destruction of traditional structures of meaning, whether from the Western heritage of the Christian religion or from the originally Greek metaphysics. But they were not prepared for the possibility that the theoretical and personal-existential nihilism, which a thinker would presuppose, could be transformed to a public power. They did not foresee the appearance of a nihilism so manipulative, neo-heathenish, and perverted by a mania for racial purity, as to cloak nothingness under historical necessity, under prospects for the future, whereby all that had once been fixed was seemingly set in motion, so that the pseudo-creative breath of nothingness could suck out the natural essence of everything and everybody.[3] This is how Bonhoeffer, on his part, experienced National Socialism and described it in a section of his ethics manuscripts on "Heritage and Decay." In this text he, as a participant in the resistance, realistically assessing the dangers, coded his statements in such a way that the State Secret Police, the Gestapo, after confiscating the ethics manuscripts when Bonhoeffer was arrested in April of 1943, soon handed them back, without recognizing them as material on which a prosecution against Bonhoeffer could be based.

In the section on "Heritage and Decay," written in September of 1940, at the peak of Hitler's successes, we read, "Faced with the abyss of nothingness, the question about the historical heritage" of the West ceases to exist. "The burden of yesterday is shaken off by glorifying shadowy times of old; the task of tomorrow is avoided by talking about the coming millennium."[4] For Bonhoeffer, National Socialism, spoken of here in code, is a manipulating variant of nihilism. While acting arbitrarily in the present, meaning is procured, on the one hand, from olden Germanic times, and, on the other hand, from the supposed dawn of a thousand-year Reich.

But this manipulative positing of meaning does not create the firm ground on which life finds the form of law and justice. Under the rulership of the Führer, everything is related to him and his lifetime. Only he stands

---

3. Dietrich Bonhoeffer, *Ethics* (Minneapolis: Augsburg Fortress, 2005), (hereafter DBWE 6), 128.

4. Bonhoeffer, *Ethics*, DBWE 6:128-29.

above the rivalry struggle of the pretenders to succession, while Himmler and Göring recklessly build up their private armies. There is no legally binding constitution that would provide rules for how to proceed when, in the event of the Führer's death, state leadership needs to be established. Amid this egocentric and cynical handling of leadership, the prerequisites for a meaningful constitutional law are lacking. The quest for meaning [*Sinnfrage*], in fact, not only pervades the personal, or even only the private or inwardly human existence, but concerns all dimensions of life, up to and including the existence of communal bodies and the realm of international affairs. To restrict the quest for meaning to the realm of the individual, and to the areas of intellectual and cultural formation, is too short-sighted. Again and again, the quest for meaning stimulates a dialogue with history, a dialogue on which, at that time, Reinhold Schneider, Jochen Klepper, and many others embarked in opposition, however much the then prevailing scholarly historicism had obscured the possibility of inquiring into history as a source for the foundation of meaning. In historicism, as well, there can be perceived, up to the present day, a slippery slope tending toward nihilism.

Awareness of the nihilistic character of National Socialism, which manipulated and cut short any honest quest for meaning, misled many in the post-Hitler era into suggesting and supporting a simple backward-looking restoration of traditional meaning. More recent resistance research in the United States and in the Federal Republic of Germany emphatically exposes the authoritarian and conservative, or even reactionary and class-centered character, of bourgeois resistance groups in the Third Reich — groups that often were not at all free from anti-Semitic notions. In fact, ample evidence for this opinion can be adduced. Nevertheless, it is necessary here to warn strictly against all-inclusive judgments, and also against the transfer of today's political science categories to the situation of that time.

The resistance could not have conceived of a democratic public order for the time immediately after the Führer and his ruling clique would have been removed. The National Socialist propaganda and practice had influenced the majority of the people far too much, especially during the time of Hitler's great successes up to the fall of 1941, but with effects extending far beyond that time. To reproach the resistance with its tie to certain groups from educated citizenry and nobility, or to some leading groups in the military and the civil service, is rather anachronistic in view

19

of the situation at that time. Already by 1933, the workers' resistance had been brutally battered.

But, above all, it is an imperative of historical fairness to discern precisely how the attitudes of the various persons and groups differed. Helmuth James von Moltke, initiator and center of the Kreisau group, aimed at very fundamental social and political changes. He attempted, as did many others, to reply out of a Christian spirit to nihilism. "The recognition that what I am doing is meaningless does not hinder me from doing it, because I am much more firmly convinced than previously that only what is done while recognizing the meaninglessness of all doing has any meaning at all." Like many Christians in the resistance, Moltke discovered within himself a "socialist trait"[5] that resulted from the critical and attentive analysis of the consequences of capitalism, an awareness that was superseded only in the years after 1945 through neo-liberalism. With Bonhoeffer, as well, we find a clear realization of the shortcomings of the property-holding citizenry, and a firm resolution to acknowledge the proletariate's importance for the future, both in the society and — particularly — in the church, and in no way to assent to simply restorative tendencies. Being committed to and highly esteeming the Western legacy, he gained distressing insights into the West's crisis and the impossibility of simply linking with and carrying on where the events of 1918 or 1933 had put a full stop. His concern was a new beginning — which hardly came about in Germany after 1945. For this reason it is meaningful to reconsider today his thoughts for a future after the Third Reich, since, in doing so, we come to view critically from a distance what today is taken to be self-evident or even irrevocable.

We can certainly no longer think in the same way as we might have thought in Bonhoeffer's situation, for whom the time after Hitler was an anticipated, but intangible future. However, we can measure what has happened from 1945 up to today by what Bonhoeffer had in mind as a new beginning, and so learn to understand more accurately the unfathomable despair that Reinhold Schneider, in 1958, perturbingly expressed in his narration *Winter in Vienna*.

2. I do not intend to treat here Bonhoeffer's concrete considerations for a new and truly worldly order of Europe under God's command. Some material can be found in his writings that were inherited and first edited

---

5. Helmuth James von Moltke, *Briefe an Freya 1939-1945*, München 1988, 300, and 609 (letter of January 10, 1945).

by Eberhard Bethge, for example, in a paper of September, 1941, entitled "Thoughts on William Paton's book 'The Church and the New Order in Europe.'"[6] I only want to point out that Bonhoeffer's considerations for the future included the concrete dimensions of political order and of a national and international constitution. To begin anew meant, to Bonhoeffer, first to pass through a process of becoming aware of and avowing guilt, of repenting, of doing real penance, and of seeking for new foundations of living together beyond nihilism. But to begin anew also meant to grapple with and clarify the concrete experiences with people under the Hitler regime. And these were, in the majority, experiences of failure, of lack of civil courage, of thoughtless complicity [*Mitläufertum*], of lies violating one's own conscience, of shutting one's eyes to obvious injustice, and of lack of concern about the suffering of others, whether because of fear or because of a narrowed range of perception. He deemed all of this possible only in a situation where people no longer felt urged, by a vital knowledge about the mission and meaning of their lives, to accept responsibility, but would accept, in thoughtless subordination, the dictate from superiors that the meaning of life lies in blind obedience.

However, according to Bonhoeffer, it was in particular the relation to death that was decisive for the quest for the meaning of life and of a new beginning. A strong tendency to heroicize death prevailed in the nihilism of the Third Reich. In his 1926 book *Being and Time*,[7] Heidegger had characterized, though in quite a different manner, the determined course of anticipating death as the royal path toward developing the capacity for authentic being. In the resistance, Bonhoeffer had to become familiar with daily thinking his own death probable, as well as the death of his friends. He did not hate death; he knew that death can extricate from intolerable conditions and thus be an expression of freedom.[8] But his thinking, by contrast with nihilism, is devoid of any trace of necrophilia. ". . . we would like to still get to see something of the meaning of our muddled lives. We also do not heroicize death; we hold our life to be too great and too precious for that. All the more do we refuse to regard danger as the meaning of life; we are not desperate enough for that, and we know too much of the

---

6. DBW 16, 1996, German draft 536-41, English version 541-49.

7. *Sein und Zeit* §§ 53 and 62.

8. In the poem "Stations on the Way to Freedom," written in prison, death is the last of the four stations. DBW 8, 571-72. LPP, 371.

goods of life. We also know too well the fear of losing one's life, and all the other destructive effects of living in constant peril. We still love life, but I believe that death cannot surprise us."[9]

Construction in a post-Hitler era, then, was to serve life — even if it be the life of the coming generations. But what kind of people would have to be taken into account in this construction?

3. Bonhoeffer reckoned with deep changes that had occurred in the minds of his contemporaries, changes that would make it difficult to bear trustworthy witness to who Christ actually is for us today. "The time in which one could say this through words — whether theological words or pious words — is past, as is the time of inwardness and conscience, and that means the time of religion all together. We are heading for a completely religionless time; the people, such as they happen to be, simply cannot any longer be religious. Even those who honestly term themselves 'religious' practice this in no way — they supposedly mean by 'religious' quite different matters."[10]

This judgment — tentatively formulated in the confidential correspondence of close friends, and not in the form of a theory safeguarded by evidence — has later been scoffed at, by pointing out this or that wave of a religious boom in our Western society, as a crassly erroneous judgment. Today (1983), a human religious need of meaning is affirmed again with enthusiasm; sociologists are gladly listened to when they describe the highly various attempts at religiously constructing meanings of reality. But in those contexts the term "religious" does not focus on what Bonhoeffer has in view. He regards religion as a supplement, an ornament, an elevation and exaltation of daily life that obeys other laws and forces, and indeed some persons and groups would rather have it religiously adorned. In the daily lives of these same people, as well as in science and technology, it is nevertheless evident "that everything also works without 'God,' and, to wit, just as well as before."[11]

So by watching the people of the Third Reich, Bonhoeffer observes the unveiled appearance of a human condition, traces of which had been perceivable long before: the immense expansion of the possibilities of the human being to take the human world into its own management, both the

---

9. "After Ten Years," DBW 8, 37. LPP, 16.
10. Letter to Bethge of April 30, 1944, DBW 8, 402-3. LPP, 279.
11. Letter of June 8, 1944, DBW 8, 477. LPP, 326.

physical and the psychic processes of human life, and in so doing take wrong trends and failures into the bargain with manly sobriety, and even to cope on its own with events as drastic as World War II. Such coping with events, however, refrains from asking fundamental questions of overall meaning. It self-assuredly claims recourse to human maturity, decision-making capability, and competence for handling the world, a world from which humans can afford to separate a quite distinct small world of entirely personal, private, inward, and intimate dimensions.

This small world remains a matter of privacy that is of no one else's concern, and yet can be stylized ambitiously so as to become the problem of a person's subjective and free conscience. But this conscience must not interfere with the practices of coping with the world. And even the churches affirm this separation of religious privacy from the reasonable and mature coping with the problems of active and public life, in that they declare, in many variations, the questions of society, of international relations, of peace, even of the earthly survival of humankind, to be, for the Christian, questions of personal political discretion, but not questions to which the common confession of belief of Christians might be relevant. The official opinions of the two great churches, Protestant and Catholic, in the Federal Republic of Germany on the question of peace in the 1980s were, until now (1983), predominantly characterized by delegating the burden of decision to the individual's political reason and personal conscience — especially when a decision had to be made whether or not to possess nuclear weapons capable of mass destruction, for the sake of deterrence, and to risk — in case of a negative decision — conflict with the strategy of the Western alliance.

But when church representatives argue like this, then they believe the political, economic, military, and judicial competence of human reason to be capable of coping with the questions of the world. This is precisely what, for Bonhoeffer, characterizes the "religionless world": the quest for meaning is no longer a fundamental question concerning the all-inclusive whole, but a narrow question that remains restricted to a particular train of actions or a living individual's attitude toward life, and cannot be heightened so as to imply the quest for God that would be relevant for the life of the whole society.

But when a human being is affected through the reality of God that is made known in Christ, then, according to Bonhoeffer, the division of the reality of human life into two realms is smashed, namely, the division into the realm of reasonably coping with the respective autonomous spheres of

23

a profane world and the realm of inwardness, a world of religious needs and emotions through which the quest for meaning is satisfied. The latter realm becomes marginal in life and is not in accordance with the full biblical understanding of reality. Bonhoeffer, in faith, confronted with the religionless world come of age, is compelled to ask: How will this world — and we in it — be addressed and claimed through Christ today? In this confrontation, he develops Christian ethics as ethics of responsibility. The withdrawal from the world of real-life problems into inwardness, or into an other-worldly orientation, is understood by him as a pious godlessness that depraves the churches. By contrast, he can speak of an anti-religious and anti-churchly godlessness of the world come of age, as being a godlessness that is full of promise.[12]

4. Here again Bonhoeffer uses the biblical word *promise,* the profane translation of which, according to him, is the concept of meaning. But how can godlessness be full of promise? It can be so because it makes evident, in protest against piously veiled godlessness, the nature of the world come of age, and exposes it in a surprising light. The religiously-Christianly embellished godlessness that withdraws from this-worldly responsibility is thus unmasked as being hopeless. Bonhoeffer refers to Luther's saying "that God would rather hear the curses of the godless than the hallelujas of the pious."[13] In the promising godlessness of the world come of age, human beings have no possibility of religiously concealing their being responsible for the world. They must answer for what they bring about in the world, and this can make them face the quest for God in a new manner. Religiosity points to God as the powerful rescuer in circumstances of predicament. It makes use of God by fitting him in as a *deus ex machina,* or God of the gaps, wherever human beings are confronted with problems that they could not yet solve. But by using the recourse to God's omnipotence in such a way, humans are offered the possibility of evading their own responsibility. God then is expected to compensate meaninglessness by providing a meaning which the world, peopled with immature human beings, does not have. Coming of age, however, leads to a new and more truthful awareness of our situation before God, as "God gives us to know that we must live as those who cope with life without God."[14]

---

12. *Ethics,* DBWE 6:124; letter of July 18, 1944, DBW 8, 537. LPP, 362.
13. *Ethics,* DBWE 6:124.
14. Letter of July 16, 1944, DBW 8, 533. LPP, 360.

Of course, Bonhoeffer knows of perverted maturity, of "the shallow and banal this-worldliness of the enlightened, busy, indolent, or lascivious" persons.[15] But this is not an adequate reason to find fault with maturity, and to point out minor human weaknesses and sins and nail a human being down to these, for the sake of religious blackmail. Confrontation with God must be brought about precisely "at the strongest point" of the human being: that is, human maturity must be recognized.[16] Granted, "The mature world is more God-less, and perhaps just because of that nearer to God, than the immature world."[17] But the human being come of age, while having learned to procure shelter from natural dangers, by means of technology and organization, nevertheless lacks shelter from the dangers of human organization. So there is no approving of an optimism of progress here, but rather the statement that the human being has coped with everything, "only not with its own self!"[18] The human being who has been able to organize security from all kinds of external dangers is able to realize that there are internal dangers to humankind, and, prepared by this insight, can be willing to be addressed and claimed precisely as a strong being. When Bonhoeffer speaks of faith lived in full this-worldliness,[19] he speaks of the human response to this address and claim to the whole human being. When laid claim to, human beings do not devise, on their own, the meaning of their own doing and living, but accept the responsibility that comes up. And hereby the human being's position in the world and among others is deeply changed. People no longer regard their own persons, in the manner of modernity, as a subject that assumes to be able to find in their own self the basis for all certain knowledge. Descartes did this once, and, following him, the whole movement of modern subjectivity, which simultaneously has immanentism as its consequence. Instead, when addressed and claimed in the middle of life, the human being experiences transcendence, that is, not an arbitrarily chosen but a meaningful claim — meaning that comes to meet the human being.

5. But how are we addressed and claimed through Christ in this world, and thus placed in relationships that have promise? Bonhoeffer answers: in that Christ calls us to suffer with him the suffering of God in the

15. Letter of July 21, 1944, DBW 8, 541. LPP, 369.
16. Letter of July 8, 1944, DBW 8, 511. LPP, 346.
17. Letter of July 18, 1944, DBW 8, 537. LPP, 362.
18. "Outline for a Book," August 3, 1944, DBW 8, 557. LPP, 380.
19. Letter of July 21, 1944, DBW 8, 542. LPP, 369-70.

godless world. By doing so, the shortcomings of the world would not be concealed religiously — as if the omnipotence of God would put everything in order — but we would be exposed to them fully with our whole lives. The Bible does not know the modern distinction between the external and the inner, and so prevents us from removing God from the realm of public human existence to the inward, private, and other-worldly realm. There is no exit for the Christian into the eternal, or into other-worldliness, but, like Jesus in Gethsemane, the Christian must taste the earthly life to the full, must stand fast in this world, and must consent to being addressed and claimed in the middle of life, and the Christian must, by a strength bestowed by God, partake of what God suffers from this world. "Here lies the decisive difference from all religions. Human religiosity will point to the power of God in the world, when the human being is in need" — as if God would be there for the sake of the human being. "The Bible points the human being to the powerlessness and the suffering of God; only the suffering God can help."[20] Only the suffering God calls the human being into the full this-worldliness of faith, so that the human being, consciously submitting to a divine judgment, and broad-mindedly and selflessly partaking of the suffering of fellow human beings, may prove to be strong in life. Likewise, not struggling for self-preservation, but being for others, accords with the church's commission; and love for the enemy is not a sign of weakness, but of strength bestowed on human beings. Bonhoeffer does not want to speak of God predominantly where the boundaries, weaknesses, guilt, and doom to death of the human being are in view; he does not want fear to drive the human being to God. Rather, he wants Christ to claim the human being wherever there is human goodness and strength.

"I believe that God is better honored when we know, and drink to the dregs, and love the life that he has given us in all of its worth, and therefore just as strongly and sincerely feel pain when the worth of life is impaired or lost."[21] "Only when we love life and the earth so deeply that all seems lost and ended when this is lost, are we allowed to believe in the resurrection of the dead and a new world."[22] In this way, Bonhoeffer feels a deep affinity with the Old Testament. Its concern is not human happiness as such, but

20. Letter of July 16, 1944, DBW 8, 534. LPP, 360.
21. Letter of January 23, 1944, DBW 8, 289. LPP, 191-92.
22. Letter of December 5, 1943, DBW 8, 226. LPP, 157.

God's blessing that includes all earthly goods. "This blessing is the claiming of earthly life for God, and it contains all promises."[23] Therefore, blessing must not be opposed to the cross, even if, in the Old Testament, blessing includes the cross, just as, in the New Testament, the cross includes blessing. Both blessing and cross do not relate to an inward province of the human being separate from the realm in which otherwise the world is coped with through human doing and suffering; rather, they have their place in the midst of a life that, as a whole, is an answer to God's addressing and completely claiming us, an address and claim that meets us in Jesus Christ, with whom ultimate reality is given. Blessing and cross allow humans to let unsolvable questions rest, and to keep in mind that our thoughts are not God's thoughts.

6. According to Bonhoeffer, the quest for meaning in Western culture has been torn into the abyss of nothingness that claimed everything for itself, a nothingness that burst forth bluntly and violently in National Socialism. We who know of Auschwitz may hardly dare to raise the question of meaning. And in view of the possibility that the system of deterrence, with its weapons of mass destruction, may fail and ruin civilization, the quest for meaning seems to be sheer absurdity. While, from our lives, the quest for meaning will arise urgently again and again, we are nevertheless unable to proceed continually from the question to an answer, including the all-encompassing answer given by the existence of God. Instead, in asking the question as we proceed on our way, we are faced ever anew with a profound ambiguity. Obviously, life-affirming and life-destroying forces constantly struggle in human life, and suspend us in an unconquerable uncertainty about the outcome. What is meaningful seems to be closed in by the waters of an ocean of meaninglessness. The expectation of earlier generations that human life would go on into infinity has lost its evidence. The meaning of our personal lives is called in question, as is the continuation of human life, and we do not have any well-founded answer.

But we have a promise in view when we learn to conceive of and live our lives as an answer to God's making himself known in the life of Jesus; for then there is hope that in this world, we may participate in God's loving entry into a world that does not deserve the suffering God receives from it — a world to which God gives compassion and blessing. The godlessness of the world, to be sure, remains perceptible, but belongs among penulti-

23. Letter of July 28, 1944, DBW 8, 548. LPP, 374.

mate things, and passes away. The fact that God holds back his omnipotence for a while and does not force but attracts the godless world makes room for the play of our freedom and our responsibility. God, who shows himself in the cross of Christ as the one who absorbs all power into powerlessness, thus sets us free, uncompelled but overcome by his love, free to accept God's grace and the meaning given to our lives, namely, that we are meant to be witnesses to him, to his loving will. The young Martin Luther, in desperation, started by asking, "How do I obtain a gracious God?" In faith, the question was transformed so as to become more encompassing, "How does God regain the creature that is fallen but loved by God?" How does it come to pass that the goodness of creation and of the Kingdom of God shines through the wrongness of the world? That God grants us forgiveness of guilt, and ends our bondage to it, sets us free to be addressed and claimed by God. Then, grace is not cheap or ineffective anymore, but joins gift and commission.

7. But where, then, does the quest for meaning remain? Obviously, it is a preliminary question that arises again and again from the disquiet of life in our modern world dominated by science and technology — but it is a question that was in no way asked at all times by the people of the West, let alone the people of all cultures. In an essay that is both cautious and visionary, Ernst Feil exposes the genealogy of this question that arose from the world experience and thought of Ludwig Feuerbach, Friedrich Nietzsche, Franz Overbeck, and then from nihilism and existentialism up to Jean-Paul Sartre and Albert Camus.[24] Feil shows that both the critical rationalism of Karl Popper, and the individualistic immanentism of Gerhard Szeszny, yield the result that meaning is set up by the human being, a result that is emphasized also by renowned philosophers who, like Leszek Kolakowski, won distance from their earlier Marxism.[25] Even in the thinking of Adam Schaff, the quest for the "meaning of life," suppressed by orthodox Marxism, gains vivid importance, contrary to the theory that the course of history will, of necessity, follow known laws. The quest for mean-

24. Ernst Feil, "On the Meaning of the Quest for Meaning," *Stimmen der Zeit*, 1977, 3-16.

25. In *Philosophisches Wörterbuch*, two volumes, edited by Georg Klaus and Manfred Buhr (Leipzig: 1975), a dictionary presenting the ideology of Marxism-Leninism, parts of the paragraph on meaning [*Sinn*] on page 1100 are underlined by Heinz Eduard Tödt. There it is stated that, for instance, life is endowed with "sense," or meaning, by the human being who is the only agent capable of doing so.

ing arises, then, from the conditions of life in the world of science and technology, and yet asks for something — for a "sense" — that can only be worded by a human being who is prudently concerned and fully committed, although the outcome can, finally, only be an asking of open questions. Such asking is in no way meaningless, neither for the individual nor for the societies and the formations of public life, including international relationships. For where questions are asked in such openness — instead of giving answers by dictates of meaning — the respect for the dignity and the destiny of the human being remains in play.

Nevertheless it should not be suggested that asking for meaning by open questions must lead to the quest for God. God is not simply the answer to the human quest for meaning. Whoever thinks so does not respect the secret of God's aseity, his being in and of himself, and of God's making himself known in Jesus Christ, only because of which the possibility of faith and life is given. This self-revelation is, at its innermost core, for the human being the promise of life that conquers death. The human quest for meaning can be decoded from this promise as possibly containing a presumptuous claim — namely, to set up meaning on one's own, instead of receiving one's own life as a gift ever anew. But what is promisingly human in the quest for meaning can also be decoded — namely, to look for a destiny we may long for, despite all the adversities and absurdities of life, a destiny that constitutes the human dignity which is not at our disposal. So, although the contexts and associations are quite different, we may repeat the ever memorable word of Aurelius Augustinus in his *Confessions,* "Our heart is restless until it finds its rest in You."

3 Belief in a Non-Religious World: Must One Choose Between Barth and Bonhoeffer?

1976

Soon after the publication of *Widerstand und Ergebung* in 1951 (English translation: *Letters and Papers from Prison*), Karl Barth had confessed to being uneasy about Dietrich Bonhoeffer's prison theology. He was still uneasy about it when he wrote his letter of May 22, 1967, to Eberhard Bethge.[1] Barth had now read Bethge's Bonhoeffer biography, and explicitly consented to the path Bonhoeffer had traveled from Christian faith to political action. But the theological letters and papers that Bonhoeffer wrote in prison still appeared to him to be an unsystematic juxtaposition of aperçus conditioned by the situation. Barth decidedly preferred what Bonhoeffer had written before the *Ethics* manuscripts. He was especially displeased at the rumors about an allegedly mature world and a non-religious interpretation that had circulated since the 1950s.

Bonhoeffer, on his part, had criticized Barth's "revelation positivism," and missed contributions to a "non-religious interpretation of theological concepts" — he did not see anything decisive from which the "religionless worker or human being in general" might profit. Barth, he stated, had begun a critique of religion, but not really elaborated it; instead, he had merely replaced religion by "revelation positivism" and the church, and had, thus, "set up a law of belief."[2]

---

1. See above, chapter 1, note 1.

2. Letters of June 8, April 30, and May 5, 1944, DBW 8, 481, 404-5, and 415-16. LPP, 328, 280, 286.

Obviously, as can be gathered from this reproach, the point at issue between Barth and Bonhoeffer is the understanding of revelation. From Bonhoeffer's point of view, their debate could be unrolled by means of the key statement from *Ethics*, "The reality of God is disclosed only as it places me completely into the reality of the world. But I find the reality of the world always already borne, accepted, and reconciled in the reality of God."[3]

Revelation, according to Bonhoeffer, is the self-disclosure of God's reality for us, as it is conveyed in the living voice of the gospel. It does not inform objectively about a world beyond this world, as if a human being could learn something about such an otherworld while keeping at a distance. Rather, the disclosure of the divine reality concerns and changes the human being. But Bonhoeffer's statement does not say that God discloses himself only as he places us into God's reality. Instead, Bonhoeffer goes on to say, strikingly, that revelation places us completely into the reality of the world. What happens here is not an escape from the world, but, on the contrary, the disclosure of the world-reality so that the human being is linked up, by a living bond, with the world of human life, and in it discovers God's reality.

This can be understood most easily when we consider love for the fellow human beings, or kindred, who form a part of the reality of the world with which we meet. So we read in I John 4:12, "No one has ever seen God. If we love one another, God lives in us, and his love is perfected in us." God discloses himself as we are placed completely into that world-reality which is experienced in the love for our neighbors. When we forgive someone for wrongs done to us, we commit ourselves to the reality of the world in such a way that we come to know the forgiving God in it. In truly accepting suffering, our life's world changes for us in such a way that we see in it God's reality disclosing itself.

The second half of Bonhoeffer's key statement says, When God's reality discloses itself to me, I find the world-reality "always already borne, accepted, and reconciled in the reality of God." So I discover something that I cannot see, or have not been able to see before having been placed into the world-reality in a certain way. Namely, I discover that the world is borne — that is, it is creation; accepted — it is justified by Christ; reconciled — it has communion with God through the Spirit. When revelation

3. *Ethics*, 1940; DBWE 6:55.

makes us partake in the world as whole human beings, and not merely "inwardly," then not any random world is disclosed for us, but a world that is accepted by God. This world experience differs eminently from a scientific one, an ideologically determined one, or one in daily life.

Bonhoeffer's statement points to a circle in life and cognition. Pursuing this circle, our thinking must take as starting-point the reality of God that discloses itself to us and changes our position in the world in which we live. Commonly, we are estranged from reality; now we are placed wholly into the world, and come to know it anew in our own activity. But — and this is the way back to the starting-point — as we are so placed into the world, and actively come to know it anew, we recognize it as being a world borne by God. This circular motion does yield a result, namely, we find ourselves to be deeply changed in our attitude to the reality of the world, to God, and to ourselves. Speaking with Bonhoeffer's words in a letter from prison, we have learned to live in faith in the full this-worldliness of life.[4]

Realizing this circle, Bonhoeffer criticizes Barth's "revelation positivism," and along with it also an earlier phase of his own theology. Barth, according to Bonhoeffer, makes revelation appear like a given entity that rests in itself, some metaphysical idea that might be conceived as devoid of any essential connection with human life, something the significance of which would be unintelligible for a religionless human being. However, so Bonhoeffer replies, revelation is an event that changes our position in the world, an event that concerns the human being wholly and not — like the religious act — only partially. Revelation proves true in the reality of the world.

The most important basis for this criticism probably was the 1942 volume II/2 of Barth's *Church Dogmatics.* Its topics, predestination and the commandment of God, are dealt with so as to lay the foundations of the objective side of ethics. Barth radically emphasizes God's sovereignty here, in opposition to religious subjectivism. He wants to prevent the pious and theologizing human being from manipulatively reversing the descent from God toward humankind into an ascent that makes of God a product, or a projection. But could Barth conceive of God's sovereignty so that the human being would not become a marionette, but the human being's position in the world that had been made possible by God — human sponta-

---

4. Letter of July 21, 1944; DBW 8, 542. LPP, 369-70.

neity, own activity, and maturity — would be brought to the fore? This seemed, to Bonhoeffer, to be lacking in Barth.

Must one now, for the sake of intellectual honesty, choose between Barth and Bonhoeffer — against the one, and for the other? We will not be allowed to regard as harmless, or to level down the criticism by each of the other one. We should ask, however, whether the fundamental positions of both, which come to expression in their understanding of the world and of revelation, are contentious or convergent. In order to find an answer, the function either of them attributes to religion must first be thought through.

"Our entire nineteen-hundred-years-old Christian proclamation and theology builds on the 'religious *a priori*' of humankind. 'Christianity' has always been a form (perhaps the true form) of 'religion.'"[5] But in to-day's transition to religionlessness, this historically conditioned religious *a priori* turns out to be without force. It can no longer be a precondition of Christian proclamation, and it is important to realize what this fact means for Christianity.

"Religious *a priori*" is a term that indicates an aptness with which human beings are endowed prior to all experience, a natural predisposition that directs them, in life and in cognition, toward God. The traditional opinion is: Only because human beings, by reason of their essence or existence, ask for God, can the gospel be an answer to this quest.

Bonhoeffer, however, declares: Interpreters who have recourse to the religious *a priori* think, on the one hand, metaphysically, and, on the other hand, individualistically. This is what he most of all objects to in religion. Bonhoeffer pays less attention to philosophical metaphysics than to metaphysics within traditional religion. He regards as "metaphysical" a "construction, being in and for itself, without any essential relationship to life." He discovers something like this in the "thinking in terms of two realms" that prevails in traditional theology,[6] where the supernatural realm is thought to have no essential relationship to life. Barth's positivistic teaching on revelation is "metaphysical" when it does not relate essentially to life to-day, that is, when the occurring revelation cannot become a human experience, and the human being is directed to have recourse to an other-worldly power. These negative characterizations of "metaphysics" are the other side

5. Letter of April 30, 1944; DBW 8, 403. LPP, 280.
6. *Ethics*; DBWE 6:58.

of Bonhoeffer's positive statement, "The reality of God is disclosed only as it places me completely into the reality of the world. But I find the reality of the world always already borne, accepted, and reconciled in the reality of God."

Individualistic orientation and inwardness are analogous to a realm of divine reality that is other-worldly, and unrelated to our lives. Either a positivistically understood revelation of the Word makes us look to this other world, or an inner voice oblivious of the world does so, or both work together. Our connection with the beyond is then mediated by an intuition, or by conscience understood as metaphysical. If this were correct, then Bonhoeffer would have had to say: The reality of God is disclosed only as it awakens my inner voice which directs me to the beyond. But he actually says: The reality of God places me completely into the reality of the world, makes me experience a living and specific bond to the world we live in, and only thus refers me back to the reality of God. The times in which the isolated inner voice seemed credible, are past. "We are approaching a completely religionless time."[7]

Corresponding to this understanding of revelation, Christian ethics is reorientated so as to become an ethics of responsibility. Responsibility arises neither from the subjective spontaneity of reason, nor from inwardness, but from the indissoluble bond connecting the human being with the world of human life. In this world-reality, the reality of God is disclosed, and in this God-reality, then, is disclosed responsibility in the world.

A non-religious interpretation of biblical and Christian concepts will understand revelation, then, as an occurrence that concerns and changes the recipients' bond with their world. The formula of "the world come of age as being addressed and claimed by Jesus Christ"[8] is one of the possible expressions for this occurrence; another possible expression is "blessing" as "adressing and claiming the earthly life for God."[9]

What does the world's coming of age have to do with this occurrence? Neither in the theory of a "religious *a priori*," nor in a "revelation positivism," is the quality of the world's condition of any importance for the disclosure of the reality of God. The world remains outside of and excluded from the religious act, as being of inconsiderable weight. But the world come of age claims to be important for everything that really con-

7. Letter of April 30, 1944; DBW 8, 403. LPP, 279.
8. Letter of June 30, 1944; DBW 8, 504. LPP, 342.
9. Letter of July 28, 1944; DBW 8, 548. LPP, 374.

cerns the human being, so that humankind without the human world is no longer humankind. This world come of age, even as a God-less world, is nearer to the biblical God than an underage world, since the latter, looking out for an other-worldly God, and presupposing a religious *a priori*, does not consider that "The reality of God is disclosed only as it places me completely into the reality of the world."

With Bonhoeffer, then, a new understanding of revelation and, simultaneously, a new understanding of the human being and of the world come into force — and this with the claim of corresponding better with the Bible. Here Bonhoeffer had, of course, still to make comprehensible how it occurs that the reality of the world, including the human beings who belong there, becomes the sphere in which the divine revelation is performed. He hints at this by means of the occurrences of blessing and of suffering, both of which manifestly belong in the context of everyday life.

Karl Barth traveled a long way since volume II of *Church Dogmatics.* He himself mentioned this at several times, as in his 1956 lecture, "The Humanity of God." Here he confesses that he was earlier in danger of isolating and absolutizing God for the sake of God's godliness, and confronting humankind with God as such, which made the human being appear as a poor wretch. But precisely this would distort the godliness of God. According to the appearance of godliness in the Christ event, God is God in his very will to be together with the human being, whom God wants to be his partner. God's godliness does not exclude but includes his humanity. God's humanity is the free affirmation of, and the entering into life for, human beings. Barth does not suppose here an abstract affirmation of the human being's inwardness, but thinks of God's participating in the whole humankind that lives, working and acting, in the world of human life, and always develops spontaneity and self-sufficiency.

In this argument, the bond connecting the human being with the reality of the world plays, initially, only a secondary role. Barth's argument still seems personalistic, restricted to a living face to face of God and the human person, and ascribes no fundamental importance to what happens in the world of human life.

However, this opinion can no longer be maintained when Barth's teaching on the parables of the Kingdom of God is included. The parables of Jesus make perceivable what knowledge of revelation is. Jesus tells of daily events, of the doings of a sower, of someone who finds a treasure buried in the field, of a reckless emancipated son whom his father accepts back.[10] Something happens in the world that is, perhaps, surprising, but understandable to everyone. And suddenly just this points to God's reality. The parable intends to say: This is how things happen in the Kingdom of God! A piece of the objective world becomes a carrier of revelation. God's reality is disclosed indirectly, in that the human being is placed by it into the reality of the world, and given to understand, in dealing with it, what there is in the world that surpasses the world. Here it becomes clear how Barth and Bonhoeffer converge in their understanding of revelation and of the world. Both recognize the religious *a priori* as unbiblical.

Then, the question arises: By comparison with Bonhoeffer, is Barth the one who is right after all? Barth seems to hold on to the godliness of God more decidedly, and, while indeed connecting it with human activity, still does not make the knowledge of God's godliness dependent on the problematic maturity and religionlessness of the human being of today.

Here we must refer back once more to Bonhoeffer's key statement, "But I find the reality of the world always already borne, accepted, and reconciled in the reality of God." This statement blocks the possibility of asserting that, with Bonhoeffer, theology dissolves in ethics, or in neighborliness [*Mitmenschlichkeit*]. The reality of the world can only be addressed and claimed for Christ because humans in faith always find it already accepted and reconciled in the reality of God. It is one single reality, wherein that which is disclosed to humans in faith — who are thus set in motion, claimed through blessing, and torn into the Messianic suffering of Jesus Christ[11] — is, however, hidden again and again. "The non-religious interpretation is . . . a christological interpretation" (Gerhard Ebeling).

But what is it that the human being in faith finds borne and reconciled in the reality of God? According to the parables of Jesus, it is the future of the Kingdom of God that is approaching in the midst of reality. In faith, people see the "this-worldly" reality in the light of the world's future, and recognize their own situation as having been opened up toward God through God's promise.

Bonhoeffer puts less stress on this aspect. He rarely employs the modes of time systematically in distinguishing within the one reality. One exception is the weighty distinction between ultimate and penultimate things that he used in his *Ethics* manuscripts and continued to use in his

10. Matthew 13 and Luke 15.
11. Letter of July 16, 1944; DBW 8, 536. LPP, 361.

papers and *Letters and Papers from Prison*.[12] Making a difference between the two, and linking them together through the process of "preparing the way,"[13] allows Bonhoeffer to expose the theological significance of the "natural" in the reality of the world.[14]

What is natural is not obvious, but rather is obscured and hidden; it must first be experienced and recognized. Faith sees the penultimate in its proper place, and is able to set free a true experience of the natural. But it also happens that "reason" and the "basic will of life," while both remain embedded in the natural, lead to a conscious perception of the natural as it is given,[15] and objectively indicate that the reality of the world is borne by God. Bonhoeffer even speaks of a "providential conformity between the contents of the second table of the Decalogue, and the law inherent in historical life itself."[16] Traditionally, such an ability to recognize the true laws of life as the "law of God"[17] was ascribed to "religion." Such religion proved true in the course of the life of its followers, notwithstanding the contact of religion with a so-called "beyond." That is, the followers experienced something in the reality of their world as put in a good and salutary order through the "law of God" and the corresponding "natural law." But the modern development of Christianity, being oriented toward inwardness, no longer remembered the context of this verification, or reduced it individualistically; thus the "beyond" was separated from "this-worldliness," and became "metaphysical," in Bonhoeffer's understanding of the term. Bonhoeffer's key statement, however, unveils again the reality of the world as the place of verification. Not each and every form of religion is criticized, then, but only the modern form that is indissolubly linked up with metaphysics, other-worldliness, partition, and inwardness. Therefore, the quest for "'natural' piety" and "unconscious Christianity" remained on Bonhoeffer's agenda in prison.[18] Bonhoeffer's interpreta-

---

12. *Ethics*, 1940, DBWE 6:146-170, and letters of December 5, 1943, and April 30, 1944; DBW 8, 226 and 406. LPP, 157, and 281.

13. *Ethics*, 1940 and 1942, DBWE 6:161-67 and 360, and letter of May 21, 1944; DBW 8, 443. LPP, 304.

14. *Ethics* 1940; DBWE 6:171-81.

15. *Ethics*, DBWE 6:176.

16. "Staat und Kirche [State and Church]" 1941, in DBW 16, 1996 (506-35), 520. *Ethics* (Touchstone edition), 336.

17. *Ethics*, 1942; DBWE 6:296.

18. Letter of July 27, 1944; DBW 8, 545. LPP, 373.

tions are "religionless" only in the narrower sense of the concept of religion in which the context of verification is forgotten.

Only when reason and the basic will of preserved life do not break loose from remaining embedded in the natural, and when reason and will do not become subjective and split from a natural that becomes objective, can they lead to a proper dealing with the natural and to genuine protection of life. They then experience the world as a reality that is destined to be a good natural thing, a reality in which the violation of the natural avenges itself on the violator.[19] Formally, the natural is determined through God's will to preserve it, and through its orientation toward Christ.[20] This, however, will not be experienced in natural piety, nor in natural religion, but in revelation as conveyed in the living Word of God addressing us.

The theological elaboration of the "natural" constitutes both a fundament for Bonhoeffer's concrete ethics, and a basis for consensus between Christians and non-Christians in practical questions. When, in speaking of God, the human being is addressed as a strong one, in the midst of life,[21] then the human sense for what is natural, good, and healthy is addressed. The "righteous deed"[22] does not refer to principles and to timeless norms, but to the natural as a dimension of God's world-reality, to be experienced ever anew, that has been revealed in Christ's becoming human. Therefore such a deed needs prayer, just as prayer is in need of such a deed.

The question of true religion, as distinguished from an arbitrary or "metaphysical" religion, must be considered anew, not only regarding Bonhoeffer, but also regarding Barth. Barth speaks of the puzzling fact that outside of the church-community there really are found true words that objectively have a direct connection with the one true Word. According to Barth, the created world — the cosmos, the nature with which the human being is endowed in the domain of humankind, and the nature of this domain as such — also has its own lights and truths and, thereby, its language, its words.[23]

---

19. *Ethics,* DBWE 6:176.

20. *Ethics,* DBWE 6:174.

21. Letter of April 30, 1944; DBW 8, 407. LPP, 282.

22. "Thoughts on the Day of the Baptism of Dietrich W. R. Bethge," May, 1944; DBW 8, 435-36. LPP, 298 and 300.

23. *Church Dogmatics* IV/3.

It might be allowed, then, to term the adequate perception of such true words "religion," just as we have done considering Bonhoeffer's experience of the unblocked "natural." By beholding undistortedly and perceiving adequately, these phenomena of the worldly reality are viewed in a manner that does not immediately issue in an arbitrary construction of religious or metaphysical systems of sense, but that holds on to the insight that "the fear of the Lord is the beginning of wisdom" (Psalm 111:10). All true religions know of this fear, and of experiences of wisdom. Such knowledge appears to be possible also in a religionless world; for precisely here, people can experience the need for an illumination of their own world through true lights and words, being aware that, at best, truth is disclosed in risky dealing with the world, and yet is not at their disposal.

Opposites remain between Barth's and Bonhoeffer's judgments on secularization and maturity of the world. Karl Barth cannot deem that which arose from such a coming of age as so revolutionarily new. Bonhoeffer, for his part, is deeply impressed by the coming religionlessness of the world. This means, above all, that metaphysical religiosity is no longer verified through experiences in the world. Bonhoeffer's prognosis of a coming religionlessness is not already refuted by the fact that there may obtain today, after a wave of progress and emancipation, a boom of new "religiosity." Bonhoeffer's criterion for judgment is not whether or not the human being is filled with religious notions, but whether human religious notions are credible, and are proven true in the reality of the world. The discussion between Bonhoeffer and Barth might be carried on by taking as a basis their converging understanding of revelation and of the world, and by examining the question of verification and probation of faith lived in the world today. Thereby it would also become recognizable what religionlessness and coming of age mean, and what they cannot mean.

4 End, or Comeback of Religion?
Forty-Five Years After Dietrich Bonhoeffer's
Thesis of a Religionless Christianity

1988

1. Did Dietrich Bonhoeffer err? Did he cause damage to religion and to the church when he saw a religionless Christianity coming? Did his prognoses about an arising mature world have the effect of a self-fulfilling prophecy that provokes what it predicts? Is it also to a large degree Bonhoeffer's fault that many people today no longer expect the church to provide their lives decisively with meaning and fulfillment? Is he partly guilty that the turbulent movements of youth-religion, transcendental meditation, new gnosis, and occultism bypass the church? Did he impress a stamp on the church that makes the irrationalisms of New Age proclaimers appear so strange and unrelated to it? Such questions were asked rather frequently, and with emotional urgency, after the failure of the cultural and student revolt in the early 1970s, and especially since the turn toward neo-conservatism at the beginning of the 1980s. Since that turn was attempted, not only many church people, but also philosophers and ideologues affiliated with politics, have endeavored to secure a firm place for religion, both in public life — the term *civil religion* was gladly adopted from the United States of America — and in the personal socialization of the individual. Obviously, religion and morals are often correlated, and a society in which religious awe and reverence are lacking, and many of the wholesome inhibitions from acting asocially have been lost, could become a society in which the egoisms of individuals and of groups are raging in immoral conduct, addiction, corruption, crime, or even terrorism — expensive and dangerous affairs for a society. In view of this, we may understand the legendary state-

ment of the notorious freethinker Friedrich II of Prussia, who is said to have told one of his ministers, "Thou hast better procure religion in my country, or else go to the Devil!" Interest in religion by politicians, economists, and the police can be just as great as the interest of representatives of the church.

It is good that Dietrich Bonhoeffer is asked these critical questions. Evidently, no one remembers today, in this respect, Rudolf Bultmann and his exciting demythologization program,[1] or Friedrich Gogarten who, in his 1953 book *Verhängnis und Hoffnung der Neuzeit* [*Despair and Hope for Our Time*, 1970], following up Bonhoeffer's vision of a world come of age, decidedly proclaimed that secularization is legitimately Christian, whereas secularism is destructive. Today, Bonhoeffer is the most widely read German-language theologian in the world. For worldwide ecumenicalism, he represents the struggle of the Confessing Church, together with the resolute resistance to the National Socialist rule of violence. He is viewed by many as standing for those who, by risking and losing their lives, bore witness to the real existence of a different Germany that was not servile to the National Socialist regime, and was not willing to silently tolerate its crimes and atrocities. Since 1986, the volumes of the new edition of Bonhoeffer's writings, *Dietrich Bonhoeffer Werke*, are appearing, in which the editors' comments place Bonhoeffer's theological statements and his church activity into the context of the times he lived in. The edition will vividly portray how, in his case, theology and biography belong together, which, so far, has not been similarly described in previous theologians.

Whoever opposes Bonhoeffer with criticisms, reproaches, and negations is facing a highly influential person, a powerful and radical theological thinker, full of fascination and authority. Already in the 1950s, and still today, many young people decide on studying theology for the ministry, because the message or the figure of Bonhoeffer has attracted or even inspired them. If he, a key figure for the postwar epoch, has erred, if he has pointed out false ways, then this would, indeed, be a burden for church, theology, and society, that must not be passed over in silence, but should be voiced in public. We have before us, then, a rather explosive topic.

2. Dietrich Bonhoeffer was a master of coining sharply pointed formulations, especially in letters and in diaries, where he was not in danger

---

1. "Neues Testament und Mythologie. Das Problem der Entmythologisierung der neutestamentlichen Verkündigung" (1941), in *Kerygma und Mythos* I, 15-53.

of being misunderstood, or accused of one-sidedness. Almost everything that is brought up against Bonhoeffer today is found in private and confidential documents, publication of which, without corrections, was never intended, and that he probably would have refused. This is especially the case with the letters and papers written in the Tegel prison. They are experimental, unguarded, bold, trusting that the reader, the intimate friend, will understand, complete, and add more to thoughts that had remained unfinished in the shortness of time. But such fragmentary and improvised statements are highly valuable when they arise from truly new considerations that amount to a kind of revolution in theological and ecclesiastical thinking. They need not be as cautious and smooth as a published text would have to be, and thus may bewilder both friends and enemies. We know how bewildered Karl Barth was when he read, after the publication of the letters in 1951, the judgments that his younger friend and comrade in the church struggle had sketched in prison and could no longer elucidate. Bonhoeffer certainly did not do justice to Barth in his prison writings. But for us, the insight into the raw, unpolished core of Bonhoeffer's considerations is of great significance. The rule for our interpretation should be to study carefully how the thoughts are connected, and not to stick to separate formulations or conceptions. To be sure, that is possible only in preparing an analytical study, not in a brief talk.

3. Let us study, then, the concept of religion that is central for our investigation. Bonhoeffer used the concept in a special, antithetically pointed sense. He conceives religion and Christian faith as opposites, and focuses his attention on what counteracts a biblically oriented life in faith, and corrupts it in the bourgeois world of the West in the twentieth century. Had Bonhoeffer wanted to deal with religion historically, that is, with the forms in which religion has appeared in Hinduism, Buddhism, Islam, and so forth, he would certainly have chosen quite different criteria. But religions were not his theme.

However, already here a warning must be heeded. I speak of religion and of religions as if this were a self-evident matter. One of the foremost experts on Bonhoeffer's theology, the Catholic theologian Ernst Feil in Munich, has shown in the first volume of *Religio*[2] that the current understanding of religion is the offspring of modern times, or, more precisely, of Protestant modernity. After approximately the eighteenth century, the

---

2. Published in Göttingen, in 1986, four volumes up to 2006.

term *religion* developed into a concept under which are subsumed any imaginable experiences and formations, including Christianity, that refer to transcendence beyond human reach. But the inclusion of Christianity contradicts the biblical understanding of faith and sanctification. Since God's revealing and making himself known in Jesus Christ, the faith that issues from this unique event cannot simply be placed into the framework provided by the modern concept of religion. At the time in which the concept developed, the persuasion was formed that the aptitude to experience fear and fascination in the presence of the transcendental, or the numinous, is innate in all human beings, an *a priori* endowment thanks to which humankind is fully human. Religious *a priori* means that the human being, prior to all experiences *a posteriori,* is receptive to religious experiences — a plausible opinion in a world in which there is no widespread, theoretically supported atheism.

The reply to this concept of religion did not take long in coming. In the second half of the eighteenth century, some of the French Encyclopedists were energetic materialists and atheists. In Germany, atheism was massively proliferated through the left-wing Hegelians, especially through Karl Marx, with the result that a more or less official ideology of atheism developed in the socialistic systems that comprise, in the twentieth century, more than one-third of humanity. Religion and atheism now confront each other. From the atheistic standpoint, the critique of religion is regarded as the presupposition of enlightenment and science. In the critical analysis of the function of religion in society, religion is assumed to be a human capability to produce, by means of psychic projection, a superstructure, or heaven, longed for by the frustrated human being as a refuge to flee to and escape from this world. Religion, then, does exist also for atheists, but as a human product that contains no other reality than that which the human being puts into it. The reproach leveled by the atheist against religious people is: You squander the treasures of the earth, the imagination and productivity of the human mind and soul, by projecting a heaven, and thus making the earth appear poor and wretched. Instead, the earth needs to be loved and handled with human imagination and productivity.

An interim result may be stated. The current concept of religion did not actually exist in all times and all cultures, but belongs in the recent centuries of the cultural milieu that bears the stamp of Western Christianity, and is also conditioned by the falling away from Christianity. Hence it is valid only in a limited historical epoch, and can lose its significance in the process of history, and in other cultural constellations.

It will be immediately objected that the Latin word *religio* is much older. Indeed, *religio*, briefly put, meant before modernity nothing other than a human virtue, namely, the precise, awesome, and respectful observance of a god, or gods, and of orders represented by them. Religion, in Latin, is observance of the *lex deorum*, the law meted out by the gods to the human beings. Here, thinking still proceeds from the gods. In contrast, the modern concept of religion proceeds from the capability and aptitude of the human being to experience, feel, and internalize that which is divine, religious, and super-worldly, and to live accordingly.

When Bonhoeffer speaks of the passing and vanishing of religion, then, he is speaking of a historical phase that is coming to an end, even if it is deeply connected with Christianity. When religion disappears, Christianity will change. Therefore Bonhoeffer inquires into a religionless interpretation of Christianity and biblical concepts. We are not in a crisis in which Christian faith will end, or the church in the biblical sense will die, but in a crisis in which two elements that historically were closely connected are painfully disassociated. If this separation or dissociation is to be avoided, then religion must be revived, restored, regenerated, and performed anew. This is the alternative to Bonhoeffer's conception, which originated in the experience that "the people, such as they happen to be, simply cannot any longer be religious."[3] According to Bonhoeffer, that form of religion which was shaped in connection with Christian faith and life in the mainstream of the Western bourgeois era can no more be genuinely and honestly filled with life, and experienced as truth, in the 1940s and subsequent times. The reason why this is impossible can only be shown by inspecting more closely the individual elements that belong to, and constitute the vitality of such religion. This is our next task. We will now consider, one after the other, the major phenomena that, according to Bonhoeffer's observations recorded in his prison writings, had been part of the form of Christian life in modern times.

4. a) The time of theological or pious words is past.[4] The ecclesiastical language in the 1930s was, in different variants, a separate language of

3. Letter from prison, April 30, 1944, in: *Widerstand und Ergebung*, DBW 8, 403. LPP, 279.

4. DBW 8, 402. LPP, 279.

piety, as if spoken in Canaan. It was especially in vogue in groups with pietistic traditions, and among members of the Christian community movement, but was also used in the Protestant religious milieu in general. This language perhaps satisfied needs of those who had grown up in it, and still understood it. But it was not a language that called for change and renewal in the world. It was a language with neither credibility nor consequences, a language that made costly grace cheap. Bonhoeffer had already exposed this in his 1937 book on *Discipleship*.[5] Now, in 1944, he countered the words that had become powerless by "prayer and righteous deeds among the people."[6] Words spoken by Christians should become credible and convincing through righteous action. In the beginning of the Third Reich, the churches had been rather verbose in paying homage to the new wielders of power, while concealing their secret reservations. But ecclesiastical language had thereby lost its force and credit.

4. b) The time of inwardness is past.[7] In German mysticism, the word cluster *innig* and *Innerkeit* had arisen, meaning an attitude of absorption, meditation, abstraction from all outward matters, and concentration on the inward spirit. Its source had been the expectation that the human being, when turning inwards, would discover there a whole world in which self-affirmation and self-sufficiency were found. Goethe, Herder, and German Romanticism secularized this mystical absorption in inwardness, and made it a characteristic of the cultured bourgeois who is mostly unpolitical, but absorbed, for example, in art, music, and poetry. In the medium of such inwardness, religion would live as a beatifying feeling for the eternal, a beholding of the universe, as depicted by the young Schleiermacher. It would live in an ocean of emotions where the ego feels supported and sheltered. Sigmund Freud wrote in his 1930 treatise "Das Unbehagen in der Kultur" ("Discomfort in Culture"), "For my part, I cannot discover within myself the oceanic feeling." The bourgeois and religious culture made people expect to float, elevated and limitless, within themselves. But when Freud probed into inward matters, he met with the unconscious, repression, and conflicts, and not with cosmic harmony. Bonhoeffer has in view, together with Freud, such disillusioning experiences with human inwardness.

---

5. *Discipleship*, DBWE 4:43-56.

6. "Thoughts on the Day of Baptism of Dietrich W. R. Bethge," May, 1944, DBW 8, 435. LPP, 300.

7. DBW 8, 402. LPP, 279.

4. c) The time of conscience is past.[8] According to the neo-Lutheran understanding that was stated impressively by Karl Holl and spread through his school, Protestantism was a culture of conscience. At the Reichstag in Worms in 1521, Luther had maintained that the conscience within him forbade him to recant his teaching. Luther's conscience was understood to be the archetype and primordial theme of Protestant religion, and also the primary theme of bourgeois individualism. In 1940, when preparing his book on ethics, Bonhoeffer wrote that the human being "whose sole support is conscience" cannot stand firm under a pressure like that exerted by the National Socialist regime. This "man of conscience" is not competent to see through the camouflage and disguise of an evil power, lacks criteria for his decisions because of such blindness, and is prone to act, or omit action, with the aim of salving his own conscience, thus avoiding feeling accountable for evil. It would be more wholesome, so Bonhoeffer says, to really look at the hard facts, and let a bad conscience speak, instead of deceiving it.[9]

In July of 1944, while pondering over religionless Christianity, Bonhoeffer put down the following note: "Conscience, the voice of that which is general and necessary." Conscience represents general principles, as, for example, Kant's categorical imperative. The note continues, "But the consent, the commission, the recognition received from the other human being, is more convincing than a good conscience."[10] Striving for a good conscience, human beings seek their own peace of mind, a concord with their own selves, and remain autistic, however much they refer to — unconcrete — generalities. What is more convincing is a behavior that relates to the other, the fellow human, remains neighborly, and can receive recognition from the other. The background to this is Bonhoeffer's understanding of transcendence. The faithful experience transcendence in an encounter with a concrete neighbor where their autistic incurvation upon themselves[11] breaks open, and a conversion of their being human happens. "The 'being for others' of Jesus is the experience of transcendence!"[12] To dismiss the traditional religious understanding of conscience does not mean that conscience is eliminated. But the voice of conscience must be

---

8. DBW 8, 402. LPP, 279.
9. *Ethics*, DBWE 6:79.
10. DBW 8, 506. LPP, 343.
11. *Act and Being*, DBWE 2:46 *(cor curvum in se)*, 2:41, note 20, and other places.
12. "Outline for a Book," August, 1944, DBW 8, 558. LPP, 381.

understood quite differently, namely, in relation to the other one who is uniquely there for us, to Jesus.

4. d) The time of metaphysics is past.[13] It is the essence of metaphysics to point to a being that is not severed by the boundary of death, but is ever present. Here Bonhoeffer comes close to Nietzsche's thinking that brings metaphysics to an end. Metaphysics did not arise in the domain of Christian faith, but from the Greek experience of the gods. It is originally related to the god of the philosophers — and Christian theology has subsequently made use of it for many centuries, at considerable costs.

The god of metaphysics appeared during the archaic era of the Greeks. According to Xenophanes, the god is essentially an omnipresent, purely spiritual beholding, the Greek term for which is *nous*. "The pure and omnipresent beholding of the divine *nous* is nothing else but the truth of being, a truth within which everything that can be at all must stay." "Everything that is met in space and time always already stands in his presence," in the presence of god/*nous,* who therefore "cannot have within space and time his pure essence that eternally remains the same. But that which is not in space and time does not move."[14] God is in the beyond as the unmoved mover of all things. He cannot become human. If everything is in the presence of the divine *nous,* when this *nous* beholds the being as it is, and when the human being is given a share in this beholding, then the guarantee for what is true and good, even for what is at all, rests in this god. But when the god of the philosophers, or of metaphysics, gets lost because he no longer comes into view for human beings such as they have become, and is dead to them, then also truth and goodness and that which fundamentally is behind the appearances get lost to humankind. Human cognition now is only a form of error that is more or less useful for human life. The domain of human knowledge is nothing other and nothing more than history, or transitory this-worldliness. This is the situation of nihilism, after metaphysics as the basis for all knowledge and orientation in life has disintegrated.

This is exactly what Bonhoeffer saw, similar to Nietzsche. What is Christian had been thought to be a religion in the categories of the god of the philosophers, the very god whose death Nietzsche had prophesied, and everything in theology and the church that had been supported by these

---

13. Letters of April 30 and May 5, 1944, DBW 8, 405 and 414. LPP, 280 and 286.

14. Georg Picht, *Der Gott der Philosophen,* in: *Wahrheit, Vernunft, Verantwortung* [Truth, Reason, Responsibility], Stuttgart 1969, 242-43.

categories had vanished. The task now is to live, express in words, witness to, and experience faith without the help of metaphysical thought. This loss frightens us, and with reason. We have already seen that, in the era of metaphysics, conscience had been experienced as the voice of God. When conscience is called in question as merely being the voice of the autistic self whose inner unity is threatened, a voice without truth, and when human inwardness that formerly was regarded as a pure and blissful beholding, analogous to the divine beholding, is declared to be a place of unsolved and repressed dividedness and conflicts, then we surely face a shocking devaluation of former values. What will Bonhoeffer put in their place? But we are not yet at an end of values lost.

4. e) The time of the human being's individuality is past. Of course, the isolated and unmistakable human individual will continue to exist. But in earlier times this individual owned the special dignity of being entitled and obliged to seek, above all else, after personal salvation, or spiritual wellbeing. Sermons preached in the times of Cultural Protestantism, and, later, of the Word of God theology, summoned the individual to do so. What Bonhoeffer has observed prompts him to ask, critically and rhetorically, "Is it not true that, for all of us, the individualistic quest for personal salvation has nearly vanished — that we, indeed, stand under the impression that other matters are more important than this quest . . . ?" "Is there any quest for salvation found in the Old Testament? Is it not true that justice and the Kingdom of God on earth are the center of everything — and that, in Romans 3:24-26, Paul's aim is to state that God alone is righteous, and not to teach an individualistic salvation?"[15]

Bonhoeffer deliberately turns to the Old Testament, texts that come from outside the sphere of influence of the god of the philosophers, the Greek God of metaphysics, against whom these texts ought to regain their weight. Old Testament faith, so Bonhoeffer insists, is "no religion of redemption," or of individual salvation on the other side of the boundary of death. Unlike myths of redemption, the Old Testament speaks of "historical redemptions" that orient the human being toward life on earth.[16] The pure *nous* of the god of metaphysics could have its analogy in the pure *nous* of the individual. In the masterwork of liberal theology, *Das Wesen des Christentums* [*What Is Christianity*], Adolf von Harnack could speak,

15. Letter of May 5, 1944, DBW 8, 415. LPP, 286.
16. Letter of June 27, 1944, DBW 8, 500. LPP, 336.

in 1899/1900, of the infinite value of the human soul. Ernst Troeltsch was even convinced that the most important contribution by Christianity to modernity had been the metaphysics of the individual. All of this is devaluated by Bonhoeffer through his Old Testament orientation and a corresponding interpretation of the Resurrection message.[17] Resurrection, that is, being created anew by God, is not due to an *a priori* aptness, or predisposition, inherent in the human being.

4. f) The time of the precedence of other-worldliness over this-worldliness is past. This is closely connected with all the other phenomena. As the unmoved mover, the god of metaphysics, the pure *nous,* is beyond time and space. The Christian individualist, whose whole concern is salvation in the beyond, can regard this world, in its relatively differing conditions, only as an insignificant transition stage to be endured patiently. Those who rely on inwardness imagine that eternity is already within themselves. But Christians see themselves, as whole human beings, first of all oriented toward this world wherein their lives are to be lived responsibly in faith amid the fullness of tasks, questions, successes, and failures, of experiences and perplexities, of mature action and accepted guilt, of health and happiness as well as suffering and harassment. Revaluation of values: this-worldly Christianity instead of otherworldliness. Occasionally, Bonhoeffer has stated, both together with and in opposition to Nietzsche, that the faithful are no backworldmen,[18] that is, people who do not really dwell in the world for which they are co-responsible, but in an imaginary world beyond the real one.

5. We will now collect the suggested phenomena of the fading and vanishing of religion. Words that are pious but not substantive, inwardness that is far from reality, a listening to conscience that causes isolation, metaphysics that evades worldly problems, concern for the beyond instead of living consciously in this world — for all that, religion appears to be the comprehensive concept, a ribbon that holds these phenomena together in a specific way, as a general view of the world, and a distinct feeling for the human being's position in the universe.

Bonhoeffer must be asked, then, what should take the place of those characteristics, or deficits, of religion. He clearly does not intend to merely subtract religion from all that, as if the remainders were all right and

17. Letter of March 27, 1944, DBW 8, 368-69. LPP, 240.
18. 1932 DBW 12, 264, and other places.

wholesome for life. Before we ask in detail what, according to Christian faith, should develop in a religionless situation, we must discuss the problem of the world's coming of age.

In the 1950s and 1960s, Bonhoeffer's formula of a world come of age was frequently mistaken for a license for an unchecked secular belief in progress, or even for a God is Dead theology[19] and the abolition of personal piety. Because of this misunderstanding, Bonhoeffer, since the turn to neo-conservatism, became the object of polemics. He himself describes how, since the thirteenth century, the human being took over more and more, and with increasing awareness, the part of one who is able and obliged to shape the human world. This became possible and necessary through "the discovery of the laws according to which the world lives in science, society and state, art, ethics, and religion, and manages to cope by itself." When world and life are shaped accordingly, a "hypothetical premise 'God'" to which to resort in case something can not (yet) be explained, appears to be dispensable. An uncanny security develops that everything will go just as well without such a god as a substitute, or stopgap, who takes action with his power when human formation fails to function. Failures are now ascribed to the human actor, and soberly taken into the bargain. To defame those who took over responsibility for the human world and act maturely, without making God religiously a factor in their calculation, is judged by Bonhoeffer to be "senseless," "ungentlemanly," and "un-Christian."[20]

But Bonhoeffer sees just as precisely — even before Hiroshima and Auschwitz happened, and the awareness of an ecological crisis arose — how deeply the human being come of age is endangered through its own autonomous deeds. The deepest reason for this is the human being's inner self-contradiction, or dividedness. There are insurances against dangers of all kinds, only not against the human being. In one place he remarks that it will be the specific task of "our church to counter the vices of the hubris of worshipping power, of envy, and of illusionism as the roots of all evil." Bonhoeffer does not harbor a one-sided optimism about maturity, nor is he of the opinion that the church should float along with the trends, and religiously legitimize worldly activities. On the contrary, the church

---

19. Among others, Thomas J. J. Altizer and William Hamilton, *Radical Theology and Death of God* (1966); Dorothee Sölle, *Stellvertretung. Ein Kapitel Theologie nach dem "Tode Gottes"* (1982).

20. Letter of June 8, 1944, DBW 8, 476-79. LPP, 325-27.

should critically confront the persons come of age, whatever their calling be, and tell them "what a life lived with Christ is, what it means 'to be there for others.'"[21] This must not be done in a patronizing way. Instead, the church should assist people in understanding their own coming of age better. Bonhoeffer, because of his view of sin, is conscious of the inclination of the human being come of age, imbued with ego-strength and power, to shape reality according to its own image and interests, without openness for and solidarity with others. However, it would be false to conclude from this insight that maturity must be met with suspicion.

6. We will now consider in reverse order the deficits that mark religion as questioned by Bonhoeffer.

On 4. f): The time when the beyond had precedence over this-worldliness is past. Bonhoeffer says expressly that he is not thinking of the shallow and banal this-worldliness of enlightened, or busy, or indolent, or lascivious people.[22] His concern is — seemingly a paradox — the this-worldliness of faith. Bonhoeffer's positive thesis is that the Old Testament and, even more, the hope for resurrection, make human beings live their lives "on earth." No "ultimate escape into the eternal" is left. "What is in this world must not prematurely be abolished."[23] Christian faith and life here on earth are linked up so tightly as was never the case in religious Christian tradition. Bonhoeffer can and must say that he sees in his own church, the Confessing Church, a remarkable readiness to "stand up for the 'matter' of the church, etc., but little personal faith in Christ. 'Jesus' vanishes from view."[24] In a this-worldly orientation, however, those who live in faith do not hang on to an imperceptible god in the beyond. Instead, it is Jesus who "addresses and claims the whole human life, in all its appearances, for himself and the Kingdom of God."[25] All weight falls on discipleship. What comes in sight first, are not sins and weaknesses of the human being, but human strengths, maturity, health, happiness, and power that issue from God's blessing.[26] Bonhoeffer calls "this-worldly" a life lived "in the fullness of the tasks, questions, successes and failures, experiences and perplexities," a life in which "no longer one's own sufferings, but God's

21. "Outline for a Book," August, 1944, DBW 8, 557 and 560. LPP, 381, 383.
22. Letter of July 21, 1944, DBW 8, 541. LPP, 369.
23. Letter of June 27, 1944, DBW 8, 500 and 501. LPP, 337.
24. "Outline for a Book," August, 1944, DBW 8, 557-58. LPP, 380-82.
25. Letter of June 30, 1944, DBW 8, 504. LPP, 342.
26. Letter of July 28, 1944, DBW 8, 548. LPP, 374.

sufferings in the world are taken seriously, and one keeps awake with Christ in Gethsemane, and I think that is faith, that is *metanoia* [change of heart], and, thus, one becomes a human being, a Christian. (Compare Jeremiah 45!)." We must listen quite closely. It is not denied that the human being is a sinner, and is weak. This emerges all too quickly. But traditionally this has made us forget that human beings are addressed and claimed by God in their strength, in their power, and in their gifts, so that they will engage themselves in affairs that pain God in the world, such as injustice, misery, oppression, emptiness, and senselessness. Human maturity and strength are needed when human beings, instead of living their lives revolving around their own problems and weaknesses and sufferings, are to tackle that from which God suffers for the sake of humankind. This course of human action, to be sure, leads to suffering, but not to a suffering of one who is occupied only with her or his own dear ego. Instead, it leads to sharing "God's suffering in one's this-worldly life"[27] — and this means to follow the path of Jesus Christ in this world.

On 4. e): In such a this-worldly life of faith, religious individualism is abandoned. The focus of concern is no longer personal salvation, but participation in the work of Jesus in this world, and, thus, in living in primary relatedness to the other human being, to the neighbor, since Jesus is the exemplary "man for others."[28] This "being for others" of Jesus and of those who follow him — who are set free from themselves — is regarded by Bonhoeffer as the genuine experience of transcendence, and as the new life. To experience transcendence means to experience what cannot be projected out of a human being's own self, not even out of the deepest inwardness. In a section of *Zarathustra*, entitled "Von den Hinterweltlern," Nietzsche wrote, "At one time, even Zarathustra threw his madness beyond the human being, like all backworld people. . . . Alas, you brothers, this god, whom I created, was human work and human madness, like all gods!" Bonhoeffer thinks of such statements by Nietzsche when he seeks genuine transcendence, a transcendence that will only be present for one who steps out from the ego-cage of individualism.

On 4. d): The time of metaphysics is past. We must keep in mind that Bonhoeffer takes his orientation from him who became human, Jesus Christ. Metaphysics knew the unity of what is true, good, and beautiful as

---

27. Letter of July 21, 1944, DBW 8, 542. LPP, 370.

28. "Outline for a Book," August, 1944, DBW 8, 559. LPP, 381-82.

the highest, absolute, divine idea, and deduced from it the orientation of the wise in the world. But the science, philosophy, and anthropology of today cannot arrive anywhere at such a unity of truth, goodness, and beauty. In a world after Auschwitz and Hiroshima, confidence in a good world order is broken; in the modern sciences, knowledge is segmented, and there are merely laborious attempts to hold insuperable inconsistencies together. Even supreme ideals, such as human dignity and human rights, are controversial. The West interprets human rights from the viewpoint that the right to freedom is dominant, and equality and participation are secondary. The East dissents one-sidedly from this interpretation. And no philosophy can provide grounds for human dignity that would be generally accepted. So people content themselves with interpreting human rights in ways that are advantageous for their respective systems of society, and practise nihilism when the question of truth comes up.

Bonhoeffer invites us to seek ultimate orientation from Jesus Christ who, according to the Gospel of John, says, "I am the way, the truth, and the life" (John 14:6). This orientation which, of course, does not issue exclusively from the authority revealed in Jesus, but also from the terrible occurrence of the crucifixion of an innocent one, seems to move God into a far distance, and alters every traditional image of God. Can God, who usually is called the Mighty, or the Almighty, suffer? Can he deliver the one he authorized into human hands, to be sentenced and put to death? The cross of Christ compels us to realize that God holds back his power, makes room for human power, and is revealed as the powerless one. Bonhoeffer formulates concisely: "God suffers to be pushed from the world onto the cross, God is powerless and weak in the world, and precisely and only as such is he with us and helps us."[29] Bonhoeffer has tried to think what is hardly thinkable — that God helps us through holding back his power, and through suffering himself. A person who is able to experience and think God Almighty in consonance with what happens in the world, does not need the crucified Jesus of Nazareth. But those who can no longer see and think God as ruler of the world, all-powerful, all-wise, all-good, should, if they do not want to fall into the abyss of nihilism, hold on to the suffering and the authority of the crucified one. In him, the turnabout from God's powerlessness to the wonder of new creation in the resurrection becomes evident. Metaphysical thinking has no room for the cross of Christ and the

29. Letter of July 16, 1944, DBW 8, 534. LPP, 360.

powerlessness of God. But for those who recognize their commission and authorization to participate in the messianic suffering of God in this world, the experience of being forsaken by God (Matthew 27:46; Psalm 22:2) is the gateway to the true experience of God.

On 4. c): The time of the autonomous conscience is past. For the religious human being, conscience represented the voice of God. The powerless God, hidden and pushed away, clearly cannot be the support for conscience. Already in 1942, for his book on ethics, Bonhoeffer showed how Christ gives orientation to the conscience of the faithful.[30]

What about — on 4. b) — inwardness? The personal relationship to Jesus Christ that Bonhoeffer lives and sees, is, indeed, an inward phenomenon. But it does not self-sufficiently and blissfully remain within, but must turn outwards. This is tersely expressed when in the letter written for the baptism of his god-child in May, 1944, Bonhoeffer speaks of praying and righteous doing among humankind. Prayer happens inwardly, but relates to the father of Jesus Christ and comes into the open in responsible action. Likewise, the time of intellectual or speculative inwardness and delight in pure knowledge, as an inner beholding, is past. Bonhoeffer predicts that the thinking of the coming generation "will only deal with what you will be responsible for in your acting. For us, thinking was frequently the luxury of the spectator. For you, it will be completely in the service of action."[31] Will meditative life be impoverished? By no means. Bonhoeffer emphasized the restitution of the arcane discipline of the faithful whose meditations on the mysteries of faith must not be proclaimed in public.[32]

On 4. a): The time of theological or pious words is past. This statement embraces all that Bonhoeffer expected and prayed and hoped for regarding the church of the future. He envisioned a church that does not defend and exonerate itself, but confesses, without any lenience toward itself, the concrete guilt it incurred by not resisting, even in martyrdom, the National Socialist regime, and failing to help those who were persecuted; a church that does not try to rescue religion, but whose proclamation aims at consequences of faith for behavior, and is marked by its standing up responsibly for others; a church that proclaims the biblical message

30. *Ethics,* DBWE 6:278-79.

31. "Thoughts on the Day of Baptism of D. W. R. Bethge," May, 1944, DBW 8, 435 and 433. LPP, 298 and 296.

32. Letter of May 5, 1944, DBW 8, 415, LPP, 286, and elsewhere.

religionlessly, and not as if it represented God's almightiness; a church that confronts the hubris of human power, instead of conforming, for the sake of its self-preservation, to the powers that be; pastors who practice worldly professions, renounce former privileges, and live by voluntary contributions of the communities; a church that takes part in "the worldly tasks of human community life, not ruling but helping and serving."[33]

In his vision of a future church after the end of the Hitler regime, Bonhoeffer did not see a secularized, spiritually weak church, conforming to the trends and powers of the times. But the Protestant church of the Federal Republic of Germany after 1945 did not follow the path that Bonhoeffer had sketched. There was no concrete confession of guilt — it would have stirred up heavy conflicts within the church. There was no change in the relation of church and state — the Roman Catholic church, with its unbroken claims, dragged the Protestants along. There was no reform of the education of theologians. There was no self-critical reticence regarding proclamation — on the contrary, the claim of the church to have a say in public was trumpeted.

Whether or not someone errs can only be established by testing, probing, and gaining experience in what he proposed. Judged by its behavior, our Protestant church did not probe into Bonhoeffer's proposal.

Besides the church, however, there are so-called religious and pseudo-religious movements a plenty. This had also been the case in the 1920s, when the society in Germany was infested with a multitude of irrational movements, including nationalistic religiosity. If I see rightly, all of these present movements are not major religions, but irrationalisms that flourish and pass; movements that supply a want caused by a sense of meaninglessness and emptiness of spiritual and emotional life; movements in which people seek a compensation for the coldness in our society, and for the immobility of our church; movements which for those who keep them going are a thriving financial religious business. But I am not knowledgeable enough in this regard for a well-grounded opinion.

Personally, I see the path of Bonhoeffer full of promise. Its future — so I think — lies still ahead. Some of what happens in the theologies of liberation, and in the grassroots communities all over the world, is connected with Bonhoeffer's outlook. So it is necessary to hand on to future generations Bonhoeffer's theology, faith, and witness given with his life.

33. "Outline for a Book," August, 1944, DBW 8, 560. LPP, 382-83.

5 Resistance by Word and Political Resistance in Ethical Responsibility: The Individual, the Groups, and the Church

1980

Preliminary Remarks

Our generation is witnessing a measureless escalation of violence in many parts of the world. Are we mistaken in regarding this as unprecedented? In earlier generations, violence was widespread, for example, in colonialism and in class struggles. But a flood of worldwide information, and an abundance of disputes about *violentia* have intensified our sensibility to this troublesome and agonizing theme. There exist in our world, of course, several major islands of prosperity where law and order rule and where citizens are, to a certain extent, protected from unlawful violence. Most of these islands are industrial nations. But even within these, prosperity and peace based on justice cannot be enjoyed lightheartedly. For these nations are accused of having exploited and impoverished, for the sake of their own prosperity, those regions of the Third World that, in dependence and in material needs, struggle for their liberation and the bare necessities of life. And there are also areas where industrial prosperity and postcolonial dependence intersect and either generate or exacerbate violent conflicts, as, for example, in Southern Africa. These conflicts concern us directly, because we influence them all the time through our decisions. By "we" I mean us citizens of nations whose attitude is either hostile or friendly to liberation movements, and us members of churches whose solidarity with the suffering people and also with the sister churches in these areas is called forth. Perhaps we wish to remain neutral. We feel not informed enough to take a stand. We would rather not dirty our hands interfering in violence and bloodshed. But whatever we wish or do, we, directly or indirectly, are always entangled. We wish for a peaceful world, but the circumstances are adverse.

Those who live in biblical traditions are reminded of the God of Israel who, working in hiddenness but irresistibly, overturns all power relationships. Luke 1:52 says of him, "He has put down rulers from their thrones, but has lifted up the humble." We, who are well-off, are faced by this God who is party to the hungry and the lowly, and whose working in the world threatens us. How should we behave in this divine world revolution, which differs crucially from the political and social revolutions that are nevertheless constantly used by God? How do we respond to those who resort to violent means in their need?

In the established churches of Germany there are two modes of response. The first one argues that the churches cannot support liberation movements that seek to gain their freedom and rights by using violence. Churches are bound on principle to give nonviolent help to nonviolent actions. This argument is, at first sight, strongly valid. Using violence always involves guilt, and it cannot be the task of the church to encourage people to act so that they incur guilt. But might there be situations in which both action and non-action entangle in guilt? And might the attitude of a church in a Western society that wishes to support only strictly nonviolent action, on principle, regardless of the concrete situation, be backed up by massive interests? A 1978 position paper on South Africa today, *Hope at what Price,* issued by the World Council of Churches in Geneva, cites Bonhoeffer who, despite his contempt for violence, participated in the attempt to kill Hitler. A speaker of the Protestant Church in Germany rejected the reference to Bonhoeffer, arguing that Bonhoeffer's action resulted from a completely personal contingent decision of conscience that was not a decision of the church.[1] This is historically correct. No resolution had been passed by the Confessing Church that could be construed as a summons to tyrannicide, thus legitimating Bonhoeffer's action. But what really matters is whether the church, in retrospection, adopts Bonhoeffer's step and recognizes it as a precedent for a possible Christian orientation in comparable future situations. This has never happened in the churches of the Federal Republic of Germany. Can we be satisfied with this?

1. See above, chapter 1, II, 1.

When a church, on principle, rejects movements that cannot or will not renounce the use of violence, a second, much older argument comes into play. It states that only Christian individuals, guided by their personal conscience, can make political decisions. The church-community cannot decide about politics. It must respect the decisions of each of its many members, and may only sharpen the consciences of the individuals with its proclamation.

To follow this basic principle strictly would mean that preaching can only call upon the individual in a formal manner to decide conscientiously. Christian preaching would, then, not concern the subject matter of the decision. It would be a call to an existence guided by conscience. Proclamation would remain on neutral ground, above factions, as if the church were equally the church of all groups in the society, and not primarily bound up with a single stratum, for example, the middle class.

This neutral understanding of the church, of preaching, and of conscience had already deeply disturbed Dietrich Bonhoeffer in 1932, immediately prior to the seizure of power by National Socialism. Bonhoeffer considered neutral preaching to be the proclamation of a faint church that abandons its commission and existence. He was convinced that the church must venture to proclaim the Christian message in its elementary sense concretely, that is, in the context of specific situations and fundamental decisions. In a letter of December 25, 1932, he regrets "that our church today cannot speak the concrete commandment" — although Christ who is present in the church commands, through his word, quite concretely, and addresses not only the individual but "also a congregation and a people" as hearers of this commandment.[2] At this time, when the National Socialists' seizure of power was immanent, Bonhoeffer was thinking of a vast and resolute partisanship of the churches in their ecumenical alliance for the promotion of peace, rejecting belligerence and the preparation for war. The Protestant churches did not respond to Bonhoeffer's challenge, and before long the National Socialists could start the militarization of the German people without objection from the church.

To this, a second problem was soon added: the persecution of the Jews, beginning in March and April of 1933. Bonhoeffer immediately challenged the church to oppose that by proclaiming the concrete commandment. Here also, the church was clearly not capable of concretely pro-

2. Letter to Helmut Roessler, DBW 12, 39-40.

claiming the Word of God. It did not even stand up resolutely in public for Jewish Christians, members of the Christian church-community, and, again, left it to the individuals to be told by their consciences how far to help in individual cases.

On the road to both the Second World War and the Holocaust, the churches did not even intervene with a resolute witness in the face of the wielders of power. Bonhoeffer viewed this as heavy guilt incurred by the church.

But we should not think this easy to judge. Are we, whose history contains such events, today in a position to proclaim God's commandment concretely? Do we, at bottom, still believe that political decisions should always be left to individual conscience, while the church has nothing to say and to confess in common? If this were so, then we would be just as weak as the church of 1932 and 1933 that could not understand Bonhoeffer's challenges, let alone muster the courage to act accordingly. We must ask ourselves whether and how we might follow Bonhoeffer's insight and intention today, or whether we can only admire him as an exceptional prophet on whom the gift was bestowed of doing what we cannot do.

Considering these questions, we meet with three key concepts: the individual, the group, and the church.

1. The Individual

1.1. No epoch has advocated the rights of individuals as resolutely as modernity. The Enlightenment set the individual's reason free by raising the courage to judge maturely (*sapere aude,* venture to know, was Kant's formula). The movement toward democracy and human rights attempted to secure the individual's legal position against the power of the state, and against societal forces, by means of constitution and legislation. "The dignity of the human being is untouchable." This is professed at the beginning of the basic law of the Federal Republic of Germany. The economic individualism of property was based on the premise that the citizen and proprietor, in competition with all others, has nothing else to seek in the market but their own advantage and profit — a legally regulated struggle of everyone against everyone, which was expected to yield the greatest benefit for the commonwealth, since competition would urge each of them on to utmost productivity. The dominant interest here is production stimulated by mutual competition. Antagonism will be made safe by the law. Immanuel Kant said, "The law is a condition in which everyman can safely have his own against the other one."[3]

How is a society to be assessed that is oriented toward economic individualism? John Maynard Keynes, the famous English political economist who died in 1946, judged that modern capitalism is completely nonreligious, without inner coherence, lacking in public spirit, not always, but often, a mere heap of "possessors and pursuers." To put it differently, individualism in economy and society will unleash the individual's productive forces, but the public spirit, the solidarity among the citizens and of the citizens with the commonwealth, in short, the emotional bonds, will waste away. Where individualism rules alone, it will make society into a mechanical social apparatus in which all are fixed on their own interests, and face each other in competition, or at a cool distance.

What type of religion fits this society? Undoubtedly, a religious individualism that regards any decision as a matter of the personal conscience of an individual who rejects interference. Bonhoeffer spoke of an individualistic religion in which all emotional needs are focused on inwardness and privacy.[4] He was convinced that this would end up in religionlessness, and that Christian faith must not depend on this type of religion.

Since 1945, individualism in all areas has rapidly increased in the Federal Republic of Germany during its Westernization and Americanization. At the same time the awareness has increased that a modern society in which individual claims and needs dominate cannot last. To give a matter-of-fact example, the average individual citizen in an industrial society can no longer supply their old age needs by their own possessions or property in the earlier sense. They need an income that is adjusted to economic development. Such an income can only be financed by solidarity between the generations. Those who are working today pay for the support of the older people, and must trust that the next working generation will support them in their old age. But where does the incentive for solidarity come from in a society that, practically and ideologically, is based on the individual's interests and claims, and fosters religious individualism?

1.2. In his early writings, Bonhoeffer shares the traditional German criticism of so-called Western individualism, capitalism, and liberalism,

---

3. *Metaphysik der Sitten* [1789, Metaphysics of Morals], AB 44.
4. Letter from prison, May 5, 1944, DBW 8, 414-15. LPP, 285-87.

because they isolate people and extinguish public spirit. In *Sanctorum Communio,* Bonhoeffer in no way eliminates the individual and the subjective spirit, but he contrasts this with the concept of an "objective spirit" that pervades a "collective person." The cool relationship between individuals that are isolated through economy and law is countered by the concept of community. Social philosophy, with its "individualistic social atomism," is mostly blind to the reality that is meant by the concept of community.[5] "The only fruitful relationship with human beings — in particular with those who are weak — is love, that is, the will to keep community with them."[6]

But even this very concept of community was unscrupulously misused and discredited by the National Socialists. They slyly mobilized emotions in the population — the elemental feeling of belonging that makes people stand up for each other — and termed it "national community" [*Volksgemeinschaft*]. As the opposite of Western individualism, the concept of community, lacking sharp contours and abounding in associations, could be used not only in a romantically blurred sense, but also for an ideological function, and become a pre-fascist slogan. Is there a pre-fascist ambiguity also in Bonhoeffer's concept of community?

1.3. In view of the fascist misuse of the concept of community, Bonhoeffer evidently looked for other terms to express the reality he saw, namely, the bond of solidarity connecting the individual with the many others in a commonwealth. These are, chiefly, the terms of history, responsibility, and guilt. In a manuscript for his book on ethics he argues that there is no such thing as an isolated individual who would choose, based on one's own conscience as if wielding an absolute criterion, between what is good or evil in and of itself. When the church demands of individuals to make all fundamental decisions on the grounds of their consciences, without offering assistance in solidarity with them, then the church follows an abstract ideology of individualism. Reality is different. "The question about the good is asked and decided . . . in the midst of our historical existence."[7]

What does history mean here? What function does it have in the life of an individual? Let us take an example. In June, 1939, Bonhoeffer decided, after a difficult inner struggle, and aware of the imminent outbreak of war,

---

5. 1927/1930 DBWE 1:33.
6. "After Ten Years," December 1942, DBW 8, 29. LPP, 10-11.
7. *Ethics,* 1942 DBWE 6:247.

to return from the United States of America to Germany. This all-but-suicidal decision will become unintelligible when reasoning starts from the individual's rights and duties. Bonhoeffer, however, was convinced that he had to participate in the fate and guilt of his people in order to be allowed to begin anew together with them after the war. History, then, is the space of concrete solidarity, and this also means that liability must really be shared, and guilt must consciously be taken on oneself. Not only the individual, but also every group and church will thus be connected with and included in a greater continuity — not blindly and involuntarily but co-responsibly. Bonhoeffer opposed the bonds of responsibility to irrational bondage. For this reason, he considered the church guilty of not having proclaimed concretely and urgently God's commandment to the German people. Already in 1941, when Hitler was at the peak of his power, Bonhoeffer wrote a confession of the church's guilt that included its being guilty of the persecution of Jews.[8] In the Stuttgart confession of guilt of 1945 by the Council of the Protestant Church in Germany, the Holocaust — this blatant iniquity in German history — was not mentioned at all.

1.4. Bonhoeffer's understanding of history, which I have just touched on, is a theological and, in particular, christological understanding. History is that reality in which Jesus Christ, in the vicarious representative action of taking on guilt, has bound himself to humankind. Through him, all human life is destined to be lived in vicarious representation. The task of Christian ethics is to make us aware of the "structures of responsible life,"[9] so as to give orientation to human life and activity. The starting point for understanding and living a responsible life cannot be the isolated individual, but must be the human being who is interwoven with the lives of the many, and aware of being bound to them.

Does Bonhoeffer's reasoning skip human individuality, or the typically modern quest for autonomous self-existence? Does the community or the state gain precedence again, and with it the legitimation to control and speak for the individual without listening, or to lay claim to the individual's life when reason of state deems it necessary? By no means. Responsible life remains individual life, but in a way that joins freedom and bonding. Freedom is proven in the self-examination of one's own life and activity, and in the venture of concrete decisions. Bonding is practiced by

8. *Ethics,* 1941 DBWE 6:138-41.
9. *Ethics,* 1942 DBWE 6: 257-89.

entering into the concrete texture of interwoven lives so as to act in accordance with reality, and in vicarious representation.[10] Bonhoeffer understands freedom as communicative freedom that is realized by each individual in togetherness. This means that conscience is not the isolated individual's, but the conscience of a human being who lives in communication with others. And vice versa, to be bound does not mean to become submerged in the tutelage of a collective, but is the responsible taking over of a bond by each one personally, a bond affirmed by the human being come of age.

This has consequences for the behavior of Christians in secular modern society. When this society is unilaterally guided by the programmatics of individual self-realization, or self-fulfillment, and of a mechanical aggregation of individuals to be regulated by law, then the Christian can strengthen the repressed elements of solidarity — of the binding community — without impairing individual rights, for example, citizens' and human rights. And vice versa, when societies today are in danger of putting individuals under tutelage and at their disposal, then the Christian will strengthen those elements that give the individual free space for the venture of self-examination and concrete decision. Individualism must be overcome communicatively, and collectivism must be overcome by the human being's coming of age. In this context, a specific weight is ascribed by Bonhoeffer to the association of bearers of responsibility — beyond individualism — and to the church as Jesus Christ's being for the world whereby human beings are allied in brotherhood with each other. In order to correct individualism, not eliminate it, I will discuss the group and the church.

2. The Group

2.1. It is abstract talk to confront the individual immediately with the state, the commonwealth, or the church, since everyone is simultaneously a member of intermediary institutions — for example, the family, or a firm as the place of work — and intermediary groups in which the individual's judgment and conscience develop. I will single out one type of group, namely, the initiative group, and consider the special group in which

10. *Ethics*, DBWE 6:257.

Bonhoeffer lived from 1938 on as participant in knowledge of the political resistance planning, and from 1940 on as participant in the conspiracy. In entering this group, he passed from resistance by word in the Confessing Church to politically organized resistance by deed. This special group, in this specific situation of life under an inhuman rule of violence, is, of course, but one instance among many other paradigms.

Resistance that is pushed into illegality needs, as a rule, small initiative groups. The individual would be incapable of actively opposing a totalitarian regime, and in larger institutions secrecy would be impossible. In a conspiratorial group, a high concentration of trust must prevail. The fate of each is dependent on that of the others. Solidarity in view of the common goal is the basic condition for all initiative groups.

Initiative groups lack the legitimation by procedure and ritual through which conscience is quieted. Family and business company, political party, the governing body of the established church and of the legal state profit from these legitimizations. In all these cases, there are departments over which somebody is in charge, with duties and rights to be observed in the respective traditional role. The initiative group, however, must legitimize itself ever anew, even in their own eyes, and on occasion in public. It is not merely a place of common information, orientation, and resolution, not only a body with the potential to take action, but a place where conscience is formed communicatively — and the more so, the less its doings are recognized as legitimate by the state and society. Irregular deed falls back on the decision of our own conscience.

2.2. The conscience is an inner voice that warns, reveals contradictions, and thus gives direction. A moving document of the wrestling of conscience in a group is found in Bonhoeffer's account rendered at the end of 1942, "After Ten Years." Here, a "we" is speaking. "We have been silent witnesses to evil deeds . . . we have learned the skills of dissimulation and ambiguous speech, experience has made us distrustful of people — are we still useful?" Useful for what? For taking over responsibility for the course of history, for acting in vicarious representation and without legal protection. Bonhoeffer did not ignore the voice of a warning conscience that advised against unavoidable guilt, but replied that "the final responsible question is not how to pull myself heroically out of the affair, but how the coming generation is to live."[11] The conscience, to be sure, concerns one's

---

11. DBW 8, 38 and 25. LPP, 16-17 and 7.

own self, but not the isolated self. It concerns a self that is conscious of the responsibility that falls to it from outside, a self that, for example, feels co-responsible for the life of the next generation.

2.3. The resistance group into which Bonhoeffer became integrated is frequently characterized and devalued as elitist, pursuing upper-class interests, and conservative. The memorandum of the so-called Bonhoeffer group of experts in Freiburg[12] bespeaks a view of history held by German cultured citizenry that is frequently at variance with Bonhoeffer. It must not be denied here that the vision and interests of the group in which Bonhoeffer participated were actually limited. No one is free from such weaknesses. What is decisive is how much the outlook and concern of the group in its situation is congruous with the general interest of the whole population. To reach this generality was surely and expressly the goal of this and other groups. On this basis, men and women from both the bourgeois tradition and the labor movement became allies. In a situation in which the wielders of power answered any alternative with the executioner's ax, it was crucial to be in agreement that, according to conscientious judgment, moral self-extermination through obedience to a criminal regime must in no way be accepted — and that meant that one's own life had to be put at stake in order to remove the criminal regime.

2.4. What Bonhoeffer conceptualized from 1940 to 1943 for *Ethics* often seems written for initiative groups of like-minded people. Here is a characteristic passage: "Extraordinary necessity appeals to the freedom of those who act responsibly. In this case there is no law behind which they could take cover. Therefore there is also no law that, in the face of such necessity, could force them to make this rather than that particular decision. Instead, in such a situation, one must completely let go of any law," that is, of legality, "knowing that here one must decide as a free venture. This must also include the open acknowledgment that here the law is being broken, violated; that the commandment is broken out of dire necessity, thereby affirming the legitimacy of the law in the very act of violating it" — and finally one will surrender "one's own decision and action to the divine guidance of history."[13]

12. Memorandum from 1943, published in Tübingen 1979 as *In der Stunde Null. Die Denkschrift des Freiburger "Bonhoefferkreises": Politische Gemeinschaftsordnung. Ein Versuch zur Selbstbesinnung des christlichen Gewissens in den politischen Nöten unserer Zeit.* [In the zero hour. Memorandum of the Freiburg "Bonhoeffer circle" on political communal order, reflecting upon the Christian conscience in the political needs of our times.]

13. *Ethics*, 1942 DBWE 6:274.

A characteristic of this ethic is that it cannot rely on principles. It even does not make Jesus' Sermon on the Mount, with its call to the renunciation of violence, into a principle. The attempt to derive the goodness of an action from its accordance with principles will make the action ideological. This will happen, for example, when a church relies on the principle of legality, or of non-violence. "Whereas all action based on ideology is already justified by its own principle, responsible action renounces any knowledge about its ultimate justification. The deed . . . is completely surrendered to God the moment it is carried out. Ultimate ignorance of one's own goodness or evil, together with dependence upon grace, is an essential characteristic of responsible historical action."[14] Here, *nota bene,* the law is not deprived of its binding force, and accountability is not cancelled. On the contrary, Bonhoeffer passionately struggled for adherence to the law, and for action guided by a conscientious rendering of account. But he came to see that, in the reality of the world in which we live, it does happen that every option of action is intertwisted with evil. Here, judgment must be ventured freely as to what action is now responsible, even if not without guilt. The conscience warns against entanglement in guilt. A scrupulous conscience will, in the end, mislead to non-action, permissiveness, and adaptation. Responsibility, however, urges to take over, with eyes open, the unavoidable guilt that is ever and again linked up with the venture to act. Faith in God's forgiveness of guilt affords the gift to bear guilt without repressing it. Therefore faith is more than conscience. It sets free the human being whom conscience accused. It thus sets the human being free to act. In such freedom for responsible action, a group will join to venture the deed in solidarity. The group does not relieve individuals of the task to examine their own consciences. But it provides space for mutual information and communicative clarification of what responsible action means here and now. So the examination of the individual's conscience is placed in a new context. The crucial problem of the resistance group to which Bonhoeffer belonged was the question of whether, and whereby, they would be empowered to remove the lawless regime by violent means and bloodshed.

2.5. Bonhoeffer considers the use of violence, not as legal power but as irregular violence. "There are occasions when, in the course of historical life, the strict observance of the explicit law of a state, a corporation, a fam-

14. *Ethics,* 1942 DBWE 6:268.

ily, but also of a scientific discovery, entails a clash with the basic necessities of human life. In such cases, appropriate responsible action departs from the domain governed by laws and principles, from the normal and regular, and instead is confronted with the extraordinary situation of ultimate necessities that are beyond any possible regulation by law." Such necessities "no longer permit human reasoning to come up with a variety of exit strategies, but pose the question of the *ultima ratio*." There is no rational legitimization for an overthrow, a revolution, or a violent struggle for liberty. It would be wrong to try to devise a Christian teaching on just revolution or — under the present conditions — on just war. *Ultima ratio* action cannot be regulated by a law. "It would be a complete and total misunderstanding if the *ultima ratio* itself were again turned into a rational law, if the borderline case were made the norm, the *necessità* a technique."[15] But neither the individual nor the group may spare themselves the conscientiously sought and found proof that here and now they deal with an *ultima ratio* case. Otherwise, they run the risk of misusing the freedom that those who are responsible have.

2.6. The structures and possibilities of groups are clearly distinct from those of both the individual and the church. Where an individual cannot accomplish anything, the group has special opportunities for information, communicative forming of judgment and will, and action. But it also has, as we saw, a special burden to bear. A justification for the group's activity can be derived neither from the necessity to preserve the moral integrity of the individual, nor from the acknowledged legitimacy of the established church. Specific reasons for its actions must be provided, in which awareness of responsibility, communication about goals and means, and accounting for the conscientiously recognized ethical necessity come together. Such specific reasoning is constantly called for, not only in resistance against totalitarian regimes, but also in the public life of democracies, as can be seen from the examples of groups that are engaged in disputes about nuclear energy, pollution, the integration of discriminated population groups, and the like. Surely, it is extremely difficult to provide justification in situations where such initiatives are pushed into illegality, as happens with dissident groups in the Soviet Union, or with human rights groups in South Korea, or with groups combatting racism in Southern Africa. In those cases, *ultima ratio* comes into view, and the pressing

15. *Ethics*, 1942 DBWE 6:272-73.

question arises as to what would authorize them to take action under such conditions. Bonhoeffer expected authorization from the clash with primordial necessities of life, as from the need that the state, commissioned to administer peace, justice, and communal life in human dignity, destroys law and order, so that an action becomes necessary that cannot be grasped by any law. The certainty that this is an emergency is the prerequisite of extraordinary illegal action. Since political and social conditions have to be judged, certainty cannot spring from a subjective intuition of conscience. In order to prevent the danger of merely judging subjectively, the judgment must be formed in common and with one accord. But common judgments need criteria. Can the proclamation of the church help to find them? Bonhoeffer did expect this from his church when he demanded that it should proclaim the concrete commandment of God today, here, and now.

3. The Church

3.1. So the question arises: How can churches deal with Christians who, in need, venture illegal resistance and use of violence? If they have nothing to say but to call upon the individual's conscience to decide on political actions, they factually distance themselves from them. The proclamation, then, seems to contribute nothing to the content of the decision, and is as neutralized and privatized as modern political and religious philosophy expects religion to be. On the other hand, the proclamation cannot wish to justify, on principle, violence in the situation of *ultima ratio*. It would thereby level down the crucial difference, emphasized by Bonhoeffer, between violence in case of need, and violence as principle, as law. The commission of the church is to proclaim the gospel and command of God concretely for a situation. Under an inhuman regime of injustice, this preaching will inevitably, and on its own authority, become resistance by word, and will, under the prevailing conditions, entail repressions and persecutions. What is needed here is not a direct political action of the church, but only the unswerving witness to the truth — and this is the primary mandate of the church.

3.2. The witness to truth will be all the more effective, the more a regime of injustice veils its rule of violence and buys off adherents and accomplices through benefits, and the more the difference between right and wrong is blurred. The National Socialists, for example, camouflaged the genocide of Jews and so-called gypsies — Roma and Sinti — with the propaganda that it would be of vital importance to eliminate elements that constantly poisoned and disintegrated the communal life of nations. The success of this propaganda even in the church is almost inconceivable for us today. Even the Freiburg Memorandum that had been requested by the Provisional Administration of the Confessing Church in the late summer of 1942, a statement coming from oppositional circles, uncritically took over the National Socialist notion of race, and deemed it the state's duty to restrain the fatal influence of a race on the national community [*Volksgemeinschaft*] — which should, however, certainly not be achieved by lawless and immoral measures. Considering how great the difficulty in distinguishing between right and wrong in the complexities of life is for one who is haunted by instincts of self-preservation and anxieties, and whose conscience can be "salved," or "deceived,"[16] the task of witnessing to the truth is immense. It is the core of the church's resistance by word.

3.3. Many people believe resistance by word is not enough. They demand liberating revolutionary action from the church. Seemingly they can appeal to Bonhoeffer's statement on the Jewish question in April of 1933, where he argued that the church, on the one hand, cannot immediately act in a political way, but that, on the other hand, it is duty-bound to act immediately politically when the state no longer keeps up law and order. In this case it is not enough to patch up the victims crushed by the wheel; rather, the wheel itself — that is, the state's doings — must be stopped.[17] By what means? At that time, Bonhoeffer thought of an ecumenical council that would set consciences free for resistance. The church would not act politically, but would resist by word, and thus, through exposing the notoriously lawless political situation as a case of need, and delegitimizing the wielders of power, would support the groups ready for and capable of taking political responsibility.

According to my understanding, the mandates of the church and of Christians in political action groups remain different even in the borderline case. But there is no difference in so far as both are bound to, and witness to, the same Christ.

3.4. This view, so it seems to me, accords with the preaching of Jesus.

16. *Ethics,* 1940 DBWE 6:79.
17. DBW 12, 353.

Jesus did not summon to direct political action. But his sermon was by no means politically neutral. Jesus' call to renounce violence (Mark 10:42-45), and to serve instead of domineering (Luke 22:24-27), simultaneously laid bare the use of violence by the wielders of power and the unjust power relations in this world. How acutely the political consequences of Jesus' work were felt appears from the fact that he was condemned as a political agitator. His voice challenged the repressions perpetrated by violent rulers. This is not done by a neutral, non-partisan sermon — at the cost that the voice of Jesus can no more be recognized in the voice of the church.

3.5. Surely the church's witness to the truth and resistance by word are accompanied by activity, for example, intercession in solidarity and care for the victims of the wielders of power, actions which are always perceived as political provocation — in National Socialist Germany, those who helped Jews were persecuted as well. The church's activity includes giving spiritual encouragement to those who look for alternatives in order to re-establish justice and peace. The church must not, for the sake of self-preservation, break with those who venture political action responsibly in illegality. They need the spiritual community of the brothers and sisters in the church.

In a letter to Eberhard Bethge, Bonhoeffer wrote on November 18, 1943, after more than seven months of imprisonment, that at first the question had disquieted him "whether it really was the cause of Christ" by reason of which he now grieved his family and friends and his Confessing Church, "but I soon put this question out of my head as a tribulation, and became certain that going through such a borderline case, with all its problems, was my commission, and became quite happy by this, and have remained so to this day."[18] The church cannot take the struggles of conscience from those who are in tribulation. But it owes them unbroken community, and consolation through the word of forgiveness of sins. This is denied when a political action, such as that into which Bonhoeffer entered, is declared to be nothing more than an individual contingent decision of conscience. Certainly it is a personal decision, but the church should help to bear the burden of it through its resistance by word. Otherwise it will become an accomplice to the wielders of power. In the beginning of the struggle of the Confessing Church, Bonhoeffer wrote to Erwin Sutz, "It is high time to break with the theologically based reticence about

18. DBW 8, 187-88. LPP, 128-29.

the doings of the state — it is nothing but fear — "Speak up for those who cannot speak for themselves," Proverbs 31:8 — who in the church today knows still that this is the very least requirement of the Bible in such times?"[19] Or, differently said, the declaration of Peter — one must obey God rather than people (Acts 5:29) — is the immovable criterion for deciding on resistance by word.

4. Conclusion

4.1. A result of our considerations is that individuals, groups, and the church cannot be separated, but must be closely correlated when responsible resistance against an inhuman and illegitimate regime of injustice is called for. All three have different responsibilities that cannot be substituted, and distinct mandates. The individual must fight in faith the trial of conscience that unavoidably accompanies the free venture of an illegitimate deed. The group is the space within which a judgment of the situation and the will to act are formed in solidarity and communication. The church is, for both, individuals and groups, the support that gives certainty through witnessing to the truth, the source of inseparable community grounded in Christ, and the place where sin and guilt are forgiven. It was a tribulation for Bonhoeffer that what belongs together was separated in and by his church, so that individuals and the groups of like-minded people had to endure the trials alone and mostly in isolation.

4.2. What does this mean for theology today? We have seen that modern individualism disintegrates the solidarity even of the faithful by privatizing religion and reducing conscience to a purely formal forum in the individual. We experience in this twentieth century, as a counter-move to individualism, various collectivisms in which the individual is but a wheel in a mechanical total context. Individualism and collectivism face each other in official opposition and clandestine complicity. Each is the other's antitype, in contrast to which each comes to look more promising. Bonhoeffer's thinking centers on a concept of responsibility for history that admits neither individualism nor collectivism. Individualism is excluded because the appeal to bear responsibility comes from history, that is, from what is going on in politics and society, and is borne in a relation-

19. DBW 13, 204-5.

ship in which the individuals, endowed as they are with knowledge, will, and conscience, deal with what happens in the surrounding world. Collectivism is excluded because responsibility cannot be shifted to the collective, and the collective cannot determine it. It is crucial that the church and Christianity neither lapse into the one or the other, but proclaim and practice a life of communication in solidarity which is the corrective necessary for every society to ward off intolerable deformations, even though no societal order will fully realize it. But is theology able to keep up and work out this perspective, or does theology, too, succumb to dictates of conformity to society, adapting unreflectedly and uncritically to current scientific reasoning and societal interests?

6 Discrimination Against Jews in 1933: The Real Test for Bonhoeffer's Ethics

1982

Ever since Eberhard Bethge's Bonhoeffer biography was published in 1967, all experts have shown their astonishment at the clear-sightedness and decisiveness with which the twenty-seven-year-old theologian Dietrich Bonhoeffer judged the political situation and the tasks of the church in the spring of 1933. Karl Barth wrote to Bethge on May 22, 1967, "What was new to me was especially the fact that from 1933 on Bonhoeffer was the first, indeed almost the only one, who so centrally and energetically focused on and acted in the Jewish question. I have felt for a long time that it was a guilt of mine that I did not also — not in public, that is — urge it in the church struggle (for example in the two Barmen Declarations of 1934 of which I was the author) as being crucial."[1]

Despite the first boycotts and violent actions against Jews beginning around April 1, 1933, and despite the so-called Aryan clause — paragraph 3 of the Law for the Reconstruction of the Professional Civil Service of April 7, 1933 — church leadership in Germany across the board were incapable of seeing the "Jewish question" as a grave ecclesiastical problem. They did notice, however, that this matter was "not a peripheral issue for the government, but a central point of its program," as Regional Bishop Heinrich Rendtorff declared in the session of the governing body of the German Protestant Church on April 26, 1933, in Berlin.[2] The number of Christians

---

1. Karl Barth (see above, chapter 1, I, 1), p. 403.
2. Minutes of the proceedings of the German Protestant Church Committee on April

of Jewish descent, especially within the Protestant pastorate, was rather small. Besides, the distance from the Jews was great, both from those who were assimilated, and from members of synagogues, and the rejection of Jews in church tradition and nationalistic thinking was deep and unreflective, so that the idea of being bound to manifest some kind of solidarity occurred only to a few.

In a book on the churches and the Third Reich, Klaus Scholder, treating the "Jewish question" of 1933, praises Bonhoeffer's short essay "The Church Before the Jewish Question"[3] of April, 1933, as "most illuminating and both politically and theologically outstanding among the productions coming from these years. Here, with incomparable precision, the theological view of problematic state action was conceptualized in a new way that still possesses validity, even under the changed conditions of the present." Scholder gives major weight to Bonhoeffer's statements on the responsibility of the church vis-à-vis the state that, in their consistency and clarity, are unprecedented in Protestant traditions, unless one goes back to the religious wars and the Monarchomachians in the sixteenth and seventeenth centuries. Scholder writes, somewhat imprecisely, that "in the spring of 1933, Bonhoeffer still without any doubt conceded to the state the right to solve the Jewish question through exceptional legislation" — like Walter Künneth.[4] Bonhoeffer himself says more cautiously that the "state is entitled to steer new courses here."[5] These new courses must not necessarily be "exceptional legislation." As Bonhoeffer continues his argument, he sets incisive bounds to such language by insisting on a constitutional rule of law. Scholder did not mention at all that Bonhoeffer names the conditions that bring the church into a *status confessionis,* namely, the compulsory exclusion of baptized Jews from Christian congregations, and the prohibition of Christian mission among Jews, by order of the state. According to Protestant understanding, a *status confessionis* can arise only when central truths of the confession of faith are endangered. This top priority was as-

25-26, 1933, in Berlin (*Evangelisches Zentralarchiv,* EKD A 2/28); excerpts printed in Armin Boyens, *Kirchenkampf und Ökumene 1933-1939. Darstellung und Dokumentation* (Munich: 1965), pp. 295-99, quote from p. 298.

    3. DBW 12, *Berlin 1932-1933* (Gütersloh: 1997), pp. 349-58.

    4. Klaus Scholder, *Die Kirchen und das Dritte Reich,* volume I (Frankfurt/Main: 1977), p. 350.

    5. DBW 12, 351; cf. Bonhoeffer, *No Rusty Swords: Letters, Lectures and Notes 1928-1936,* trans. Edwin H. Robertson and John Bowden (London: Collins, 1965), p. 223.

cribed by Bonhoeffer to the "Jewish question" — in contrast even to those of his fellow theologians and church leaders for whom an exclusion of baptized Jews was out of the question.

Attention to such subtleties had perhaps not been urgent before Eberhard Bethge, on the occasion of his being awarded the Leopold Lucas Prize on October 24, 1979, gave a moving lecture that provides the groundwork for further studies. In it, he showed in all frankness that many a criticism of Bonhoeffer's statements on the "Jewish question" had been voiced by Jewish contemporaries under the impression of the Holocaust. Emil Fackenheim, once an inmate in the Sachsenhausen concentration camp, and afterwards a philosophy professor in Toronto, wrote in an inquiry in 1979, "I heard Christians say that Bonhoeffer the person was better than Bonhoeffer the theologian, for his theological concern had been to struggle only for non-Aryan [or Jewish] *Christians*. If it could be shown that he had gone beyond this [and had struggled theologically for non-Christian Jews], then I would gladly emphasize it." Even more, Eva Fleischner and William Jay Peck, Ruth Zerner and Walter Harrelson point out "anti-Judaisms" implied in Bonhoeffer's essay. Frank Littell also draws the conclusion that "Bonhoeffer's deeds were better than his theology."[6] Eventually it is observed that Bonhoeffer traveled the path of a deep change of mind in his attitude to Jewry, away from the traditional Lutheran position to an enhanced sensibility to the Jews, up to his statement of 1941: "Driving out the Jew(s) from the West must result in driving out Christ with them, for Jesus Christ was a Jew."[7] Pinchas Lapide can refer to such statements when he says, "From the Jewish view, he [Bonhoeffer] is the pioneer and forerunner of steps toward a re-Hebraization of the churches in our day."[8]

We have no reason to ascribe to Bonhoeffer a legendary perfection, and to leave out of account the possibility that he, too, like almost all other German theologians in his time, in education, studies, and ministry, took over, at first quite unwittingly, anti-Judaistic elements, which he got rid of only gradually, and perhaps only partially. New Testament exegesis gave occasion enough for such adoption. It needs to be clarified, however, what can count as Anti-Judaism, and how Bonhoeffer actually thought and argued.

---

6. Ernst Feil and Ilse Tödt, eds., *Konsequenzen. Dietrich Bonhoeffers Kirchenverständnis heute* (Munich: 1980), pp. 172 and 175.

7. DBWE 6, *Ethics* (Gütersloh: [1992] 1998), p. 105.

8. *Konsequenzen* (note 6 above), p. 174.

In the American discussion — but not only there — one can observe that anger and disdain against the neo-Lutheran two-realms teaching are to some extent also projected onto the Lutheran theologian Bonhoeffer. It is mostly overlooked that the neo-Lutheran teaching differs from Luther's authentic teaching and Bonhoeffer's interpretation of it.[9] In many instances the neo-Lutheran two-realms teaching helped people adapt to National Socialist totalitarianism. It is false to devalue Bonhoeffer's theology because of this teaching — which he combatted. Not a few German publications follow such criticism as came up in the United States of the Lutheran Bonhoeffer that allegedly was undemocratic and not free from anti-Judaisms. So Bonhoeffer might have a right to a clarification, as precise as possible, of his human and theological approach to the "Jewish question."

The contribution I would like to make is limited to one particular point. I want to examine whether, and how, the decisions of Bonhoeffer in the beginning of 1933 are connected with the development of his theological ethics. Can one separate the good person from the theologian Bonhoeffer, allegedly more questionable? Can one interpret his brave decisions simply as consequences of lucky inconsistencies? This pattern of interpretation seems applicable occasionally to some of his contemporaries, for example, the young Martin Niemöller. But I felt compelled to form the hypothesis that Bonhoeffer's early ethics and his perspectives, intentions, and decisions in the spring of 1933 are closely related.

Surely my hypothesis covers only one aspect that I in no way wish to understand as exclusive. In the case of hardly any theologian does the unity of biography and theology show so clearly and dramatically as in Bonhoeffer's case. The influence of the family that, among other assets, embodied the best traditions of educated citizenry, the politically and socially well-informed group of friends, and many other things, should of course not be underestimated. It might also be surmised that his behavior in 1933 was spontaneously determined so that it could not be derived biographically and hardly be fathomed rationally, and only a forced interpretation could see his decisions as the plausible consequences of preceding developments and insights. But such alternative considerations will be put aside here. We will examine the hypothesis of a relationship between

---

9. See Heinz Eduard Tödt, *Die Bedeutung von Luthers Reiche- und Regimentenlehre für heutige Theologie und Ethik*, pp. 52-126 in N. Hasselmann, ed., *Gottes Wirken in seiner Welt*, volume 2 (Hamburg: 1980).

Bonhoeffer's early ethics and his decisions in 1933. The English title chosen for the present text, "The Real Test for Bonhoeffer's Ethics" — together with the original German title "Ethics in Emergency" *(Ethik im Ernstfall)*[10] — suggests that an ethical theory may result in decisive behavior when the concrete situation demands it.

I. Bonhoeffer's First Draft of a Christian Ethic in 1929

I must begin with a document that in Bonhoeffer research is often approached with uneasy and sad feelings, and occasionally also with apologetic attempts at exoneration. The twenty-three-year-old Bonhoeffer, as assistant pastor of the German congregation in Barcelona, Spain, gave a series of three lectures for the parishioners. The concluding lecture, held on February 8, 1929, was entitled, "Basic Questions of a Christian Ethic."[11] The hearers were merchants, craftsmen, and many Germans living abroad who needed encouragement in the economically difficult situation of that time. Bonhoeffer's preceding lecture had ended, with reference to the Constantinian legend, pathetically but in existential earnest, "German people [*Volk*], this is your God, he formed you, and he will be with you. In the struggle with fate, look to the cross, the most wondrous symbol of your God, and know this, Only in this sign will you conquer."[12]

By contrast with the hearers of that time, we could hardly be motivated by these sentences to attend and listen to the following ethics lecture. They seem to be penetrated all too much with confused theological right-wing ideas. One year later, Erik Peterson, who later converted to Catholicism, bitingly stated in a letter to Adolf von Harnack, "Spiritually and sociologically," the Protestant church corresponds approximately to the spiritual and sociological status of the German National Peoples Party."[13] At first glance, the

10. The title of the lecture underlying this essay, given in Erlangen on May 17, 1979. See also Tödt, *Kirche und Ethik. Dietrich Bonhoeffers Entscheidungen in den Krisenjahren 1929-1933*, pp. 447-63 in D. Lührmann and G. Strecker, eds., *Kirche (Festschrift* presented to Günther Bornkamm on the occasion of his 75th birthday) (Tübingen: 1980). "Dietrich Bonhoeffer's Decisions in the Crisis Years 1929-33," *Studies in Christian Ethics* 18/3 (1965), 107-24.

11. *Grundfragen einer Christlichen Ethik*, pp. 323-45 in DBW 10, *Barcelona, Berlin, Amerika 1928-1931* (Munich: 1991).

12. DBW 10, p. 322.

13. Peterson, *Theologische Traktate* (Munich: 1951), p. 301.

reader might find this confirmed by Bonhoeffer's lecture on Christian ethics. Some scholars do voice the opinion that elements of a "pre-Fascist ideology," of a "nationalistic irrational decisionism," or of a titanic "ethic of the moment" appear in the lecture.[14] Doubtless, some of the phrases in the lecture were, at that time, in current use in national Protestantism, and are in continuity with neo-Lutheran opinions on war. They must, however, not be torn out of their specific context, and attention should be paid to the function they have in this lecture. Otherwise we would all too naïvely measure the statements of that time by our political notions and categories that are imprinted with the horrible experiences of the Hitler regime and the Holocaust, and that arise from a modern common understanding of democracy. In his lecture, the assistant pastor Bonhoeffer intended to speak concretely. This meant, at that time, to treat three major problems. First, war, for the end of the First World War, the 1919 Versailles Treaty — called "treaty of shame" — with its consequences, and above all the "war guilt lie" that was felt to be a dishonor to the nation still, or anew, outraged the German soul. Second, the economic struggle of competition that escalated with the impending world economic crisis. Third, the sexual revolution of the 1920s, which Bonhoeffer treated as secondary, compared with the other two themes.

Before Bonhoeffer tackles these themes, he gives a methodological introduction. Ethics is not a subject of principles and norms, but "of blood and history." There is, then, a German, as well as a French or an American ethic — this sounds like an echo of Max Weber's famous lecture of 1919, "Politics as a Vocation." The Christian, however, recognizes the will of God by means of Scripture. But Scripture does not offer principles. It offers statements that concern the human being who must listen to, and absorb them in each situation ever anew. The recurring ethical precepts in the whole gospel have one message for us, namely, "be mindful in your actions that you are acting under God's eye, that God has his will which he wills be done." Here Christian ethics moves beyond what is traditionally good or evil; it is, in a certain sense, amoral. Bonhoeffer is not willing to surrender this discovery of a beyond of good and evil to Friedrich Nietzsche in his enmity toward Christianity. The Christian does not follow fixed ethical principles, but is facing the concrete situations of life. "There is always only the crucial moment, which is any moment that can become ethically valuable."

14. See among others Tiemo Rainer Peters, *Die Präsenz des Politischen in der Theologie Dietrich Bonhoeffers* (Munich: 1976), pp. 33-36.

This statement, so it seems, links most closely up with Rudolf Bultmann's language, inspired by Søren Kierkegaard, in his 1926 book *Jesus*.

Obviously, Bonhoeffer is here, on the whole, close to the decisionism of the 1920s, echoes of which, at that time, also still ring in Barth's ethics of revelation. It is characteristic of Bonhoeffer that he conceives of this type of ethic, decisionism, in the way of voluntarism. "The moment will tell you of what kind God's will is; one only needs to realize that one's will must each time be forced into the divine will." This ever renewed process of uniting with the will of God sets boundaries for decisionistic arbitrariness. But where the faithful human being's own will has acquiesced in the will of God, it gains an eminent authority for the revaluation of all values, an authority that is equal to the liberty of which Nietzsche is aware, just as Luther understood faith as an authorization even to create new Decalogues better than that of Moses.

The conclusion — important for the treatment of the war question — is, "There are no actions that are bad in and of themselves. Even murder can be hallowed. There is only faithfulness to or deviation from God's will. There simply is no law in the sense of concrete contents, but only the law of freedom, that is, to bear one's responsibility alone before God and oneself. . . . It is the greatest misunderstanding to make, for instance, the commandments of the Sermon on the Mount into a law again by applying them literally to the present."

All this seems to express a young man's strong awareness of his own authority — and who would deny this to the youthful Bonhoeffer? But it is only one side of the matter. Bonhoeffer is haunted by the question of whether the open-ended hearing of the word of Scripture, as the self-revealing will of God in the present moment, yields unambiguous concrete directives in the midst of the pressing problems. "Day by day, hour by hour, we are being led to face situations that are without precedent, in which we must make a decision, and in which we again and again go through the same surprising and frightening experience that the will of God does not reveal itself as clearly to our eyes as we had hoped, obviously because the will of God seems to be self-contradicting, within two seemingly antagonistic orders of God, so that we are not in a position of having to decide between good and evil, but have to choose between evil and evil. And here lie the virtual and most difficult problems of ethics."[15] This tragic or realistic

15. DBW 10, pp. 323, 329-30, 332-34.

view that the human being often has no other choice but between alternatives that each contain evil, will accompany Bonhoeffer's lifetime. So he had to reject the illusion of a guiltless life, but all the more passionately had to discuss the question of what, in view of such inescapable entanglement in guilt, the responsibility of the human being in faith then is.

For the assistant pastor Bonhoeffer, the two conflicting orders in God — seen in human perspective — are the order of love in the Sermon on the Mount and the order of history. Here he argues indeed in line with neo-Lutheran tradition. Even in wartime, the commandment in the Decalogue and in the Sermon on the Mount remains valid for the faithful, Thou shalt not kill! Do not resist evil! Love your enemy! And yet, according to Bonhoeffer's judgment then, to interpret the command as pacifism on principle does not fit in with God's real will for this specific situation, since such an interpretation is not concrete. Not to protect one's family, friends, or fellow citizens by handling a weapon would mean loveless abandonment of the nearby neighbor. The result is, "I will raise the weapon in the dreadful awareness of doing something horrible, but not being able to do anything else . . . the love for my people will hallow murder, will hallow war."[16] Indeed, here one can only choose between evil and evil. Bonhoeffer does not shy away from this insight. To kill one's enemy, even when one does not hate him or her, remains, in his view, "murder" — a shockingly harsh word in the context of the discussions on war at that time.[17] Wartime killing is burdened with guilt, and needs to be hallowed by God, that is, atoned for by forgiveness. The practical consequence, however, remains the same, namely, participation in the war of one's own folk, even in case it must wage a war of aggression for the sake of its historical growth, in the conviction that it thereby is following God's guidance of history.

At this point in the lecture, statements follow that make interpreters easily forget how strongly Bonhoeffer feels the human condition of being bound to God's will for history, and having to distance oneself from God's will of love, as tragic. He says, "God calls the people to valor, to fighting, and to victory. Also strength and power and victory come from God, for God creates youth in humans and in the people, and loves youth, for God himself is forever young, strong, and victorious."[18] Fifteen years later,

---

16. DBW 10, p. 338.
17. See Günther Dehn, *Die alte Zeit, die vorigen Jahre* (Munich: 1962), pp. 247-85.
18. DBW 10, p. 339.

Bonhoeffer will likewise reject any faultfinding with the human being's strength and health in Jesus's name. Precisely the world that has come of age, the human being full of life and strength, is to be claimed by Christ. But then — in 1944 — strength is no longer the youthful vigor of the people, but empowerment to participate in the suffering of God in this world.[19]

In 1929, Bonhoeffer, prompted by Friedrich Naumann, also sees the rigors of economic life. He takes the fact that the minor entrepreneur is ruined by the major to be a law. Here also, nothing but the obligatory choice between evil and evil is left. Charity done by the winner to the loser does not make good the evil of ousting, even if it is to the interest of the economic commonweal that many must succumb in the struggle of competition. Having to pass over the life of other nations, and of other participants in the economic struggle, corresponds with God's order of history. Is this a fate to which a Christian must utterly surrender? Maybe not. In the concrete situation, in the ambiguity of circumstances, the Christian must struggle ever anew toward a decision springing from God's will. Not as if problems could be solved by "ethics," which is "a demonstration of the weak will that arises from the thankfulness for what God has done for us." Ethics does not find solutions that spare human guilt. "Only the one who has thoroughly tasted the whole earnest, depth, and need of the worldly realm, the ethical realm, longs for leaving it and knows nothing but the one wish that our world waste away, and Your Kingdom come."[20]

No doubt, here Bonhoeffer comes quite close to the attitude of Reinhold Seeberg, Paul Althaus, and Emanuel Hirsch, and to that of many national Protestants. The struggle among peoples [*Völker*] and the economic struggle are simultaneously seen in the perspective of social Darwinism and as God's order of creation and history. Decisions on what to do concretely are made by way of reflecting on the bonds that tie us to this order. But different from these voices, Bonhoeffer names the facts at issue more honestly and frankly. He does not exonerate killing in war from the harsh word *murder,* and calls the struggle for existence in economy and elsewhere ruinous. Nevertheless, had Bonhoeffer continued to adhere to this notion of God's order of history, he would have had trouble getting rid of a series of presuppositions for treating the Jewish question when it became

19. DBW 8, pp. 504, 511, 534; *Letters and Papers from Prison* (New York: Macmillan, 1972), pp. 341ff., 344ff., 369f.

20. DBW 10, p. 345.

acute in 1933 because of National Socialist anti-Semitism. Bonhoeffer had to go beyond this stage of ethical judgment-forming. This view of history, together with its ethical consequences, contradicted the Sermon on the Mount and the commandment of neighborly love too much. How could the contradictions be resolved? Bonhoeffer's engagement in developing a Christian ethic that he later regarded as his real legacy[21] can indeed be interpreted as the attempt to unravel what had become so badly twisted in the Barcelona lecture.

II. The Breakthrough to an Ecumenical Ethic of Peace, 1930-1932

Bonhoeffer's year in Barcelona ended in January, 1929. Beginning with the 1929 summer semester, and lasting until September, 1930, Bonhoeffer was an assistant to Wilhelm Lütgert, professor of systematic theology in Berlin, and qualified as a university lecturer with his book *Act and Being*. During this time, a turning happened that Bonhoeffer mentioned years later in a letter. "I had not yet become a Christian, but was my own wild and unruly lord. . . . For all my loneliness, I was quite pleased with myself. The Bible freed me from this, especially the Sermon on the Mount. . . . I suddenly came to see Christian pacifism, which I had only shortly before . . . passionately fought, as self-evident. And so it proceeded, step by step. I no longer saw or thought anything else."[22]

Having been granted a fellowship, Bonhoeffer studied at Union Theological Seminary in New York for one academic year until June, 1931. His addresses to American congregations and youth groups show that his thinking had changed deeply since the time in Barcelona. He expressly spoke as a German, and accordingly rejected the ominous article 231 of the Versailles Treaty that ascribed to Germany the sole guilt for the First World War, but

---

21. 1943 DBW 8, p. 188; *Letters and Papers* (note 19 above), p. 129.

22. Letter of January 27, 1936, p. 113 in DBW 14, *Illegale Theologenausbildung Finkenwalde 1935-1937* (Gütersloh: 1996). [This breakthrough seems to have occurred during Bonhoeffer's "trip abroad" in 1930-31 to Union Theological Seminary and Harlem. See especially Ruth Zerner, "Dietrich Bonhoeffer's American Experiences," *Union Seminary Quarterly Review* 31/4 (Summer, 1976), 268 and 270; also Bethge, *Dietrich Bonhoeffer*, pp. 154, 206. Some have thought his trip to Rome in 1924 might have been the time of this breakthrough, but this seems less likely to me. It did influence him significantly, however; see Bethge, pp. 56-65.]

he did so for the sake of reconciliation and understanding. A passage from a sermon says this clearly enough. "You have brothers and sisters in our people and in every people, do not forget that. Come what may, let us nevermore forget, that our christian people is the people of God, that if we are in accord, no nationalism, no hate of races or classes can execute its designs, and then the world will have its peace for ever and ever."[23]

Now, the one Christian people [*Volk*] of God, and not each person's own folk, was of paramount value, entrusted with the ecumenical commission to promote peace between the nations instead of each nation's struggle for self-preservation. Now Bonhoeffer took interest in Gandhi's non-violent struggle. The French Christian pacifist Jean Lasserre became his friend. Now he saw the importance of the kingdom of God no longer merely in the beyond, but for the earthly reality. "Taking the kingdom of God seriously as a kingdom on earth is biblical, and is in the right, whereas an otherworldly understanding of the kingdom is in the wrong."[24]

While he was still in America, Bonhoeffer learned that Paul Althaus and Emanuel Hirsch had severely attacked the German members of the ecumenical movement who were preparing a meeting of the World Alliance for Promoting International Friendship through the Churches, to be held in Cambridge in September, 1931. The ecumenical work, they wrote, would veil the "murderous policy" of the others against the German people through an "artificial semblance" of ecumenical community. They would "confuse consciences" — this is one of the strongest traditionally Lutheran reproaches — both at home and abroad, and would deny the "German destiny." Only the rupture of relations even between the churches could now "honor the truth."[25]

---

23. Sermon originally preached in English on November 9, 1930, p. 581 in DBW 10; *A Testament to Freedom: The Essential Writings of Dietrich Bonhoeffer*, ed. Geffrey B. Kelly and F. Burton Nelson (New York: HarperSanFrancisco, 1990), p. 104.

24. See above, chapter 4, section 6, 4e, Nietzsche on "backworldpeople." The end of the 1929 Barcelona lecture (DBW 10, p. 345) reminds of escapism from the world. In 1931, Bonhoeffer and Lasserre addressed students in Victoria, Mexico, on the subject of peace. Lasserre remembered that "for the people of Victoria it was a tremendous event to listen to a German and a Frenchman together!" Germany and France had at that time the image of hereditary political enemies. Quote from p. 152 of Bethge, *Dietrich Bonhoeffer: A Biography*, (Minneapolis: Fortress Press, 2000), the revised edition of the English translation of Eberhard Bethge, *Dietrich Bonhoeffer. Theologe — Christ — Zeitgenosse. Eine Biographie* (München: 1967; ninth edition Gütersloh: 2005).

25. Bethge (see previous note), p. 195.

Deeply offended, the ecumenists, almost branded traitors to their fatherland after having promoted, in recent years, understanding for Germany in all the world, asked in return whether or not this absolutizing of the German destiny would aid and abet the National Socialists. Althaus, who did not belong to this party, wrote, "One has rightly said that National Socialism consists, in its innermost core, in the national youth's resolute will to freedom. . . . In National Socialism, the injured pride of our great people, but also the Germans' brutal existential need, have found their strongest and most passionate expression."[26]

While Althaus and Hirsch presumably spoke for a majority of the Protestant theologians in Germany, Bonhoeffer without delay decided for the minority. From here on, he was an ecumenist, an active participant in the work of the World Alliance, a part-time youth secretary for several European countries, fully exposed to Althaus' attack against political Westernization. But, after one year's work, Bonhoeffer had to acknowledge in the fall of 1932 that the ecumenical peace promotion through the churches had no success in Germany. The influence of Althaus, Hirsch, Gogarten, and their like-minded national-Protestant anti-Western colleagues was too strong. They were not even able to recognize how successful Stresemann's and Brüning's policy of rapprochement, connected with American economic interests, was for Germany.

Bonhoeffer approached the peace promotion of the World Alliance not pragmatically, but from the bottom of theology, and yet with concrete aims. He systematically established fundamentals of an ecumenical ethic of peace, that simultaneously was a political ethic. Bonhoeffer research did not pay much attention to this. For example, in Tiemo Rainer Peters' stimulating 1976 study on the presence of the political in Bonhoeffer's theology[27] this central dimension in Bonhoeffer's thought is nearly completely lacking. But the ecumenical peace ethic came to be fundamental for his decisions in 1933.

Compared with the ethics lecture in Barcelona, the type of ethic that Bonhoeffer now develops has not changed. Methodologically, he follows

26. *Allgemeine Evangelisch-Lutherische Kirchen-Zeitung,* volume 65 (1932), pp. 63-64; Albert Schäfer, *Die theologische Beurteilung des Krieges in der deutschen protestantischen Theologie zwischen den Weltkriegen, dargestellt an den Beispielen Paul Althaus, Emanuel Hirsch, Dietrich Bonhoeffer und dem sogenannten Fall Dehn* (dissertation, Heidelberg, 1978), pp. 170-187.

27. See above, note 14.

the same lines. But the contents are radically different. Bonhoeffer now understands the biblical texts much more concretely, and as much more binding. Now begins the increasing christological concentration, described in Ernst Feil's book *The Theology of Dietrich Bonhoeffer*.[28] And now the understanding of the church in Bonhoeffer's *Sanctorum Communio*[29] becomes more concrete. There he had written that humankind is brought into real community with God in Christ so that the church is the new will of God with the human beings. Now the church referred to is no longer understood as being based on the national church of the Germans, or other peoples' national churches, but as the church that is becoming ecumenical. The confession to a (concrete) unity of the church now comes to be necessarily included in every true Christian confession of faith.

Among the many important texts by Bonhoeffer written in these years before 1933, two are especially noteworthy regarding the ecumenical ethic of peace. These are the July 26, 1932, lecture on the Theological Foundation of the Work of the World Alliance, and the report on the theological conference of the mediation office for ecumenical youth work held in Berlin on April 29-30, 1932.[30] We will focus on what is new and different from the ethics lecture in Barcelona.

First, Bonhoeffer has now discovered that the then widespread theological notion of the nation as God's order of creation is scarcely biblical. Second, he gives up the idea that a people, or nation, will receive its respective call within God's order of history which must be obeyed unconditionally, even by putting other nations down. Instead, he seeks a theological criterion that allows the Christians to be critical of the existent political structures. The criterion cannot be found in an *order of creation*, because this term covers up the human sin that drives much of the activity of a people, organized in a nation-state. The consequences of sin are taken into account in the concept of an *order of preservation*. This term, even if it

28. Philadelphia 1985; German original, *Die Theologie Dietrich Bonhoeffers*, fourth printing 1991 (see chapter 1, I, 1).

29. See chapter 1, I, 2.

30. DBW 11, *Ökumene, Universität, Pfarramt 1931-1932* (Gütersloh: 1994), pp. 327-44 *(Zur theologischen Begründung der Weltbundarbeit)*, and pp. 317-27 *(Bericht über die theologische Konferenz der Mittelstelle für ökumenische Jugendarbeit)*; in *No Rusty Swords: Letters, Lectures and Notes 1928-1936*, trans. Edwin H. Robertson and John Bowden (London: Collins, 1965), pp. 153-73.

sounds conservative today, functions in Bonhoeffer's language to criticize the religiously nationalistic and national-Protestant traditions by disclosing how limited, ambivalent, and temporary any earthly order is. The term states that a certain measure of juridical and political ordering should remain in force to check human sin in a people and a state, and to avert a decline into a destructive chaos. But these orders are not ends in and of themselves. Instead, they are external means to preserve justice and peace until the coming of Christ. This is the goal by which they must be measured. They are not supposed to be Christian orders. Any religious glorification of an organized nation-state is out of the question. Moreover, where orders are no longer open to the proclamation of the gospel and, thus, to the coming of Christ, Christians will demand that they be forced open or destroyed. The concept of orders of preservation, derived from Lutheran traditions, did not have this critical function when used by other contemporary Lutherans, as, for example, by Walter Künneth. So Bonhoeffer dropped it a few years later.

What would be a concrete order of preservation in the situation of that time? Bonhoeffer considered certainly not only a people or a state to be such an order, but thought much more of an international order of life, outlined as an order of peace. Bonhoeffer research has frequently spoken of the young Bonhoeffer's pacifism. We have already cited the letter in which Bonhoeffer mentions "Christian pacifism."[31] Nevertheless, this term connotes something that diverts from his way of thinking. Bonhoeffer dismisses supreme principles, even if they are pacifism or peace, from his ethics. Instead he asks for the concrete commandment of the living God that must be heard in the present situation. And this he perceives to be the rejection of war, and the promotion of an order of peace through the church in its ecumenical alliance, in the awareness that Christ crucified is the bringer of peace.

This accords with the development of international law, both at that time and today. In the Briand-Kellogg Pact of August, 1928, the states that concluded the treaty solemnly declared that they condemn war as a means of international conflict resolution, and renounce it as an instrument of national policy in their mutual relationships. Bonhoeffer wrote in 1932, "Today's war destroys both soul and body. Since we can in no way understand war as God's order of preservation and therefore as God's com-

31. See above, note 22.

mandment, and since war, on the other hand, requires idealization and idolization in order to have life, today's war, that is, the next war, must be put under the *ban* of the church. . . . The full force of resistance, refusal, and banishment" should be turned against the next war, not because of a "enthusiastic raising of one commandment — for instance, the fifth commandment — above others, but in obedience to God's commandment addressing us today, that war should be no more, since it blinds us to revelation."[32] Even peace is no absolute supreme value, but is limited by truth and justice. Nevertheless, God's present-day commandment, as Bonhoeffer perceives it, gives utmost urgency to the order of peace.

Here we meet the strongest characteristic of Bonhoeffer's ethics. He sees the church authorized by the gospel to recognize, in common, concrete commandments of God, and to proclaim them here and now. In a sermon of June 19, 1932, Bonhoeffer preached, "Must Christianity, which formerly, in its beginnings, was revolutionary, now be conservative for all time? Must it be that every new movement must blaze its own trail without the church; that the church will realize only twenty years later what happened? If this must really be so, then we may not wonder when times in which martyrs' blood will be demanded will come again also for our church."[33]

Prophetic words from one ready to vouch for this with his own life. In the church, confession and promise must be concrete. There is concrete promise in the celebration of the sacraments. Bonhoeffer expressly draws a parallel between the sacraments and the venture of concrete and binding proclamation and confession by the church. A church that evades this venture by merely preaching general truths is regarded by him as weak and faithless. God's commandment must become concrete in its contents through the proclaimer, that is, through the church. "What the sacrament is for the proclamation of the Gospel, is the knowledge of concrete reality for the proclamation of the commandment," namely, it is that which gives certainty. *"Reality is the sacrament of the commandment"* — not simply an empirically existing reality, but reality disclosed in faith. But since concrete recognition of reality is always a venture in the fallen world, the church cannot proclaim the commandment as concrete directive other than "in faith in the word of forgiveness of sin."[34]

32. DBW 11, p. 341.
33. DBW 11, p. 446.
34. DBW 11, p. 334.

Bonhoeffer's understanding of the church and of ethics is a whole, and has concrete consequences for political orientation as well. The ethics with which Bonhoeffer was to meet the events of 1933 was outlined in 1932, and was stated in public in the context of peace promotion.

III. Bonhoeffer's Position on the "Jewish question" in April, 1933, Compared with Official Church Proceedings

1. Bonhoeffer's Specific Prerequisites

Though National Socialism appeared on the scene in 1933 with vigor and splendor as the rescuer of the German people, it could not tempt Bonhoeffer; for he was convinced, along with his family and friends, that Hitler meant war. What direction our history — especially that of the German and Jewish peoples — would have taken had the two great churches in ecumenical alliance been as convinced of God's commandment of peace as Bonhoeffer was, is unimaginable. The price the Roman Catholic and the Protestant churches in Germany would have had to pay at that time for their objection to war would surely have been great, but certainly incomparably smaller than the cost of Hitler's warmongering. But these are anachronistic considerations. The churches were not ready, and Christendom knew little of their responsibility for peace.

Bonhoeffer got into his first concrete conflict with the Third Reich not over the peace question, but, surprisingly, over the "Jewish question." Had he been the normal product of academic theological education, this would not have happened to him. The Old Testament, or Hebraic Bible, had long been put in the shade, Israel's significance for salvation history had widely been forgotten, the German Jews, in their diversity from the strict orthodox to the nearly assimilated Jews, had — according to the current opinion in theology and church — little to do with the people of promise, and much to do with opposition to faith in Christ. This was true, as I have verified, for the majority in all theological disciplines.[35] And even the New Testament theologian Gerhard Kittel, an expert in Jewish literature, uncommonly prominent as the single editor of the huge *Theological*

---

35. See on that point Marikje Smid, *Deutscher Protestantismus und Judentum 1932/1933* (Munich: 1989), pp. 221-320.

Dictionary of the New Testament,[36] who before 1933 had eagerly participated in the cooperation of Christians and Jews, in 1933 took the point of
view of a "Christian anti-Judaism" that he saw as being based on the New
Testament and church tradition. Correspondingly, in a peculiar manner he
agreed with the legislation on Jews as a way to repeal Jewish emancipation.[37] How did it happen that, contrary to the prevailing mentality in theology and the church, the Jews became for Bonhoeffer already in April,
1933, a question of confession?

I will not reconstruct the historical context once more — this has
been done especially by Eberhard Bethge, and also by Ernst-Albert
Scharffenorth[38] — but restrict myself to considering Bonhoeffer's theses
and behavior in the spring of 1933 in the light of the 1932 outline of his ethics, assuming that he did not revise it substantially in the meantime.

However, I have to add a remark on Bonhoeffer's relationship to
the Old Testament and to Judaism before 1933. The evidence is clear.
Bonhoeffer unambiguously rejected the devaluation of the Hebraic Bible that was customary in neo-Protestantism and had been executed, in
different ways, by Julius Wellhausen and Adolf von Harnack. The introduction to one of Bonhoeffer's lecture courses in the winter semester of
1932-1933 ends with the dictum, "in the whole of Holy Scripture, God is
the one and only God. With this belief, the church and theological science stand or fall."[39] This makes it probable that he, summarizing one
of the lectures on recent theology in another course in the same semester, used words noted down by a student, "the Jews' God and the God of
the New Testament. We must not split [in two] . . . God is one."[40] Moreover, in the agitated political situation of the National Socialists' imminent seizure of state power with their anti-Semitism, the conspicuous

36. *Theologisches Wörterbuch zum Neuen Testament*, 10 volumes (Stuttgart: 1932-
1979).

37. Leonore Siegele-Wenschkewitz, *Neutestamentliche Wissenschaft vor der Judenfrage. Gerhard Kittels theologische Arbeit im Wandel deutscher Geschichte* (Munich: 1980),
pp. 85-111.

38. Bethge, *Dietrich Bonhoeffer und die Juden*, pp. 171-214 in *Konsequenzen* (note 6
above), and Scharffenorth, *Die Kirche vor der Bekenntnisfrage. Bonhoeffers Aufruf zur
Solidarität mit den Juden*, pp. 184-234 in W. Huber and I. Tödt, eds., *Ethik im Ernstfall.
Dietrich Bonhoeffers Stellung zu den Juden und ihre Aktualität* (Munich: 1982).

39. 1933 DBW 3, *Schöpfung und Fall* (Gütersloh: [1989] 2002), p. 23; DBWE 3 (Minneapolis: Fortress Press, 1996), p. 23.

40. DBW 12, p. 157, note 20 (Klara Hunsche).

expression "the Jews' God" [*Judengott*] was bound to arouse the listeners' attention.

So it is no accident that it was Bonhoeffer who, around the end of March and the beginning of April, 1933, came to contribute the introductory statement to a discussion of the "Jewish question" in a group of theologically interested pastors who met regularly in Gerhard Jacobi's parsonage at the Emperor William Memorial Church [*Kaiser-Wilhelm-Gedächtniskirche*] in Berlin. The plan to discuss this question together scandalized members of the group, and caused Leonhard Fendt to leave it.[41]

Finally, there is the following highly significant passage in a letter of April 14, 1933, to Erwin Sutz: "A great reorganization of the churches is imminent. . . . On this occasion, the German-Christians[42] will hopefully withdraw on their own initiative from the two confessional churches — as awful as that is, on the other hand — and so we will once again salvage the church, *hominum confusione et dei providentia* [through human confusion, and thanks to God's providence]. The Jewish question, too, troubles the church a great deal, and here the most reasonable people have completely lost their heads and their Bibles."[43]

2. The Theses on the Church Membership of Christians of Jewish Descent

Bonhoeffer published his essay "The Church Before the Jewish Question" in the June, 1933, issue of the journal *Vormarsch*. Its section II, the older part, consists of theses on the church membership of Christians who are of Jewish descent. This part develops what Jewry, Jewish Christianity, and heathen Christianity mean, "seen from the church of Christ." According to Bonhoeffer, they are not so-called racial but religious concepts. To speak of "Jewish race" is "biologically questionable." A Jewish Christian is not a Christian with Jewish ancestors, but one for whom "membership in the

---

41. Bethge, *Biography* (note 24 above), p. 272.

42. Translator's note: This does not mean (all) Christians who were Germans. The "German-Christian" movement advocated a nationalistic ideology, and readily adapted to National Socialism and its anti-Semitism.

43. DBW 12, pp. 57-58.

44. DBW 12, pp. 355-58; *No Rusty Swords*, pp. 227-29.

people of God, in the church of Christ, is conditioned by observance of a divine law." "Only this difference in understanding Christ's epiphany" has historically led to splits that have mutually been regarded "partly as an intolerable heresy, and partly as a tolerable schism."

Bonhoeffer transfers this course of events in Early Catholicism by analogy to the present. Where a church group would "let membership in the church be conditioned by the observance of a divine law, for example the racial uniformity of the members of the congregation," the Jewish Christian type would reappear today.

There is a widespread tendency to see in this argument of Bonhoeffer's a trick of polemics and discrimination against the German-Christians as "Jewish Christian." It should, however, be noted that the theses were intended for internal discussion and clarification in the Jacobi group, and were, at first, not addressed to German-Christians. Accordingly, the reference to the historical type of "Jewish Christian" cannot have intended a depreciation, as if Bonhoeffer had wanted to apply to the German-Christians something that he, in covert anti-Judaism, considered an invective. Instead, he definitely hoped that the German-Christians would separate from the churches of Reformed and Lutheran confession,[45] and grasp the enticing chance of being fostered by the party and the state. Then, the confessional churches would exist without the favor of the party or the state, whereas the other church would be synchronized with the regime, which was one of the basic goals of German-Christians.

While all this seems possible to Bonhoeffer, he declares it impossible for the church to exclude members of Jewish ancestry from the church-community for the reason that their membership would clash with the Jewish Christian claim that observance of a law is a prerequisite. To comply with that claim would turn the heathen Christian community into a Jewish Christian community, which would be unacceptable to heathen Christians. Here Bonhoeffer intercedes for the right of the heathen-Christianly minded Jews, undoubted members of the heathen Christian church-community along with the members of German ancestry. Their expulsion would result in schism. The problem was not whether parishioners of German ancestry could still bear with Jewish co-parishioners. Church is "here where Jew and German stand together under the Word of

45. See the phrase "the two confessional churches" in the letter of April 14, 1933, to Sutz (quoted above), DBW 12, p. 58.

God, and here is the proof whether or not church still is church." Those who separate themselves from such a community of Jews and Germans must be told that they themselves put into practice the Jewish Christian notion of a religion of law, and lapse into modern Jewish Christianity. The verb "to lapse" is a pejorative. But what is depreciated? Not the original but the copy, in which the questionable datum "race" is treated like a law of God — as an order of creation — while the genuine Jewish Christianity takes its orientation from the true law of God. The argumentation seems not yet touched by either the boycott of Jewish businesses on April 1, 1933, or the Law for the Reconstruction of the Professional Civil Service of April 7, 1933. There is only the warning at the beginning of the theses that "The church cannot allow the state to prescribe for it how to deal with church members. The baptized Jew is a member of our church." The substance of the theses is that heathen Christianity's freedom from the law is the one and only option for the members of a true church of the Reformation. Therefore those who wish to restrict the freedom from law should withdraw from this church.[46] It is self-evident that an Aryan clause can by no means be imposed on pastors and officials of a church understood in this way. Church membership is bound up, on principle, with the distinction between heathen Christians and Jewish Christians. This is a strong and fully consistent position — including the hoped-for withdrawal of the German-Christians.

Nevertheless, there is a difficulty that Bonhoeffer did not make clear. Can the racial uniformity of the parishioners that would come to be observed in a German-Christian separate church, can this nationalistic law be equated to the Jewish Christian law, revealed by God to Moses on Mount Sinai, and fulfilled in Christ? Wilhelm Stapel and Emanuel Hirsch could draw such a parallel. But Bonhoeffer thought much too biblically of the law, or Torah, to consider this comparison sound. The fact that he uses it, in spite of this difficulty, suggests that his concept of Jewish Christian does have a negative connotation, so to say a stain come off from the dye with which the concept of German-Christian is imbued, namely, the missing freedom to disregard any prerequisite for belonging to a people other than the perceived Word of God in Christ. For this reason, Bonhoeffer

---

46. In a June 22, 1933, gathering of about two thousand students and theologians at the University of Berlin Bonhoeffer demanded that a council be called to deliberate and pronounce binding decisions on unity or schism of the church (DBW 12, p. 85).

must ask whether such a new German-Jewish-Christian church would be a tolerable schism or an intolerable heresy. So a religious deficit is here implied in Bonhoeffer's concept of Jewish Christian. At the same time, Hans Ehrenberg, a pastor of Jewish ancestry, saw a fundamental positivity in the fact that a Jewish Christian still lives in the continuity of God's faithfulness to the people whom God has chosen and to whom God has given his law.[47]

3. The Deliberations in the German Protestant Church Committee Based on a Paper Submitted by Walter Künneth

A treatment of the "Jewish question" as bold as Bonhoeffer's could be expected neither from the General Superintendents and Consistory Presidents of the regional church of the Old Prussian Union who met on April 11, 1933, in Berlin, nor from the thirty-six members of the governing body of the Protestant church in Germany as a whole, who deliberated on April 25 and 26. Both times, an at first anonymous paper on "The Church and the Jewish Question in Germany" by Walter Künneth, director of the Spandau Apologetic Center in Berlin, was discussed. It is unlikely that Bonhoeffer did not hear of this paper after the discussions of April 11. So he supposedly wrote the later part of his essay, section I, completed on April 15, in knowledge of the substance of Künneth's considerations. Künneth later expanded his paper and published it in the different revised editions of the volume *The Nation Before God* of which he, together with Helmuth Schreiner, was the editor. Künneth's first, then unpublished, statement already takes into account expressly the so-called Aryan clause in the Law for the Reconstruction of the Professional Civil Service of April 7, 1933, and its concept of "non-Aryan descent."

Künneth awkwardly begins his paper with a rather unguarded reference to the National Socialist revolution, and infers from it everything else. "The national state's self-reflection on the peculiarity of the German people leads, by necessity, to the task of regulating the Jewish question in Germany in a new way." The task must be tackled because of the overgrowth of Jewish influence, stifling the German spirit and public life, and the proportional discrimination against German civil servants, doctors, and holders

---

47. Ernst-Albert Scharffenorth in *Ethik im Ernstfall* (note 38 above), pp. 213-14, 217-19.
48. Künneth's paper is printed in *Ethik im Ernstfall*, pp. 255-57.

of public offices. The new measures would have to protect the security of the German folk — as if such measures were urgent in 1933. The point of view of national politics, and the concept of non-Aryan descent in paragraph 3 of the new Civil Service law, should be decisive.

Argumentation within the Lutheran tradition would have started strictly from the commission for the sake of which, according to Romans 13:1-7 — the powers that be — and other verses from Scripture, the state is established. In that case, the lawfulness and legitimacy of state actions would have been the foremost issue, rather than the consequences of national self-reflection. But Künneth adopts the self-interpretation of the wielders of power, and this predetermines the course of his argumentation. Several years earlier, in an essay on "Race and God," published in the Apologetic Center's journal *Word and Deed* (number 12), Künneth had appropriated a teaching on race. "In the light of the Christian belief in God, race appears, first, as a primordial datum of creation, a special expression of the divine creative will" (p. 6). Strangely enough, the many inconsistencies of the teaching on race — Künneth considered the Germans a conglomeration of Nordic, Alpine, Westic, and Dinaric races — did not bother him.

As to church membership, Künneth exclaims, "Equality, according to the equal confession of heathen Christians and Jewish Christians in the church! A deviation means abandonment of the Gospel." A flaw in this seemingly resolute basic statement is the inaccurate and unfortunate use of "Jewish Christians," as a combination of (Jewish) origin and (Christian) confession when speaking of the baptized church members of Jewish descent who, by joining a church of the Reformation, have become heathen Christians, as Bonhoeffer has made clear.

Künneth extends his basic statement — equality! — to the question of who should be installed in a ministry. Here, however, the first qualifications arise, with grave consequences. The church should be on guard lest an overly prominent Jewish Christian element hamper the proclamation in Germany's people — as if the tiny numbers of pastors and parishioners of Jewish descent at that time would bring about such a danger.

For Künneth, the church and the state take different stands on the "Jewish question." The church must raise certain claims, which are: 1. Distinction between Jews and Jewish Christians through gradation in legislation. 2. No unworthy treatment of church members of Jewish descent, which might contradict the recognized dignity of the Christian church and sacraments in the nation's life. That is, Jewish church members and "members of the synagogue" are clearly distinguished. 3. Undiminished ecclesiastic service to "Jewish Christians" and Jews (mission to Jews), while conversions must be examined conscientiously. 4. Distinction between old-resident Jews who have become Christians earlier, and immigrants after the November Revolution 1918, since, through Christian belief, the "Jewish Christians" have come closer to the German people and culture.

Finally, "With regard to the outer and inner need of the Jewish race in Germany caused by the exceptional legislation and the public attitude toward boycott thereby facilitated, even if one may understand it as being in the interest of the state, the church is obligated to a special responsibility." Künneth does not say what everybody knew, namely, that the boycott was organized not by the public, but by the party. He wanted Christian charity to be bestowed primarily to the Jewish Christians in need, for example, in the form of a "Jewish Christian collection." The church would have to remonstrate against violent persecutions of the Jews, which would discredit the state and the right to defense against an overpowering foreign influence.

Künneth's theses speak for, or rather against, themselves. What remains to be considered is their direct effect. At the beginning of the meeting on April 26, 1933, Baron von Pechmann had stated emphatically, "Our church owes its own loyal members, at long last, the consoling and uplifting word of protection."[49] Künneth's paper did not encourage acting accordingly, and even less encouraging were the Church Committee's deliberations. In addition to the "private work" (by Künneth), a statement coming from the regional church of Baden was discussed. It portrayed the church members of Jewish descent as victims of the racial struggle in this unrighteous world, guaranteed none of their legal claims, but affirmed that the church would never forsake the commandment to love the neighbor and the brethren. For today's reader, this statement is embarrassingly painful. The young Protestant author Jochen Klepper, at that time recently married to a Jewish woman, wrote in a March 29, 1933, diary entry, "On the whole matter of the boycott, I have but one thing to say: I mourn for the Protestant church."[50]

49. Boyens (note 2 above), p. 296.
50. Scholder (note 4 above), p. 325.

The most telling contribution to the discussion, according to the minutes, came from Heinrich Rendtorff, bishop of the regional church of Mecklenburg, who at this time was under heavy National Socialist pressure. He requested that, for the time being, no stand be taken in public.

> Not out of hesitancy, but out of fundamental considerations of belief. The public would listen only to the "yes" or "no" spoken to state measures. Everything else would be completely unimportant. Therefore it should be spelled out in more detail what was meant. The church had welcomed thankfully that at long last an authority existed again. If such was the case, then the attempt to halt the worldly sword would be contrary to belief, the more so as this was a central item of the government's program, and not a peripheral matter. Speaker warns against calling the current judgment of the Jewish question un-evangelical. For seventeen hundred years, the Jews had stood unter exceptional law with the full approval of the church. Their liberation was connected with the Enlightenment mentality of progress. The notion of progress must not be identified with evangelical norms. Today, a spiritual combat between two completely different vital dispositions was happening: on the one hand emphasis on the prerogative of the free personality, and on the other hand preference for the preponderance of the state as representing the whole. Speaker refuses to take sides in this fight as a theologian, and to call one of the two views the specifically Christian one. Personally, he would strongly lean towards the second view, which in his opinion was closer to the Bible. He therefore requested to refrain from a public pronouncement, and to continue in the previous line, especially in warding off hardships from case to case.[51]

Here, the problem is placed into the context of modern history and Christian resistance against its trend toward Enlightenment. Such a broad perspective renders superfluous any fundamental and, simultaneously, concrete position taken on the question. Bishop Privy Church Councilor Professor Heinrich Rendtorff points out a connection between the treatment of the Jews in Germany and an eventual new minority law for Germans abroad. "Therefore the speaker finds it extraordinarily hard not to vote for a public stand."

51. Boyens, p. 298.

At the conclusion of the meeting, the Church Committee declared informally and without public effect "that the Protestant church will continue to regard its own members of Jewish descent as its own, sympathizes with them, and stands up for them within the boundaries of what is possible in practice. The Church Committee also feels urged to address to the governmental powers a word of Christian admonition not to leave the commandments of righteousness and Christian love out of consideration, even in a justified correction of a state of disorder."[52]

4. The Substance of the "Jewish Question" in 1933 and Bonhoeffer's View of How the State Is in Charge of It

Against the background of these church proceedings, the uniqueness of Bonhoeffer's essay "The Church Before the Jewish Question" can be seen more sharply. We will now turn to the later written part, completed on April 15, published as the preface and section I.[53] Here the anti-Jewish boycott of April 1, the Civil Service law of April 7, 1933 with its Aryan clause, and probably also Künneth's paper and the proceedings of April 11 are considered, but of course not the proceedings of April 26.

First of all, Bonhoeffer, in contrast to Heinrich Rendtorff, does not see in the state's anti-Jewish exceptional legislation the resuming of a 1700-year-old tradition, but "a fact that is unique in history," because now Jews are placed by the state under an exceptional law independent of their religious affiliation, solely on racial grounds (350) — an assessment that in this confused situation is as correct as it is sagacious. Here, as in section II (356), Bonhoeffer severs the fateful link between looking at the matter in the perspective of the church, and judging it in a — questionable — racial perspective. The latter kind of judgment is intruding into the state and the church as the influence of the party and the German-Christians increases. Bonhoeffer's assertion that "without a doubt, the state is entitled to steer new courses here" (351) has caused much offense. Eberhard Bethge reports from the American discussions since the 1960s,

---

52. Boyens (note 2 above), pp. 298 and 299.
53. DBW 12, pp. 349-55; *No Rusty Swords*, pp. 221-27. DBW 12 page numbers are inserted in the following text.

What was felt to be upsetting in this first position taken by Bonhoeffer on the Jewish question in the Third Reich, was obviously only, first, that Bonhoeffer, as an obstinate Lutheran, could concede to the state so much right to establish regulations — even for the treatment of the Jews, and, second, that he unmasked himself to be an utterly unadvised advocate of Christianity's usurpation of Jewry's inheritance, and a proclaimer of a punishment theology, which opinion he then retained to his end.[54]

The Luther-phobia is too widespread, and, above all, the reputation of the Lutherans' attitude to the Third Reich and the powers-that-be is too catastrophic almost all over the world, to adequately treat here the problem of the "obstinate Lutheran" Bonhoeffer. We will focus on the Lutheran Bonhoeffer who constantly combatted neo-Lutheranism. How does he see the responsibility of the church vis-à-vis the state in April, 1933? The existence of a "Jewish question" was evident from the boycott of April 1 and the Civil Service law of April 7, and it was obvious that it had only been made into a state problem of the first rank by the National Socialist German Worker's Party. But now it was a political reality. Who should be in charge of treating and solving this question amid the so-called national revolution? The party organizations, or the state bodies?

In the literature up to the present, it has been overlooked that it was this alternative that came up acutely in the first months of the Third Reich, and that Bonhoeffer must have had this alternative in view. In order to make the context clear, we must consider how the "Jewish question" was put in Germany and Central Europe at that time, and what experiences had been made with it up to 1933.

In one of the volumes on the history of the Jewish people, edited by Haim Hillel Ben-Sasson, Shmuel Ettinger discusses the situation of the Jews in Eastern and Central Europe, both in Soviet Russia and in the European democracies. "Never before in European history had so many Jews played such an active role in political life, and held such influential positions as in the first years after the Russian Revolution, and after the end of the First World War (1917 to 1922)."[55] But precisely this fact exacerbated the differences between Jews and those among whom they lived. Depending

54. *Konsequenzen* (note 6 above), p. 185.

55. P. 272 in volume III of Ben-Sasson, ed., *Geschichte des jüdischen Volkes* (Munich: 1980).

on the respective political situation, Jews were considered to be partisans either of the revolution or of the capitalist reaction, and in the new national states, especially in Poland and the Baltic nations, hatred of Jews was a feature of patriotism. Pogroms and encroachments were the order of the day, and efforts for protection of minorities through international law remained largely powerless. State interventions impoverished broad Jewish strata of society, and restricted their participation in higher education.

Because of these living conditions, an enormous migration to the west began in Eastern Europe, to which the Western European nations reacted, again, with restrictive measures. The rejection of the Jews who, by various means, were denied entrance into many professions, and then denounced as concentrating in certain other professions, was mainly stirred up by anti-Semitic propaganda. Prominent evidence were "The Protocols of Zion," probably composed at the end of the nineteenth century in Paris by members of the Russian secret police, in order to suggest a threat to the Christian peoples by an allegedly uniform world Jewry striving for domination. Alfred Rosenberg and other National Socialist Party idealogues, but also followers of Erich and Mathilde Ludendorff as well as other anti-Semites, again and again fed their suspicions on these protocols. The National Socialists, after having gained four million six hundred thousand votes in 1930, and having come to rule the streets more and more through their terror, began to boycott Jewish shops, and contrived pogroms against the Jews, for example, in September, 1931, in Berlin.[56] The great scientific and cultural accomplishments achieved by Jewish citizens during the time between the wars, especially in Germany, were either not noticed, or else disparaged.

It was easy to see that, in most countries, Jewry was divided into many competing or hostile factions, ranging from the strictly orthodox to the religiously indifferent or assimilated, from the communistic to the German-conservative Jew. After the Balfour Declaration of 1917, in which the Jews were promised a "national home" in Palestine by the British Secretary of State for Foreign Affairs Arthur Balfour, and after the immigration from the east, the Zionist movement in the Weimar Republic became a considerable factor in Jewish life in Germany. Especially here, Jewry reached a nearly singular legal status. Max Birnbaum described it in his book on the state and the synagogue in the years

56. P. 364 in Ben-Sasson (see previous note).

from 1918 to 1938, "In contrast to the Jewish communities in most other countries, (German Jewry) had legally recognized public [*öffentlich-rechtlich*] representative bodies, both in its individual congregations and in the larger district associations of congregations. They had been granted rights and given functions to which otherwise only government or communal boards had a right." "The legally recognized public character of the congregations and associations led to a unique contest with the government boards. After long and difficult struggles, these efforts culminated, in the early part of the Weimar Republic, in the legally and fiscally equal status of the Jewish religious community with the churches. Thus, emancipation reached its final phase, namely, the emancipation not only of the Jews, but of Jewry." "The Prussian Regional Association of Jewish Congregations included approximately seventy-five percent of German Jewry, or almost four hundred thousand Jews, and has the historic merit to have created, in form of its annual meetings, a platform, based on strictly democratic elections, where, along with regular business, the great spiritual contests between the different streams in Jewry could take place."[57]

57. Max P. Birnbaum, *Staat und Synagoge 1918-1938* (Tübingen: 1981), pp. 1 and 2. Within German Jewry, the Zionist Union for Germany fought, especially at the beginning and at the end of the Weimar Republic, for the Jews' legal status with national self-assurance. The documents number 116 and 117 in J. Reinharz, ed., *Dokumente zur Geschichte des deutschen Zionismus*, 1981, concern the early phase after November, 1918 (especially pp. 253-54 and 256). On August 12, 1932, an article in the *Jewish Review* appealed to the authorities — von Hindenburg, von Papen, Schleicher — to request guarantees, in case Hitler would come to be a member of a future government, against measures blemishing Germany's name through injuring German Jewry's status as citizens of the state, their honor, and their existence (p. 528). When millions of Germans living abroad claimed, as nationals, equal rights in other states, then, logically, the legal status of the Jews who openly professed their particularity must not be infringed. The lawyer and Zionist leader Siegfried Moses insisted, as late as January 8, 1933, on fighting vigorously for the maintenance of full equality and free development of Jewish distinctiveness in Germany, notwithstanding the primacy of development work in Palestine. On March 22, 1933, in a letter to the Zionist Union, treating the "basic view held by the German Zionists at a moment of threat and danger," he demanded "active participation in the German Jewish tasks set by the present hour." "Common to Zionism is the recognition that the German Jews, when participating in the public life surrounding them, and especially when exercizing their civic rights, should voluntarily keep within certain bounds" — a restriction that, *mutatis mutandis*, was soon demanded by several church bodies and, for instance, Walter Künneth, from church members of Jewish descent. Siegfried Moses, however, pointed out the difficulties in setting such bounds. "In my opinion, a boundary providing for full exercise of political rights, while prohibiting any participation

What, then, really was the "Jewish question" for Bonhoeffer in April, 1933? First of all, that Jews were placed by the state under exceptional law. Künneth named reasons for a re-regulation of the "Jewish question." Bonhoeffer names none. But neither does he declare that there must not be any change. This would hardly have been reasonable in view of the public pressure exerted by the National Socialist Party. Along with the boycott and the Civil Service law, the national meeting of the German-Christians on April 3 and 4 in Berlin, in which one group had protested against "foreign blood" in German pulpits,[58] made a new regulation necessary. The question now was who should take the initiative. To leave it to the National Socialist Party organizations would mean boycott, terror, and lawlessness for the Jews. The alternative was to have the state tackle the task, whose bodies had arrived, in the previous decades, at legal regulations with the authorized Jewish representative bodies.

Bonhoeffer judged, "without a doubt, the state is entitled to steer new courses here" (351). This rules out the possibility that the party might alone be in charge of the "Jewish question." In April, 1933, the state bodies and the legislation mostly still followed constitutional regulations, and Bonhoeffer's essay urges the importance of holding on to such constitutional rule of law [*Rechtsstaatlichkeit*], especially when pressure is exerted on it, which is obviously done by the party. Bonhoeffer does not suggest, as Scholder inferred, "to solve the Jewish question through exceptional legislation."[59] The range of state measures on which consultations could be held — and should be held, in order to be legally valid — with the Jewish representative bodies was rather wide. Such representations continued to exist even after the state apparatus had almost completely fallen into the

in the German cultural life — in exchange for a grant of cultural autonomy — is hardly less wrong than, for example, a delimitation that tries to hold on to economic positions." The Zionists were conscious of the fact that their argumentation differed from that of other Jewish groups, and they reflected carefully how far to cooperate with non-Zionist Jewish authorities. "In the first rank, we must strive for actions taken by the congregations and their alliances," to whom precedence should be given because of their status as legally recognized public bodies. The letter concludes, "It is not our task to polemicize against a government. It is and remains our right to delimit our world view from other views" (quotes from pp. 554-55). This claim implied loyalty to the state and government, but delimitation from the National Socialist party and its anti-Semitic world view.

58. So S. Nobiling for the Berlin Group of German-Christians, according to Scholder (note 4 above), p. 369.

59. Scholder (note 4 above), p. 350.

hands of the National Socialists. In a speech on September 10, 1935, Adolf Hitler made brutally known, "What can be resolved by the state will be resolved by the state. What, because of its essence, the state is incapable of resolving will be resolved through the movement,"[60] that is, the party.

5. Bonhoeffer's Understanding of the Action of the Church Vis-à-Vis the State

When Bonhoeffer ascribed the competence to deal with the Jewish question to the state, in order to withdraw it from the National Socialist Party — that would of course expect the state to tolerate or even support pogrom solutions — he must not be reproached with overstating the rights of the state in a Lutheran Prussian tradition. This can be more precisely shown, as Bonhoeffer treats explicitly the responsibility of the state in an ethical perspective from the point of view of the church. These statements are no ad hoc formulations, but determined by the insights won up to 1933 for his ecumenically oriented political ethic. Concerned about his fellow Christians, and above all about the unnerved minds of theologians and church leaders, Bonhoeffer starts with the "proper concept of the church." He does not ask generally the ethical question how state action in the "Jewish question" should be judged, but asks specifically, "How does the church judge this state action, and what task follows from that for the church?" (350). Künneth's starting-point, namely, the "national state's self-reflection" in the so-called German revolution, is out of the question for Bonhoeffer.

In accord with Reformation tradition, Bonhoeffer states, first, that the church, affirming the state as "God's order of preservation in a godless world," must not interfere in the state's specific activity. Certainly, every strong state needs humanitarian associations, and also Christian personalities, that bring "the moral side of its respective measures into view." The "finer art of state" will know how to profit from such "interference by word [*Einrede*] in its relative significance." Bonhoeffer thus points out the function of a critical public [*Öffentlichkeit*], a participant of which is a church that is essentially regarded as a "cultural function of the state."

60. M. Domaris, *Hitler. Reden und Proklamationen 1932-1945* volume I/2 (Munich: 1965), p. 525.

But the true church of Christ cannot criticize here by moralizing humanitarianly. "It has neither to praise nor to censure the laws of the state." Bethge comments, worried, How would such a statement have rung in Bonhoeffer's ears ten years later![61] Such statements, however, serve to clarify the church's and the state's respective commissions, and prepare a much more fundamental questioning of state activity. The church should not lapse into moral-clerical schoolmastering. "History is made not by the church, but by the state; but certainly, only the church that witnesses to God's entering history knows what history is and therefore what the state is."

Bonhoeffer seems to speak rather restrictively. "The church cannot primarily act *directly* politically; for the church does not pretend to know the necessary course of history. It cannot *directly* interrupt the state in regard to the Jewish question, and demand that the state act in a certain different way." But this statement — that the church will not be able to propose distinct laws to the state — preludes severe remarks. The church must ask the state again and again whether its actions are such as a legitimate state is responsible for, namely, "activity in which law and order, and not lawlessness and disorder, are created." The church must ask the state whether a certain state activity makes the state "appear to be threatened in its essence as state [*Staatlichkeit*], that is, in its function to create law and order through its power." The church's criticism does not aim at this or that questionable action, but at dangers to the foundation of the state — and this in the instance of the "Jewish question" that seems to be but a minor piece of ideology. The church can and must bear witness that much more is at stake. By concretely alerting to the fact that the state's essence is endangered, the church "makes the state bear the whole weight of responsibility for its peculiar manner of acting."

In principle, the state may create new laws. However, "Both, too little order and law, and too much order and law, compel the church to speak" to the state. The sentence at the beginning of section I, "Without doubt, the church of the Reformation is not called to speak to and interrupt directly the state's specific political activity" — also in the "Jewish question" — here finds its strict limitation. Now follow examples for "too little" and "too much." When "a group of people is made lawless," there is too little law. A reintroduction of serfdom — in Bonhoeffer's view an analogy to the introduction of an exceptional law for Jews — would be regarded by the

---

61. Bethge, *Dietrich Bonhoeffer: A Biography* (note 24 above), p. 274.

church as an action of a lawless state. Too much law would exist "should the state interfere in the essence of the church and its proclamation, for instance through the compulsory exclusion of the baptized Jews from our Christian congregations, and the prohibition of mission to Jews. Here the Christian church would be in a *status confessionis,* and here the state would be negating itself." A "three-fold possibility of action by the church vis-à-vis the state" arises, namely, (1) to make the state, in public, responsible for the (il)legitimacy of its action; (2) to aid all victims of state action, including the Jews "who do not belong to the Christian church-community"; (3) when facing an unchecked state of injustice, to take hold of the spokes of the wheel, which means direct[62] political action of the church, for example, in the sense that the illegitimacy of a regime will be proclaimed according to the resolution of an evangelical council.

This is a perfectly clear and decisive statement. It gives the church full authority to articulate ethical decisions in the political arena, when the state becomes a state of injustice, as a confession of faith in God whose commandment addresses us here and now. Only because Bonhoeffer's theology had closely linked the church together with an ethic of listening to God's commandment in the present situation, such conspicuous conclusions could be and had to be drawn. *Status confessionis* in favor of the few church members of Jewish descent; lawlessness, comparable to a reintroduction of serfdom today, as the brand that would mark any exceptional law for Jews — Bonhoeffer's contemporaries could hardly imagine such a radicalization of the "Jewish question," which had turned into a questioning of the legitimacy of the state. It seems that Bonhoeffer did recognize that anti-Semitism and hostility to Jews were not accidental, but substantial features of National Socialism and a state dominated by it.

---

62. In the first printing in 1959, a typographical error had occurred that distorted the meaning. Ernst Feil discovered it, and corrected it in his 1971 book *Die Theologie Dietrich Bonhoeffers* (see chapter 1, I, 1), p. 264, note 105. The third possibility is not an "indirect" [*mittelbar*] but a direct [*unmittelbar*] action of the church. Bertold Klappert, p. 97 in *Ethik im Ernstfall* (note 38 above), found Bonhoeffer's illustration for the third possibility of action used in the reverse sense in a lecture on Jewry in Public Life as a Danger for the German Reich given by Adolf Stoecker on February 3, 1882. The same picture was used by Max Weber in the lecture on Politics as a Profession, given in 1919 and published in second edition in 1926, "Here we enter the realm of ethical questions, for there the question belongs what kind of human being one must be [namely, one who takes up politics as a profession] in order to be allowed to put one's hand in the spokes of the wheel of history." Quote from p. 167 in Weber, *Soziologie. Weltgeschichtliche Analysen. Politik* (Stuttgart: 1956).

We have shown that Bonhoeffer cannot be reproached for granting the state too much control over law and order. The other reproach, mentioned above, suspected him of anti-Jewish theologizing. Does some "anti-Judaism," as problematic as this concept might be, keep sticking to Bonhoeffer? Again, we must try first to interpret, and then to judge, and remain aware of the fact that such a judgment will also yield an orientation for our own behavior and thinking.

6. Bonhoeffer's Judgment of the Jewish Question in Terms of Salvation History

In the last paragraph of section I, Bonhoeffer remarks that there is still another context in which the church sees the state measures against Jewry. He refers to the notion which, as he states, never got lost in the church of Christ, that the "'chosen people' who nailed the Redeemer of the world to the cross, must bear the curse of this deed in a long history of suffering." Here appears an accumulation of elements that are suspected of bespeaking a Christian anti-Judaism. This traditional notion must certainly be corrected, since, historically, the main legal and political responsibility rested upon the Roman occupation force, and not simply the Jewish people, but certain groups and wielders of power among them were responsible for delivering Jesus up to the Romans. Bonhoeffer does not correct this, but in the first place pleads for human compassion through citing from Luther's table talks [*Tischreden*], "Jews are the poorest of all people on earth. . . ." It should be noted that he chose this quote, and not one of Luther's wicked pronouncements on Jews. And, continuing in this decidedly one-sided tendency, he at once places the "history of suffering of this people, loved and punished by God, under the sign of the last homecoming of the people of Israel to their God. And this homecoming occurs in Israel's conversion to Christ." Ulrich Wilckens renders the text in Romans 11:12b about the *pleroma* of Israel, to which Bonhoeffer alludes, "what fullness of blessing will arise from Israel's complete homecoming (into the community of the chosen people of God)!"[64] Through his addition in parentheses,

---

63. DBW 12, pp. 354-55; *No Rusty Swords*, pp. 225-27.

64. Wilckens, *Das Neue Testament. Übersetzt und kommentiert* (Gütersloh: 1970), p. 540.

Wilckens lets the reader suppose that Israel's path would have reached its goal in membership in the church. Bonhoeffer, however, is closer to the Pauline text when he emphasizes — through quoting the renowned theologian of salvation history, Gottfried Menken — Israel's conversion to the Lord. Only in this connection can the question of Israel's relationship to the church make any sense at all. The end of the quote from Menken's 1795 text is, "Happy the people for whom the *Lord* is their God!" The goal of the homecoming is, in Bonhoeffer's understanding, not the church, but the Lord of the church.

The church sees, Bonhoeffer says, that God's history with "this enigmatic people" goes on. "Every new attempt to resolve the 'Jewish question' is shipwrecked by the significance of this folk for salvation history; nevertheless, such attempts must again and again be made." Bonhoeffer is not thinking of an end to the history of this people through an assimilation, as if the church would have taken their place. But when a state must make attempts to create order because disorder reigns in the "Jewish question," and leave out of account exceptional legislation that would mean lack of law, then there would supposedly have remained, in 1933, only the alternative between support for the gathering of the Jews in Palestine[65] where, at that time, the Jewish community numbered two hundred fifty thousand people, and the stubborn struggle for autonomy was gaining slow progress; or to grant the Jews a guest status in Germany with full rights that protected them from anti-Semitic persecutions. But these are mere assumptions that proceed from the supposition that Bonhoeffer had thought of concrete attempts at a resolution. The supposition is, indeed, corroborated by the striking statements that "the state is entitled to steer new courses here," and that a preliminary solution to the "Jewish question" must again and again be sought. Preliminary, because no attempt will bring to a close this people's significance for salvation history.

The term *salvation history* indicates that Bonhoeffer, in this place, rather than making proposals for legal solutions, thinks something else more important, namely, to ask, How does the church see the history of suffering of God's "chosen people"? What is the church told by its knowledge "of the curse that burdens this people"? In no way does Bonhoeffer's text suggest that the answer would be: The salvation history of Israel has ended, Israel will no more come home to their God. Quite to the contrary.

---

65. Ben-Sasson (note 54 above), pp. 266-362, especially pp. 328ff.

The church cannot get stuck in self-conceited "cheap moralizing." Instead, "looking at this rejected people, the church, aware of being unfaithful to its Lord again and again, knows itself to be humbled together with them."[66]

The reader of the Bible is familiar with the notion that human life is lived under the curse and God's judgment of wrath. There is the curse on the soil because of humankind's fall into sin (Genesis 3:17), the curse on Cain (Genesis 4:11), the curse on the depraved humankind and the deluge (Genesis 6:5-8), the prophets' announcements of the coming judgment and curse on Israel and Judah (Jeremiah 26:6; Malachi 2:2), the curse on the one who does not do the commandments (Deuteronomy 27:26, cited in Galatians 3:10). When the curse is to be understood in such an all-encompassing sense, as the reverse side of the bestowal of grace by God while humankind turn their back to God, then the church that is again and again unfaithful to its Lord is deeply hit by the curse, and humbled together with Israel. And yet, the promise of homecoming into the life of faith in, and loyalty to the Lord is kept up. As Paul said, Christ let himself be burdened with the curse that is bound to hit unfaithfulness, "in that he became the curse for us, for it is written, 'Cursed is everyone who is hung on the wooden cross'" (Galatians 3:13). The church that knows of salvation history knows of the bond connecting, as kindred, those who may come home, shamed by grace.

Does some anti-Judaism creep in nevertheless? It becomes crucial now to determine precisely what this concept means. If anti-Semitism indicates an ideological racist hostility to Jews, then anti-Judaism obviously indicates a religious hostility. It will hardly be correct to classify the prophets' announcements of curses on Israel in old Israel as anti-Judaism, and the original proclamation of Jesus and the Apostles does not deviate in principle from this line. However, the bitter separation from the synagogue in the early period of Ancient Christianity occasioned mutual reproaches of being cursed. Several New Testament phrases, formulated in this context, do contain an anti-Judaistic component. But Bonhoeffer, like Paul, holds firmly that Israel has a lasting significance for salvation history, and will come home to God, and he bases his thinking on the premise of a fundamental solidarity between the church and Israel. This cannot be labeled anti-Judaism. The theories of disinheritance and substitution that are be-

---

66. In the sermon of June 19, 1932 (note 33 above), Bonhoeffer speaks of a guilty church from which martyrs' blood could be demanded (see chapter 1, II, 2).

ing discussed today — the church sees itself as having taken Israel's place, Israel is thereby disinherited and outdated — should not be projected too unequivocally into Bonhoeffer's text. It was much too clear to him that the conversion of both Israel and the church to the Lord, to the "true God in Christ," is an eschatological occurrence. Christian anti-Judaism develops where the solidarity of the church with Israel is cancelled; it germinates where Christians no longer understand the death of Jesus on the cross as his dying for the "chosen people," and as such for all of us; where Christians push away the hope for Israel, expressed in Romans 9 through 11 in terms of salvation history; where Christians moralizingly assess the predicament of Jews, deeming it their fate to be punished. Bonhoeffer affirms none of this.

IV. Results

Bonhoeffer's judgments of the "Jewish question" in April, 1933, are distinguished by their fundamentally theological character, by surprising perspectives, and clear resolution. For a young, twenty-seven-year-old theologian, the convergence of these characteristics is quite unusual, especially in a situation in which general confusion reigned. I have started from the hypothesis that Bonhoeffer's clear-sightedness and decisiveness are largely due to the lucidity achieved in the development of his theological ethics up to 1933. Now in summary it should be shown how far this hypothesis has been verified.

1. Künneth's argumentation in April, 1933, takes its stand from the start on the basis of the so-called national German revolution, accepts its terminology (non-Aryan descent) and logic, and ponders on the claims the church should raise. Bonhoeffer refuses at the outset the basis of the new ideology, and argues at once that an exceptional legislation for Jews because of their race is unheard-of in history. All questions that now arise have to be answered on the grounds of "a proper concept of the church," including the question of how to judge the state's activity. Bonhoeffer thus proceeds from a basis attained in his ecumenical ethic of peace in 1932: Ethics grows out of common confession. The biblical Word passed on through the tradition and proclamation of the church yields insights and directives that help decide questions arising in the present. Based on its own insights, the church must question the state about its specific respon-

sibility, and must in case of need resist the state even by the most extreme means specific to the church. The church is undoubtedly competent to judge whether the state becomes lawless.

Künneth confirms the state's right to exceptional legislation for Jews, but demands a graded distinction between Jews (whom he exposes to state action almost without protection), and Jewish Christians (whom he, in order to be theologically correct, should have identified as Protestant Christians of Jewish descent). He inadmissibly confuses belief and belonging to a people by arguing that the Jewish Christians, because they had come into a closer relationship with the German people and culture, should be granted a reduced version of exceptional law and charitable church aid. For Jews who are still either directly or indirectly influenced by the synagogue, Künneth only rejects violent persecution of Jews when they, being "a foreign body in the life of the people," are eliminated from it. Bonhoeffer, uncompromisingly, sees the church obligated to ask the fundamental question of whether the state, as a state of justice [*Rechtsstaat*], keeps up the law, and to reject everything that abolishes the constitutional rule of law [*Rechtsstaatlichkeit*]. This view corresponded to Reformation tradition that, while distinguishing between a spiritual and a worldly regime, and acknowledging, accordingly, a specific commission given by God to each, the church and the state, nevertheless ascribed to theological knowledge and church teaching the task of judging whether the state adhered to its commission of safeguarding justice, peace, and the protection of its citizens. In 1933, Friedrich Gogarten and many others, declaring the *nomos* of the people to be God's law, abandoned this Protestant understanding of the moral state as a state of justice. Bonhoeffer consistently persisted in this tradition, but developed, more clearly than traditionally understood, the church's responsibility and ethical authority.

3. We discovered that Bonhoeffer wanted the churches, in regard to the "Jewish question," to appeal to the obligation of the state of justice to take action against the pogroms of National Socialist Party organizations. Künneth and the Church Committee also knew of the violent persecution of the Jews, and feared that it would go on and grow worse. Already in February, 1933, "the National Socialist propaganda spread unscrupulously, and the terror of the party's SA and SS organizations was now no longer restrained by any state power."[67] The Emergency Decree (the Reich Presi-

---

67. Gebhardt, *Handbuch der deutschen Geschichte*, volume 20 (no date), p. 81.

dent's Edict for the Protection of People and State) of February 28, the Enabling Act (Law to Relieve the Emergency of the People and the State) of
March 23, 1933, and other measures opened the way more and more for the
arbitrary rule of the party, although by far not all the state institutions, the
administration, jurisdiction, the police, and the Reich Defensive Forces
[*Reichswehr*] had as yet been synchronized with that rule. So, in April, 1933,
an appeal to those responsible to keep up the constitutional rule of law was
possible and necessary. Bonhoeffer saw a situation arise in which the state's
essence appeared to be threatened — threatened by an inhuman ideological fanaticism, and by party organizations that had the option to resolve
the "Jewish question" through continuous pogroms, lawless excesses
against citizens whom they hated.

4. Bonhoeffer endeavored to argue in line with Reformation traditions. His argument that it was the function of the state to create law and
order did sound conservative. His assertion that in case the state would become lawless by administering either too much or too little law and order,
church action would become necessary, up to clutching the spokes of the
wheel, went far beyond the horizon of church leaders in 1933. Five years
later, such considerations prompted Bonhoeffer to participate in preparations to overthrow Hitler, now without any support from his church. A political ethic that could include an overthrow in the utmost case of need was
without precedent in the German Reformation tradition.

5. Regarding both the problem of peace and the "Jewish question,"
Bonhoeffer developed his political ethic strictly from the viewpoint of a
church that is earnestly obedient in its confession of faith. So there is a
double parallel. In both cases, Bonhoeffer wants the church to speak up for
the cause of a lawful order [*Rechtsordnung*]: in the first case, for an international order of peace, and in the second case, for a state of justice in Germany. In both cases, Bonhoeffer saw an extreme challenge to the church,
and called for a council.[68] It is evident that Bonhoeffer's approach to the
"Jewish question" accords with his overall thinking that conceives church
and ethics as a whole.

6. It is wrong to suppose, as has been done occasionally, that Bonhoeffer had "fought merely for the non-Aryan Christians."[69] In Bonhoef-

68. DBW 12, p. 354 ("Protestant council"); 1934 DBW 13, p. 301 ("ecumenical council").

69. Cited in *Konsequenzen* (note 6 above), p. 172.

fer's view, the church has the duty of making the state responsible for justice in general. By contrast with Künneth, Bonhoeffer knows no gradation of justice for Jews of Christian descent, and Jews who are members of the synagogue, or non-religious Jews. This shows that an ethic that is strictly based on the obedient church's confession of faith can indeed be an ethic "for others."[70] But since, for Bonhoeffer, the core of the "Jewish question" is the significance of this people for salvation history, it is impossible to resolve the question. The problem would be resolvable if complete assimilation and integration of Jewry into society could be advocated. Bonhoeffer, on theological grounds, cannot do so. Being convinced that this people, constituted by God's law, will continue its path in salvation history, Bonhoeffer thinks of new preliminary regulations by state law. A second problem for the theologian is to consider, based on a "proper concept of the church," what the bonds of church membership mean for the attitude to the baptized Jews in 1933. In that part of his paper which is related to this, section II, Bonhoeffer conspicuously avoids distinguishing sharply between God's people and Christ's church, and instead juxtaposes "membership in the people of God, in the church of Christ."[71]

7. Bonhoeffer's theological-ethical argumentation on the "Jewish question" was consistent in the situation in 1933, long before visible steps toward the "Final Solution" were taken — but it found no recognizable assent. A year and a half later, Bonhoeffer wrote to Erwin Sutz, "'Speak up for those who cannot speak for themselves' (Proverbs 31:8) — who in the church still knows today that this is the minimal action requested by the Bible in such times."[72]

---

70. Cf. August, 1944, DBW 8, p. 558 ("being for others").
71. DBW 12, p. 356.
72. Letter of September 11, 1934, DBW 13, pp. 204-5; *Testament to Freedom*, p. 435.

7 Dietrich Bonhoeffer's Ecumenical Ethic of Peace

1982

We Europeans live in a time and a region in which a war carried out with weapons of mass destruction would tear us into a horrible downfall of human life. This view is not debated. What is debated are the ways and means to prevent such a war. Is striving for security through armament and deterrence a must, or would it bring about what it is meant to prevent? Can we develop a new international political culture in which cooperation in the partners' mutual interest would exclude the outbreak of wars and stabilize at least outward peace?

There are no sure answers to these questions. We must orient ourselves in a situation of objective uncertainty, and we must be aware that every one of us shares in the responsibility for the course of events, whether we participate in, separate ourselves from, or work against the European peace movement. As Christians, we hold that faith empowers us to take responsible steps also within the unknown.

In quest of a grounded orientation regarding the issues of armament, war, and peace we turn to Dietrich Bonhoeffer. Not in the hope that we might simply adopt a conception that dates back some fifty years, but in the expectation that Bonhoeffer's attempts to find answers, and his experiences with them, will be illuminating and important to us. Bonhoeffer deserves precedence over others because he, in the beginning of the 1930s, developed an ecumenical ethic of peace that was no mere addendum but a central part of his theological thinking and political orientation.[1] This has been neglected even by some Bonhoeffer scholars who are especially interested in the political Bonhoeffer.[2] My thesis is that the path Bonhoeffer traveled in his life as a Christian and as a theologian, in faith and in deed, is only disclosed when we also probe into his turning toward and development of an ecumenical ethic of peace. In particular Bonhoeffer's close bond to the Sermon on the Mount becomes clear in this context.

I. The Justification for Participating in War in Bonhoeffer's Barcelona Lectures as Starting Point for the Path He Took in Theological Ethics

In the winter of 1928 to 1929 Bonhoeffer, during the one year of his ministry as assistant pastor, lectured on "Need and Hope in the Religious Situation of the Present" to the parishioners of the German congregation in Barcelona. Under this overall title, the twenty-three-year-old theologian

1. This chapter, like the previous one, deals with the time from 1928 to 1934. Bonhoeffer's treatment of both the "Jewish question" and the peace problem exhibits the stringency of his ethical judgment-forming [*Urteilsbildung*]. I want to show that Bonhoeffer's texts on ethics during this time, while treating concrete problems, are strongly continuous in both the motives and the methodology of his systematically consistent approach. A later chapter will prove that this is true up to and including the *Ethics* manuscripts of the years 1940 to 1943. By that, I want to refute a widespread opinion that was even shared by Barth. In his May 22, 1967, letter to Bethge, he wrote that he "would venture to doubt somewhat whether theological systematics (here I am thinking also of his *Ethics*) was truly his strong point." Barth stated this, however, under the impression of the debate about Bonhoeffer's aperçus (see above, beginning of chapter 3) of a "world come of age," "non-religious interpretation," and so on which then was in fashion, but he rightly protested against the attempts to see Bonhoeffer all of a sudden "in line with Tillich and Bultmann." *Gesamtausgabe* V (see above, chapter 1, note 1), p. 406.

2. Tiemo Rainer Peters, treating "The Presence of the Political" in Bonhoeffer's theology, does not mention his ecumenical peace ethic (see above, chapter 6, note 14, and the text preceding note 27). Hanfried Müller praised Peters's book under the heading "The Theological Discovery of the Political Bonhoeffer in the Federal Republic of Germany" in *Theologische Literaturzeitung* (periodical for theological literature) number 102, 1944, pp. 321-36, without bringing this topic up. In his own book *Von der Kirche zur Welt* (from church to world) that first appeared in Leipzig, German Democratic Republic, in 1961, Müller mentioned only briefly Bonhoeffer's commitment to the "question of peace," on p. 172 in the West German edition (Hamburg-Bergstedt: 1961).

who was for the first time on his own — far away from his teachers in Germany — expressed his theological convictions in three lectures. They are regarded in Bonhoeffer research as the biggest stumbling block. But just for this reason they must be interpreted carefully.[3]

(1) In the lecture on the prophets' tragedy and its lasting sense[4] Bonhoeffer explains the present crisis of bourgeois existence through following the traces of God's paths with his people. Beginning with the crisis of Israel in the eighth century BC, the great prophets confronted the people, and introduced a term that was to become a guide through world history for more than two thousand years, the term *faith* [*Glaube*]. In opposition to the war faction that intended to cope with the situation militarily, Isaiah exclaims, "if you are not in faith, you will not remain" (Isaiah 7:9). To go with God as the prophets do means to travel a hard path of sacrifice. God distinguishes between nations only according to whether or not they do his will.

(2) The second lecture speaks of Jesus Christ and of the essence of Christianity.[5] Bonhoeffer begins by stating "that Christ has actually been eliminated from our lives." Human beings today want to travel their religious path on their own, and lapse into hubris all over — in religion, morals, church, humanism, and mysticism. In direct opposition to his great teacher Adolf von Harnack (and Harnack's book on the essence of Christianity[6]) Bonhoeffer objects that "the affirmation of an infinite value of the soul is un-Christian." The path of Jesus led through real despair, the cross, and nothingness. Accordingly, faith will arrive only when the human being becomes nothing, completely empty, because God himself will then make all things new. Bonhoeffer asks, "Will the twentieth century be Europe's and Germany's hour of death?" and concludes that there will be a victorious future only when the sign of the cross is in view.[7]

---

3. See also above, chapter 6, part I.

4. *Die Tragödie des Prophetentums und ihr bleibender Sinn*, pp. 285-302 in DBW 10.

5. *Jesus Christus und vom Wesen des Christentums*, pp. 302-22 in DBW 10.

6. *Das Wesen des Christentums*, see above, chapter 4, section 4e.

7. DBW 10, pp. 302, 317, 322. Carl-Jürgen Kaltenborn published in 1973, in (East) Berlin, his book on *Adolf von Harnack als Lehrer Dietrich Bonhoeffers*. Reinhard Staats examined it in an essay on "Adolf von Harnack in Dietrich Bonhoeffer's Life," pp. 94-122 in *Theologische Zeitschrift Basel* number 37, 1981. Aided by Hans Christoph von Hase's and Bertha Schulze's recollections, he arrives at the conclusion, "Bonhoeffer's theological thinking was decisively influenced since 1924 by Adolf von Harnack more than by others, since 1931 by

(3) On February 8, 1929, Bonhoeffer lectured on basic questions of a Christian ethic.[8] His approach to ethics here is determined primarily by dialectical theology. Ethics speaks of human paths to God. Therefore innumerable forms of ethics exist which are not Christian. For there is only one path from God to the human being, and this does not depend on human good or evil. Nietzsche is not the first from whom the Christian has to learn what is "beyond good and evil." Christianity is a-moral. The many ethical precepts in the New Testament are found elsewhere, too, with Rabbi Hillel the commandment to love, and with Seneca that of love for the enemy. The Sermon on the Mount only advises the Christian to be mindful that it is God's will that his will be done, that each time the human will must be "forced into the divine will." But what, then, is the will of God? "The moment will tell you of what kind God's will is." No ethical principles, no generally valid law, no moralizing of life exists for the Christian. "There is always only the crucial moment." With this ever new and immediate orientating toward God, Jesus gives back to humankind, as the mightiest of gifts, the lost freedom, and therein creativity. In this freedom, Christians create standards for measuring good and evil; they create, as Luther said, new tables of the law, new decalogues.[9] Whoever, together

---

Karl Barth" (p. 116). The 1928-1929 Barcelona lectures can hardly be squared with this thesis. The first two of them follow the language of dialectical theology in that there is, on the one hand, critique of religion, of the church, ethics, humanism, Greek spirit, mysticism, on the other hand, insistence on God's sovereignty, on revelation, and on faith characterized as emptiness, and devaluation of the *Leben-Jesu-Forschung* (research on the life of Jesus) by arguments from *Formgeschichte* (form criticism), along with emphasis on post-Easter *kerygma*.

8. *Grundfragen einer christlichen Ethik*, pp. 323-45 in DBW 10. In Peters' opinion (p. 36 in *Die Präsenz des Politischen*, see note 2 above), Bonhoeffer did not resume "the democratic elements" of his dissertation *Sanctorum Communio*, "but rather its sporadic and untypical nationalistic-irrational implications." Hanfried Müller characterizes ideas in the third lecture as indeed "pre-fascistic" (p. 327 in *Theologische Literaturzeitung*, see note 2 above). Bethge sees in the lecture formulas of German nationalistic origin (in line with the *Deutschnationale Volkspartei*), borrowings from Friedrich Naumann and Max Weber, and conventional Lutheran statements, embellished with a titanic ethic of the moment (pp. 119-20 in Bethge, *Biography* English 2000, see above, chapter 6, part II, note 24). I am, in part, of a different opinion.

9. Pp. 327-29 in DBW 10; compare DBWE 9, *The Young Bonhoeffer 1918-1927* (Minneapolis: Fortress Press, 2003), p. 346 (from 1926), and DBWE 6, p. 288 (from 1942). The "crucial moment" is explained as "any moment that can become ethically valuable." This reminds of the passage written in the 1927 dissertation, printed in *Sanctorum Communio*, p. 48

with Tolstoy, relates the Sermon on the Mount directly to the present makes it a law. Surely, this resolve of the ego to force one's own will into the divine will may not be far from Heidegger's summons to exist essentially *(eigentliches Existieren)*, and shares with it that the normative contents remain indefinite. Bonhoeffer does not repress this lack of concreteness, but speaks now of the frightening experience that God's will is disclosed to us not unequivocally but contradictorily. It is the most severe problem of a Christian ethic that, in human eyes, God's order of love and God's order of history are antagonistic. History and love will "find their synthesis only in eternity,"[10] obviously an allusion to the relationship between virtue and blissfulness *(Glückseligkeit)* according to Kant. Order of love means Sermon on the Mount. The basis of God's order of history is the Old Testament. God travels his path in history not only with each nation but also with each individual. The antagonism of the two orders has found its strongest expression in Lutheranism, where it appears as the antagonism of *deus revelatus* and *deus absconditus*. Not for nothing had Bonhoeffer studied Luther under Holl and Seeberg.

What follows from this ethical-theological conception is acutely evi-

---

in DBWE 1, "At the moment of being addressed, the person enters a state of *responsibility* or, in other words, of decision." The person is "in a state of responsibility in the midst of time; not in time's continuous flow, but in the value-related — not value-filled! — moment. *In the concept of moment, however, the concept of time and the moment's value-relatedness are set in one.* It is not the shortest possible span of time, an atom mechanically conceived, as it were. The 'moment' is the time of responsibility, of value-relatedness — let us say God-relatedness — and, what is essential, it is concrete time, and only in concrete time ethic's real claim comes to pass, and only in responsibility am I fully conscious of being bound to time." This reminds of Søren Kierkegaard's analysis of the concept of moment in *The Concept of Anxiety* (1844), where it is, for instance, stated that "sensuousness, temporality, and the moment can only be understood in the context of Christianity, since only there does eternity become essential." Bonhoeffer refers to Kierkegaard (in note 12 to p. 56, on p. 57, in DBWE 1), "Our argument is close to his in its critique of the idealist concepts of time and reality." In Bultmann's 1926 book *Jesus* (English, *Jesus and the Word,* which Bonhoeffer cites in note 28 on p. 170 in DBWE 1), Kierkegaard's "moment" is alluded to, for instance, in the passage, "But what, then, does intelligibility of God's claims mean? . . . They cannot be developed in a general ethical theory . . . they grow quite simply from the situation of decision before God in which the human being is placed," whereby "this moment of decision contains everything that is necessary for the decision, insofar as the entirety of existence is at stake." See pp. 56-57 in Heinz Eduard Tödt, *Rudolf Bultmanns Ethik der Existenztheologie* (Bultmann's ethic of existence theology, Gütersloh: 1978).

10. DBW 10, p. 340.

dent in the war problem, which Bonhoeffer had to treat in the first place, since the consequences of the World War still irritated the Germans. He clearly knows that the churches and Christianity are accused of having justified murder in war in "the holy name of Jesus Christ." He knows of the objection to military service in war on the grounds of the Sermon on the Mount, and sympathizes with it. Yet he says that this objection lacks what is crucial in that it is unconcrete, and thus contradicts (as it seems to him) the methodological basic claim of his ethic of the moment. "Standing in the very midst of the need of decision whether to expose my own brother, my own mother to the attacker's hands, or to have to oppose the enemy with my own hands, then the moment will certainly tell me which is and must be my neighbor, even before God's eyes. God has given me to my mother, to my people. Whatever I have I owe to this people. Whatever I am came through my people. So whatever I have shall belong to my people again. That is divine order, for God created the nations."[11] Surely, the enemy is in just the same need. Therefore no hatred of the enemy, and therefore even within the struggle the prayer for him and his soul.

It is not easy to detect the fine rift cracking the argument here. That which tells me what to do is no longer the moment. The decision is determined by a para-situational order. I will "certainly" be told that belonging to my brother, my mother, and my people will be decisive. We today must ask the additional question, Have we in the Second World War been able to protect with our weapons, and will we in the "Third" World War be able to protect our mother and our nation with weapons of mass destruction?

Bonhoeffer himself regards the decision for weapons as something horrible, as violation of the conscience by the course of world events, as the terrible need to have to choose merely between "evil and evil."[12] But when God is forcing my will, even "murder" can be "hallowed." Bonhoef-

---

11. DBW 10, pp. 335-37.

12. A struggle with Max Weber's view of political "responsibility" can be inferred from Bonhoeffer's horrified statement "that, seemingly, good is realized only through evil" (DBW 10, p. 342). In his 1919 lecture on politics as a profession *(Politik als Beruf)* Weber refuted Friedrich Wilhelm Foerster's, a pacifist's, "simple thesis that from good can only follow good, from evil only evil," by stating, "Even the ancient Christians knew quite well that the world is ruled by demons, and that whoever engages in politics, that is, in using power and violence, concludes a pact with diabolic forces, and that for such a person's actions it is not true that good can only come from good, evil only from evil, but that often the opposite is true. Who does not see this is in fact politically a child."

fer does not make use of the traditional criteria of the teaching on just war. He even considers the possibility of armed participation in a war in which one's own nation, for the sake of its living conditions, tramples down the life of other nations.[13] The traditional German example for this was, until the First World War, Poland — its partitions to the interests of other nations — and the dictum, supposedly said by Bismarck in 1886, on the Polish fate in history, "Beat the Poles until the lust for life deserts them! My compassion for their situation is great. But if we wish to exist, we must exterminate them. The wolf cannot be blamed for being a wolf, because God created it so."[14] A peculiar contradiction remains. Christian ethics affords the freedom to decide in the moment. But God's will binds this freedom to the earth, to the nation, to the laws ruling the course of the world. So there is nothing left but the hope that God's forgiving grace will allow us to take part in that Kingdom which is exempt from the need of these times.[15]

Bonhoeffer's conception of 1929 was certainly not "pre-fascistic."[16] It lacked, for example, the racial component that is typical of fascism. But it did partake, in a modified form, of the neo-Lutheran religious enhancement of the idea of nation. As such, it could find assent from a majority in German Protestantism of that time. Bonhoeffer, however, made the tensions inherent in this ethos stand out in sharp relief. His intellectual honesty in the lecture pressed beyond the position marked in the lecture.

II. Bonhoeffer's Ecumenical Ethic of Peace and Theological Ethic of State till the End of the Weimar Republic

In the early 1930s a turning happened in Bonhoeffer's life which resulted in a revision of his theological-ethical conception. Speaking of it in a letter to a friend, he calls it a liberation through the Bible, and especially through the Sermon on the Mount. "I suddenly came to see Christian pacifism . . . as self-evident."[17]

13. DBW 10, pp. 332-33, 338-39, 341; DBWE 1, p. 119.

14. In Bismarck's works, however, the end of the dictum is that the wolf, in recompense, should be "shot dead, if one can do so."

15. DBW 10, pp. 344-45.

16. Hanfried Müller, see note 8 above.

17. See above, chapter 6, part II, note 22, and the paragraphs following there.

1. *The Significance of Bonhoeffer's Stay in America*

Bonhoeffer had prepared himself carefully for the academic year 1930-1931 that he was to spend at Union Theological Seminary in New York. When he then spoke to American audiences, he did so as a messenger from Germany, depicting the hardships of German families in the war and in the still continuing times of need. It is surprising how strongly he emphasized the German leaning toward peace that existed in the working class and the Youth Movement, as well as the beginning of the work of the World Alliance of churches for peace through international friendship.[18] Bonhoeffer was no longer convinced, as he had been in the third Barcelona lecture, of the absolute claim that one's own nation seemed to have on each of its citizens. Now the Christians' awareness of belonging to the one people of God took precedence. On November 9, 1930, in an Armistice Day Service, he preached, "Come what may, let us never more forget, that our christian people is the people of God, that if we are in accord . . . then the world will have its peace for ever and ever."[19] Wishful thinking? In any case, such statements contain Bonhoeffer's commitment to work for peace. A manuscript for addresses to congregations concludes, "We know, it is not enough only to talk and to feel the necessity of peace, we must work seriously."[20]

Jean Lasserre, a French pacifist and theologian, who studied together with Bonhoeffer at Union Theological Seminary and became his friend, lived a simple obedience to the Sermon on the Mount and Jesus' commandment of peace. After the end of the academic year, in May, 1931, the two traveled to Mexico. In the city of Victoria in the state of Tamaulipas the Quaker Héberto Sein had organized a public meeting for peace promotion. Lasserre and Bonhoeffer were the speakers. The common lecture of a Frenchman and a German, from nations regarding each other at that time as hereditary enemies, deeply impressed the hundreds of listeners — and certainly also the lecturers themselves.[21]

Bonhoeffer could hardly deem his cooperation with the Frenchman

18. The World Alliance for Promoting International Friendship through the Churches, founded in 1914, had prominent German members; see Bethge, *Biography,* pp. 190-93.

19. DBW 10, p. 581 (Bonhoeffer's English).

20. DBW 10, p. 388 (Bonhoeffer's English).

21. Oral information by Lasserre on the occasion of the celebration of Bonhoeffer's seventy-fifth birthday, 1981. Compare above, chapter 6, part II, note 24.

a pacifistic idyll. News from Germany showed that the deadly enmity between France and Germany had not yet healed. The dispute about Günther Dehn, who had criticized the naïve veneration of the soldiers killed in battle, was in full swing.[22] On June 2, 1931, a newspaper article on the Protestant church and international reconciliation *(Evangelische Kirche und Völkerverständigung)*, written by Paul Althaus and Emanuel Hirsch, mobilized the entire right-wing press, and a considerable part of the church press, against the German ecumenists who had met in Hamburg to prepare a World Alliance conference to be held in September. The article argued that a war against Germany was being waged now, in peace times, by means of war contributions under the name of reparations *(Wiedergutmachung)*, that would effect Germany's downfall. And this was happening amid the blatantly broken promise of disarmament on the part of the victors. Under such circumstances an understanding was impossible. Instead, lies about the real situation must be unveiled. The article ends, "Whoever believes that understanding can be better served otherwise, disowns the German destiny and confuses consciences at home and abroad, because in this he does not honor the truth."[23]

Althaus and Hirsch regarded an identification with the fate of the German people simply as a precondition for ecumenical church community. The partners abroad were confronted with the alternative either to accept the German-national view or to risk the rupture of relations between Christians. When the ecumenists, suspected of "political Westernization," suggested that such an attitude might lead to a victory of the National Socialists, Althaus replied that the National Socialists' appeal to the "injured pride" and "brutal existential need" of the German people was understandable.[24]

Bonhoeffer, back from America, decided to participate in the 1931 Cambridge conference of the World Alliance, and was elected as one of three part-time youth secretaries. This decision was surely not beneficial for an academic career. But Bonhoeffer was henceforth fundamentally bound to Christian ecumenism. This bond was expressed in the ethic of peace which he now developed. He could no longer say, "God created the

---

22. Dehn, *Die alte Zeit, die vorigen Jahre* (times bygone, the previous years, München: 1962), pp. 247-85.

23. See Bethge, *Biography*, p. 195.

24. See above, chapter 6, part II, note 26.

nations,"[25] nor draw seemingly assured conclusions from such an assumption, as he himself had done in Barcelona, conclusions that motivated Althaus and Hirsch to decide against the ecumenists.

2. Theological Presuppositions of an Ecumenical Ethic of Peace

Ernst Feil has pointed out in his book *The Theology of Dietrich Bonhoeffer*[26] that after Bonhoeffer's return from America and during his lecturing at the University of Berlin Christology moved into the center of his theology. This is evident from the documented lecture courses.[27] The christological concentration corresponds to the immediacy with which Bonhoeffer from now on listened not only to the promise of grace but also to the challenge to be obedient in the Sermon on the Mount. This has consequences for ethics.

In July 1931, Bonhoeffer paid a visit to Karl Barth, who was teaching in Bonn. For some time afterward, Bonhoeffer criticized Barth for excluding "any concrete" ethic, while rightly fighting an ethic of principles.[28] Bonhoeffer insisted that concrete revelation happened and is happening in Jesus Christ. The Word of God really enters empirical history. Jesus Christ is indeed the "anti-logos" within history who contradicts the human logos. He is the incarnate Word, really present in what happens. "Christ as God's Word in the sense of address does not mean Christ as timeless truth, but means God's addressing us with the truth that breaks in upon the concrete moment."[29]

The moment, as the source from which ethical decision springs, had been conceived in Barcelona programatically to be without a certain content that could be known beforehand. Practically, however, a (supposed) para-situational certainty — "God created the nations" — determined the content. Now, in christological concentration, it becomes clear how concrete the address by Christ in the moment is, an address that both demands and brings into being. (No longer are "historical growth and divine

---

25. DBW 10, p. 357.

26. See above, chapter 1, part I, 1.

27. Feil, *Theologie* (German), from p. 161 on; DBW 11, *Ökumene, Universität, Pfarramt 1931-1932* (Gütersloh: 1994), pp. 139-215, 239-313; DBW 12, pp. 153-99, 279-348; DBWE 3.

28. DBW 11, p. 212.

29. DBW 12, pp. 282 and 298.

commandment of love" two antagonistic orders, as, in Barcelona, they had appeared to be.[30]) Hence, the Sermon on the Mount gains new binding force. It is heard as a call to simple discipleship in faith. "Faith must be single-minded. Otherwise it brings about reflection instead of obedience, otherwise the left hand knows what the right hand does, which is no discipleship, for discipleship knows nothing of good or evil." There are no human means to secure peace. "The Christian can only venture peace in faith." There is no other "access to the enemy" than "via the prayer to the Lord of all peoples."[31]

3. The Development of an Ecumenical Ethic of Peace

(A) Both as youth secretary for the World Alliance and as lecturer and preacher in Berlin, Bonhoeffer felt impelled to develop ethics that would be, in parallel, an ethic of international peace and a theological ethic of the state. The Weimar Republic's inner crisis and its situation in the international system interacted closely.[32] Had the victorious nations granted con-

---

30. DBW 10, pp. 333-34.

31. DBW 17, *Register und Ergänzungen* (indices and supplements, Gütersloh: 1999), p. 117 (compare DBW 12, p. 233). Bonhoeffer now deals with the problem, which arose in Barcelona, of arrogating to know good and evil beforehand. Later in 1942 he states, "The knowledge of good and evil appears to be the goal of all ethical reflection. The first task of Christian ethics is to supersede [do away with, *aufheben*] that knowledge" (DBW 6, p. 299).

32. Bonhoeffer developed his ecumenical peace ethic in a specific way. The problem he treated was the middle one of three relationships of public law that Kant had distinguished in *"Zum ewigen Frieden"* (On eternal peace) 1795-1796. Between the human beings' rights as citizens in a nation-state *(ius civitatis)*, on the one hand, and, on the other hand, the worldwide rights of human beings and states insofar as they are regarded as citizens of a universal human state, influencing each other in an external relationship *(ius cosmopoliticum)*, there is the international law *(Völkerrecht, ius gentium)*. The fact that Bonhoeffer did not speak of peace in general, but tackled a specific problem, was noted — in part with displeasure — by some of his contemporaries. Hans Schönfeld in Geneva, having looked into the theses Bonhoeffer had sent for the address he was to give on the church and the world of nations *(Kirche und Völkerwelt)* in Fanø on August 28, 1934 (see DBW 13, pp. 298-304), forwarded the theses, on August 10, to Wilhelm Menn with the remark, "I must say that I am rather aghast, also at that which Mr. Bonhoeffer presents here, confining himself narrowly to the problem of war" (DBW 13, p. 184, note 3). Bonhoeffer's specific ethic of peace, as a *pax gentium* ethic, is at present (in the 1980s) especially up to date, since this is the aspect of peace that is almost exclusively seen today. In the meantime many have come to feel

cessions to those Weimar governments that were recruited from parties loyal to the constitution, even if the concessions would have been by far not as big as those which the National Socialists quickly bullied from the victors, then the Weimar Republic would have had good chances to survive, in spite of the world economic crisis of 1929 and political left-wing and right-wing extremists. Then the Second World War, insofar as it of necessity followed from the National Socialists' seizure of power — the Bonhoeffer family, like many others, saw already in 1933 that Hitler "means war!"[33] — would not have had to break out.

(B) On July 26, 1932, Bonhoeffer delivered a lecture on the theological foundation of the work of the World Alliance *(Zur theologischen Begründung der Weltbundarbeit)* at the youth peace conference in Ciernohorské Kúpele, Czechoslovakia.[34] Bonhoeffer starts from the thesis that "There is not yet a theology of the ecumenical movement." But when this movement arises out of a new self-understanding of the church, then it will bring forth a new theology. Otherwise, it remains an organization for a purpose which, for example, in Germany will not attract the youth dominated by National Socialism. The World Alliance has done good practical work while being at a loss in basic questions. Its work is based, according to Bonhoeffer, on the view that the individual churches are locally limited, whereas the one church is not. It has to express the claim of its Lord to the whole world. Bonhoeffer denies — two years earlier than the Barmen Theological Declaration of 1934 — "that there are God-willed autonomous spheres of life which are exempt from the lordship of Christ, and do not need to listen to this Word. What belongs to Christ is not a holy sacred district of the world, but the whole world."[35] The one church is Christ *praesens.* Therefore it proclaims with authority the gospel and the com-

---

that the institution of war is as urgent a problem as Bonhoeffer saw it to be, and can no longer continue to exist. When focusing on a *pax gentium,* however, only a fraction of that which an ethic of peace has to consider will come into view. Results of decades of peace research in the Protestant Institute for Interdisciplinary Research *(Forschungsstätte der Evangelischen Studiengemeinschaft)* in Heidelberg are summarized in the article by Heinz Eduard Tödt on peace *(Frieden)* in volume 13 of the encyclopedian library on Christian faith in modern society, *Christlicher Glaube in moderner Gesellschaft* (Freiburg: Herder, 1981), pp. 79-119, and reprinted in Tödt, *Perspektiven theologischer Ethik* (München 1988), pp. 237-68.

33. Bethge, *Biography* (above, note 8), p. 257.

34. DBW 11, pp. 327-62.

35. DBW 11, p. 331.

mandment — not principles which are ever true, but commandments that are true today, because God is always precisely today our God. But does the church proclaim concrete commandments with the same certainty with which it proclaims the gospel?

Exactly this is the typical Bonhoeffer question, by which he was haunted like no other theologian. The beginning of a sentence by Gerhard Ebeling, who was a candidate in the 1936-1937 course of the Finkenwalde preachers' seminary, directed by Bonhoeffer, of the Confessing Church, serves to show the acuteness of this question. Ebeling wrote in 1982, "The task of ethical judgment-forming gets more thorny the deeper it enters into concreteness, and the farther it thus ventures into the public. . . ."[36]

Bonhoeffer, on the contrary, said in 1932 that a commandment is Christ's commandment only when it is proclaimed concretely. "The Gospel becomes concrete with the hearer, the commandment becomes concrete through the proclaimer." The proclamation of the commandment must incorporate the real facts in the commandment so that it will hit the situation itself. The church cannot just say in general that there ought to be no war, but should be able to say concretely, "go into this war, or do not go into this war." The church proclaims to the community God's definite demand. Bonhoeffer explicitly rejects the path which the churches have almost always traveled, namely, "evading and retreating to the base of principles behind the front." He sees that the church's commanding thus becomes dependent on the knowledge of reality. He demands of the church "either a conscious and qualified silence of not knowing, or a venturing of the commandment in all conceiveable concreteness, exclusiveness, and radicality." Since the church can err, it needs faith in the forgiveness of sins. But the church does not content itself with judgments based on an empirical knowledge of facts. It embeds this knowledge in a knowledge of reality that is oriented to Christ.

This authorization of the church to command concretely belongs to the heaviest problems in Bonhoeffer's writings. Bonhoeffer debated with Barth about it in 1931. Because of this view he was soon reckoned among

36. *Zeitschrift für Evangelische Ethik* (journal for Protestant ethics) number 26, 1982, p. 18. The sentence continues, ". . . which fact surely does not entitle us to renounce any attempt at establishing a consensus with regard to what is concrete, but rather warns against overestimating the possibility of a general consensus in concrete ethical questions and the necessity of a corresponding consensus within Christianity, and admonishes us to keep to the distinction between faith and work also in this respect."

the radicals in the Confessing Church and the ecumenic movement. But apart from this view his ethics and behavior cannot be grasped.

The recognition of God's commandment here and now is an act of God's revelation in the present. That means even the Sermon on the Mount is no biblical law, no absolute norm for our action. It is, instead, "in its commandments the illustration of what God's commandment can be" today, precisely for us.[37]

(C) All existing order, including that of the nation, loses in the moment[38] its absolute authority. It is only part of the fallen world, and not an order of creation. We must understand the orders of the fallen world in their orientation to Christ, to new creation, to the future. For some years, and so in 1932, Bonhoeffer used the term *orders of preservation,* but later dropped it because of the neo-Lutheran misuse of it. By preservation, Bonhoeffer said in 1932, God warrants the possibility that new things come. What is not open to the revelation of Christ must be broken. On this depends the judgment of the church. No war tasks of nations can be inferred from the orders. Instead, the recognition is coming up in the World Alliance that "The order of international peace is today God's commandment for us."

How is this peace to be understood? Anglo-Saxon theological thinking in the World Alliance regards that peace which now is to grow as a "piece of the Kingdom of God on earth," so that it is "absolutized" into an "ideal." International peace, an order of preservation, is misunderstood as a "final order of consummation, valuable in itself, a breaking in of an order from beyond upon the fallen world." The establishment of an order of preservation can attain absolute urgency, and this is the case for the order of international peace, *pax gentium,* in 1982 as it was in 1932. Nevertheless, international peace as an order of preservation must be established within the boundaries of truth and justice. "Where a community of peace endangers or stifles truth and justice, the peace community must be broken, and struggle announced. When both sides then really struggle for truth and justice, the peace community, even if broken externally, is realized more deeply and strongly in the struggle for the same cause." Struggle can be an order of preservation. But the "justification of struggle" in no way includes "the affirmation of war on principle." "Our war today can no longer be

37. DBW 11, pp. 332-35.
38. DBWE 1, p. 48, compare above, in note 9.

subsumed under the concept of struggle, because it is the assured self-destruction of both combatants," and thus by no means an order of preservation. War today destroys the inner as well as the outer human being, soul and body. It needs idealization and idolization (Ludendorff's teaching on "total war" is a probable background for this statement). Today's war, that is, the next war, must be banned by the church, because it obstructs the view of revelation. We need not shy away from the term *pacifism,* even if the ultimate pacification is done by God. This term challenges us to overcome war. The "re-creation of conditions" that must be achieved today needs the churches' "great proclamation in common" that results in international thinking, which "costs hard work and hard struggle." The terrible need of the church is that it appears incapable of common recognition of the truth. Only where the church knows of its guilty condition of being torn apart, and yet "feels compelled under God's commandment to speak out," is forgiveness and redemption promised to it.[39]

(D) Around this core of Bonhoeffer's peace ethic statements crystallize other considerations, as in the lecture in February, 1932, on the right to self-assertion *(Das Recht auf Selbstbehauptung).*[40] One of humankind's answers to the quest for this right is represented by Gandhi, namely, it is better to suffer than to assert oneself through violence. The other answer is that of European and American civilization. Modern "war stems from times when Europeans thought they could create living space *(Lebensraum)* for themselves only by killing others." Machines work in a similar manner, inconsiderate to nature. "Therefore catastrophe arises where the machine is intentionally placed in the service of the destruction of human lives."[41] Bonhoeffer demands from the individual, as from the nations, something which is resolutely denied by national Protestant theology, namely, readiness for sacrifice instead of the will to assert oneself.

It is evident that this peace ethic is connected with the Sermon on the Mount — to wit, not in the sense of letter-bound directives, but as illustrating what God's commandment can be when heard concretely today and here.[42] This interpretation must be seen together with the other one that the Sermon on the Mount unmistakably demands single-minded

39. DBW 11, pp. 336-44.
40. DBW 11, pp. 215-26.
41. DBW 11, p. 224.
42. DBW 11, p. 335; compare above, end of section B.

obedience and committed discipleship.[43] Already in 1932, Bonhoeffer warns against making grace "cheap," a thought that he later elaborated in his 1937 book *Discipleship*.[44] "Any service in war — unless it be Samaritan service — and any preparation for war — is forbidden to the Christian. A belief that considers an arbitrary disposal of this law to be freedom from the law . . . defies God."[45] Bonhoeffer's resolve not to assent to being drafted to armed military service was already settled in 1932 through his recognition of God's concrete commanding at a particular time.

4. Bonhoeffer's Theological Ethic of State

A peace ethic is incomplete without a corresponding political ethic. When during the crisis of the Weimar Republic terror from right and left controlled the streets and paralyzed the law, Bonhoeffer pleaded that the constitutional rule of law [*Rechtsstaatlichkeit*] be kept up. The church would have to admonish the national power state to stay within its limits. It would have to tell the state that "nationalistic defiant insisting on flesh and blood is sin against the Spirit."[46] It is the state's specific commission to restrain blind nationalistic zeal. In a sermon of June 12, 1932, Bonhoeffer warns the nationalist government under Reich Chancellor Franz von Papen not to try to tear a whole people from collapse by means of the "Christian *Weltanschauung*" (worldview). Such soothing religious talk would be but a flight from the living God who is dangerous.[47] Neither would the Protestant church hear "God's protest" against it.[48] The church, supposedly a fresh power in politics, must beware of being played as a trump card in the struggle of the parties, or of being used for a "Christian political ideology," which would mean to "Christianize politics."[49] After all, God acts on his world also by using the state. The church is doubly bounded, on the one hand by the Kingdom of God, which is not at the church's disposal and yet wishes to be present among us, and on the other hand by the state, which has a spe-

---

43. DBW 17, pp. 117-18; see above, note 31.
44. DBWE 4.
45. DBW 17, p. 118.
46. 1932 DBW 11, p. 232.
47. DBW 11, pp. 440-41.
48. DBW 12, p. 426, in a Reformation Memorial Day sermon (November 6, 1932).
49. 1933 DBW 12, p. 239.

cific objective commission. The church cannot dominate the state, but can serve the state by "proclaiming Christ's lordship over all the world in faith and in word." Conflict will arise only when the state endangers this word.[50] It almost seems as if the state might function, by reason of its specific commission, in secular autonomy [*Eigengesetzlichkeit*]. But Christians, as citizens, can neither escape into the "otherworld of pious bliss" where the earth is abandoned, nor drift into the "this-worldliness of a secular utopia" that would only surrender the human being to the earth's "enslaved finitude." So Bonhoeffer can say, "The Kingdom of God is in our world not otherwise than in the duality of church and state."[51] The people stands in both, state and church, because it is called to the Kingdom of God.

With this concreteness, Bonhoeffer confronts the tendency that prevailed in German theology at that time to shift the Kingdom of God to the beyond, or to a final eschatological future, or to inwardness. In a 1932 memoir on the "social gospel," Bonhoeffer wrote, "Taking the kingdom of God seriously as a kingdom on earth is biblical, and is in the right, whereas an otherworldly understanding of the kingdom is in the wrong."[52] So Bonhoeffer sees the state commissioned, as an order of preservation, to guarantee law and external order and to provide neither too little nor too much of both. There would be too much law and order if the state would develop into a *Weltanschauung* state, and let its matter-of-fact activity become ideologically heated up. There would be too little of them if the state would not protect the rights of all sections of its population.[53]

It is decisive that Bonhoeffer denies the state the right to wage war. In this, the state has to listen to the proclamation of the church, and the church, if it wishes to remain loyal to its commission, can tell the state only that God commands international peace.

In the time of the Weimar Republic, Bonhoeffer was the only German theologian who developed an ethic of peace theologically. It should not be forgotten, however, that peace work done by Christian groups and churches, not only in the ecumenical movement but also within Germany, was widely spread, and of course was accompanied by theological and other reflections. Many important contributions appeared in the journal

---

50. 1932 DBW 11, pp. 301 and 303.
51. 1932 DBW 12, pp. 269-70 and 273.
52. DBW 12, p. 210.
53. 1933 DBW 12, pp. 353-54; compare above, chapter 6, part III, 5.

Die Eiche (the oak tree), edited by Friedrich Siegmund-Schultze. The general superintendent of the *Kurmark* (the main part of the March of Brandenburg) Otto Dibelius, a widely known speaker of the church of the Old Prussion Union, published in 1930 a popular book dealing with practical questions, *Friede auf Erden* (peace on earth)? and before that a booklet on the church and the League of Nations, *Kirche und Völkerbund*. Some paragraphs from the booklet will convey an impression of the atmosphere in church and theology in Germany already before the rise of Hitler's party and, intensified, after the party's sensational success in the November 30, 1930, election — instead of the previous twelve seats, now one hundred seven seats in the Reichstag. The great dispute about the ecumenical Life and Work conference in Stockholm, 1925, has yielded, so Dibelius thinks, some clarity. "German Lutheranism rises against an Anglo-Saxonism that is decisively shaped by Calvinism and Methodism. German Lutheranism refuses to participate in a struggle for the betterment of the world. For, as the Lutheran spokespeople say, the world lies in wickedness, and this aeon, in which sin rules, will never become a paradise. Whoever wants to abolish war, or even only to fight war in the name of Christianity, confuses the sphere of faith that is commended to the Christian with the sphere of the world where, according to God's will, things develop autonomously [*eigengesetzlich*].

"It is doubtless the mission of German Lutheranism to work out, in utmost acuteness, this separation of God's Kingdom and the world, of faith and the law of nature. However, to express this separation is not as easy as it is often supposed to be. . . .

"That the basic attitude of German Lutheranism has led to such an acute opposition against the League of Nations is to be explained by the historical situation, . . . especially by the concern that the rationalism of certain Anglo-Saxon circles could gain ground in Germany."

Dibelius counters this attitude of German Lutheranism by stating, "No word in the League's statutes suggests that the League of Nations should represent God's Kingdom on earth. The League's work concerns nothing other than the sober question, Shall, or shan't there be cooperation toward obstructing war?" In the name of Protestant Christianity, Dibelius answers in the affirmative, "Yes!"[54]

The Lutheran Bonhoeffer is certainly not in opposition to Dibelius

---

54. *Kirche und Völkerbund* (Berlin: 1927), pp. 23-24.

as regards this practical worldly side of peace work. But he cannot content himself with excluding this worldly side from theology. Hence his critique, on the one hand, of an Anglo-Saxon pragmatic and yet idealizing treatment of the peace question, and, on the other hand, of drifting into a "backworldly" conception of the Kingdom of God.

III. Ecumenical Peace Ethic and Theological State Ethic After Hitler's Seizure of Power

1. The Situation After January 30, 1933

Hitler's seizure of power meant preparation for a war of expansion. Bonhoeffer, convinced of this, set out, after the seizure of power had happened, to gather the means of church and theology to combat Hitler, and thus to struggle for peace. His leading viewpoint is today readily characterized as a "conservative notion of order."[55] It is more precise to characterize it as the theological notion of orders of preservation in Bonhoeffer's political ethics. In the radio talk of February, 1933, and the longer version given in the College of Political Science in the beginning of March, Bonhoeffer confronts the *Führer* cult, or leadership cult, by strictly distinguishing between an authority that accrues to the *Führer* out of the masses of his followers, and the authority of office [*Amt*] that is founded on God's commission for the state. *Führer* cult, on the one hand, becomes seduction, while mirroring, on the other hand, the arbitrariness of those who are led. A genuine leader must be able, on the grounds of responsibility and objectivity, to "disillusion" those who are led.[56] It is futile to measure these maxims of Bonhoeffer's by liberal democatic criteria. They belong in a concrete situation where Bonhoeffer faced a nationalistic movement fanaticized by the National Socialist Workers' Party.

This confrontation also enlightens Bonhoeffer's argumentation on the "Jewish question" in April, 1933. His judgment that "without a doubt, the state is entitled to steer new courses here"[57] has provoked vehement

---

55. Even Bethge, *Biography* (see above, note 8), pp. 259-60, albeit referring to theological counterpoises.

56. DBW 12, p. 258.

57. P. 351 in *Die Kirche vor der Judenfrage*, DBW 12, pp. 349-58; compare above, chapter 6, part III, 4-5.

contradiction. He is blamed for supporting a concept of state authoritarianism and denigrating civil rights. But Bonhoeffer does not speak in general terms. His judgment implies that the Party's attempts at resolving the "Jewish question" through boycott, terror, arbitrary arrests, and pogroms must be averted. Hitler expressly announced that the Party would resolve what the state was incapable of resolving.[58] Faced with this concrete alternative, Bonhoeffer demanded that the still functioning constitutional powers of the state should solve the problem by means of law. And he demanded that the church ask the state whether depriving the Jews of their legal status could be considered a state's legitimate action, since the state is commissioned to administer law and order — but neither too much nor too little of it — and thus to guarantee external peace. If the state, by failing to do so, becomes a state of injustice, the church is eventually challenged to take hold of the spokes of the wheel of the state's unlawful activities.[59]

This consideration is doubly new in the history of German Protestantism. First, it is considered a duty of the church, and not only a duty of the citizens or office holders, to resist state powers that practice injustice. Second, the resolution to resist a state of injustice is considered as having to be made by an "evangelical," or rather an ecumenical council *(Konzil)*.[60] At the 1934 ecumenical conference of Fanø, Bonhoeffer appealed to an "ecumenical council" in the matter of international peace.[61] Whoever attributes to Bonhoeffer a conservative notion of law and order must disregard his insistence on the relative right of the revolutionary new, grounded on the better righteousness demanded by Jesus in the Sermon on the Mount (Matthew 5:20), and the concomitant critique of "Christian conservativism" found in his university lecture course on recent theology in the winter of 1932-1933. The church preaches that the order of the state, recognized as an order of preservation, is continually "eschatologically broken." "The church is not merely there to support the state. Friction between church and state is natural."[62]

58. September 10, 1935; see above, chapter 6, part III, 4 note 59.

59. DBW 12, pp. 351-53; see above, note 53. Compare above, chapter 6, part III, 5, note 61, Max Weber's statement that one whose profession is politics is "allowed to put one's hand in the spokes of the wheel of history."

60. DBW 12, p. 354; 1932 DBW 11, p. 286 ("ecumenical gatherings").

61. DBW 13, p. 301.

62. DBW 12, pp. 167-68.

Bonhoeffer can only be reproached for having presented, during these years, the state problem, and widely also the peace problem, only from the viewpoint of the church, without developing sufficiently what is problematic within state and peace. So he does not quite satisfy his own postulate that the judging and commanding church must have looked into the details of the matter.[63] Of course, a detailed elaboration can hardly be expected from an individual when multidisciplinary cooperation is missing. But Bonhoeffer, through the continuous dialog within the group of family members and friends, was well-informed about many matters, especially about what happened in Hitler's so-called national revolution.

2. Bonhoeffer's Peace Commitment
at the Fanø Conference in August, 1934

(A) While the Fanø conference of the World Alliance together with the Life and Work movement was prepared, dramatic political events took place that threatened peace. Under the pretext of suppressing the putsch attempted by Reich minister Ernst Röhm, Hitler saw to it that more than one hundred of his political opponents were liquidated on June 30 and July 1, 1934. On July 25, Austrian National Socialists attempted a putsch, and chancellor Dollfuss was assassinated in Vienna. Italian troops were deployed along the Tyrolean border. On August 2, Reich chancellor Hindenburg died, and Hitler merged the two highest state offices into his own new capacity of "Führer and Reich chancellor," to whom the armed forces had to swear an oath of allegiance. With this, the Führer dictatorship was established.[64]

Bonhoeffer, since October 17, 1933, a pastor in London, had struggled in Fanø for the acknowledgment of the Confessing Church as the sole representative of the German Protestant churches with some slight success in the youths' pre-conference. He believed that it was high time for an ecumenical and binding proclamation of Christ's commandment of peace to the nations. His lecture on the church and the world of nations is lost. We only have the brief theses he sent to the research department of the Ecumenical Council in Geneva. Seen methodologically, the relationship be-

63. 1932 DBW 11, p. 333.
64. Bethge, *Biography* (above, note 8), pp. 372-73.

tween theses and lecture probably was similar to the relationship between the 1932 texts for Ciernohorské Kúpele, namely, that no detailed reasons are given in the theses.

(B) The theses[65] are titled, "The Church and the World of the Nations (On the Theological Foundation of the Work of the World Alliance)." Against the wishes of the Geneva research department, Bonhoeffer focuses exclusively on "the overcoming of war." The initial thesis states, Only in being a church, and not as an association pursuing a goal, is the World Alliance authorized to proclaim the word of Christ to the nations. In the public opinion of that time, war was understood in a threefold way, (1) as intentional human deed, for which the human will is fully responsible, (2) as a work of demonic forces in this world that are inimical to God, (3) as unveiling a world that has fallen under the law of death. Accordingly, war was publicly justified at that time in a threefold way, (1) as an intentional moral deed to preserve the state and attain peace, (2) as an irresistible course of events that, in the judgment of the realists or rather naturalists, the human being cannot control, (3) as an indication of the heroic world of sacrifice.

Bonhoeffer argues that secular pacifism's denial of such justifications does not suffice, because in this pacifism human power is reckoned to be supreme. The church's threefold reply is, (1) human will must be confronted with the commandment "Thou shalt not kill." The God of the Sermon on the Mount judges the guilty human being, and the church tells the human being that war creates destruction, not peace. The answer to those who think that a nation must protect itself with weapons is, "Did you ever venture, in faith, to leave your protection to God, in obedience to God's command?" (2) No organization will overcome demonic powers. Their banishment is God's own deed. Even if the establishment of an international peace order as an order of preservation is urgently commanded (here we adduce a clarification from the 1932 Ciernohorské Kúpele lecture), the organization of it would lapse into a misleading illusion in case it would imagine to be capable of doing more than establishing external conditions.[66] The deliverance from evil cannot be organized, but it may be

---

65. In German, DBW 13, pp. 295-97.

66. In 1932 (DBW 11, p. 339), Bonhoeffer admonished the World Alliance to do the commanded work for international peace soberly, in contrast to an idealizing "enthusiastic" [*schwärmerisch*] pacifism, and to bear in mind that this necessary world-wide peace is "no

prayed for. (3) The abolition of war is a deletion of a "dreadful symptom" in this world that has fallen into death, but not an "abolition of the cause of the evil," as pacifism all too easily imagines. Even when a war can no longer be declared and waged, the human being has still not become lord over the real cause of belligerent destruction.

Bonhoeffer's immediate concentration on the commandment "Thou shalt not kill" is astonishing. In the 1932 theses he had spoken more constructively of the state's task to change conditions that could cause war.[67] In 1934, in a situation of acute danger, he urges passionately the single-minded obedience of the Sermon on the Mount.

(C) It is reported that his August 28, 1934, morning address — later called a peace sermon — on "The Church and Peoples of the World"[68] impressed the audience even more deeply than his lecture. The address began with the promise in Psalm 85:9, "I will hear what God the Lord will speak: for he will speak peace unto his people, and to his saints." Peace is not a question open to discussion, but is strictly God's commandment given with the epiphany of Christ. The fifth commandment of the Decalogue is filled christologically. No hypocritical problematizing is allowed, as, for instance, invoking the neighbor who has to be protected with weapons. Bonds that connect us in our world are valid, but not ultimate. When we question the commandment of God before obeying it, we have already denied God. This is in fact the language of Bonhoeffer's 1937 book *Discipleship*. Brothers in Christ cannot take up arms against one another, for they know that in doing so they take up arms against Christ himself. In all secular endeavors, peace and security are confounded. There is no path to peace by way of security. For peace must be ventured. Who of us can say what it might mean for the world if a people would meet the aggressor — not with weapons in hand, but — praying, defenseless, and precisely for that reason armed with the

---

absolute ideal condition." Compare the first thesis of the so-called Heidelberg theses of 1959, "World peace becomes a vital condition of life in the technological era. . . . To call world peace a necessity is no saying of Christianity, and much less an enthusiastic saying, but is a statement of profane reason. The world peace of the technological era is not paradise on earth." These theses are printed for instance in Carl Friedrich von Weizsäcker, *Der bedrohte Friede* (threatened peace, München: 1981), the first thesis on p. 95; compare on p. 126, "World peace is not the golden age."

67. P. 346 in DBW 11, pp. 344-47.

68. Title (on p. 302) of the English version (DBW 13, pp. 302-5) of the German address on *Kirche und Völkerwelt*, DBW 13, pp. 298-301.

only true defense and weapon? Not the individual Christian, not the individual church, but only the one great ecumenical council of the holy church of Christ all over the world can with authority proclaim to the peoples of the world the commandment of peace, and take the weapons from their youth's hands. This must be done now. The trumpets of war can be blown tomorrow. Do we wish to get involved in guilt greater than ever before?

I have only paraphrased Bonhoeffer's text, because the language of analysis and interpretation is insufficient to convey what impressed then, and impresses now, the hearers of his words — though without decisive success. In 1934 in Fanø, no ecumenical declaration against war was passed that might have had an effect on the European churches. History took the seemingly compulsory course that Bonhoeffer had apprehended. The victors' promised disarmament remained undone. Taking this breach of promise as a justification, Hitler proclaimed seven months later, when the law on general military conscription went into effect on May 1, 1935, Germany's rebirth as a military power. This did not provoke any resistance on the part of the churches — and at that time they could in no way justify a German rearmament by pointing to the Soviet Union's military pressure (as they much later did in the Cold War).

Nevertheless there were in Fanø indications in the direction of a "re-creation of conditions."[69] In the youth conference, a majority supported resolutions that a civil service for conscientious objectors to military service be acknowledged by the state, and that the state's striving for sovereignty be accorded only a relative right,[70] two moments of a renewed concept of nation-state in which the state's claim to a right to war is abrogated.

I will not pursue further the effects of Bonhoeffer's peace ethic after 1934. A paper submitted by the Confessing Church to the 1937 ecumenical conference in Oxford includes a reduced version of Bonhoeffer's thoughts.[71]

69. 1932 DBW 11, pp. 341-42.

70. DBW 13, pp. 193-95.

71. The section *Krieg und Frieden* (war and peace) of the report of the ecumenical committee of the Provisional Church Administration of the German Evangelical Church, pp. 280-82 in DBW 14, *Illegale Theologenausbildung* (illegal theological education): *Finkenwalde 1935-1937* (Gütersloh: 1996). Eberhard Bethge described Bonhoeffer's path from pacifism to conspiration in pp. 119-36 of *Frieden: Das unumgängliche Wagnis. Die Gegenwartsbedeutung der Friedensethik Dietrich Bonhoeffers* (Peace — the inevitable venture. The significance of Dietrich Bonhoeffer's peace ethic for the present), edited by Hans Pfeifer (München: 1982).

He himself retired in 1937 from the office of ecumenical youth secretary. The ecumenical movement had not ventured to decide exclusively for the Confessing Church in Germany. So the influence of the *Kirchliches Aussenamt* (foreign office of the church) on the ecumenical bodies in Geneva came to prevail till 1945, and this *Aussenamt* was definitely synchronized with National Socialism.[72]

3. The Prospects for Dietrich Bonhoeffer's Summons to Ban War

Bonhoeffer's statements and actions at the Fanø conference show how little he was ready to bend to the dictatorship of so-called political and historical realities, and how eagerly he expected a similar attitude from the followers of Jesus Christ and from a church under the presence of the Holy Spirit. In Fanø and in the years to come, the Confessing Church in Germany disappointed him. Did this happen by reason of an unavoidable historical necessity?

Theologians and theologies, church leaders and churches often display little courage to oppose alleged realities with their own analysis and definition of the facts of the matter. The 1928 sociological Thomas theorem (named after William I. Thomas) states, "If men define situations as real, they are real in their consequences."[73] Those who act determine the significance of events, attribute a meaning to them, and thus make them components of social reality. This is also expressed in Robert K. Merton's theorem of self-fulfilling prophecy.[74] Of course a definition of a situation is not arbitrary, but is, in turn, also determined by many factors. For in-

72. Compare Eugen Gerstenmaier's 1981 report on his life, *Streit und Friede hat seine Zeit* (there is a time for strife and a time for peace), in which all reasons for exoneration are adduced, especially pp. 72-77 and 269-70 (and pp. 265-70 including the notes) of Gerstenmaier's 1938 book *Die Kirche und die Schöpfung* (church and creation) where he theologically justifies and limits the "totalitarian attempts at reintegrating state and people" with the central statement, "Wherever there is struggle about God's creation, about its lasting existence [*Bestand*], there the church has to bless the weapons and to join in battle."

73. W. I. Thomas and D. S. Thomas, *The Child in America: Behavior Problems and Programs* (New York: 1932), p. 572.

74. See p. 426 in D. Martindale, *The Nature and Types of Social Theory* (London: 1967), who quotes p. 179 in Merton, *Social Theory and Social Structure* (Glencoe, Illinois). According to Martindale, the self-fulfilling prophecy is "a false definition of the situation evoking a new behavior which makes the originally false conception come true."

stance, it becomes a component of social reality only when a sufficient number of people act accordingly.[75]

Bonhoeffer refused to accept the judgment, prevailing in the world in which weapons and mistrust reigned, that the present situation was a prewar situation. He demanded instead that the ecumenical council of the church oppose this mood resolutely in faith and proclaim God's peace commandment to the world. Nobody can know what would have happened if the Protestant and Roman Catholic churches, comprising large sections of the European population, had adopted Bonhoeffer's biblical definition of the situation, and had banished war. It was clear to Bonhoeffer that the Christians' and the churches' witness to peace as God's will for the world under the present conditions would tear them into suffering. He was ready for that. But obviously neither the speakers and decision makers in the churches nor the people in the church were ready. The perception of the political and social reality even in the churches was adapted to the attitudes dominant in the societies.[76]

IV. Critique of Bonhoeffer's Ecumenical Peace Ethic

1. Discontinuity and Continuity in Bonhoeffer's Conception of Ethics

(A) The change of attitude to war that happened after Bonhoeffer's Barcelona lectures needs no further comment. But there is a noteworthy continuity in the formal approach to ethics. It is from the start determined by presuppositions which Bonhoeffer shares with dialectical theology. In Barcelona, the moment in and of itself would have (supposedly) told the Christian how to decide ethically. Later, faith will hear in the moment what the gospel of the present Christ commands, and hear it concretely and thus in relation to the real living conditions. Henceforth Bonhoeffer's ethics is concerned with the concreteness and binding force of Christ's command-

---

75. Examples given by Martindale are: A financially stable bank is ruined when its customers presuppose the opposite, withdraw massive amounts of money from it, and thereby cause the bank's bankruptcy; and, where black people are supposed to be strike breakers, they are not accepted into trade-unions, which fact impels them to break strikes in order to have a job at all.

76. Compare above, chapter 6, beginning of section III, 1.

ment for those who follow him. The most elaborate core of Bonhoeffer's ethics in the years around 1932 is his ecumenical peace ethic.

(B) Bonhoeffer demanded unconditional obedience to the commandment of peace. This attitude sprang from his experience of contacts with persons from other nations. In the extant texts, however, the connection between the perception of reality and the orientation of the will is not clearly established. In his peace ethic, Bonhoeffer focuses in a somewhat one-sided manner on the obedience of the will, and treats the quest for knowledge needed in obedient responsible action as secondary. This has consequences for his criticism of Anglo-Saxon Christian and secular pacifism.

2. Anglo-Saxon Humanitarianism and the Flashes of Truth about the World's Reality

(A) Bonhoeffer criticizes the Anglo-Saxon-dominated World Alliance for conceiving the problem of war and peace only "as a problem of action, but not as a problem of essence."[77] We can, in return, ask Bonhoeffer what should follow practically in politics from the authorized proclamation of the peace commandment through the one church of Christ. Bonhoeffer does not consistently refer to the banishment of war in the Kellogg-Briand pact of 1928, nor does he appreciate the endeavors to develop an international humanitarian law to avert war, and to establish institutions for its promotion. It seems that Bonhoeffer still traditionally restricts God's commission for the political powers-that-be, according to Romans 13:1-7, to the national state, instead of extending it to international organizations. The critical and solidary relationship of church and state developed by Bonhoeffer regarding the *ius civitatis* — both related to and rendered relative through the Kingdom of God — should be transposed into the dimension of the *pax cosmopolitica*.[78]

In assessing secular peace efforts, Bonhoeffer almost always emphasizes deficiencies. To me, a theology seems possible which not only shows where the secular and humanistic peace efforts differ, but also emphasizes what is in common. Bonhoeffer's later theological reflections on the world

77. 1931 DBW 11, p. 127.
78. See Kant, above, note 32.

come of age point in this direction. In this way, a constructive relationship between theology and peace research might be established. But at the beginning of the 1930s, Bonhoeffer still shares the tendency toward delimitations that was emphasized by dialectical theology. So he could not yet gain a full view of both difference and convergence of Christian and secular peace efforts.

(B) Later, Bonhoeffer came to see analogies. In 1942, he speaks of the "most astounding experiences we have had" that in the face of barbarism and violence an "appeal to culture and humanity . . . , to freedom, tolerance, and human rights . . . was sufficient to evoke immediately awareness of some kind of alliance between the defenders of these threatened values and Christians." This was no "goal-driven alliance." Instead, "Reason, justice, culture, humanity . . . found new meaning and new strength in their origin" — which ultimately means, in Jesus Christ.[79] These are gifts, aren't they, that counteract the doom of belligerent confrontations in our world, and thus promote peace. These gifts probably were alive in Anglo-Saxon thinking in the 1930s, and probably overlaid with ideologies of humanitarianism. They might have been hardly recognizable from the viewpoint of traditional German culture *(Bildung)*.

When Bonhoeffer visited Barth in Bonn in July, 1931, their friendly controversy concerned concrete ethics. Barth reproached Bonhoeffer for making grace into a principle and thus killing everything else. What was killed? Barth spoke of "relative ethical criteria," of many "little lights" along with "the one great light," that are also necessary for our orientation in faith.[80] So Barth argued already in line with the teaching on lights *(Lichterlehre)* which he developed twenty-eight years after his conversation with Bonhoeffer in his *Church Dogmatics*.[81] Unexpected enlightenments, truths, lights that arise in the course of world history can again and again be related to and decoded by the one great light Jesus Christ. In 1959, Barth speaks of worldly parables of the Kingdom of Heaven that shame the Christian church-community, and he understands them as free manifestations of Jesus Christ in world history. This is in accord with Bonhoeffer's later thesis, "The reality of Christ embraces the reality of the world."[82]

79. DBWE 6, pp. 339-41.
80. DBW 11, p. 20.
81. Volume IV, part 3, § 69.
82. DBWE 6, p. 58.

Prior to this extension, Bonhoeffer's ethics is restricted to church ethics. This may be true also of his 1937 book *Discipleship,* "dangers" of which he recognized later, without abandoning its basic concerns.[83]

3. Limits of Bonhoeffer's Exposition of the Sermon on the Mount

Although the Sermon on the Mount was of crucial importance for Bonhoeffer's turning toward an ethic of peace, a concrete and detailed exposition of it is found only later. As a result of long years of work, the section on "The Enemy — the 'Extraordinary'" in *Discipleship*[84] deals with the peace problem. A central thesis is, "In the New Testament, the enemy is always the one who hates me. Jesus does not even consider the possibility that there could be someone whom the disciple hates. . . . Jesus speaks of enemies, that is, of those who will remain our enemies, unmoved by our love; those who do not forgive us anything when we forgive them everything; those who insult us all the more, the more we serve them."[85] In today's peace ethic, these statements must be related to what Carl Friedrich von Weizsäcker calls "intelligent love of the enemy."[86] This is to say that even the Sermon on the Mount does not only address the will, calling for obedience, but also calls for knowledge, for human insight combined with a disposition, that comes to be an orientation in faith and life.

4. The Significance of Bonhoeffer's Statements on Peace

Is it correct to speak of Bonhoeffer's ecumenical peace ethic? He did not put any of his texts under this title. But while he revised the contents of his first draft of a Christian ethic that he had presented in Barcelona, he continued in the same formal line. The 1932 university seminar on the topic of

83. Letter from prison, July 21, 1944, DBW 8, p. 542.
84. DBWE 4, pp. 137-45.
85. DBWE 4, p. 139.
86. *Der bedrohte Friede* (see above, note 66), pp. 533-38; p. 533, "Where knowledge is needed, practical love of the enemy begins with learning to understand our enemy. He will presumably still remain our enemy, will continue to fear us, and for that reason to hate us. But at least we will then begin to no longer make all those moves that continuously give him the impression that he rightly fears and hates us."

"Is there a Christian ethic?"[87] was closely connected with the 1932 lecture on the theological foundation of the work of the World Alliance, that is, with Bonhoeffer's peace ethic.[88] From the notes taken by a student in the last seminar session it can be inferred that Bonhoeffer refused to have recourse to any of six possibilities, be it orders of creation, conscience, the Christian principle of love, the situation, faith in the forgiveness of sin, or even the Sermon on the Mount, to secure the goodness of an action. "The possibility of the judgment that what we do is good rests alone in Christ."[89] Action in faith is determined by Christ to venture the peace given by Christ in the contexts of life, and especially as a "peace of nations" [*Frieden der Völker*].[90] The concept of ecumenical peace ethic does not suffice to characterize Bonhoeffer's reflections on theological ethics as a whole — we then might have to speak of a Christ ethic. It does suffice, however, to name the prominent specific feature of his concrete ethical reflection in the early 1930s. In Bonhoeffer's ethics manuscripts from the early 1940s, the terms *war* and *peace* had to recede into the background. Out of regard for his co-conspirators, such themes could not directly be treated in papers that might fall into the hands of the Secret State Police [*Gestapo*] or the Secret Service of the SS. But the matter is not outdated for him — and much less so for us in the 1980s. Surely, we must with greater intensity, in a Christian perspective, inquire into which, and how, concrete conditions must be changed so that peace can grow in all dimensions of life in the international system. In order to attain knowledge that might properly steer our activity — a knowledge that always remains a venture — we need to open up to the peace that surpasses all reason (Philippians 4:7).

87. DBW 11, pp. 303-13.
88. Compare DBW 11, in note 1 on p. 304.
89. DBW 11, pp. 311-12.
90. 1932 DBW 17 (see above, note 31), p. 118.

8 Dietrich Bonhoeffer's Theological Ethics and Human Rights

1989

1. National Socialism and fascism in Europe, Japanese imperialism in East Asia, and Soviet Stalinism in the 1930s and 1940s deeply shook the sense of justice in the world community. The proclamation of the Universal Declaration of Human Rights by the United Nations on December 10, 1948, and the commitment to human and basic rights included in the German and Japanese constitutions, were reactions to this crisis. Doubtless, a Western understanding of human rights, predominantly influenced by the United States, was dominant. Previous to the epoch of fascism and imperialism with its persecutions of churches, the major Christian churches had criticized or even rejected the human rights movement, because they had not forgotten that human rights had been interpreted in the French Revolution as inimical to the churches. Now they supported the proclamation of human rights and their juridical codification in the postwar constitutions. It may seem that, both in the Federal Republic of Germany and in Japan, the inclusion of basic rights in their constitutions did not result from their own traditions, but from outside influences. In Germany, they did have remarkable precursors in the constitution drafted by the citizens' revolutionary Paul's Church meeting in Frankfurt on Main in 1848, and in the Weimar Republic's Reich constitution of 1919. But the end of the Weimar Republic had shown that the constitution, providing for basic rights, was not deeply rooted in society, and its suspension was combatted with only weak determination. This holds true also for Protestant churches and groups. Only minorities among them, like liberals, Christian Socialists,

and, in part, Karl Barth's followers, appreciated the value of constitutional liberty rights.

Until now, the influence of Protestant personalities and Protestant convictions on the basic law [*Grundgesetz*] of the Federal Republic of Germany of May 23, 1949, has hardly been investigated. Surely, the most important student of the theologian and politician Friedrich Naumann, namely, Theodor Heuss, as the leading politician of the liberals — the Free Democratic Party — and as a member of the Parliamentary Council, had a significant part in the development of the basic law. Also, members of the Confessing Church who went into politics after 1945, as, for example, Hermann Ehlers, influenced the construction of the Federal Republic of Germany momentously. But they could not rely on established Protestant convictions regarding human and basic rights. This is clearly shown in the Protestant ethics that were published in Germany during the first decade after the end of the war. These ethics, including Helmut Thielicke's voluminous work, do not at all discuss the constitution and its section on basic rights. Also otherwise, it seems that plans and considerations developed by resistance groups against the National Socialist regime within Germany — aside from economic politics, which was decisively influenced by the Freiburg group around Walter Eucken — had little direct impact on the constitution and construction of the Federal Republic of Germany. Until today, the (Western German) Federal Republic has not really succeeded in appropriating the struggle of this minority as a tradition that would mark German self-understanding or "identity" in the second half of the twentieth century.

It may, then, be surprising that in Dietrich Bonhoeffer's *Ethics,* in the partially fragmentary manuscripts from the years 1940 to 1943 that Bethge first published in 1949, a long chapter on natural rights is found. Until now, it has not been noticed even in research on the contemporary history of church and theology, and has hardly been noticed in Bonhoeffer research. This chapter, in its handwritten original, bears the title, "The natural life." After introductory reflections on the concept of natural life, the rights of bodily life are treated, and then a section on the rights of the life of the spirit is begun.[1] Six detailed working notes on slips of paper [*Zettelnotizen*], written by Bonhoeffer while he composed this manuscript, contain three arrangements of topics that pretty well agree with one an-

---

1. "Natural Life," pp. 171-218 in DBWE 6, *Ethics.*

other. These show that, in the extant manuscript, not even the treatment of the first of seven topics came to an end. Bonhoeffer had to interrupt this work in the Ettal cloister, where he had stayed since November 17, 1940, when he, on February 23, 1941, started on his first trip to Switzerland as an agent of William Canaris' Military Intelligence, or rather as a representative of the group of conspirators in this office [*Amt Ausland/Abwehr*]. After his return to Germany on March, 24, 1941, he did not resume work on this manuscript. Presumably, conversations with Karl Barth and other Swiss friends made him see that the question of the Christian's responsibility in history was a problem of utmost urgency. He discussed this theme in the two versions of the manuscript "History and Good," which contains the fundamentals of Bonhoeffer's ethic of responsibility.[2]

Even though it is true that only the smaller part of Bonhoeffer's planned chapter on "Natural Life" is worked out as a manuscript, it can without exaggeration be stated that, in it, quite a special outline of an ethic of human rights is presented, informed with Christian tradition and German experiences, that is to be read as a conscious completion and alternative to an Anglo-Saxon and Western European understanding. As far as I know, this is the only ethical elaboration on this theme by a theologian in German-speaking Protestantism before the end of the Second World War, the only systematic Protestant attempt to conceive of human rights.

2. I do not offer here a detailed interpretation of the extant manuscript and working notes. Instead, I want to show, by delineating characteristics of Bonhoeffer's exposition, that this chapter on "Natural Life" in Bonhoeffer's *Ethics* deserves fresh interest and can yield far-reaching insights.

In the manuscript written during the winter of 1940 to 1941, Bonhoeffer begins by stating that the concept of that which is natural has either been lost or is badly misused in Protestant ethics. The concept gets lost when knowledge of the sinfulness and fallenness of the human being and of reality passes an overly generalizing verdict on all that is natural which hides from view the relative differences within the penultimate. The concept is misused when what is natural is transfigured religiously and awarded the glory of primal creatureliness untouched by humankind's fall. In both instances, theology fails to put that which is natural in its proper place, namely, in the penultimate. The penultimate's particularity and ori-

2. DBWE 6, 219-45 (first version), and 246-98 (second version).

entation toward the ultimate must be maintained precisely for the sake of the ultimate, or eschatological realm, and must neither be skipped nor exalted to the realm of transcendence. Bonhoeffer had developed these theological determinations in the preceding chapter on "Ultimate and Penultimate Things."[3] What is natural is in no way identical with what is creaturely, because it belongs to the reality after humankind's fall. But, as the underlying Latin word group *nasci, natura* already indicates, it is gifted with a moment of independence and self-development. It is that form of the fallen world's life which is preserved by God, and is open and oriented to justification, redemption, and renewal through Christ. Its opposite is the unnatural, namely, that which destroys the form of life. The natural is recognized by reason that does not presume to be superior to the natural, and does not aim for the absolute, but understands itself to be a part of the life that is preserved after the fall, a part that is enabled to "perceive" that which is given, or rather to recognize in what is given that which is universal, or determined by a general law or regularity, as distinct from that which is individual.

What corresponds to the recognition of the natural by reason is the affirmation by preserved life of the "basic will" inherent in it that is directed toward preservation. Unnaturalness is the will or drive to destruction or self-destruction, which is certainly at work in the fallen world and must be countered. Destructive unnaturalness in no way exhibits or even declares an intention to destroy. Instead, it often appears as the unintended outcome of organization and mechanization, of human errors and delusions, and of human striving for self-justification. Its peculiarity is that it intends to make life available, although something is given with life that needs to be acknowledged and affirmed as unavailable. It thus oversteps the limits of availability, instead of affirming them in self-limitation.

The overstepping of boundaries is inherent in vitalism, which absolutizes earthly life by taking it to be an unquestionable ultimate reality. In vitalistic affirmation of life always a part is set as the measure, and erected destructively against other life. In vitalism, life makes itself an absolute end in itself. Thus vitalism ends in nihilism, in the loss of measures that are wholesome for life, in the disintegration of what is natural, and becomes an abyss, a nothingness. At the other extreme, in the mechanization of life, life is reduced to its usefulness in the plan for an overall organi-

---

3. DBWE 6, 146-70.

zation, made into merely a means to an end, so that it is no longer respected as also an end in itself. This, again, means an unnatural destruction of the undisposability of life.

Between the extremes of vitalism and mechanization, natural life is simultaneously an end in itself and a means to an end. It is a means to an end in its service to other life, and also as it is destined to participate in the Kingdom of God. It is an end in itself as a gift of the Creator, whose will is to preserve life beyond the fall until the coming of Christ. In the framework of natural life, life's being an end in itself is expressed in rights, while life's being a means to an end is expressed in duties given with natural life.

Since the eighteenth century, human rights have been treated as "inborn" rights. Bonhoeffer, on the basis of his suppositions, is ready to accept this view. He relates these rights to two dimensions of human life, namely, the body and the spirit. He had to interrupt his work on the manuscript about natural life before he could exposit the latter dimension. But he thoroughly treated the "right to bodily life." "This is not a right that we have stolen or earned for ourselves, but is in the truest sense a right that is 'born with us,' that was there before our will, that rests in what actually exists. Since by God's will human life on earth exists only as bodily life, the body has a right to be preserved for the sake of the whole person. Since all rights are extinguished at death, the preservation of bodily life is the very foundation of all natural rights."[4]

3. Before we follow Bonhoeffer's manuscript further, we must consider briefly its relationship to the Western conception of human rights. Traditionally — in its liberal version — the Western starting point is the individual who is taken to be, by birth, the bearer of all rights. According to the theory of the social contract, the individual surrenders certain negotiable rights to the commonwealth to which the individual is affiliated, in order to retain for lifetime a basic set of inalienable rights, and among them human rights. Bonhoeffer's exposition differs from the Western conception in that he takes "natural life" to be the primary bearer of rights. Surely, it is peculiar to natural life that it comes to be the life of an individual, and that the individual cannot and must not be absorbed into the life of the community, that is, into the collective. The individual's right to life is not only grounded in reason, but is also valid in a theological perspective. "It follows from the will of God, who creates individuals to give them eternal life, that

4. DBWE 6, 185.

there is a natural right of the individual."[5] But this individual is not unquestionable, but, as a bearer of natural life, also a harborer of rights. The individual, then, can be opposed by the natural life's right. This is most clearly evident in the case of growing life in the body of the mother. Further, the human being in general — as distinct from the animal — possesses life in relative freedom, including the possibility of suicide. But the bodily life's right opposes every potential "self-murderer," and wards off suicide, while in an individualistic-atheistic ethic the decision for suicide can well stand good before one's own moral judgment. Ultimately, "The right to self-murder breaks down only before the living God."[6] But also the natural recognition that my life has its own value over against me is an argument against suicide, unless killing myself is demanded as a self-sacrifice. As we become aware of the ecological crisis, we are strongly motivated to take natural life seriously in its self-regulation and its own weight, and to accord to it a dignity and worth that transcends its usefulness for the human being.

When the natural life's rights are, as with Bonhoeffer, the starting point, then it is impossible to interpret, for example, the liberty rights in isolation and individually, and thus egocentrically. Such an interpretation has been a constant danger under liberal-capitalistic conditions. Whoever understands himself to be a bearer of the gift of natural life knows himself to be fundamentally connected with others to whom the same gift has been imparted, and feels obliged to respect and serve the right of other bearers of natural life.

4. According to Bonhoeffer, the rights of bodily life are grounded in this life's being an end in itself. "The body is always 'my' body," the body of an individual, and every encroachment on my body is an interference in my personal existence. In opposition to tendencies toward hostility to the body in some Christian traditions, Bonhoeffer sees the "right to bodily joys" and the right to pleasure and happiness grounded in the body's being an end in itself, just as the affirmation of that which is natural is inherent in the "basic will" of preserved life. It is a second thing — which does not invalidate this first thing, namely, the right to happiness — to renounce voluntarily, or feel compelled to renounce, in faith, this or that kind of bodily happiness for the sake of a higher happiness.[7] In each of Bonhoef-

5. DBWE 6, 183.
6. DBWE 6, 202.
7. DBWE 6, 188, 186, 176, and 214.

fer's three arrangements, on working notes slips, of topics to be treated in the planned part on the natural rights of the life of the spirit, "happiness" appears as the title of a separate section.[8]

When pursuing the specific themes chosen by Bonhoeffer for his ethical explication of the right to bodily life, one recognizes quickly how intensively he includes in his systematic discourse the consideration of unjust National Socialist activity. The themes discussed in this manuscript are (compulsory) euthanasia and eugenics, suicide and the sacrifice of life, marriage, reproduction, abortion, birth control, sterilization, rape, exploitation, and torture.[9] In many of these fields, the racist-eugenic worldview of the National Socialist regime had introduced laws, orders, and extrajudicial special actions, which Bonhoeffer countered by insisting on the rights of bodily life. Direct polemics were impossible for him as one who knew of concrete plans for a coup d'état, since his manuscripts could not be secured against seizure by the secret state police [*Gestapo*]. Not on any account should he make himself and his co-conspirators suspect. Nevertheless, the manuscripts, protected by handwriting that is very difficult to read, and by a deftly encoded terminology, speak a clear language for those who could see the practices of the National Socialist regime from an oppositional perspective.

The same holds true for the planned part on "The Natural Rights of the Life of the Spirit." The human spirit shows up in the capability of human beings to encounter the reality, to which they themselves belong, in relative freedom. Precisely this is a proof of their being human. Bonhoeffer distinguishes between three fundamental ways of behavior in the spirit's life vis-à-vis reality, namely, judging, acting, and enjoying. These are three ways of coping with reality, that is, of relating oneself properly to reality.[10] On the working note slips, topics are noted that impair the freedom and the rights of the life of the spirit, as for example, "uniformity," "the stoppage of sources of knowledge," "the 'spiritual' killing of those who are inferior," and "spiritual rape." In the Third Reich, uniformity was enforced through ideological propaganda and schooling. Sources of knowledge were stopped by not permitting newspapers and books from other countries in Germany. Authors and artists were killed spiritually by declaring

8. Compare DBWE 6, 217 and note 159.
9. DBWE 6, 189-217.
10. DBWE 6, 217-18.

their works to be "degenerate" and outlawing them. Spiritual rape was practiced by threatening and punishing any utterance of divergent views. Further, the remark is found in the notes, "the breaking of character." What Bonhoeffer understood by this is illustrated in the section of the chapter entitled "Ethics as Formation" about the failure of those who, faced by the brutal reality of the Third Reich, looked for orientation in traditional morality.[11]

Bonhoeffer had the violations of human rights in view that were continually practiced by the National Socialist regime. He pondered on the rights of the natural bodily and spiritual life that had to be clearly and bindingly established in opposition to these violations. The violations of rights with which Bonhoeffer was confronted have in no way vanished from today's world. Torture, exploitation, ideological compulsion, restrictions on freedom, and many other infringements are universal phenomena, or rather plagues, that are combatted also today, always with a merely partial success. Precisely because Bonhoeffer's considerations developed in the face of the concrete unjust praxis of a regime of violence, they are significant far beyond those times of the Third Reich. Simultaneously, they do not encourage imposing the requirements of human rights like an abstract system of norms on foreign cultures and societies, but investigating how, under their own cultural and political conditions, the natural rights of human beings can properly be understood and protected.

5. Bonhoeffer treated life's natural rights in the context of ethical discourse without being able or obliged, in his situation, to search for how a juridical codification of human rights in international treaties, or of basic rights in the constitutions of nations could be accomplished. The juridical treatment of these matters raises further questions — for example, how a right should be formulated so as to enable citizens to bring their claim actually into court, in order that the right they seek be realized. Ethical discourse on human rights can in no way replace juridical formulation and realization, but can provide support and points of orientation.

In the framework of a Christian ethic, as elaborated by Bonhoeffer, the relationship of theological cognition and cognition by natural reason is of major significance. To some statements on the penultimate, which is what reason is able to grasp, Bonhoeffer immediately adds theological arguments. This is not surprising in a first draft of an exposition, but it does

---

11. DBWE 6, 76-82, and 84-87.

not correspond with Bonhoeffer's methodological intention. Precisely by distinguishing between the penultimate and the ultimate, by expounding natural life as life after the fall and thus under the conditions of the penultimate, and by advocating this natural life's own rights and message, he creates a platform for discourse among all who oppose insights of relative reason and affirmation of life to that which is destructive in reality. This platform of discourse may not be skipped prematurely in deducing certain kinds of determinations from theological statements and forcing them on argumentation based on reason. But when reasoning comes to an end and has to state final alternatives or even antinomies, then the placement of the problem in theological perspectives assumes its legitimate function, which accords with keeping the penultimate open and oriented to the ultimate. As "the concept of the natural must be recovered from the gospel itself,"[12] and since Bonhoeffer endeavored to do so, he opened up the possibility of lucidly and legitimately relating natural reasoning and theological statements to one another, and ascribing to the phenomena of natural reality the "reasonable," as well as the encompassing "theological" significance due to them. Herein also, Bonhoeffer's exposition of human rights as rights of natural life is an advance into new ground, and a suggestion that we can hardly do without. It was certainly not to our country's advantage that this exposition remained widely unnoticed while the Federal Republic of Germany was built up, and especially when its constitution was written, as the Protestant actors did not know that a Protestant theological view on pressing problems was possible, and had in some respects been provided.

12. DBWE 6, 173.

9 Dietrich Bonhoeffer's Practice of Conscience and Ethical Theory of Conscience

1988

Conscientia, translated by Luther as *Gewissen,* is a word that is widely known, but its meaning is difficult to comprehend. The concept was formed in the languages spoken in the ancient Mediterranean area. The Latin term — *conscientia,* a loan translation from the Greek — is a legacy inherited by the areas of European and American culture and ecumenical Christianity. In these areas, everyone understands what speaking of a bad conscience means. An intellectual and an emotional component are involved. Persons who are worried by a bad conscience are aware of something they either have done or neglected to do, and in connection with it consciously judge themselves negatively. This intellectual judgment contains a displeasure that impairs their emotional well-being. Pangs of conscience are painful. One reacts to a bad conscience. One appeases or suppresses it, or one tries to compensate, for example, by asking for forgiveness of one's wrong-doings, and when the one who has been wronged does forgive, one feels pacified. We should speak of conscience not as if it were an organ of the human soul, but as being a process of some length in time, a process with characteristic structures.

Scholarly literature shows that we are moving in a labyrinth as we try to determine the essence, function, origin, evolution, and constitutive conditions of conscience. We see ourselves confronted by a conceptual and factual pluralism. There is no evident universal understanding of conscience. Our problems of conscience challenge our own responsibility to develop a right understanding of conscience. For this endeavor, experiences with conscience in other times and by other human beings, and their interpretation, are an indispensable help. In this sense we will inquire into the understanding of conscience that Dietrich Bonhoeffer struggled for, both in the conflicts he lived through in resistance and conspiracy, and in his theological work.

Four dimensions of the understanding of conscience that are especially hotly debated must be considered.

First, the modern civil and human rights movement. It has procured for conscience an extraordinary public significance, for example, by introducing liberty of conscience into constitutions and international conventions. There is a subjective public basic right to liberty of conscience.[1]

Second, culture influenced by humanism. It proclaims the autonomous personality's human dignity. This personality is concerned about its own integrity and unity and its inwardly felt violation of self-esteem, and therefore listens to the voice of conscience.

Third, psychology, psychoanalysis, and other sciences concerning the human being. Here, models of the formation of conscience in the socialization of the individual are developed. Fundamental anthropological statements are made, for example, by determining the relationship between superego and conscience. The importance of other people, such as the father, for the development of conscience is examined.

Fourth, Christian preaching and teaching. Especially in the Reformation tradition, the relationship between faith and conscience is a fundamental problem. In Lutheranism, some even try to identify faith and conscience.

Dietrich Bonhoeffer refused to accord this overly central position to conscience, rooted in Lutheran tradition, and assigned it a different place. In trying to comprehend and critically assess his conception, we can take advantage of an unusual possibility. The extant source material allows not only a reconstruction of his theory, but also insights into his practice of conscience, to be inferred from diaries and letters. In his research on practice and theory of conscience in Dietrich Bonhoeffer's life and theology, Peter Möser found that his practice was hardly expressed in his theory.[2] In

1. Compare article 4 I and III in the basic law [*Grundgesetz*] of the Federal Republic of Germany.

2. Möser, *Gewissenspraxis und Gewissenstheorie bei Dietrich Bonhoeffer,* theological dissertation (typescript, Heidelberg, 1983).

the following, I will argue with Möser's result, though restricted to the time from the summer of 1939 to April of 1943.

I. The Inner Call to Return from Emigration

A. In the spring of 1939, the German occupation of the remainder of Czechoslovakia[3] and aggressive agitation against Poland increased the probability of an outbreak of war. Bonhoeffer, who conscientiously objected to military service and to swearing the military oath to Hitler, seemed no longer to have a place in Germany. In his radical attitude, he stood largely alone. American friends feared his impending end in a concentration camp. The fellow fighters in the Confessing Church led by the Councils of Brethren urged him to travel to the United States of America. Objection to military service earned the death penalty. A "Bonhoeffer case" would have substantiated the widespread National Socialist accusations against the Confessing Church of being unpatriotic, un-German, even traitorous to the fatherland. With all of this in view, Bonhoeffer went on June 7, 1939, with ambiguous feelings, aboard the ship that brought him to New York.

B. Bonhoeffer's diary bespeaks the impact of the doubts which now assaulted him. His thoughts often proceed from the Moravian daily biblical texts [*Losungen*].[4] On June 9, he encourages himself with the consideration that Christ is with those who belong to him — everywhere. But instantly the question arises within him, "Or have I nevertheless evaded the place where He is? where He is *for me*? No, God says [in the watchword from Isaiah 41:9], 'You are my servant.'"[5] He vehemently struggles against the self-reproach of having evaded the place where he was meant to be, but the reproach is there, and torments him.

---

3. The regions with German population (Sudeten) were claimed as German territory in October, 1938. At the Munich conference of September 29, 1938, the rest of Czechoslovakia had been promised a guarantee against an unprovoked attack. In spite of that, German troops occupied Czechoslovakia on March 15, 1939.

4. Daily watchword, drawn by lot from the Old Testament for each year anew, since 1728, in Herrnhut, Upper Lusatia, Germany, with an interpretive verse selected from the New Testament.

5. DBW 15, *Illegale Theologenausbildung: Sammelvikariate 1937-1940* (Gütersloh: 1998), 218.

In New York, he begins at once to revoke the decision to emigrate. He does not want to be bound for a longer time. Tormenting homesickness for the brothers in the Confessing Church, and for Germany, comes over him, to his own astonishment, being an experienced world traveler. Surely, from this travel to the United States there might be no returning. On June 15, he notes, "The whole impact of self-reproaches because of an erroneous decision comes up again, and almost overwhelms one. I was very desperate."[6]

Such pangs of Bonhoeffer's conscience are strange indeed. Judging by human standards, his situation in Germany was hopeless, if he would not and could not give up basic convictions. Since centuries, the *ius emigrationis* — the most longstanding human right — applies to such cases. But a conscience does not take its orientation only from that which is right in general; it speaks quite personally, elementarily, related to each one's own life. Bonhoeffer notes on June 20, "How strange — in all my decisions I am never quite clear about the motives. Is that a sign of vagueness, of inner dishonesty, or is it a sign that we are guided beyond our recognition, or is it both?" For Bonhoeffer, life decisions are not the direct result of rational ethical argument, but happen also under the influence of an uncontrollable awareness of being guided. On the same day, the diary entry follows, "Today's watchword speaks dreadfully hard of God's incorruptible judgment. He certainly sees how much personal sentiment, how much anxiety, is included in today's decision, however courageous it may seem. The reasons for an action that one offers to others and to one's own self are surely inadequate. One can give reasons for everything. In the end, we act from a level which remains hidden from us."[7]

Is conscience a voice that arises from this deeper level that is hidden from the human being's rational reasoning? Bonhoeffer's entry was written after his decision was made, after he had refused the offer of a profession in the United States of America on that fateful June 20, 1939. The central argument given for the dangerous return to Germany is, "We can no longer get away from it. Not as if we were necessary, as if we were needed (by God!?). But simply because our life is there, and because we leave behind and destroy our life if we are not with it again. It is not anything pi-

---

6. DBW 15, 223.

7. DBW 15, 228. Compare the theme of *actus directus,* the act in faith "that can never be captured in reflection" in Bonhoeffer's 1931 book *Akt und Sein;* cf. DBWE 2 *Act and Being* (Minneapolis: Fortress Press, 1996), 160.

ous, but something almost vital. But God does not act only through pious impulses, but also through such vital ones."[8]

This is strange as well. When examining himself, Bonhoeffer does not resort to the noble reason that the Confessing Church in Germany would need him — which would truly not have been exaggerated — but he says, unsparingly and disarmingly, I must go back because my life is there. At his departure from Germany, it was by no means clear that he could not inwardly break away from this life together with his brothers in the spirit, with his church, and with his family — not even when this life was acutely threatened with death. Now, this was clear to him.

Was this a decision of conscience? Is conscience an inner voice that warningly reminds the human being of what life consists in?

C. In his self-examination, Bonhoeffer did not refer to a commission he had in Germany. But to his disappointed and dumbfounded American friends, who had taken much trouble for his sake, he had to give reasons for his sudden decision to return. His central argument is found in a letter written in the beginning of July to Reinhold Niebuhr: "I have come to the conclusion that I have made a mistake in coming to America. I must live through this difficult period of our national history with the Christian people of Germany. I will have no right to participate in the reconstruction of Christian life in Germany after the war if I do not share the trials of this time with my people."[9] Obviously, this statement is not at all identical with the considerations in the diary. The diary has no mention of a necessary inner authority in a time after Hitler. May one give to fellow people, even friends, other reasons than those that are decisive in one's own eyes? I think one even has to do so, in order to remain understandable, if only the reasons accord with truth, even though they differ from the personal reasons. Talking with oneself is different from talk among friends in that it is immediately related to conscience. Soliloquy in Bonhoeffer's American diary frequently ends with words similar to prayer. On the crucial day of June 20, they are, "At the end of the day, I can only ask that God might judge this day and all decisions mercifully. It is now in his hand."[10]

D. On July 7, already on the return voyage, the diary entry says, "I am

8. June 26, 1939, DBW 15, 234.
9. DBW 15, 201 (in English).
10. DBW 15, 229.

glad that I was there, and glad that I am on my way home again."[11] Bonhoeffer will later speak of a freed conscience. The doubting and self-
tormenting tone of the diary entries prior to the decision is absent from
the last entries that follow the decision — although he is now heading for
danger. Now, he is at one with himself.

May we regard this diary, supplemented by letters, as the unintended
documentation of a process of conscience, even though the word *decision*
occurs frequently, while the word *conscience* occurs almost not at all? I
think so. It is a document which implicitly shows how someone deals with
what we call an appeal [*Anruf*] of conscience, with a call from the bottom
of that which Bonhoeffer calls his "life." We must examine now whether
some of this recurs in *Ethics* texts on conscience.

II. On the Instability of the Isolated Conscience

One year after the painful decision process in New York, Bonhoeffer, now
already deeply involved in the coup d'état plans of the resistance group in
William Canaris' Military Intelligence Office [*Amt Ausland/Abwehr*],
wrote the first paragraphs of the manuscript "Ethics as Formation."[12]
How urgent the problems treated here were for him can be seen in the famous essay "After Ten Years."[13] For this account rendered two years later,
in December, 1942, he rewrote these paragraphs. Deeply concerned,
pained, and angered, Bonhoeffer had witnessed that many honorable
men, of whom more steadfastness had been expected, had "toppled" in
the end, that is, they either had cautiously adjusted to the Hitler regime,
or entered into active complicity with it. Later generations have asked and
are asking, Were these men, who had seen so many Nazi crimes — for example, the pogroms against the Jews in November of 1938, the attack on
Poland in September of 1939, camouflaged with lies, and the acts of annihilation there — and nevertheless cooperated with this regime, were they
without conscience? It is to Bonhoeffer's credit that he did not speak in
tones of contempt about people who deeply disappointed him, but really

11. DBW 15, 240.

12. DBWE 6, *Ethics* (Minneapolis: Fortress Press, 2005), 76-102.

13. *Nach zehn Jahren. Rechenschaft an der Wende zum Jahre 1943*, pp. 19-39 in DBW 8
(letters and papers from Tegel prison; Gütersloh: 1998); LPP 1-20; compare above, chapter 5,
note 6.

sought to comprehend what happened in and with these men. He analyzed their fate with an intensity found in hardly any other contemporary text. Bonhoeffer speaks not at all of convinced National Socialists, nor of characterless opportunists, but of representatives of a "noble humanity," of a remarkable ethos. He characterizes the attitudes and failures of three times two correlated groups of persons as representative types. Among the six is "the man of *conscience*," the inwardly counseled person, whose polar opposite is the person on the *"way of duty"* who follows outward commands. "Men of *conscience*" are "counseled and supported by nothing but their own conscience." Can they stand fast in exigencies that demand decision, in the conflicts tearing at them, as the person is totally claimed by the Hitler regime? According to Bonhoeffer, what happens is, "The countless respectable and seductive disguises and masks in which evil approaches them make their conscience anxious and unsure, until they finally content themselves with a salved conscience instead of a good conscience, that is, until they deceive their own conscience in order not to despair. Those whose sole support is their conscience can never grasp that a bad conscience can be stronger and more wholesome than a deceived conscience."[14]

How does this failure come to pass? The first factor is the successful disguise of the regime. Clad "in the garment of relative historical and social justice,"[15] the regime gave the unsettling deceptive impression of working, despite its evil deeds, ultimately for a cause that, at its core, was good and beneficial for the German people. Today, in hindsight, it seems inconceivable to us who think we know with certainty what in those times was not known, that persons of high culture and integrity could be so deceived. But even the most brilliant minds in German intelligentsia, men such as Carl Schmitt, Martin Heidegger, Emanuel Hirsch, and some famous theologians and church leaders, were deluded, especially as long as the regime made use of them and let them hold prominent positions.

These famous men and the man of conscience have the weakness of being deceived in common. The person of conscience is troubled by exigencies that demand decision. Exigency [*Zwangslage*] means that any of my options for how to act will offend my conscience. I choose the less evil

14. 1940 DBWE 6, 78-80.
15. Paper of September 1941, in DBW 16, *Konspiration und Haft 1940-1945* (Gütersloh: 1996), 538.

option and forget, because I avoid what is more evil, that it is evil as well. This was the great temptation for those who stayed in responsible positions during the Hitler regime, increasingly collaborated with it contrary to their convictions, and subjectively quieted their consciences with their still good intentions. But objectively they became accomplices to unprecedented crimes, to which they shut their eyes. Bonhoeffer's judgment is — if only these collaborators had remained honest and aware of a bad conscience on account of their behavior, instead of deceiving themselves by lies! But precisely this cannot be done by those whose only support is a good conscience. They want to and have to remain honorable and uphold their self-respect at all costs. Thus they must play down the evil reality to harmlessness. A bad conscience might have exerted a wholesome compulsion to switch from collaboration to dangerous opposition.

In the text "After Ten Years," Bonhoeffer states that only those will stand fast "for whom the final measure is not their reason, principle, conscience, freedom, or virtue, but who are ready to sacrifice all of this when they are called in faith, and being bound to God alone, to obedient and responsible action."[16] May I really sacrifice my good conscience to an exigency? In asking such a question, I refer to an egocentric, autistic conscience. This is done by those who quite uncommunicatively, quite self-relatedly, seek support from their conscience alone. A conscience that is not egocentric, but in accord with reality, must always be related to others. Bonhoeffer reproaches both the ethical theorist and this person's conscience with remaining abstract, that is, severed from concrete reality.[17] How can a conscience be one's most personal inner voice, and yet simultaneously communicate with and relate to others and to events that appeal to one's responsibility? Here, we should remember Bonhoeffer in New York in June, 1939. His conscience warns against separation from that in which his life consists, from the community with the brothers in the Confessing Church, and from the fate of Germany and Christian civilization. However, could human conscience perhaps be incurably egocentric, since it speaks in the sinful human being in a fallen world?

16. DBW 8, 23; LPP 5.
17. DBWE 6, 77.

III. On the Damage to Conscience
in the Situation of Disintegration

In the *Ethics* manuscript "God's Love and the Disintegration of the World,"[18] Bonhoeffer does not speak directly of the situation in the Third Reich, but at first, referring to the biblical relation of humankind's fall into sin (Genesis 3), of the basic human situation. Before the fall, Adam lived in the immediate knowledge of God as his origin. In Adam's contact with reality, human knowledge of good and evil was not required. Mysteriously, Adam in his freedom wanted to master reality himself. For doing so, specific knowledge was needed, namely, the ability to distinguish between good and evil. The grasping of this knowledge deeply changed the human being's place in reality. Bonhoeffer writes, "To know good and evil means to understand oneself as the origin of good and evil, as the origin of an eternal choice and election."[19] To the human being who knows in an egocentric way, reality appears no more in its original form, as creation. It now is seen only as a construct of the human being who arbitrarily chooses between good and evil. The human being, as the designer and estimator of everything, can now perceive reality only anthropocentrically. But this is always a construction in a one-sided perspective. Today, we become aware of this one-sidedness, for example, as we recognize that an anthropocentric dealing with nature results in a destruction of nature. Humans have lost their original place in reality so thoroughly that they can no longer even imagine it. They know themselves only as divided, as estranged from the origin, from reality, and from themselves. Humanly constructed reality is contradictory, and human beings are completely entangled in these contradictions. The result is destructiveness. According to Genesis 4, the next step is Cain's fratricide of Abel. Moving beyond homicide, human dealing brings death to fauna, flora, and the environment. What does this mean for conscience? Is it forced into the destructiveness of divided reality, without an alternative?

According to Bonhoeffer, shame is deeper and more comprehensive than conscience. Shame at least still reminds us of the whole human life that is now divided from the origin, from God, from the other person,

18. DBWE 6, 299-338.
19. DBWE 6, 302; compare DBWE 3, *Creation and Fall: A Theological Exposition of Genesis 1-3* (Minneapolis: Fortress Press, 1997).

from reality, and from itself. Shame calls for veiling, covering up, or even masking, since humans cannot "endure themselves" as divided beings. They refuse "to become consciously aware of everything that is germinating within themselves," or they repress what they truly are, and appear on the stage as somebody else who is not guilty of all of this. But precisely shame, impelling human beings to hide themselves, is an indication of the original reality in which shame was not needed.

Conscience, less comprehensive than shame, is primarily only concerned "with the relationship to one's own self." But it is bolder. It claims to be the source of religion. "It portrays the relationship human beings have with God and with others as emerging from the relationship they have with themselves. Conscience claims to be the voice of God and the norm for relating to other human beings." It pretends that humans have come to be like God, knowing about good and evil, and thus about the origin of everything. "They do not deny their own evil. But in the voice of their conscience those who have become evil call themselves back to their authentic self, their better self, to the good."[20] Conscience bears witness to the truth that humans are destined for that which is good. But at the same time it pretends that humans can overcome the division and attain the unity of the origin on their own. This striving is transfigured into a religious and ethical endeavor, and yet it is *hubris.* Human beings cannot free themselves of being *incurvatus in seipso,* inevitably turned in upon themselves,[21] and thereby entangled in unforeseeable conflicts with their surroundings. Based on a biblical-theological analysis of conscience, Bonhoeffer can penetrate the blatant failure of the "man of conscience" in the Third Reich. Persons of conscience who encounter such a reality cannot but conceive of it as a conflict that would tear them up unless they could deceive their conscience with lies. The reality to which they have access is devoid of potential to cope with the exigencies under the Nazi regime.

The biblical-theological critique of conscience in the manuscript "God's Love and the Disintegration of the World" seems to be devastating. There is no longer room for the Protestant — and also the Catholic — "myth of conscience." But does this mean that conscience as an anthropological datum is eliminated from Bonhoeffer's thought?

20. DBWE 6, 304-5, 307-8.
21. Compare *cor curvum in se* (heart turned in upon itself), DBWE 2, 46 and elsewhere.

IV. On the Role of Conscience in Responsible Life

In the account "After Ten Years," Bonhoeffer notes that Germans, although selflessly ready for subordination, traditionally lack a decisive basic knowledge, namely, "that of the necessity of free responsible action even contrary to vocation and commission."[22] In view of this deficit, which under Hitler is fatal, Bonhoeffer explicates in a 1942 *Ethics* manuscript "The Structure of Responsible Life."[23] Since manuscripts could — and did — fall into the hands of the Gestapo, Bonhoeffer had to speak in code about the situation in which he is thinking and acting. But he surely or even predominantly speaks about the free responsible deed that is planned for overthrowing the Hitler regime. When preparing Bonhoeffer's *Ethics* manuscripts for the first printing, in 1949, Bethge chose "conscience" *(Das Gewissen)* as a subtitle for a section of "The Structure of Responsible Life." According to Bonhoeffer's own disposition, the topic of this section is *Selbstzurechnung*, "*my accountability* for my living and acting."[24] Comparable sections in the manuscript "God's Love and the Disintegration of the World" deal with discerning and doing the will of God.[25]

Responsible action is not possible without readiness for bearing unavoidable guilt. Especially in regard to the overthrow — but not exclusively related to this extreme situation — Bonhoeffer says that "Those who, in acting responsibly, seek to avoid becoming guilty . . . place their personal innocence above their responsibility for other human beings and are blind to the fact that precisely in so doing they become even more egregiously guilty. They are also blind to the fact that genuine guiltlessness is demonstrated precisely by entering into community with the guilt of other human beings for their sake." The view that one takes guilt on oneself in acting as required by one's own responsibility is, naturally enough, ethically contested. Can killing the initiators of monstrous genocides, and rescuing the lives of millions of people, make one guilty? Such a deed could, on the other hand, cost many innocent lives, as it could probably not be done without a civil war and unforeseeable effects. And killing without legal proceedings and sanction by law remained an offense, because good ends

22. DBW 8, 24.

23. DBWE 6, 257-89.

24. DBWE 6, 257; on pp. 275-83 the topic of "conscience," self-accountability, or "willingness to become guilty" is treated.

25. DBWE 6, 323-26 and 328-31.

cannot justify evil means. Bonhoeffer saw tyrannicide as an action that was laden with guilt, but inevitably required in a situation when being bound by oath to Hitler, the *Führer,* blocked many a German's decision for a coup d'état.

Against intentionally taking on guilt [*Schuldübernahme*], there is "an objection of indisputable gravity. It springs from the lofty authority of conscience, which refuses to sacrifice its integrity to any other good, and refuses to become guilty for the sake of another human being." Loftiness of conscience — this sounds like Kant. But also, "All Christian ethics agrees" that "it can never be advisable to act against one's own conscience." This is unmistakably reminiscent of Luther's declaration at the Diet of Worms on April 18, 1521, "I remain overcome by the texts from Scripture I have adduced, and my conscience remains caught by God's Word. Therefore I cannot and will not recant anything. For to act against conscience is troublesome, unwholesome, and dangerous."[26] Bonhoeffer explains that conscience remains a binding authority in the "formal definition" that it protests against activity that threatens the person's "being in unity with one's own self." To act against it "is similar to suicidal action against one's own life."[27]

But how can we define the content of this unity with one's own self? "The call of conscience has its origin and goal in the *autonomy* of one's own ego." As it observes a self-found law, and is the self-justification of the fallen human being, it is deeply entangled in sin. Nevertheless, the call is to be respected, even if it cannot aid in achieving the unity to which it calls. Unity is gained where it is seemingly surrendered, namely, where conscience no longer aims for the unity of the isolated self, but addresses the self in the community with Jesus Christ. In faith, "I can only find unity with myself by surrendering my ego to God and others. The origin and goal of my conscience is not a law but the living God and the living human being as I encounter them in Jesus Christ." This transforms our relationship to all norms which conscience has appropriated, including "the law," in a manner that is recognizable for us when looking at Jesus. By breaking the Sabbath law and many others in order to hallow the law of love for God and human beings, Jesus became the liberator of conscience for the service of God and neighbor. "The freed conscience aligns itself with the responsi-

---

26. Luther, Weimar edition, volume II, 555 and 581-82.
27. DBWE 6, 276-77.

bility, which has been established in Christ, to bear guilt for the sake of the neighbor,"[28] a guilt that, in 1941, obviously consists in breaking the law that forbids high treason and killing.

Bonhoeffer here describes how Christians deal with their conscience in the new freedom vis-à-vis the law. Traditionally this was treated under the topos of *tertius usus legis,* or *usus in renatis.* This teaching concerns the function of the law of God for those who are reborn, the faithful. The autistic character of conscience, which "the law" is unable to remove, here is overcome. Reconciliation with God through Christ annuls our human state of being curved inward on ourselves, and opens us to community with God and our surroundings. It helps to find a new self that understands itself to be a gift of grace. Conscience goes along with this renewal of the human being. The other's concrete need becomes weightier than the human being's allegedly guiltless accord with an isolated self of its own. This turning had considerable concrete consequences in the situation of conspiratorial resistance.

From the first overthrow plan in 1938 to the last one for July 20, 1944, the officers in command in the military, whose initiative was necessary for a coup d'état, could not resolve on taking personal responsibility for the order [*Befehl*] that would initiate the actions. Some of them were ready to act if they were ordered to do so by an authority. They did not want to break the soldiers' law that connects order and obedience. They did not feel free from the oath of allegiance they had sworn, although Hitler, as the administrator of the oath, had long destroyed the foundation of the oath through many crimes. To intervene on their own in the course of history and take on themselves all of the guilt connected with it — this was too much for the inner authority of men in key positions. With them in view, Bonhoeffer taught, "Those who refuse to be relieved of the responsibility they share for the course of history by whatever might happen, because they know this responsibility to be imposed on them by God, will win a fruitful relation with events in history beyond fruitless criticism and equally fruitless opportunism. . . . The ultimate responsible question is not how I might heroically back out of the affair, but how a coming generation's life will go on."[29]

Bonhoeffer attempted to unite the responsible deed that is connected

28. DBWE 6, 277-79.
29. *Nach zehn Jahren,* DBW 8, 25. LPP, 7.

with taking on guilt and the freed conscience. A union is possible where conscience is no longer egocentric but opened through relationship with Christ to include responsibility for the neighbor and for the ongoing life of a coming generation in one's "self-examination."[30] It is possible where those who are responsible do not remain alone with their guilt, but are promised forgiveness.

Such union notwithstanding, Bonhoeffer sees an unremovable tension between freed conscience and responsibility. Taking on guilt has its limits. The call of conscience must not be skipped when it warns that the ego, in its relationship to Christ, will be destroyed by the coming action. Even the freed conscience that is no longer autistic calls the faithful to unity with themselves, a unity found not in themselves but in Christ. Further, the fact must not be repressed or subdued that even the freed conscience confronts responsible action with the law, which is indeed the "law of life" [*Lebensgesetz*].[31] Law, as the guardian and preserver of life, must be taken most seriously. It may be broken only if an unavoidable and only temporary breach will not destroy it, but will establish it in its true sense. The justice system and the laws which secured the power of the unjust National Socialist regime had in fact to be broken in order to restore validity to justice. Bonhoeffer is convinced that freedom and authority even vis-à-vis the law will be gained by responsible persons when they orient themselves toward Christ. When conscience admonishes us to heed the law of life, it must be heard, but only as a penultimate word, because the law of life must also be related to Christ as the ultimate Word.

Bonhoeffer's result is that those who accept guilt in responsibility must account for it. They do so because they see the necessity of accepting free responsibility. "Those who act out of free responsibility are justified before others by dire necessity. Before themselves they are acquitted by their conscience. But before God they hope only for grace."[32] How can conscience acquit them when they must admit they are entangled in guilt? An acquittal is possible because guilt was inevitable, and because freed conscience hopes for forgiveness of guilt.

30. DBWE 6, 325.
31. DBWE 6, 282.
32. DBWE 6, 282-83.

V. Novelty and Unity in Bonhoeffer's Understanding of Conscience

Doubtless, the enormous pressure of the conspiratorial situation made Bonhoeffer rethink the relation between responsibility, taking on guilt, and conscience. I know of no text in modernity in which there is a similarly vital interplay of personal decisions of conscience and theological reflection on conscience. And yet, Bonhoeffer did not let theological insight be dictated to him by the pressure of events. Instead, he retained a wide space of freedom for his theological thinking. This thinking is biblically inspired and biblically bound, and can, precisely as such, deal with concrete reality.

Bonhoeffer's understanding of conscience is undoubtedly a direct rejection of all variants of the neo-Lutheran view. It is characteristic of this view that conscience is seen as a fundamental datum, because the law of God is expected to make itself known in conscience in such a way that the human beings are defeated every time they are confronted with it, so that they, alarmed, can be shown the access to the gospel and to full faith. This is emphasized by the stubborn insistence that the sequence law-gospel can, on principle, not be reversed. Human beings who hear in the law the unconditional claim of God and are broken down by this claim, recognize that they are sinners and depend on justification through Jesus Christ. They recognize this in their consciences. Here, conscience is specifically linked with the *usus theologicus legis,* or *usus elenchticus.* Human beings are frightened in their consciences by the recognition that they are sinners, whereas faith in justification and forgiveness frees them. Bonhoeffer denies such a primary link between conscience and law. For him, conscience is primarily bound to Christ.[33] Thus he opposes the view that the sequence law-gospel is irreversible, and sides with Karl Barth who does reverse it. Why?

In Luther's worldview, the law had a clear place and function. Luther did not know atheism, not even in the form of modern indifferentism. Nihilism was absent from his worldview. For Luther even those who, in the Christian sense, were unbelievers and godless, were confronted by the law of God in so far as this law of God became concrete in natural law — which was consonant with the Decalogue. The law of God had power and significance for everyone, and was internalized in the personal as well as the collective consciousness. Preaching had to confront the people with

---

33. DBWE 6, 278 ("Jesus Christ has become my conscience").

the vividly portrayed law of God again and again, awakening and sharpening their bad consciences to make them recognize their sin.

In Barth's and Bonhoeffer's world, there was no longer a universally valid and evident law of God, or law of nature. It was precisely neo-Lutheranism that confirmed this fact involuntarily. Combating the 1934 Barmen Theological Declaration, leading Lutherans stated in the Ansbach Recommendation of June 11, 1934, what in their view was the concrete law of God in the National Socialist state. The law "binds us in duty to the natural orders to which we are subjected, such as family, nation, and race (that is, blood relation)." The natural orders "make known to us . . . God's demanding will," the law of God.[34] This interpretation of the law with reference to nation and race, in the sense of modern ideologies, confirmed that the world in which these Lutherans lived was no longer the world of Luther in which the law of God, together with the corresponding conscience, had been universally valid and evident like a law of nature. In the contemporary world, such "ground under the feet"[35] was lacking. There was no longer a basis for a universally valid ethic and a corresponding conscience. The world had become religionless in so far as laws of nature and evolution, but no universally valid law of God could be discovered in it. The metaphysical support of the theory that human beings had to be defeated by the law in order to be prepared for faith had vanished. "Ultimate reality" had now to be found in a different way.[36] Conscience would win authority and orientation no longer by itself, or by its relationship to law, but only in Christ.

In no way does Bonhoeffer deny that conscience, this antagonism of inner voices in the human being, is a general phenomenon. He interprets the "natural conscience" as a warning "not to violate the law of life."[37] He expressly discusses the laws that are inherent in life and indispensable for its preservation in the chapter fragment on "Natural Life."[38] That which is unnatural is destructive to life. Life is, to a certain degree, capable of resisting that which is destructive. A regime that suppresses all justice must, in the

34. The Ansbach Recommendation is found in Kurt Dietrich Schmidt (editor), *Das Jahr 1934*, volume 2 of *Die Bekenntnisse und grundsätzlichen Äußerungen zur Kirchenfrage* (Göttingen: 1935), 103.

35. *Nach zehn Jahren*, DBW 8, 20. LPP, 3-4.

36. See Bonhoeffer's 1940 introductory manuscript for his *Ethics*, "Christ, Reality, and Good," DBWE 6, 47-75.

37. 1942 DBWE 6, 282.

38. 1940-1941 DBWE 6, 171-218; compare above, chapter 8.

long run, destroy itself, as the Antichrist destroys the world. It is difficult to recognize the laws of natural life. They are contradictory, or antinomian, in themselves. In order to expound them, they must be seen in the perspective that has been opened through Christ's coming into this world. Christ has promised, "I am the life" (John 11:25 and 14:6).[39] The secret of true life is paradoxically stated in the saying of Jesus, "whoever wants to save his life will lose it, but whoever loses his life for my sake will save it" (Luke 9:24). Life perceived as natural life and as given in Christ is not two different kinds of life, but one that comes to clarity and unity in Christ. The same is true for conscience in Bonhoeffer's interpretation. "Even in its liberated form, conscience still has the function it had in its natural state, namely, to warn us not to violate the law of life."[40] The freed conscience not only warns; it authorizes free responsibility. Luther spoke of such authority and freedom when he said in 1533, if we have but Christ alone, we can even make new laws, new decalogues, that are clearer than those of Moses.[41]

Can connections between Bonhoeffer's experiences in 1939 and statements in *Ethics* manuscripts 1940-1943 be perceived? Here and there we witness a process of self-examination. Not only the voice of reason, with arguments pro and con, is heard. Quite a few emotions come up, represented, for example, by Bonhoeffer's tormenting homesickness. It points out to him what his life really consists in — the community in discipleship with brothers in Germany. In *Ethics*, then, we read that conscience warns us "not to violate the law of life," or the law of one's own life. Moral doubts worry him during the voyage to America in 1939. He asks whether or not he is, in the end, dishonest with himself. Dishonest are those who refuse to admit the truth of their lives that makes itself warningly felt. In *Ethics*, then, conscience calls to unity with one's own self. Already on the ship, after having left dangerous Germany, Bonhoeffer had questioned himself, "Or have I nevertheless evaded the place where He is? where He is *for me?*"[42] In *Ethics*, he says that the freed conscience is "calling me to unity with myself in Jesus Christ."[43]

39. 1942 DBWE 6, 249-53.

40. 1942 DBWE 6, 282.

41. Luther, Weimar edition, volume 49, I, p. 47, theses for the promotion disputation of Hieronymus Weller and Nikolaus Medler (*de fide* 52-54). Compare 1942 DBWE 6, 288, and 1925-1926 DBWE 9, 359-60.

42. See above, note 5.

43. DBWE 6, 278.

Peter Möser is skeptical about a connection between Bonhoeffer's practice and theory of conscience. Since I find the main moments of his 1940-1943 teaching on conscience also in the 1939 process of conscience, I am of a different opinion. In accordance with Karl Barth's basic understanding, Bonhoeffer had to reject the neo-Lutheran teaching on conscience. But at one point he sets out on a path that is not Barth's, namely, in thinking through the conscious acceptance of guilt attached to the required deed done in free responsibility. Here he pursues the Christian self-examination into a dimension that had not been disclosed previously. To become guilty by doing what is a moral unconditional necessity is usually deemed tragic. The entanglement in guilt of the men in the resistance against Hitler also appears to be tragic. Bonhoeffer refuses this interpretation. That which the Bible — and Luther — ultimately takes seriously, is not tragedy, but is the reconciliation of the world with God through Jesus Christ who took on guilt and brought forgiveness, and is the single-mindedly obedient life lived in the power of reconciliation that authorizes free responsibility. This is at stake in the self-examination of the Christian, and thus in the conscience that has been set free in Jesus Christ.

10 Conflicts of Conscience in the Resistance Against the National Socialist Regime of Injustice: Dietrich Bonhoeffer's Account "After Ten Years"

1987

In the first decade following the end of the Second World War, the resistance in Germany against Hitler's regime was preferably characterized as an "insurrection of conscience." Later research on contemporary history began to use other categories. Historians then preferred to inquire into the interests of those who participated in the resistance and into their affiliation with groups, with power elites who were concerned about their influence, or with lines of policy. It was and is necessary to clarify these topics. However, the attention paid to the inner problems of members of the resistance, and to the moral quality of their commitment, has somewhat receded into the background, and the distance to them has considerably grown — despite all official honors. An ethically admirable behavior often remains influential in later decades and generations. But political interests and conceptions are regarded by later generations as being tied to times and circumstances, and as barely intelligible under contemporary conditions. Today, for example, the lack of a democratic theory and will is regarded as being one of the strangest deficiencies of the German resistance after 1933. How far such finding of deficits from today's perspective does justice to people operating under the conditions of that time is a question that will not be treated here. I want to examine the ethical problems in which persons who decided to join conspiratorial resistance came to be involved.

Of course, circumstances differed in the respective groups and lines and with each personality in the resistance. The communist resistance, so far as it followed the directives of Stalin and operated in strictest party discipline, had problems different from those of the social democratic or the trade union resistance. The so-called "bourgeois" resistance, including the national-conservative resistance, was much more closely connected with the state apparatus and the armed forces than the left-wing resistance was, and had much greater inhibitions about operating in ways regarded as high treason or state treason. In one respect, however, all were alike. They all risked their own lives, the lives of their wives, children, friends, and comrades, and continually had to ask themselves if they could answer for this, given the always uncertain prospects for success of the conspiratorial resistance. The death sentences pronounced by the courts were continually renewed warnings.

There were quite a few whose resolution to do away with National Socialism was so firm that they no longer asked whether the risk was worth it. One of these was Dietrich Bonhoeffer. His brother-in-law Hans von Dohnanyi had informed him about conspiratorial plans in 1938, and had seen to it that Bonhoeffer was placed in the service of Canaris' military counterintelligence office for operations abroad [*Amt Ausland/Abwehr*] in 1940. There, Bonhoeffer used his ecumenical connections above all for the conspiratorial group around Colonel Hans Oster.

Hans Oster had taken an unrecallable step when, after the end of the Polish campaign in the autumn of 1939, he had informed the Dutch of dates of the German military's coming attack. According to the laws that were in force, he thereby had committed state treason.[1] He was convinced that Hitler, intoxicated by success, and the fascination of the German people with him, could be stopped only by military failures. These would hopefully end or shorten a long and bloody war that was bound to be catastrophic for the German Reich. One of Oster's conflicts was that he, through his information, strengthened the Western Allies' defense, without being able to avoid exposing many of his comrades to a greater danger than they would have incurred in a surprise attack. Only seldom do people write down the conflicts of conscience that they have to endure. It is very difficult to make clear in words what is at stake and which motives, often contradicting each other, come into play. This can to a certain extent be achieved in letters or diary entries. But in order to understand such statements, previous knowledge of

1. Romedio G. Graf von Thun-Hohenstein, *Der Verschwörer* (the conspirator). *General Oster und die Militäropposition* (pocket book edition München: 1984). Compare below, chapter 13, note 20.

a rather personal kind is needed in most cases. However, there does exist an almost unique text from the resistance, namely, the manuscript, which in print fills less than twenty pages, of Dietrich Bonhoeffer's account rendered at the end of the year 1942, "After Ten Years."[2] This text is known all over the world, but is rarely interpreted.

Bonhoeffer gave an account of the experiences, the inner history, and the conflicts of a small group of friends in the conspiracy and handed the manuscript to Hans von Dohnanyi, Hans Oster, and Eberhard Bethge — of course in full awareness of what would have happened had these considerations come into the hands of the Gestapo and been used in court as evidence for the prosecution. One copy is extant that had been hidden under the rafters of the house in Berlin Charlottenburg, 43 Marienburger Allee, where Bonhoeffer's parents lived.

Bonhoeffer was in on the overthrow plans, but was himself known to the Gestapo under whose observation and prohibitions he had come in the struggle of the Confessing Church. So he could not write openly about the conspirators and partisans of National Socialism and those who, while rejecting it, inactively tolerated it, nor about the resistance. The Gestapo or the Security Service of the SS might at any time confiscate and examine his manuscripts — which did happen after his arrest on April 5, 1943. He had to encode much of the self-critical considerations he wanted to share with his friends. This text, then, is in a wider sense cryptic, and to interpret it precisely and in relation to the situation is difficult. But it is not encoded in the narrow sense that a code which had been agreed upon is needed for deciphering it.

Nevertheless, in many places the words do not fully convey the meaning. Only one who reads them in a perspective similar to that of the writer, "like-mindedly," will immediately perceive where the author criticizes National Socialism and those who submit to it, or where he encourages doing at long last what had been prepared by the resistance, urging "the necessity of free responsible action even contrary to vocation and commission."[3] All of that would remain veiled to the outsider, and, because it was made ambiguous by generalization, could not be used in court

---

2. *Nach zehn Jahren. Rechenschaft an der Wende zum Jahre 1943*, DBW 8, 19-39; LPP, 3-17. In the following text, page numbers from *Nach Zehn Jahren* — and the corresponding page numbers in *Letters and Papers from Prison* (New York: Touchstone, 1997) — are included in parentheses.

3. DBW 8, 24; compare above, chapter 9, note 22.

as evidence against the author and his friends. It requires a high degree of linguistic virtuosity to put oppositional thinking into harmless words. Writers in all countries where censorship, in the alleged interest of a party or state, does not allow them to say openly what they really mean, develop such a virtuosity. Bonhoeffer was well prepared for it, as he had been writing manuscripts for a Christian ethic since the summer of 1940, and had discussed similar problems in one of them.[4] For Bonhoeffer, criticism of the National Socialist regime was no longer a pressing task in December of 1942. Warmongering, euthanasia murders, organized deportations of Jews from the Reich and the occupied areas, and information that had transpired about the extermination of Jews and some Eastern European peoples, were sufficient evidence that this regime was — not occasionally but on principle — a system of injustice which no longer deserved to be called a state. It was likewise evident that the oath of allegiance to the Führer was no longer binding. So the text "After Ten Years" could simply use the word *evil.* "That evil appears in the form of light, of beneficence, of what is historically necessary and socially just, simply bewilders those who come from our traditional world of ethical concepts. For the Christian who lives by the Bible, precisely this is a confirmation of the unfathomable wickedness of that which is evil."[5] But the friends in the resistance have continually to do with people who still rely on traditional ethical concepts for their orientation, people who are hindered by grave inhibitions from joining the resistance and from being ready for "free responsible action." Bonhoeffer characterizes the different types of their behavior.

Many people still surmised that they would be able, in their cooperation with this regime, to make the voice of *reason* heard and thus avert the catastrophe. Bonhoeffer speaks of their "naïve mistaking of reality" and "defective vision" (21; LPP, 4). These *"reasonable people"* "fall helplessly captive to the stronger party." Those for whom a good *conscience* is supreme react quite differently. Ever-new exigencies demand decisions of them which are ideologically veiled but cannot be made with a good conscience. Being urged to decide, they do what is required, and salve their consciences by lies, refusing to make themselves accountable for cooperating in evil activity. We think, for example, of the tens of thousands of helpers in the clockwork of the deportation machinery, who partially

---

4. DBWE 6, *Ethics,* 77-80.
5. DBW 8, 20. Compare above, chapter 9, note 15.

knew, and partially could sense, where these trains were going. Bonhoeffer states "that a bad conscience can be stronger and more wholesome than a deceived conscience" (22; LPP, 4).

Those who consider the ethically required path to be the "way of *duty*" are in a similar situation. In their view, the giver of the order is responsible, and any venture of a responsible deed on their very own is out of the question. The reader today may think of high-rank civil servants, diplomats, and above all generals, who could not brace themselves to initiate the coup d'état. Many explained that they could not act without an authorized order from higher ranks. Bonhoeffer comments laconically, "The man of duty will in the end have to fulfill his duty even to the Devil" (22; LPP, 5). This, then, was the way of the generals up to the bitter end.

Still others permitted themselves to operate in the jungle of the National Socialist polycracy, where a plurality of powers combatted each other, in their respective positions according to their own judgments, without regard to conscience and reputation. They had again and again to "consent to evil, in order to prevent what is worse." This was certainly one of the most frequent self-justifications of those who were in no way convinced of National Socialism, but remained at their posts. For example, they commented on the anti-Jewish Nürnberg race laws of 1935 so as to make them as mild as possible, and were of the opinion that the National Socialists who would be successors to them would publish worse commentaries and issue worse decrees — which seems plausible. Bonhoeffer asks those who "act in their very own *freedom*" whether precisely that which they intend to avoid, as being worse, might have been better (22; LPP, 5). And indeed, many oppositional national-conservative personalities who, even if full of doubts, did cooperate since 1933 or 1934, enabled Hitler, who had their special knowledge at his disposal, to firmly establish his regime, to rearm the Reich, and thus to install the worst. But also those who fled from public life and reserved for themselves a "sanctuary of *private virtuousness*" could not do so without keeping their mouths shut "to the injustice around them" (22; LPP, 5).

Bonhoeffer portrays people who pick out and raise for themselves a particular historic piece of traditional ethics. They struggle in their respective ways for their moral integrity. But all of them, in all their morality, at best are onlookers amid evil events who do not expose themselves, but objectively become accomplices to the criminal regime, cannot extricate themselves from collaboration, and nevertheless make themselves believe that they are personally respectable. Bonhoeffer does not analyze this from a detached distance. Every piece of tradition the failure of which he states is living within himself. He sympathizes with the tragedy of the wreckage of each of them. He recognizes that a wreckage is unavoidable when such people are faced by the evil power to which all of life is chained in National Socialist Germany. When this is taken into account, it will be recognized that an inevitable necessity urged the theologian Bonhoeffer into the foreign business of conspiratorial resistance. Considering what he observed and recognized, he had no freedom of choice in this matter.

Bonhoeffer knew that what he saw was not obvious to all. His surprising thesis in the section on *stupidity* [*Dummheit*] is that stupidity "is not essentially an intellectual defect, but a human defect," and "not so much a psychological problem as a sociological problem. . . . On closer examination, it appears that every strong external exhibition of power, be it political or religious, stupefies a large section of the people." Under the "overwhelming impression of the exhibition of power," people often lose their "inner independence" and refrain from "finding an authentic way of responding to the given circumstances of life" (26-27; LPP, 8-9). This could be observed with many who fell under the spell of Hitler, for example, in conferences with "the Führer in person." Only in this way could it happen that the German general staff, famous for its concentration of intelligence, when planning the aggressive campaign against Russia in 1941, did not take substantial preventive measures to protect the front-line troops from the onset of the Russian winter cold. They should at least have supplied the troops with adequate clothing, even without or contrary to the order of the Führer. The Führer, however, had declared that the war in the Soviet Union would be won before the winter, within four months. Intelligent generals, struck with stupidity by the exhibition of a single person's power! A people "of poets and thinkers," stupefied by slogans and orders of the day. Bonhoeffer concluded that no "act of instruction," but only "an act of liberation" could overcome such stupidity and give back to those who had been misused their inner independence. Precisely and only under these conditions did he deem it unnecessary to know what "the people" was thinking (27-28; LPP, 9). "The resistance" has been reproached for lacking a democratic attitude. Considering these — stupefying — circumstances, one can see that the conversion to democracy did not appear to be the first and most necessary step. A people manipulated to the innermost core is not capable of democracy, and can develop only through a longer process the preconditions that are necessary for this political form.

Did Bonhoeffer simply dismiss the wrecked old virtues? Should traditional ethics be thrown on the heap of antiquated trash? By no means. Amid "evil's great masquerade" (20; LPP, 4) which swirled and twisted the old ethical concepts, the traditional virtues were shipwrecked because they had been practiced in isolation and lacked something crucial, namely, the capability to see through the sham and disguise of evil that was staged as historical necessity. In one of the *Ethics* manuscripts, Bonhoeffer writes, "The person is wise who sees reality as it is, who sees into the depth of things."[6] Bonhoeffer charges that in none of the analyzed ethical attitudes is reality faced in this way. The persons resemble Don Quixote in many respects. The reality that is not seen through is, on the one hand, the political situation under National Socialism, but on the other hand also the persons' own inner situation. The combination of both brings about the delusion that entails failure. Both deficits are, again, not so much intellectual but human deficits. The man of reason, for example, puts reason in the service of overly optimistic attempts at compromise — pulling together what is inconsistent. Hjalmar Schacht, with his great capabilities, established and carried through the economic policy of the National Socialists, who were completely unprepared in this regard, thinking he could lead Hitler economically — until, aware of Hitler's intention ruthlessly to subordinate the economy to the preparation for war, he finally felt compelled to quit his influential offices. This, however, happened only after he had made Hitler's successes possible. The lack of courage to face reality rules inwardly as well. The man of conscience and the man of strict fulfillment of duty do not realize how they, through mere obedience, help to make possible or even participate in criminal actions, and they perceive their inward reality as falsified, having deluded their consciences with lies. An impaired and selective perception of both the outward and inward reality arises when intelligence is blurred by wishful thinking, anxieties, and mechanisms of self-protection. Here also, acts of liberation are required in order that reality and truth might be viewed clearly. "The saying of the Bible that 'the fear of God is the beginning of wisdom' [Psalm 111:10] states that stupidity is really overcome only by the inner liberation of the human being to responsible life before God" (28; LPP, 9). Here it becomes evident that, according to Bonhoeffer, ultimately faith, or a clarified relation to God, will liberate the human being for an unobstructed view of reality, and

---

6. DBWE 6, 81.

assign to the traditional virtues their appropriate functions in accordance with reality.[7] Such basic insights may well be gained by criticism of others, but it is hard to apply them to one's own person. We will examine whether or not consequences can be identified in Bonhoeffer's thinking and behavior. Then, the function of faith and religion in the context of resistance will come into view.

There exist laws and rights of life an offense against which is not only unlawful but also unwise. In the long run, such an offense will result in counteracting one's own interest in self-preservation. Hitler had disregarded these laws in domestic and foreign politics recklessly, but cleverly and at first successfully. At the end of the year 1942, the impending catastrophe of the German army in Stalingrad indicated that something like an "immanent justice of history" (30; LPP, 11) does exist. But also the members of the conspiratorial resistance saw themselves forced to break some of the laws and rights of human living together. Instead of playing this offense down before himself and his friends, Bonhoeffer unsparingly exposes it. He is willing to face reality within and without. "We have been dumb witnesses to evil deeds, we have learned the arts of cunning [*mit vielen Wassern gewaschen*], dissembling and ambiguous speech; we, taught by experience, have become mistrustful of people, and often had to withhold from them the truth and the free word we owed them. Through unbearable conflicts, we were worn down, or perhaps have even become cynical — are we still useful?" (38; LPP, 16). In this encoded text, Bonhoeffer could not openly state that the resistance was bound to collide with the laws on high treason and state treason — already because arrangements, for example, with the British government, were almost indispensable for the planning of an overthrow — nor that the resistance had to take into the bargain the risk of civil war or fighting of Germans with one another. But he did not treat this as harmless. Instead, he tried to deal in a Christian manner with the unavoidable guilt incurred through such activity, a guilt by which many of his friends together with him felt to be burdened. "Certainly no activity of historic importance can do without transgressing from time to time the boundaries of these laws [of human living together]. But the crucial difference is whether such a transgression of the drawn boundary is understood to be its nullification on principle, and thereby is made into a law of its own,

7. Compare DBWE 6, 257 ("*accordance with reality*" [*Wirklichkeitsgemäßheit*]) and 270 ("*appropriate to the subject matter*" [*Sachgemäßheit*]).

or whether one remains conscious that this transgression is a perhaps unavoidable guilt, justified solely in the immediate reestablishment and observance of the law and of the boundary" (30; LPP, 10-11).

Bonhoeffer in no way considered his and his friends' activity in the resistance to be "justified," or as needing no justification, merely on account of the fact that Hitler's regime was a regime of notorious injustice and violence. Many today consider this fact a justification. Bonhoeffer, however, thoroughly pondered the problem of becoming guilty here and in the *Ethics* manuscripts. This shows how conscientiously, self-critically, and near to reality members of this resistance group saw the problems of their own entanglement in guilt. The freedom to do so is obviously connected with an awareness of living before God. This awareness repels the proneness to self-justification that is deeply rooted in the human being, and gives courage to recognize, confess, and seek forgiveness for one's own guilt. But there is a decisive presupposition that must be heeded.

In today's general discussion in the field of philosophy of religion, a neo-conservative concept of religion has come to the front, from which Bonhoeffer's understanding of faith must be distinguished. Religion is preferably seen as helping "to cope with contingency," with buffets of fate and circumstances of life that are not rationally fathomable. Burdened by these, the human being needs consolation, encouragement, and forgiveness, and an established way to nevertheless discover a meaning [*Sinn*][8] in that which is inconceivable. Human beings are viewed here exclusively in their passivity, in accepting that which meets them from outside. The ethos corresponding to this view is that of obedience in one's vocation, in the field where one is in charge, in the commission one is assigned to. Bonhoeffer remarks that the highest danger of an attitude that had developed in German tradition, a readiness for subordination up to risking one's own life obediently, is revealed when this readiness is misused "for evil." "It had to become evident that the Germans traditionally lack a decisive basic knowledge, namely, that of the necessity of free responsible action even contrary to vocation and commission" (24; LPP, 6). According to Bonhoeffer's understanding, religion that only presupposes the passive human being's need for meaning and consolation will result in cheap grace. Grace will cost the human being nothing, its fruits will not be passed on to others, it will become the isolated individual's concern.

8. Compare above, chapter 2.

Bonhoeffer, however, sees Christian faith as the answer given with the human being's whole life to God's claim and address.[9] Faith by which the human being is bound to God alone calls for responsible and, as such, obedient action. Here, responsibility that is freely taken in the courage of one's convictions is crucial. "It rests in a God who demands the responsible deed freely ventured in faith, and promises forgiveness and consolation to the human being who through the deed becomes a sinner" (24; LPP, 6). Forgiveness and comfort are offered here as well. This function of religiosity does not disappear. But the context becomes different. Here, forgiveness is related to unavoidable personal guilt incurred by those who expose themselves, who venture free responsibility, and whose consciences are burdened with it. The fact that this relation has receded into the background in the religious traditions of Germany is regarded by Bonhoeffer as being the essential cause for the lack of "civil courage," and by this he means the lack of strength to withstand the tempting and overwhelming power of National Socialism. With this in view, Bonhoeffer outlines his *Ethics,* and one-and-one-half years later his "new theology" expressed in *Letters and Papers from Prison.*[10] In biographies written about men and women of the resistance — with the partial exception of representatives of the left-wing resistance — the biographers establish with astonishing frequency that the ultimate decision for the resistance was religiously motivated.[11] Bonhoeffer discloses how, under the hardly bearable pressure of unresolved problems and seemingly senseless alternatives, Christian faith can become the call, the impetus, the encouragement, and the accompanying strength for a resistance that is able to remain unsparingly self-critical. In this respect, the account rendered "After Ten Years," after a decade of National Socialist rule, is perhaps a singular document of the reflection and attitude of a group of people who were centrally involved and lost their lives in the conspiratorial resistance.

9. Compare DBWE 6, 254.

10. Beginning with the letter of April 30, 1944, DBW 8, 401.

11. Compare, for example, the biographies in R. Lill/H. Oberreuter (editors), *20. Juli: Porträts des Widerstands* (Düsseldorf and Wien: 1984) [and David Gushee, *Righteous Gentiles of the Holocaust* (Paragon House: 2003); GHS].

11 The Bonhoeffer-Dohnanyi Circle in Opposition and Resistance to Hitler's Regime of Violence: Interim Report on a Research Project

1987

I. Recent Research Questioning the Resistance against the Hitler Regime

Not the memorial celebrations, but the scholarly congresses on the occasion of the fortieth anniversary of July 20, 1944, have made public what had long been discussed and disputed among experts. Some critical schools of research into contemporary history have called in question the "bourgeois" *(bürgerlich)* resistance. For decades after the war, the resistance had represented the "other," that is, the better Germany, in contrast to the National Socialists' Germany. It had been understood as an admirable "uprising of conscience," and so as one of their best roots of the two German postwar states served to legitimate the Federal Republic of Germany — and the German Democratic Republic — as "antifascist" resistance. Today, in the light of more recent studies and judgments, the question comes up whether the resistance should better be forgotten and put on the scrap heap of history. The bourgeois resistance is represented as, for the most part, a "national conservative" undertaking that was characterized in no way solely by its opposition to National Socialism, but just as much by a long, and frequently only at a late date revoked, cooperation or even *entente cordiale* (coexistence agreement) with the Hitler regime. It is said that this resistance agreed to a large extent with the leadership of the Third Reich on political aims, up to the ostracism of the Jews from the German people. At some point, however, the unimaginably brutal methods of the

National Socialists provoked an awareness that one could no longer cooperate, but had to proceed to opposition and resistance. But the break often came quite late, as for instance only when Hitler intended to draw Germany into a seemingly hopeless war, or even only when, after highly successful campaigns, the reverse toward defeat became apparent. Those "national conservative" resistance members who then had the chance to revolt and collaborate in overthrow planning belonged to the old "power elites," were directed by interest in their own influence, and reasoned in political and worldview categories not at all in accord with today's democratic values, neither in domestic nor international politics. After all, the potentially most influential power elite, the military and generals, did not bluntly reject as murder, and as contrary to soldiers' honor, Hitler's barbaric directives of extermination in the attack against the Soviet Union, but unwillingly or willingly incorporated those directives into their own commands. The commanders in chief of the armies and army groups passed on the "commissar order," let the murderous "task forces [*Einsatzgruppen*] of the Security Police and the SS Security Service" and the "cleanup" [*Säuberung*] commandos of the SS do their evil job in their own military area, and, as a rule, did not deny them the necessary external support or even the participation of army units in such operations.[1]

At the international scholars' conference on the fortieth anniversary of July 20, 1944, in Berlin, the view of the resistance which I have just sketched in broad strokes, and still inadequately, stood out especially clearly in the contributions of the two historians Hans-Jürgen Müller and Hans Mommsen, who have introduced the collective label "national conservative" for the bourgeois resistance.[2] Of course, the family members of resistance participants who had become victims reacted with deep dismay or upset to this historical view, which places the national conservative resistance so close to the Hitler regime. Personally and morally, they remem-

---

1. H. Krausnick and H.-H. Wilhelm, *Die Truppe des Weltanschauungskrieges: Die Einsatzgruppen der Sicherheitspolizei und des SD 1939-1942* (Stuttgart: 1981).

2. In the book that documents this Berlin conference, *Der Widerstand gegen den Nationalsozialismus. Die deutsche Gesellschaft und der Widerstand gegen Hitler*, edited by J. Schmädeke and P. Steinbach (München and Zürich: 1985), cf. H.-J. Müller, "*National-konservative Elite zwischen Kooperation und Widerstand*," 24-49, and his "*Zur Struktur und Eigenart der nationalkonservativen Opposition bis 1938. Innenpolitischer Machtkampf, Kriegsverhinderungspolitik und Eventualstaatsstreichplanung*," 329-44, as well as H. Mommsen, "*Der Widerstand gegen Hitler und die deutsche Gesellschaft*," 3-23.

bered the events and their relatives' ways of behavior quite differently, and could only protest — against projecting back into the former situation today's categories that are inevitably linked with value judgments.

But those scholars of contemporary history who hold the view sketched above had strong backing from the source material they analyzed, even if they did not meet only with assent among expert colleagues. The presentations and proceedings of this conference show paradigmatically that the consensus in resistance research, in research on anti-Semitism and the persecution of the Jews, and similarly, by the way, in research concerning the German Church Struggle, is by no means broad. Inquiry into further sources of all kinds — files, literary legacies, documents — and the examination of the categories, premises, and (often more subconscious) evaluations effective in one's own research are urgently necessary, indeed also in theological research, and especially in studies of contemporary church history. From 1933 to 1945 in the churches, even including the Confessing Church, there occurred not only worried adaptation and opportunistic cooperation but also (partial) collaboration because of partially converging conceptions, for example, regarding the exclusion of the Jews from the German people, or regarding the right of the totalitarian state, unrestricted by any earthly authority, to do whatever would serve its own political interest. An *entente cordiale* was offered to the churches only during the early years 1933-1935, and only on the condition of their far-reaching synchronization [*Gleichschaltung*] with National Socialism and adaptation to nationalistic religiosity. After 1935 the un-Christian worldview characterizing the Party and the state could no longer be overlooked.

It would not be fair to exempt the circle around the Bonhoeffers and the Dohnanyis straight away, and not to ask the critical questions that have come up through research into the national conservative resistance. Surely it is correct that the members of this circle were neither nationalistic in the sense of National Socialism, nor conservative in the sense of being indissolubly bound to earlier conditions and power distribution, nor anti-Semitic. But every one of them also had to face, since 1933, the problem of cooperation and/or resistance. Today, many a reader of texts they wrote feels these to be authoritarian, elitist, and anti-egalitarian. Reason enough, then, to inquire very critically into the actual attitudes and motives for behavior prevailing in this circle.

Bethge's great Bonhoeffer biography that appeared in its first edition in 1967[3] has thoroughly clarified these questions for Dietrich Bonhoeffer. But the focus on one person's biography, with its numerous aspects, excluded a detailed examination and representation of the whole circle together with which Bonhoeffer stayed in opposition, and eventually participated in conspiratorial resistance. The task of studying the circle was taken over by a research project that was sponsored since 1983 by the Volkswagen Foundation. The project members have the special opportunity of access to the literary legacy of Hans and Christine von Dohnanyi, almost unused and unpublished until now, which is in process of being put in order. It contains some 1,500 documents, for example, letters, papers, clandestine notes [*Kassiber*] from prison, drafts of juridical defenses, and highly valuable records by Christine von Dohnanyi from the time immediately following the war. The transcription of these in part almost unintelligible documents was the work of several years.

In addition, the project members made use of the "service journal" [*Diensttagebuch*] in which Hans von Dohnanyi, as personal information officer to Reich Minister of Justice Franz Gürtner, documented from 1934 to 1938 National Socialist crimes, offenses, and persecution measures. This journal was apparently the basis for the "Crime Chronicle" with which General Ludwig Beck intended to confront the German people in a planned overthrow, in order to lay open the true character of the Hitler regime. Further search brought to light yet more documents on the life and work of Dohnanyi, among which are his juridical fights in the Criminal Law Reform Commission of the Reich ministry of justice from 1934 to 1936 with Secretary of State Roland Freisler. This source material shows that Dohnanyi, with his function in the ministry of justice from 1929 to 1938, and since 1939 in Admiral Canaris' counterintelligence office, was the key political figure in this circle of friends. For this reason we speak of a Bonhoeffer-Dohnanyi resistance circle.

Among the further source material that benefited the research group I mention here only the literary legacy of Friedrich Justus Perels, legal counsel [*Justitiar*] to the Confessing Church. Perels was arrested on October 5, 1944, as a participant in preparing the overthrow. He was sentenced to death. In the night of April 22 to 23, 1945, an SS commando took him out of the prison on Lehrter Street and shot him, along with

---

3. See Eberhard Bethge, *Dietrich Bonhoeffer. A Biography* (revised edition Minneapolis: Fortress Press, 2000).

sixteen other political prisoners. His legacy was organized and used for the first time.

Many unpublished or as yet unused sources are available to this research project for the attempt to develop, step by step, a description of the Bonhoeffer-Dohnanyi circle in opposition and resistance. Three individual studies have been finished as dissertations in the summer of 1986:

1. Marikje Smid, *Deutscher Protestantismus und Judentum 1932/33. Dietrich Bonhoeffers Wendung gegen die Diskriminierung des Judentums zu Beginn des Dritten Reiches.*[4]
2. Christine-Ruth Müller, *Der Kampf Dietrich Bonhoeffers und seiner Freunde gegen Diskriminierung und Verfolgung der Juden in Staat und Kirche.*[5]
3. Christoph Strohm, *Theologische Ethik des Politischen in der Auseinandersetzung mit dem Nationalsozialismus. Dietrich Bonhoeffers Weg in den Widerstand im Gespräch mit seinen als Juristen tätigen Freunden.*[6]

Marikje Smid is doing research on the importance of Hans and Christine von Dohnanyi for this circle's resistance.[7] Matthias Schreiber and Andreas Kersting are examining the path and the significance of Friedrich Justus Perels and of the legal struggle [*Rechtskampf*] of the Prussian Confessing Church.[8] Ernst-Albert Scharffenorth, besides his partici-

---

4. Published as volume 2 of the series *Heidelberger Untersuchungen zu Widerstand, Judenverfolgung und Kirchenkampf im Dritten Reich* under the title *Deutscher Protestantismus und Judentum 1932/33* (München: 1989).

5. Published as volume 5 of the *Heidelberger Untersuchungen* (above, previous note) under the title *Dietrich Bonhoeffers Kampf gegen die nationalsozialistische Verfolgung und Vernichtung der Juden* (München: 1990).

6. Published as volume 1 of the *Heidelberger Untersuchungen* under the title *Theologische Ethik im Kampf gegen den Nationalsozialismus. Der Weg Dietrich Bonhoeffers mit den Juristen Hans von Dohnanyi und Gerhard Leibholz in den Widerstand* (München: 1989).

7. Marikje Smid's book *Hans von Dohnanyi — Christine Bonhoeffer. Eine Ehe im Widerstand gegen Hitler* has appeared (Gütersloh: 2002). Likewise, Elisabeth Chowaniec's law-historical study *Der "Fall Dohnanyi" 1943-1945. Widerstand, Militärjustiz, SS-Willkür* (*Schriftenreihe der Vierteljahrshefte für Zeitgeschichte*, volume 62) has been published (München: 1991).

8. Volume 3 of the *Heidelberger Untersuchungen:* M. Schreiber, *Friedrich Justus Perels. Ein Weg vom Rechtskampf der Bekennenden Kirche in den politischen Widerstand* (München: 1989). Volume 4: A. Kersting, *Kirchenordnung und Widerstand. Der Kampf um den Aufbau*

pation in the project leadership, is dealing with Gerhard Leibholz in his English exile of 1938-1945 and his impact on the resistance and the Confessing Church.[9] Maria Nilius Staub is working on a concisely annotated edition of the most important documents from the Dohnanyi literary legacy. In the following, I will not refer explicitly to these individual studies, and also will forgo detailed references to archives, legacies, and so forth. My treatise is only a preliminary report in the course of a research process that is far from being finished. The purpose of this study of mine will be to sketch the fundamental traits of the opposition and resistance that can be discerned in the Bonhoeffer-Dohnanyi circle, and to expose these to ways of questioning and categories characteristic of today's resistance research, thus testing the productiveness of the latter.

II. The Members of the Bonhoeffer-Dohnanyi Circle

Long before the National Socialists came to power, there existed an informal circle of family and friends of which the home of the renowned professor of psychiatry Karl Bonhoeffer in Berlin formed the center. Members were, in addition to the children of Karl and Paula Bonhoeffer, the brothers-in-law Rüdiger Schleicher, Gerhard Leibholz, and Hans von Dohnanyi, as well as the friend Justus Delbrück, whose sister Emmi was married to Klaus Bonhoeffer. Jurists predominated in this circle, for the eldest of the Bonhoeffer brothers, the physicist Karl Friedrich — inclined, by the way, toward Social Democracy — did not live in Berlin, and Dietrich, the theologian, was, so to speak, the exception to the rule.

This circle expanded very little during the Third Reich. After 1935 Eberhard Bethge joined as Dietrich Bonhoeffer's friend, and later became son-in-law to Rüdiger Schleicher. Around 1937 Friedrich Justus Perels, the jurist working for the Confessing Church, was accepted as a friend to the circle through Dietrich, but also through Hans von Dohnanyi. Ernst von Harnack, Karl Ludwig Freiherr von Guttenberg, the brothers Hans and Otto John, as well as Josef Wirmer were closely connected to members of

---

der Bekennenden Kirche der altpreußischen Union aufgrund des Dahlemer Notrechts von 1934-1937 (Gütersloh: 1993).

9. Compare his *Die Aufgabe der Kirche in Kriegszeiten. Der Einsatz von George Bell und Gerhard Leibholz für eine konstruktive Deutschlandpolitik Großbritaniens 1941-1943*, in: *Kirchliche Zeitgeschichte*, volume 1 (1988), 94-115.

the circle. Especially in the first years of the war, contacts with Helmuth James von Moltke were closer than previously recognized.

The circle thus maintained an informal character, despite the many oppositional activities, and finally those directed toward the coup, that involved or were arranged by the group. There were no attempts to establish a formal organization. But a high degree of "likemindedness" prevailed. From an examination of the individual biographies up to the end of the Weimar Republic, an astonishingly homogeneous picture emerges. All were averse to militant nationalism, nationalistic thought, and anti-Semitism, as well as to the "conservative revolution." They proved to be determined republicans who appreciated the constitutional rule of law in a proper state of justice *(Rechtsstaat)*. As a rule, they voted for the German Democratic Party, which after 1930 called itself State Party, or for the German People's Party, not least of all because of Stresemann's achievements with regard to international agreements.[10] They certainly thought in patriotic terms.

But it was, surprisingly, the theologian in this circle, who in 1928-1929, twenty-two years old, influenced by the overwhelming trend in the Protestant church and its theological university departments, appeared for a short time affected by national Protestant ideas of unreserved assent to the German people's self-assertion by expansion. Dietrich Bonhoeffer thoroughly revised this approach in 1930 to 1932 on the basis, as we can infer from his letters and writings, of new theological insights. He discovered the meaning of the Sermon on the Mount for his life's direction and did not content himself with relegating its promises and demands — as was common in church and theology — to private inwardness. And he recognized, not least of all in the course of his studies in the United States of America, that the church of Jesus Christ, being deeply bound to the one common redeemer, may never be a national church, but must always prefer an ecumenical alliance of all partial churches in the one worldwide Christendom. This had significant consequences. From now on, he demanded his church work for international agreement and peace, and became active in the World Alliance for Promoting International Friendship through the Churches.

This brought him quite close to the position of the jurists in the fam-

---

10. [Gustav Stresemann was perhaps the most outstanding statesman of the democratic Weimar Republic in Germany — which, had it retained power, would have avoided Nazi takeover. He became chancellor and foreign minister in 1923, successfully leading Germany to join the League of Nations and winning the Nobel Prize for Peace, but died in 1929. The parties named in the text above supported the democratic Weimar Republic. GHS]

ily, his brother Klaus and his brothers-in-law. All of them accorded high significance to international law, besides national political law [*Staatsrecht*]. Since the 1928 Kellogg-Briand Pact, international law outlawed (offensive) war. Convergent with this trend in international law, Dietrich Bonhoeffer fought on ecumenical-ecclesiastical grounds for a theological outlawing of war — with only limited resonance in the nationalistic and later National-Socialist German climate, and with equally limited ecumenical support from churches in other countries. Thus, even prior to 1933, Bonhoeffer washed his hands of any ties with national Protestantism, which from 1933 on entered into an alliance with Hitler and tried to maintain it for many years.

The recognizable signs of the Weimar Republic's dissolution had to alarm, after 1930, each attentive republican. Gerhard Leibholz, who was a respected expert in political law already at a very young age — whom even the famous Carl Schmitt had tried to woo, which ended abruptly in 1933 because of Leibholz's Jewish origins — critiqued parliamentary democracy in his writings, with constructive intent. He attempted to determine afresh the role of political parties under conditions of mass democracy. While criticizing liberalism's one-sided preference for individualistic bourgeois property-holding and capitalistic profit-seeking, he strongly emphasized as indispensable the "liberal heritage of modernity." In his view, as well as in Dohnanyi's, it was this heritage that had made possible the constitutional state of justice, human rights, religious freedom and freedom of conscience, and many other modern achievements. What was most difficult was the formation of democracy. How could parliamentary democracy persevere when aside from the Social Democrats, the (Catholic) Center Party, and the bourgeois middle parties, all others agitated against parliamentary democracy with popular success, resulting in an anti-democratic attitude of "the masses"? Under today's circumstances and value judgments, it is easy to accuse those who were active in the last days of the Weimar Republic of an insufficiently democratic attitude and to stamp their thinking as authoritarian and thus as pre-fascist. When Leibholz, who knew Italian fascism well, finally came to regard the strengthening of the authority of the constitutional state of justice as the task appropriate for those times, he did not prepare the way for Hitler's totalitarian state, but consciously countered it by the only remaining realistic alternative that appeared suited for preventing the establishment of Hitler's reign.

It was the dissolution of the Weimar Republic and the impending "seizure of power" by Hitler that turned this circle of family and friends, joined by personal and familial bonds, into a politically relevant group as well. Once the ruling power was handed over to the National Socialists, the judgment of the Bonhoeffers was unanimous: Hitler meant war. From beginning to end, the opposition to war was one of this circle's primary motives for opposition and resistance. The threat of an imminent war that had to be prevented by all available means drew the group closer together.

There were other important motives that ruled out any trust in Hitler's tempting promises during the early part of his regime, and any simple toleration of the lawless misdeeds first of the National Socialist Party, and then also of the state bodies, that were commonly portrayed as "growing pains" of the "national awakening." After August 10, 1932, when five National Socialists had trampled a Communist to death in his own apartment and Hitler had approved of the cowardly deed with unrestrained cynicism and covered the perpetrators,[11] no doubts remained with Hans von Dohnanyi, the personal information officer to the Reich minister of justice, and with the Bonhoeffers, about Hitler's brutal conception of justice. This was revealed, a mere month after Hitler's "seizure of power," in the lawless persecution of delegates and functionaries of the Communist Party of Germany, in the introduction of "protective custody" [*Schutzhaft*], arbitrary arrest without judicial checks (by the middle of March, 1933, already more than 10,000 individuals were in this kind of "custody" in Prussia), in the establishment of concentration camps, and in many further measures. The circle members were certain that Hitler's rule would spell the end of the state of justice. Dietrich Bonhoeffer had foreseen the erosion of the state as such which thus had been initiated. He had recognized the nationalistic messianic notion of (a Third) Reich, the pseudoreligious myth, and the hubristic leader cult in the National Socialist movement. Bonhoeffer's February 1, 1933, talk on Radio Berlin concerning the transformations of the concept of leader in the younger generation[12] referred so clearly to the dangerous bondage to the Führer that the broadcast was cut short — apparently out of fear of National Socialist sanctions.

11. Regarding this "Potempa case," cf. Gerhardt, *Handbuch der deutschen Geschichte*, volume 19 (Deutscher Taschenbuch Verlag), 297-98.

12. *Wandlungen des Führerbegriffs in der jüngeren Generation*, cf. pp. 242-60 in DBW 12, *Berlin 1932-1933* (Gütersloh: 1997).

Moreover, Bonhoeffer had come to accept quite early that persecution of churches and unavoidable martyrdom might happen, as sermons from the summer of 1932 demonstrate.[13] And finally, the Bonhoeffers were clearly aware that anti-Semitism was not an incidental addition to National Socialist thought as a whole, but an important part of the ideology. Disdain for the anti-Semitic ideology can be found, for example, already in letters written by Christine Bonhoeffer, who studied biology in Heidelberg before she married Hans von Dohnanyi. When Gerhard Leibholz was courting Sabine Bonhoeffer, Karl Bonhoeffer inquired in a serious conversation of both of them whether they were ready to accept all the undeserved discrimination that a jurist and university teacher of Jewish descent would encounter under the conditions that existed in the Weimar Republic. Despite openness toward Jewish fellow citizens, welcoming them into one's own family through marriage was far from being a matter of course. Quite a few were prepared for the increase of anti-Semitism through Hitler's accession to rule. Yet what really happened exceeded the worst expectations by far.

All four motives for opposition, namely, Hitler's warmongering, the destruction of the state of justice, the conflict with the churches, and fanatical anti-Semitism, were already alive in the Bonhoeffer-Dohnanyi circle, and worked together toward the rejection of the National Socialist regime, when Reich President Paul von Hindenburg handed the power over to Hitler. These were the motives to which the members of the circle appealed in the final interrogations,[14] when there was nothing left to hide from those who led the investigations after July 20, 1944, and the September, 1944, discovery of the Zossen files, of which more will be said later. A fundamental opposition to the Hitler regime characterized this circle from the beginning. But what at the end of January, 1933 was mere apprehension and extrapolation from experiences with the National Socialists and their literature up to that time was soon to be confirmed and surpassed in almost every respect, regardless of how deftly Hitler gave his actions the appear-

13. Cf. the June 19, 1932, sermon in Berlin, pp. 444-53 in DBW 11, *Ökumene, Universität, Pfarramt 1931-1932* (Gütersloh: 1994), and see above, chapter 6, text before footnote 33, "times in which martyrs' blood will be demanded" (p. 445).

14. Cf. H.-A. Jakobson (editor), *Spiegelbild einer Verschwörung*, volume I, pp. 519-20, the statements of Hans von Dohnanyi, Rüdiger Schleicher, and Klaus Bonhoeffer regarding the reasons for their opposition to the National Socialist regime, documented in the December 9, 1944, SS Security Service report.

ances of historical necessity and ultimate benefit for the German people. The readiness to cooperate with the National Socialists, for which today some of those who later entered the "national conservative" resistance are justly blamed, was basically absent from the Bonhoeffer-Dohnanyi circle. That aggravated their situation, since they were trained as jurists and prepared to take responsibility in government positions. The dilemma that arose out of this will be discussed later on.

How might the members of this circle be classified socially? The societal stratum to which they belonged can probably be best characterized with the concept of "cultured bourgeoisie" [*Bildungsbürgertum*] in its perhaps singular development and historical significance in Germany and Prussia. The scholarly intelligentsia and civil servants had enacted the Prussian reforms after the collapse of Prussia in 1806 — against a majority of the nobility and also of the royalty — and had prepared the wars of liberation against Napoleon. From that time on, favored by the institution of university education and the selection of higher civil servants, they formed that stratum of cultured bourgeoisie far more clearly set apart from the capitalist property-holding or upper-class citizenry in Germany than in the Western European nations. They knew themselves called to take on governmental and public responsibility for the commonweal. The cultured bourgeoisie as such was not one of the traditional "power elites," as were, for example, the high generals, the big industrialists, and the leading officials of the political parties. Yet access to important positions of power was often facilitated. No member of the Bonhoeffer-Dohnanyi circle attained a personal power position. Even the politically most influential among them, Hans von Dohnanyi, who firmly objected to joining the Party, was promoted only to the relatively junior position of senior government official [*Oberregierungsrat*]. His influence on justice ministers, especially on Gürtner from 1933 to 1938, was nevertheless significant, not by reason of his position, but thanks to Gürtner's boundless personal trust, against whose yielding to and cooperation with the wielders of power Dohnanyi asserted strong reservations in several fundamental discussions.

Dietrich Bonhoeffer, likewise, was not called into any position of church leadership and power. Aside from his youth — he was murdered at age thirty-nine — this was hindered by his radical rejection of national Protestantism, the theological leaders and representatives of which were from 1933 on quite inclined to form a new alliance of the church with the National Socialist state and agreed to an *entente cordiale*. The emergence of opposition by the Confessing Church shattered all plans for an alliance of that kind, and Bonhoeffer became one of the most radical representatives and voices of this opposition.

The most likely answer to inquiries about the piety or religiosity predominant within the Bonhoeffer-Dohnanyi circle is that they favored a kind of Protestantism that was not un-churchly but certainly distanced from the church, and far too reserved to show itself outwardly in day-to-day life. Dietrich Bonhoeffer's decision to study theology was a surprise for the family, who tolerantly accepted it rather than finding it reasonable. This kind of Protestantism was accustomed to hiding pious or religious feelings, and to conceiving the ethical aspect as that for which one had to take a stand in the world. Only imprisonment and situations of utmost danger occasionally allowed feelings to be verbalized that otherwise would have been perceived as a violation of personal boundaries and as embarrassing.

III. The Areas of Conflict

The attitudes prevalent in the Bonhoeffer-Dohnanyi circle were such that conflicts with the National Socialist wielders of power had to be expected. The only question was where they would first surface and how they could be weathered. Every one of them, just like the rest of those Germans who were inclined toward opposition, had to endure friction with the new wielders of power in their everyday lives, and especially in their jobs. How this ought to be most skillfully done, without overly large forfeitures, damages, or dangers, was naturally a constant subject of family consultations, which often concerned the question of how far one could go in making concessions without losing moral integrity. A family member might even be advised to join the Party for the sake of remaining in the profession. But such a nominal membership touched the uttermost limit, and Hans von Dohnanyi, despite pressure from the ministry of justice, always objected to taking that step.

In our sources we find enough material to describe the conflicts of Dietrich Bonhoeffer and Hans von Dohnanyi adequately. Only the former provided detailed writings in which the internal aspects and ethical problems of these conflicts are carefully reflected, theologically meditated on, and formulated beyond mere personal experience. In this section, we shall first discuss the external aspect of some of these conflicts.

1. Here the temporal sequence is important. The first great conflict noticeable for us is addressed in Bonhoeffer's essay on the church before the Jewish question.[15] This essay has been so highly and so frequently praised in the literature on contemporary church history that I can restrict myself to a few remarks.[16]

It was no accident that the church's initial decisions in favor of National Socialism, and Bonhoeffer's never-revised decision against the Hitler regime were made already in March/April on the subject of the "Jewish question." Anti-Semitism belonged to the core of the nationalistic worldview and was utilized again and again by the National Socialist leadership in order to mobilize the German population emotionally. While the majority of the church leaders classified the anti-Jewish excesses and the boycott of April 1, 1933, as transitory phenomena in a time of revolution, Bonhoeffer recognized in them an issue which, both for the church and for the state, meant "to be or not to be." This view was regarded by most of his colleagues in the church as an enormous exaggeration. Bonhoeffer claimed, when governmental encroachments upon the church (by means of the law for the Reconstruction of the Professional Civil Service of April 7, 1933, with its Section 3, the so-called Aryan clause) led to the exclusion of baptized Jews from the Christian congregations and to the prohibition of mission to Jews, then the church is in a *status confessionis,* a situation of utmost emergency, in which it is not permitted to back down under any conditions, lest it lose its character as a Christian church. By forcing something of this nature on the church, the state executes an "act of self-negation," and destroys its own character of state of justice. The church must then confront the state with authoritative objection, must help all victims of such state actions, and must deliberate in a church council [*Konzil*] about its eventual obligation to combat the state with direct political means. Bonhoeffer grounded this radical decision on the salvation-history bond uniting Israel and the church, and thus on a theological argument that, as such, had consequences for action up to a frontal clash with the new worldview-based state. But the conflict did not flare up in 1933. The church representatives could not bring themselves to share Bonhoeffer's theological view, and at this early stage Hitler avoided pres-

---

15. *Die Kirche vor der Judenfrage,* pp. 349-58 in DBW 12, *Berlin 1932-1933.*

16. See K. Scholder, *Die Kirchen und das Dritte Reich* volume I, 350-52 (cf. above, chapter 6, notes 3 and 4), and M. Smid, Chr.-R. Müller, and Chr. Strohm (notes 4-6 above).

sure on the church that would cause escalation into a conflict. Ten years later, when the "final solution" to the Jewish question, namely, physical extermination, was in full swing in Europe, it was much too late for the churches to object. Only a few spokespeople such as Regional Bishop Theophil Wurm in Stuttgart, or the October 17, 1943, Confessing Synod of the Church of the Old Prussian Union in Breslau, were in a position to say an open word of protest — but nothing more. For a decade, until his arrest, Bonhoeffer fought untiringly for the church's solidarity with the Jews, and gave practical help wherever this was possible for him. He included the theme "Israel — Jews — Christians" innumerable times in his theological training of candidates for the ministry, in his sermons and his devotionals. His 1933 essay was not the product of a merely temporary effort, but rather the decision for a life's task that he never relinquished.

On this path, Hans von Dohnanyi was his constant, highly active, juridically and organizationally talented companion, or rather co-fighter. In the Reich ministry of justice, Dohnanyi steadfastly impeded and sabotaged the National Socialist legislation for the Reich, with some success. Secretary of State Freisler found Dohnanyi's influence on the Reich ministry of justice in this matter insufferable. Moreover, Dohnanyi, through legal counseling, helped Jewish fellow citizens in countless instances to defend their last remaining rights, and to emigrate.

Bonhoeffer and Dohnanyi were no Semitophiles, although they had many friends with partial Jewish ancestry. While the anti-Semite regards the so-called "Semitic race" as negative, the Semitophile acknowledges the same pseudo-biological point of view by evaluating it as positive. Bonhoeffer, however, explicitly declared the Jewish question to be not a biological or racial question, but, on the one hand, a religious question that had to be settled religiously, and, on the other hand, a question of the state's consistent legislation. The state, in order to remain a state of justice, had to issue uniform laws — including fellow citizens who understood themselves to be Jews, who must not be degraded to citizens under a different law.

The actual development of the Third Reich had the astounding result that no other group was as hopelessly and fatefully abandoned as was the group of baptized Christians who were classified by the National Socialist authorities as Jews, non-Aryans, and "mongrels" of different degrees. This assertion requires a more detailed explanation. A book by Kwiet and Eschwege on the struggle of German Jews for existence and human dignity contains the following statement, formulated from an intra-Jewish perspective: "A person who confesses himself to belong to the Jewish community is a Jew," a German Jew. In addition, according to Kwiet and Eschwege, there was the German of Jewish ancestry, that is, a person whom the surrounding people classified and treated as Jew.[17] Those who confessed themselves to be part of the Jewish community, and understood themselves as a Jews, at least enjoyed this community's solidarity and help in the midst of all the horror. But those who understood themselves not as German Jews, but as Christians in Germany, and for whom — subjectively — their (partial) Jewish ancestry did not matter, now suddenly, despite their baptism and their self-understanding, were made Jews, non-Aryans, mongrels, through completely heteronomous determination. They could not enjoy the solidarity of the Jewish community that was foreign to them, and in addition lost much, if not all, of the solidarity of the Christian church to which they belonged. Often enough, the attitude of church representatives was similar to that of Hanover Regional Bishop August Marahrens, who in bondage to the powers that be eventually felt compelled to officially recognize this governmental classification in his church. "Already from 1942 on, the Hanover regional church no longer collected church taxes from Jewish Christians, since it no longer considered these people to be its members."[18] One can hardly imagine a more desperate loneliness than that of the many Christians of Jewish ancestry, who lost all solidarity and must have felt betrayed and exposed, regardless of whether their path led directly into, or passed by, the gas-chambers. Already in 1933, Bonhoeffer was convinced that the church ceases to be the church when it limits its solidarity with those Christians who were made Jews by heteronomous determination. He could not and did not want to avoid the conflict with the state in this matter even for the church's own sake. But he was equally ready to help those who knew themselves to be Jews, especially as members of the Jewish community. Christians ought to see in them Jesus Christ's persecuted kindred, while their acknowledgment as fully equal fellow citizens had to be demanded from the state. Bonhoeffer only conceded to the new state the option to negotiate with the Jewish community, as with the churches, new treaties, and legislate accordingly.

17. K. Kwiet and H. Eschwege, *Selbstbehauptung und Widerstand: deutsche Juden im Kampf um Existenz und Menschenwürde 1933-1945* (*Hamburger Beiträge zur Sozial- und Zeitgeschichte* volume 19; second edition Hamburg: 1986), 19.

18. Chr.-R. Müller, *Diskriminierung* (above, note 5), 264.

2. The second conflict in which Bonhoeffer, like all members of the circle, was involved broke out when, in the summer of 1933, the Party, by way of the state and the German-Christian organization which was servile to the Party, attempted to force the "synchronization" [*Gleichschaltung*] of the Protestant Church. Here for the first time in the Third Reich energetic objections and large protest meetings of broad sections of the population happened — the onset of a new "movement," although initiation of new parties and organizations was strictly forbidden. The Confessing Church was established, with its own organization and partial financing. None of this was intended as a struggle against National Socialism, but rather as a defense against encroachments upon the church.

Because of this distinction between political and supposedly purely ecclesiastical matters, and because of the complicated church relations, many scholars of contemporary history are not sure how to assess the resistance potential of the Confessing Church, thousands of whose members were, over the years, interrogated, subjected to prohibitions, arrested, taken to court, and some to concentration camps. But the bare fact that broad sections of the population registered here a blatant act of injustice on the part of the Party and the state, and distanced themselves from it, at least internally, was of eminent significance, considering the high degree of the population's identification with the Third Reich which the Party had by that time effected. Bonhoeffer resolutely combated from the beginning the foreign penetration of the Protestant church with nationalistic German-Christian and national Protestant ideology, and its domination by Party-servile churchmen.

The Party's church politics in the first years was not homogeneous; no outline had been conceived, neither by the Party nor by Hitler himself. At first, it appeared to be enough to force the adaptation of the church to the state, by promises or threats, to make the multitude of regional churches into a centrally controlled "Reich Church" to be utilized as a counterweight to the unbroken Roman Catholic church, and to leave the rest to ideological development. This general line was thwarted by strong-willed and resolute minority groups. These made the transformation of the church and the recognition of their leading representatives dependent on trustworthy loyalty [*Bindung*] to the Holy Scripture and the church's confession of faith, and thus effectively ruled out both Party-servile church leadership and ideologization.

The 1934 Barmen Theological Declaration's statement that Christ alone is Redeemer and Lord of the church, and that this has consequences for all spheres of life, confronted the National Socialists' totalitarian claim with a completely different challenge that could not be forced into conformity. To be sure, the basic National Protestant — mostly national conservative — orientation was so effective that the church majorities, including the few regional bishops who, supported by the congregations, remained in their leading positions despite the German-Christian attempts to conquer their territories, did not at all wish to object to the measures of the national state, not even in regard to the Jewish question and in regard to the lawless persecution of the left-wingers.

But one thing was clear: The church must remain the church! Only a few churchmen understood in the first years that even this was an eminently political claim, because it objectively countered the National Socialists' synchronization (forced conformity) activities and claims to total identification. The fact that the political character of the Church Struggle was not comprehended was even more surprising as, since June, 1933, the state's encroachments and the Party's barely veiled influence exercised through the Führer's confidant in the church, the later Reich Bishop Ludwig Müller, and through other middlemen of the Party, were visible to everyone. But the leaders and theologians of the Confessing Church judged their own actions by their motivation, and found them to be determined by the faith and confession of the church. Karl Barth, the leading theologian of the Church Struggle until his 1935 expulsion to Switzerland, and Dietrich Bonhoeffer, were aware of the inevitable political implications of this struggle, and therefore pleaded against addresses and promises of loyalty to the state. They pleaded for clearly stated claims by the church which would make obvious the conflict between the Party and the state on the one hand, and the Confessing Church on the other hand.

Yet the Nazi regime wanted to avoid at all cost fighting with the church in an open struggle of ideology versus faith. Instead, Section 24 of the Party program, which proclaimed a "positive Christianity" for tactical reasons, was adduced to conceal the trend in broad sections of the Party, probably including Hitler himself, toward a neo-pagan religiosity inimical to the church. Since the surprise synchronization attack had been only partially successful, discrimination and persecution of the Confessing Church with laws, decrees, the establishment of church offices and authorities under Party domination, such as the all-controlling "finance departments," took the place of worldview confrontations. To these was added an abundance of administrative and police measures against persons and governing bodies of the Confessing Church, reaching into every local congregation, prohibitions of assembly, expulsions from the area of residence, prohibitions of speech and of publication, searches of homes, interrogations and arrests in large numbers, as well as concentration camp internments that cost some lives. These and similar measures formed a net with fine meshes which, in the course of the Third Reich, was cast over the church, especially its confessing parts, and was drawn more and more tightly with the intent to stifle it. All this happened in the name of "deconfessionalization," or rather of an almost total exclusion of the churches from public life.

Those who took seriously their tasks in the church were eventually almost unable to avoid conflict with state measures, and had to practice, as we would say today, "limited civil disobedience." Thus they constantly had to put up with possible sanctions against themselves and their families. Since these events happened in a large part of the church-communities in the German Reich, and, in spite of the Party's intention to keep them secret, were widely noticed by the population, the SS, its Secret Service, and the Gestapo classified these confrontations as highly political, as can be seen from extant reports.[19]

Dietrich Bonhoeffer was considered one of the "radical" theologians of the Confessing Church. In 1933, in Berlin, he struggled against the German-Christians' seizure of power in the church by many means, up to the distribution of flyers. He intractably made the church bodies face the decision for or against the Aryan clause in the church under the motto that by assenting to the clause the church would cease to be a true church. As a parish minister in London — from the fall of 1933 to the spring of 1935 — he did his best to mobilize the foreign member churches of the ecumenical movement to take sides in the German Church Struggle with the Confessing Church as the only true church. At international church conferences, he sought to obtain binding resolutions from the churches that might have the objective effect to counteract, above all, the militarization of Germany. But only few persons abroad recognized the impending dangers of Hitler's regime. Besides this, Bonhoeffer saw to it that ecumenical resolutions were passed that — being noted and handed on by the Foreign

19. Cf., for example, H. Boberach (editor), *Meldungen aus dem Reich. Auswahl aus den geheimen Lageberichten des Sicherheitsdienstes der SS 1939-1944* (München: 1968).

Office — discouraged the application of the Aryan clause in the German churches.

In all of this, Dietrich Bonhoeffer had strong support from his family and circle of friends. Since 1934, Hans von Dohnanyi, as personal information officer to the Reich minister of justice until 1938, wrote a "service journal"[20] in which he recorded, besides the many injustices perpetrated by Party men, also the persecution measures against the Confessing Church, as far as they became known to the ministry from the whole Reich. In 1935, when cases concerning the Confessing Church were withdrawn from the justice system and the Reich ministry of justice through the establishment of a "decision office" [*Beschlußstelle*] for lawsuits concerning the church, the stream of such reports in the service diary dried up.

Pressed by the tight net of the measures described, the Confessing Church had to fight out its confrontations with the Party and the state largely as a legal struggle [*Rechtskampf*]. Wherever possible, it sought protection in the ordinary courts through charges and processes against intra-church encroachments by German-Christian wielders of power, as well as against bodies of the Party and of the state. In this, it found help and advice from civil servants in ministries and high public boards and, in the justice system, especially from the judges, from free-lance lawyers and teachers of political-ecclesiastical law [*Staatskirchenrecht*], such as Erik Wolf, and from jurists in church service who were employed either full-time or part-time as legal counsels [*Justitiare*] by the Confessing Church or the so-called "intact regional churches." These groups, in quite different positions, were closely connected with one another through various — mostly informal — relationships. On the basis of personal trust, they could impact legal proceedings and administrative as well as police measures in favor of the Confessing Church, in thousands of cases. Without this aid in its legal struggle, the Confessing Church could hardly have survived the twelve years of the Third Reich. Strictly speaking, the Confessing Church was from 1938 on already a tightly restricted and also divided "movement," shattered into fragments, and only rarely "capable of action." It nevertheless gained public notice again and again, and was still seen by the Party as a danger. Its being dangerous was due to the fact that in decisions for opposition and resistance to this regime the persecution of the church became a distinguishing mark for the fundamentally unjust char-

20. Chr. Strohm, *Juristen* (above, note 6), 243ff.

acter of the regime, and with that, a motive for action. In almost all of the biographies of those who directly or indirectly participated in the July 20, 1944, coup attempt, for example — with the exception of the extreme "left-wing resistance" — one comes across the remark that ultimate reasons for the decision in favor of overthrow were religious Christian motives. But as a rule, these had taken shape and gained force only through the Church Struggle.

The Party attempted to suppress the Church Struggle as an ideological debate and keep it out of the public eye. Only the non-public training in the Party organizations spread the neo-pagan religiosity, the "Myth of the Twentieth Century,"[21] and urged people to leave the church, and only a few Party organs, for example, the "Black Corps" of the SS, openly argued ideologically against Christianity. The Confessing Church, however, had to bring the Church Struggle at least to the ecclesiastical public's attention. Sermons in the worship services (even though they were regularly watched by informers), announcements from the pulpit, some publications, and word-of-mouth distribution of such information were the church's main measures in this struggle.

As director of an "illegal" preachers' seminary, which in 1935 began in Zingst on the Baltic See and continued in Finkenwalde near Stettin, Dietrich Bonhoeffer aimed at preparing the candidates for the hard way of discipleship [*Nachfolge*][22] under the conditions of discrimination and persecution, by making them capable of resistance through theological education and spiritual meditation. Most of them had little prospect of being placed as pastors and being paid sufficiently so as to be able to start a family — if they did not submit to the state-controlled "church committees" [*Kirchenausschüsse*]. Resistance here did not first mean action, but rather strengthening of faith, theological insight, and personal readiness for enduring the already visible and yet-to-be expected disadvantages and oppressions. It was not necessary in this church training to refer explicitly to political questions. They were indirectly present everywhere. One is mistaken, then, if one thinks that this time of spiritual concentration in the Finkenwalde seminary was a time of political abstinence for Bonhoeffer. The worldview confrontations and the pressure of state mea-

---

21. Alfred Rosenberg, *Der Mythus des 20. Jahrhunderts* (München: 1930).

22. Cf. DBWE 4, *Discipleship* (Minneapolis: Fortress Press, 2001), the book Bonhoeffer wrote in Finkenwalde, first published in 1937.

sures were present daily. Together with his candidates, Bonhoeffer visited synods in order to influence their decisions effectively. In the years 1935-1938, no end was in sight for the extremely successful Hitler regime, a regime that itself acted in the perspective of a "Thousand-Year Reich," for the sake of which all rigors, misdeeds, and atrocities in the present seemed justified. When the preachers' seminary was closed by the Gestapo in 1937, a still less conspicuous and looser form of education was chosen for the candidates of the Confessing Church, the so-called collective pastorates, spread out over several parishes. Only in 1940 did the Gestapo put an end to this activity of Bonhoeffer's.

Dietrich Bonhoeffer's part in the Church Struggle with the Party and the state had, of course, to be fought through in conjunction with his professional partners, the "brothers" in the Confessing Church. But he had constant support in his family circle, a place where information was exchanged and a common judgment and will could be formed, regardless of how informally this took place. Our sources show that Hans von Dohnanyi, when he rejected the National Socialist racial policy in the ministry of justice, referred to the teaching of the Protestant church,[23] a partial example of common opinion-forming in this circle. Precisely because its members were active in different professional fields — Klaus Bonhoeffer and Rüdiger Schleicher in the Lufthansa and the aerospace ministry, Justus Delbrück in the economy, Friedrich Justus Perels as legal counsel to the Council of Brethren of the Church of the Old Prussian Union — the exchange of information was advantageous, and the common judgment-forming was of great significance for the shaping of every member's own attitude.

3. A further area of conflict was the ongoing injustice of the National Socialist state, in which Party comrades were constantly favored, while those who distanced themselves from the Party were ignored, and oppositionists as well as certain groups of persons were discriminated against and deprived of their rights. The unjust character of this state could not be changed, unless the regime would be brought to an end either by a coup or by a war. But as long as this regime lasted, mutual solidarity, help for the oppressed and disadvantaged, legal advice and spiritual strengthening were daily tasks for those who could not identify with

23. Cf. the Party expert opinion that is mentioned in note 32 below; more about this later on.

the rulers. Not only the charitable aspect of such behavior should be emphasized, but its political function should be noted as well. The Party strove systematically for the defamation, isolation, and social ostracism of the groups it intentionally oppressed. These groups were not only — albeit most significantly — the Jewish fellow citizens, but also Sintis and Romas ("gypsies"), homosexuals, of course Communists, Socialists, Social Democrats, and also pacifists, internationalists, Liberals, and generally everyone whose outlook [*Gesinnung*] was suspected of being disagreeable to National Socialism. Unadapted persons were reproached with their (earlier) convictions and attitudes, and thus were isolated psychologically and practically; for who would like to be seen in the company of an "incriminated" person who could at any time lose his professional position or even be arrested? Who did not know of the dangers imminent for everyone who was denounced by an informant? And informants were everywhere. Many lists of "enemies to the state" existed, most of them with a short "warrant" [*Steckbrief*] attached. A characteristic sample is that of Bonhoeffer's superior in the church who promoted his contacts with the ecumenical movement.

"Diestel, Max, born on November 11, 1872, in Tübingen.

"Prior to 1933: Vice-chairman of the World Alliance for Promoting International Friendship through the Churches. Was in a leading position in the League for Human Rights.

"Post 1933: Maintains good relationships with English church groups, is an exponent of the intentions of the Oxford Group, fanatical minister of the Confessing Church, does not recognize the Aryan paragraph for the church, and stands in sharp opposition to National Socialism, lives today as superintendent in Berlin-Lichterfelde."[24]

This is how Superintendent Diestel was registered in July, 1939, in the Reich Central Security Office [*Reichssicherheitshauptamt*] as an enemy to the state. Almost all of these characteristics were also true of Dietrich Bonhoeffer.

The fact that someone was branded an enemy to the state was often made known by Party organs in the area where the individual in question lived, so that this publicity would cause the person's isolation. By even helping such an individual who was arrested or taken into protective cus-

---

24. Taken from G. Buchstab, B. Kaff, and H.-D. Kleinmann, *Verfolgung und Widerstand* (Düsseldorf: 1986), 70.

tody, the helper incurred suspicion and danger. Those who nevertheless maintained solidarity with suspected enemies to the state, visiting with them and providing them with assistance, counteracted the policy to isolate these people and at least lessened the psychological pressure on them that was intended by the Party. But at the same time they attracted the attention of the Gestapo and the Party organs to themselves. Thus quite a few were sentenced because of helping Jews.

It is not possible to cover even approximately the cases of assistance for harassed people provided by the Bonhoeffer-Dohnanyi circle during the Third Reich. Dietrich Bonhoeffer could devote himself to this activity most intensely in London in 1933-1935. During this time, help was mostly needed by persons who sought admission into England, or emigration to other countries from there. Hans von Dohnanyi had extraordinary opportunities to help by virtue of his position in the Reich ministry of justice until the fall of 1938, and thereafter as "Special Leader" [*Sonderführer*] with the rank of major in the military counterintelligence office for abroad [*Ausland/Abwehr*] of Admiral Canaris. The sources show that Dohnanyi made thorough use of these opportunities, intensively and extensively. In reliance upon the justice minister's trust, he was active in the 1933 Reichstag Fire trial, as well as in clarifying unfounded suspicions raised in 1938 against the supreme commander of the army, Baron Werner von Fritsch, an intrigue contrived in Himmler's and Göring's circles. In the Fritsch crisis, Colonel Oster took favorable notice of Dohnanyi and decided to call him up to the counterintelligence in the event of an impending war. These spectacular cases were supplemented by hundreds of "smaller" individual cases. The members of the Bonhoeffer-Dohnanyi circle had personal connections to almost all oppositional sections of society and of the state, so that through these relationships the necessary aid could be brought about confidentially, undocumented in writing.

One instance of help reconstructible from the sources concerns the effort especially by Pastor Braune of Lobetal to end the euthanasia actions of 1940. Many people learned about this systematic removal of "worthless life" by hearsay, without being able to find more precise information. Braune, recommended by Dohnanyi, got access to the Reich minister of justice, who until then had been fully uninformed, and who had to confess himself unable to redress the situation. Assisted by Dohnanyi, Braune drew up a memoir of twelve pages, completed on July 9, 1940, which stated the actual facts and the absence of any legal basis for the extermination actions organized since October, 1939.[25] This memoir was written one year earlier than the sermons preached by Count Clemens August von Galen, Catholic Bishop in Münster, which would later become famous. Braune himself was taken into "protective custody" on August 12, 1940, and spent some time in a concentration camp. After Braune's memoir had been presented to the Reich Chancellery, Württemberg Regional Bishop Wurm sent a written protest to the minister of the interior. The result was that the euthanasia actions were officially discontinued, and "only" continued on a smaller scale in secret. Even these short remarks show that helping those deprived of protection and rights did have political implications, and the helper, as a rule, got into conflicts with the Party and the state.[26] But these conflicts forced the National Socialists either to disclose their true intentions, or, as in the example of the euthanasia actions, to officially break off measures that had been introduced — which seldom happened.

One example that shows the dangers of helping persecuted people, especially Jews, in the Third Reich is the story of the "Grüber office." Because churches under German-Christian leadership would not provide any special help for Jews or Christians of Jewish descent, and because the "intact regional churches" and church charities also held back, a group in the Confessing Church took the initiative. Superintendents Martin Albertz and Max Diestel, the legal counsel to the Confessing Church Friedrich Perels, pastors Braune (Lobetal), Maas (Heidelberg), and Grüber (Berlin) drew up in 1938 a memoir about the desperate need of non-Aryan Christians [*Not der nichtarischen Christen*]. Grüber was commissioned with the directorship of the help station that was established in the Berlin street *"An der Stechbahn."* Until 1940, the regime tacitly tolerated the "Grüber office" which — in cooperation with the Reich Association of Jews in Germany — especially assisted in emigration, irrespective of confession. Bonhoeffer used his connection with Bishop George Bell in England for the benefit of the help station; in one instance, forty-five blank visas were issued by the English Home Office. Grüber protested against persecutions of Jews which began after the conquering of Poland, was given a warning on December 19, 1940, and interned in the concentration camps Sachsenhausen and Dachau for two-and-one-half years. In February of 1941, the office was finally closed by the Gestapo. Of the approximately thirty staff and helpers

25. Chr.-R. Müller, *Diskriminierung* (above, note 5), 291-92.
26. Chr.-R. Müller (cf. previous note), 174ff. and 233ff.

who themselves were partially of Jewish descent, only three survived the time of the Third Reich.

Even disclosure of National Socialist measures and actions counted as a deed inimical to the state. It was sharply sentenced by the courts, mostly the special courts, according to the Malicious Practices Act of March, 1933, or similar laws and decrees. Nevertheless, the Confessing Church again and again found ways to make known what the public was not supposed to know, and thus to protect persecuted people to a certain degree. Parishioners and pastors arrested in the Church Struggle were included in the "intercession list" read in worship services and meetings. In the obsequies for victims of the euthanasia actions, biblical texts and appropriate allusions were chosen which indicated — as harmlessly as possible — that this life did not die a natural death. There were many possibilities to spread information indirectly, because the people who were members of the Confessing Church or oppositional groups, as a result of long years of practice, understood allusions that we today can hardly decipher.

The effort to help those oppressed by the National Socialist regime created a feeling of concord, solidarity, and mutual vicarious representation in opposition groups that was an important basis for existing in political dissidence. In the Bonhoeffer-Dohnanyi circle, this awareness of belonging together arose early, since, on the one hand, group members were conspicuous exponents of the Church Struggle, and, on the other hand, Gerhard and Sabine Leibholz had to suffer fully the measures for discrimination and ostracism of "the Jews," and were in danger. From the summer of 1933 on, Leibholz no longer could give his lecture courses in the faculty of law at the University of Göttingen. In 1938, he emigrated with his family to England. There he advised Bishop Bell, the fatherly friend of Dietrich Bonhoeffer, on questions of the German Church Struggle, the resistance, German peace plans for a time after Hitler, and other matters. Thus, his influence was considerable.[27]

In prison, each member of the group was dependent on both the steadfast and clever secrecy of all the others and on the aid without which a prisoner could barely survive and could not maintain even minimal communication to the outside world. The prisoners' respective testimonies had to be coordinated through clandestine notes [Kassiber] and encoded messages, lest the interrogators pit the one against the other. For those who

27. E.-A. Scharffenorth, *Bell* (above, note 9).

had to endure the spiritual burden of this situation and of impending death, unbroken trust in one another, and common faith, outlook upon life, and personal ethos were highly important.

The necessity to help so many innocent people in need in the years 1933-1945 — at personal cost and risk and in civil disobedience against many state regulations — was one of the basic marks that confirmed again and again the notoriously unjust character of the regime, and motivated people to resistance and eventually to actively planning an overthrow. But the path to reaching this decision was hard to travel. Even after having made it, the going was hard, and it led through many an ethical and spiritual dilemma.

IV. The Ethical Dilemma in Opposition and Resistance

Those who were caught up in the whirl of contemporary events cannot have seen as clearly and unambiguously the character of Hitler's regime, the ethical obligation to resist, and also many problem constellations, as the historically informed person sees in retrospect. It appears almost impossible to judge fairly, retrospectively, or even to understand decisions and behavior at that time. This applies to big decisions — like fatal failure to take responsibility — but also to small everyday actions, for example, entrance into the Party, or the minimal concession of joining the National Socialist Public Welfare, in order not to lose one's employment and the means for the bare existence of one's family. Some in the Bonhoeffer-Dohnanyi circle were quite rigorous in this respect. Hans von Dohnanyi, with his brilliant gifts, for example, renounced the career he could have counted on because he did not make the required concessions to the Party, and turned a cold shoulder on Heinrich Himmler's and Roland Freisler's wooing. And so, despite his generally acknowledged proficiency, he was still a senior government official in 1938, and could no longer be retained in the ministry of justice by the minister, who had relied on him in crucial questions.

Certainly, no one who held a position of responsibility in the Third Reich got around certain concessions, such as an ostentatious readiness to cooperate even with fully convinced National Socialists, or substantial detractions from having one's own good intentions realized. One was forced to make one's behavior look "affirmative to the state" [*staatsbejahend*] and to provide proof by acting accordingly in certain cases. This became harder the more sharply one realized that the regime was unjust, and the more clearly one saw the inhuman features of National Socialism. Then those who endeavored to be honest to themselves were more and more frequently assailed by the question, "Are you making yourself an accomplice to this system of violence, and thus guilty?"

To be sure, every position of responsibility offered opportunities to do what made sense, and to avert, impede, or perhaps even sabotage evil developments — already through merely remaining in one's professional place so that no "wildly committed Nazi" could come in. This was regarded by many as a justification for their behavior — and who might judge in retrospect that they were in the wrong? But such an attitude unavoidably entailed an objective complicity with the National Socialist regime. The consequence was that those who remained in their positions and did solid matter-of-fact non-ideological work in effect strengthened the regime. A widespread slogan recommended, "Endure in order to prevent the worse!" But rather than justifying cooperation with the National Socialists, it only pointed out a dilemma that for the most part could not be solved at that time. Dietrich Bonhoeffer questioned this slogan and asked whether consenting to an evil (partial complicity), with the purpose of avoiding the worse, would obscure the insight that it might be better in the long run if the worse would happen,[28] because the worse would expose the injustice of the regime unsparingly.

Whoever wanted to remain "decent" ("decency" was at that time a predominant moral term indicating the integrity and identity of a person) did not take part in certain activities and actions that were required in the wake of the National Socialist ideology, and observed limits. But no one got through without dissembling in some situations and among some people. Because of the ubiquitous informers, one had to stay "under cover" vis-à-vis anyone whom one did not know well and could not trust. The more oppositionally-minded one was, the more one had to dissemble, and awareness of the discrepancy between one's mental attitude and outward behavior became all the more painful. But whoever intended to resist, or even to be active in a coup d'état, was practically duty-bound to dissemble,

---

28. Cf. DBW 8, *Widerstand und Ergebung* (Gütersloh: 1998), 22 (*Letters and Papers from Prison*, 5), and DBWE 6, *Ethics* (Minneapolis: Fortress Press, 2005), 79-80: "They will easily consent to the bad, knowing full well that it is bad, in order to prevent the worse, and no longer be able to recognize that precisely the worse choice they wish to avoid may be the better one."

to speak deceptively, to camouflage — up to a limit set by oneself. This was necessary not only in prison or during interrogations, but also in the daily life in the Third Reich.

Much had to be kept secret by the churches as well. After 1934, the Confessing Church hardly ever took part in the customary addresses of loyalty to Hitler, which in itself was a telling omission. But the famous Barmen Confessing Synod on May 30 and 31, 1934, could not and would not risk to declare a theologically grounded solidarity with the Jews. A protest against the Aryan clause appeared improper, since the clause had shortly before been rescinded as not applying to the churches — only temporarily, which soon became obvious.[29] Neither was there an open declaration that not only the German-Christians, as a church party, but bodies of the Party and the state, illegitimately encroached upon church affairs, although everyone knew it. A reference to this encroachment would have made noticeable that the apparently only inner-church opposition was at the same time a political opposition. Such a statement was missing not only out of fear of the power of the state, but also because the majority at the Confessing Synod were subjectively unwilling to realize the political dimension of the church conflict, that is, they fell into self-deception or felt it necessary for tactical reasons to keep silent.

Oppositionals who, like Hans von Dohnanyi, held high civil service positions and actively participated in overthrow planning, were under a special necessity of dissembling. They could not avoid a considerable amount of cooperation with convinced National Socialists. Dohnanyi was deeply depressed by this plight. He repeatedly thought of changing over to a position in the economy, where, however, not all the difficulties would disappear. The decisive reason for Dohnanyi's remaining in the Reich ministry of justice was his relationship of trust with Minister Gürtner, a genuine national conservative, whom Dohnanyi, in personal and friendly conversations, reproached for adapting too much to the wielders of power. After the murders on the occasion of the so-called Röhm putsch on June 30, 1934, had been legalized, Dohnanyi called on the minister to resign. The minister took Dohnanyi into his confidence in many weighty matters, and this made it difficult for him to end his work in the ministry. Christine

---

29. Actually, the legal situation was confused. Only a law dated August 21, 1934, clarified that "the Aryan clause, in so far as it was included in the regional churches' laws, was again valid." Cf. *Junge Kirche*, 1934, 720-21 (citation from p. 721).

von Dohnanyi, who was informed of top-secret events in the resistance, and judged matters soberly, wrote in 1946 about the activity of her husband that "being able, on the one hand, to sabotage the National Socialist madness, and, on the other hand, to help by means of his power those who were harmed" had been regarded by him "as the only justification for a man of his mental attitude to occupy such a position in civil service."[30] Numerous letters of gratitude, contained in the literary legacy, from Jews and other persecuted persons testify that this help was very effective. Dohnanyi usually showed himself to be rather reserved and guarded, and also defensive through arrogance. Ministry Officer Dr. O. Riese reported on October 1, 1946, to have been astonished how "resolutely and intransigently" Senior Government Official von Dohnanyi, in the consultations about a National Socialist bill of criminal law, picked a fight with the "then-powerful Secretary of State Freisler."[31]

Dohnanyi's dissembling clearly had limits. Thanks to information from Lothar Gruchmann, Peter Möser found in the files of the Party Chancellery of the National Socialist German Workers' Party a fifty-five-page document dealing with Dohnanyi. Dated April 30, 1937, attached to the record sheet, there is a judgment by the director of the department group [*Fachschaftsgruppe*] of the ministry of justice named Friedrich, which begins with the following sentence, "Von Dohnanyi is a man with a very sharp mind, with admirable perceptiveness, great industriousness, dexterity in oral and written presentation, gifted in the art of handling superiors." The latter remark alludes to Dohnanyi's position of trust with the minister. Then follow negative judgments, culminating in the statement that Dohnanyi has "no appreciation for the Third Reich's racial legislation, to which he is inwardly opposed. Thus he has expressed the view that the racial attitude of National Socialism is impossible because it stands in contradiction to the Christian view of the Protestant church."[32] Few Protestant theologians openly spoke in this way; Dietrich Bonhoeffer, however, was among these. Dohnanyi obviously referred to views like those held by his brother-in-law, and saw them as representative for the church. He dared to assert such an oppositional stand in the ministry. One can therefore be

30. Dohnanyi legacy, folder 26, number 14, p. 4.

31. Dohnanyi legacy, folder 23, number 24.

32. Expert opinion by the *NS-Fachschaftsgruppenleiter des Reichsjustizministeriums* Friedrich, dated April 30, 1937, *Akte der Parteikanzlei der NSDAP*, IFZ, fiches volume 1 (1983) 101 18478.

quite sure that his limited occupational cooperation with the National Socialists did not arise out of opportunism or mere need of protection. In the long run, the minister was unable keep him in the ministry against the attacks from Party groups. Dohnanyi went to Leipzig in 1938 as Reich judicial official, and from there he was called up to the counterintelligence in 1939. Such a decided attitude to National Socialism meant a great risk for the entire family, and gave rise again and again to the question whether "it was worth it," or made sense in the light of the National Socialists' permanently established power. For a person greatly interested in maintaining one's own ethical integrity, the question whether it was worth the trouble certainly could not be of primary importance. After the shift from mere oppositional attitude to active overthrow planning, such a person had to keep up camouflage and outward dissembling consistently.

All oppositionals shared the basic problem of how far the unavoidable cooperation with the National Socialists was already a guilty complicity. An accomplice is one who takes part in a crime as an informed person [*Mitwisser*], an abettor, or an accessory. Those who considered the National Socialist regime to be criminal could not but regard any behavior fostering the regime or helping it to exist as complicity. To be sure, there were many activities that only very indirectly benefited the regime, and many possibilities to work against it under cover. Many resorted to the motto, "We are patriots, we foster the German state and the interests of our fatherland, not the interests of those who at present have usurped power." But in the unclear circumstances, the fostering of the one was entwined with the fostering of the other. So this was no real solution to the moral problem that came into play everywhere in daily life.

Resistance research today pays much attention to the problem of the old power elites' and the national conservative opposition's "entente" with the National Socialist movement. But the treatment of this problem must be very careful, and should in no way lead to sweeping generalizations concerning the "bourgeois" resistance. When the National Socialists had established their power everywhere in the state and in society, almost all Germans were forced to cooperate with more or less intensity. Only the military had then still a real chance to overthrow the regime, and Hitler did everything to bring the military under the command of those who were servile or at least not dangerous to him. The clarification and formation of the mental attitudes of the commanders in chief toward Hitler's regime of violence and toward the plans for a coup d'état depended on many factors which we cannot consider here. In the Bonhoeffer-Dohnanyi circle, the decision for the shift from opposition to active participation in overthrow plans came with Dohnanyi's (1939) and Dietrich Bonhoeffer's (1940) entrance into the counterintelligence. Being informed of and participating in the overthrow plans only sharpened the basic ethical problem. Dietrich Bonhoeffer reflected on this problem theologically, of course encoded, and yet still interpretable today.

V. Bonhoeffer's Theological Account of Existence in Resistance

Dietrich Bonhoeffer was not at the mercy of the Hitler regime without alternatives. Of his own free choice he returned to Germany from London, where he had been a parish minister, in the spring of 1935, called by the Council of Brethren of the Prussian Confessing Church to lead one of its new preachers' seminaries. The establishment of such seminaries had its only legal basis in the "emergency law" [*Notrecht*] of the Confessing Church. According to state law they were illegal.

Bonhoeffer returned to Germany a second time on his own initiative, after difficult struggles of conscience, in early July of 1939. Since he was determined to refuse military service in the event of war — which objection usually was followed by capital punishment — American friends who saw him in great danger offered him a position as pastor to refugees in New York. Leading men of the Confessing Church were happy to know him in a safe place; the objection to military service of one of their widely known theologians would have attracted too much attention. But soon after his arrival in the USA, Bonhoeffer realized that he had to go back before the outbreak of the war to "share the trials of this time with my people," since he would otherwise "have no right to participate in the reconstruction of Christian life in Germany after the war."[33] By his entrance into the military counterintelligence, the problem of objection to military service was avoided and active participation in the conspiracy was opened up.

Bonhoeffer contemplated his friends' and his own situation in sev-

---

33. Letter by Bonhoeffer, end of June, 1939, as recorded by Reinhold Niebuhr, p. 210 in DBW 15, *Illegale Theologenausbildung: Sammelvikariate 1937-1940* (Gütersloh: 1998). Cf. above, chapter 9, part I, C.

eral texts in which he is relentlessly frank with himself. The account "After Ten Years"[34] depicts a late stage of these reflections. It is an almost unique document — I found no parallel in resistance texts of which I know — of fundamental self-clarification within a small circle, highly personal and at the same time universal. It is encoded, because it could have fallen into the hands of the Security Service or the Gestapo. Bethge remarks in his Bonhoeffer biography that this piece of writing was given to Hans Oster, Hans von Dohnanyi, and Eberhard Bethge.[35] In the most intimate family circle around Karl Bonhoeffer, sections of this account were read aloud.

One might see this text as an occasional writing the literary genus of which is near that of diary entries. But what speaks against this is that Bonhoeffer writes of a "we," of a "group of like-minded people" who during the last ten years, since 1933, have had common experiences and won results in the field of what is human. Neither can this account be compared to a letter to close friends. We find information about personal experiences in the resistance situation mostly in letters. An excellent example are the letters which have been abstracted, commented on, and published in the Moltke biography.[36] But already in the fall of 1940 Bonhoeffer had written a manuscript for the *Ethics* he was planning, in which entire parts of the 1942 text appear word for word. The older manuscript has the heading "Ethics as Formation."[37] It was meant to be published in a book on theological ethics. This was not to be an academic textbook, but was to address the reality filled with concrete ethical problems which pressed upon that generation. The coincidence between the two texts shows that Bonhoeffer pondered over these thoughts for years. There is, however, no equivalent in the 1942 text to the second part of the 1940 text which concerns theological considerations on "how Christ may take form among us today and here" and what this would mean for Christian ethics.[38] In the

---

34. *"Nach zehn Jahren,"* an account rendered at the turn of the year 1942 to the year 1943, printed as a prologue to the letters and papers from Tegel prison, DBW 8, 19-39 (LPP, 1-17). Compare above, chapter 10.

35. P. 787 in Bethge, *Biography* (above, note 3).

36. Freya von Moltke, M. Balfour, J. Frisby, *Helmuth James von Moltke 1907-1945. Anwalt der Zukunft* (Stuttgart: 1975). Cf. also H. J. Von Moltke, *Briefe an Freya 1939-1945* (München: 1988).

37. DBWE 6, *Ethics,* 76-102, especially 77-80.

38. DBWE 6, 99 and 102 ("Here [in our world] we must risk making concrete judgments and decisions").

following, I will focus on the 1942 text, but will on occasion add clarifications from the 1940 text.

Presently, in Bonhoeffer's judgment, "evil's great masquerade" has swirled and twisted all the old ethical concepts. It is deeply perplexing that "evil appears in the form of light, of beneficence, of that which is historically necessary and socially just" — fully covered with a respectable mask. But actually, everything by which life was kept in order has begun to slide. There hardly ever was a generation that had so little firm ground under its feet. Now, "all alternatives in the realm of what at present is possible" seem "equally intolerable, contrary to life, and devoid of meaning."[39]

To bring about a meaningful alternative through a coup d'état thus did not seem to lie within the realm of the possible in 1942 — a realistic judgment at which Bonhoeffer, however, does not tarry. He rather sketches out the failure of six traditional types of ethical behavior in this situation. The man of reason hopes to be able to bridge the contrasts to some extent through compromise, but fails to recognize the present reality in its unreasonableness. He runs aground with resignation or falls helplessly captive to the stronger party. The ethical fanatic who wants to maintain his principles gets caught in insignificant details or in traps that are set for him. The man who primarily wants to keep his conscience clean must lie to himself, since each of the alternatives in the quandaries that demand decision would cause him a bad conscience. The bad conscience, however, would be healthier and stronger than the deceived conscience that has suppressed reality. Only to do one's duty seems safest, for then all responsibility lies with the one giving orders. But "The man of duty will in the end have to fulfill his duty even to the Devil."[40] The one who, in autonomous freedom, consents to the bad in order to prevent worse, fails to see that precisely the worse choice he wishes to avoid may be the better one. Finally, the one who only has his private virtue in view closes his eyes and shuts his mouth to the injustice around him.

Bonhoeffer draws a typology of failure here, not of the opportunists' but of the ethically striving and conscientious persons' failure. That all of them must so hopelessly fail shows the deep perversion of the existing reality. "It is the best, with all they are and can do, who thus go under."[41]

39. DBW 8, 20; LPP, 4.
40. DBW 8, 22; LPP, 5.
41. DBWE 6, 79-80.

Well-known men of those years who might be seen as the embodiment of the respective types could easily be named. Whoever studies the interrogation records of prosecutor Robert Kempner[42] and reads the self-justifications of those who were interrogated after 1945 will find, precisely with the more conscientious ones among them, confirmation of the inescapable dilemma that Bonhoeffer depicts: There was no way to remain free of guilt. Considering this typology, Bonhoeffer's guiding question is: Who stands fast? His answer: Only the responsible person who, for the sake of the necessary deed, is ready to sacrifice his moral integrity — reasonableness, loyalty to principles, uninjured conscience, the arbitrariness of freedom, unsullied virtuosity — well knowing that he, too, becomes guilty and dirties his hands. This person believes his authorization to renounce all this, in the interest of the responsible deed, to be the gift of Christian faith, a faith that allows the commitment to oneself of even and especially the ethical person to be disregarded. He stands fast who wills his life to be nothing other than "an answer to God's question and call."[43]

As informed [*Mitwisser*] about the overthrow plans that could not succeed without Hitler's death, Bonhoeffer and his friends necessarily had to take upon themselves the responsibility for this murder and, with it, the unavoidable deaths of others in Hitler's company. In the winter of 1939 to 1940, Hans Oster had informed the Dutch military attaché Sas several times of the date, which was postponed again and again, of the start of the German campaign across the Western border. He had done so aware of the fact that many of his companions would fall, because a warned enemy could fight much more successfully. His expectation had been that an unsuccessful offensive would bring Hitler's regime to a quick end, so that the sacrifice of millions of lives in a long war could be avoided. Bonhoeffer's conception of a free responsible deed concerned such kinds of actions done in resistance and conspiracy — so a deciphered reading of the text "After Ten Years" must state. Especially the conscientious persons felt bound by their oath to the Führer, by their normal patriotic duty in a war, and by the "God-guided" path of history that must not be arbitrarily interfered with. Bonhoeffer's intention in this text was to release people from these bonds that had become perverted in National Socialism. He there-

---

42. R. M. W. Kempner, *Das Dritte Reich im Kreuzverhör. Aus den Vernehmungsprotokollen des Anklägers* (Königsstein/Taunus and Düsseldorf: 1980).

43. DBW 8, 23; LPP, 5.

fore had to push ahead beyond the ethical dimension into the religious dimension. "Only today do the Germans begin to discover what free responsibility is. It rests in a God who demands the responsible deed freely ventured in faith, and promises forgiveness and consolation to the human being who through the deed becomes a sinner."[44] Such statements could not be found at that time in traditional texts on Christian ethics, which either did not have the reality in view that Bonhoeffer saw, or paid no attention to the unfathomable perversity of a reality in which an honorable officer, out of duty and conscience, must commit "treason," and in which those who helped persecuted people themselves risked ending up in a concentration camp.

Bonhoeffer continues the text by discussing a number of problems which have to do with the free responsible deed, often contrasted with its opposite. He attempts to explain the lack of civil courage, evident all over, as an outcome of German traditions. These included the moral contempt for the success of actions, a contempt that indicated a missing awareness of being responsible for the consequences of one's behavior. When bad means lead to success — and that was quite obviously the case with Hitler's regime from 1939 to 1942 — "this creates a problem," namely, that of the ethical evaluation of success. Resistance without success, the consciously heroic downfall — that wasn't the aim of Bonhoeffer and his friends. "The ultimate responsible question is not how I might heroically back out of the affair, but how a coming generation's life will go on."[45] The argument has a strictly theological background. In traditional religiosity, the soul flees from the world in order to seek shelter with God. Bonhoeffer, however, sees the human being standing before God not unrelated to the world, but together with his relationships within the world which he has realized in one way or another, that is, together with what he has done or failed to do for his fellow human beings or for the world around him. Co-responsibility for the course of history is imposed on everyone — in very different ways — by God, so that no one can be relieved of it. From this faith grows a "fruitful relation to history" that would not grow out of a religion of pure inwardness, an introverted religion of conscience, that was prevalent in much of Lutheranism at that time.

Bonhoeffer had surprising experiences with stupidity. It "is not es-

---

44. DBW 8, 24; LPP, 6.
45. DBW 8, 25; LPP, 7.

sentially an intellectual defect, but a human defect." He found that people allowed themselves to be stupefied by certain circumstances. "On closer examination, it appears that every strong external exhibition of power, be it political or religious, stupefies a large section of the people." "The power wielded by some needs the stupidity of the others." Does Bonhoeffer allude to the relationship of the German population to the Führer? Surely that as well. But a more specific interpretation is at least just as probable. Nothing caused more trouble for the conspiracy than the indecisiveness of the generals. People like Hans von Dohnanyi have spoken of them time and again with scorn. Bonhoeffer may have thought of an event that happened on November 5, 1939. Walter von Brauchitsch, commander in chief of the army — with overthrow plans in the background — went to the Führer in order to convince him that an offensive against France, England, Belgium, and Holland would militarily be all-too-dangerous. Brauchitsch returned from the audience as a broken and confused man, infected with his panic Franz Halder, the chief of the general staff, and demanded the incineration of all overthrow plans. From then on, he gave in to even the most hazardous of Hitler's plans. Stupidity develops, according to Bonhoeffer, when an "overwhelming impression of the exhibition of power" robs people of their "inner independence" so that they — more or less intentionally — refrain from "finding an authentic way of responding to the given circumstances of life." Having become "an instrument without a will, the stupid person is then capable of committing all evil, and at the same time not capable of recognizing that it is evil."[46] The men in the resistance knew that neither Brauchitsch nor any other of the generals had hindered Hitler's barbaric directives from becoming military commands before the start of the campaign of extermination against the Soviet Union. The military leadership and the general staff were so "stupefied" that in 1941 no preparations were made for the foreseeable winter war in Russia, and the frontline troops were pitiably left in the lurch. The authority for freely doing the responsible deed — independent of a command issued by the topmost commander who was legally in charge but obviously criminal — was no longer present at the top of the military leadership, and Bonhoeffer attempted to analyze this lack in the section on stupidity or folly.

Bonhoeffer wanted to expose the inevitable ethical dilemma that had to be faced by those who submitted to the Hitler regime and became its ac-

---

46. DBW 8, 27; LPP, 9.

complices, as well as by those who planned the violent overthrow. Both could not avoid incurring guilt, for the behavior of both would cost the lives of many. Removing Hitler was not possible without resorting to bad and deadly means. Bonhoeffer included himself and his friends in this diagnosis. Thus he ended his text with asking the question of one's own corruption. "We have been dumb (non-protesting) witnesses to evil deeds, we have learned the arts of cunning, dissembling and ambiguous speech, we, taught by experience, have become mistrustful of people, and often had to withhold from them the truth and the free word we owed them, we, through unbearable conflicts, were worn down, or perhaps have even become cynical — are we still useful?" "Will our inner strength to resist that which was forced upon us have remained strong enough, and will our honesty to ourselves have remained relentless enough to find our way back to the path of simplicity and straightness?"[47]

In no way did Bonhoeffer claim all that was right and good for the side of his friends. In order to acknowledge one's own entanglement in guilt one needed a freedom the source of which Bonhoeffer saw in faith — faith in God who calls for responsibility and promises forgiveness. One should certainly not salve one's own conscience but expose it to relentless examination. The resulting recognition of sin then had to be dealt with in a Christian way.

Of course it cannot be assumed that the other members of this circle shared Bonhoeffer's specifically theological thoughts in their entirety. Only Perels and, to a certain extent, Gerhard Leibholz, did some theological thinking in the sense of theoretical reflections along the lines of traditions of Christian teaching. Yet every conduct of life in a Christian sense is accompanied by intuitive thoughts which amount to an elementary "theological" meditation. This is indeed recognizable in statements of all the members of this circle, which will become evident later in our dealing with letters from prison.

Dietrich Bonhoeffer pushed forward into new dimensions of theological thinking with his ethics of responsibility. A discussion of this is beyond the task of the present study. It should be mentioned, however, that thoughts similar to Bonhoeffer's occur in other Christian resistance groups. Moltke wrote on August 26, 1941, when the public was still in a euphoria of victory because of military successes in the Soviet Union, "The

---

47. DBW 8, 38; LPP, 16-17.

news from the East is awful again. We apparently have very very high casualties. But that would still be bearable, if only our shoulders were not burdened with massive sacrifices of slaughtered bodies. Again and again, one hears of news that only twenty percent of the transported prisoners or Jews arrive, that hunger rules in the prison camps, that typhus and all other deficiency epidemics have broken out, that our own people collapse from exhaustion. What will happen when the whole population realizes that this war is lost, and indeed lost in quite a different way than the last one? — with a guilty bloodshed that can never be atoned for in our lifetime and will never be forgotten, and with a totally shattered economy? Will men rise up who are in a position to distill repentance and remorse from this punishment, and with that, little by little, new vitality?"[48]

The inevitability of being dragged into universal guilt moved broad groups of ethically sensitive Protestants to empathize deeply with the ethical dilemma of each stance, including that of the resistance. In one of the manuscripts for his *Ethics,* written after the great military victories in the West in 1940, Bonhoeffer formulated a confession of the church's guilt which reflects the reality in Germany at that time. One of the ten points of this confession is, "The church confesses that it has witnessed the arbitrary use of brutal force, the suffering in body and soul of countless innocent people, that it has witnessed oppression, hatred, and murder without raising its voice for the victims and without finding ways of rushing to help them. It has become guilty of the lives of the weakest and most defenseless brothers of Jesus Christ."[49] Whoever knows Bonhoeffer's terminology at that time, immediately thinks of the Jews.[50] His church's failure, because of its lack of authority and readiness to suffer, to accuse the "powers that be" [*Obrigkeit*] urged Bonhoeffer to participate himself, as a pastor of the Confessing Church, in active resistance, even if it would use violent means. "The church was mute when it should have cried out, because the blood of the innocent cried out to heaven."[51] Joining the resistance outside the church was necessary for Bonhoeffer since the church as a whole did not act according to its confession, but left the task of crying out in protest to

48. *Briefe an Freya* (above, note 36), 278.
49. DBWE 6, 139.
50. DBWE 6, 105 ("Because Jesus Christ was the promised Messiah of the Israelite-Jewish people, the line of our forebears reaches back before the appearance of Jesus Christ into the people of Israel").
51. DBWE 6, 138.

some boards of the Confessing Church and to some personalities — like, for example, Niemöller — and even isolated those who openly raised their voice. In the resistance Bonhoeffer, among other tasks, took responsibility as counselor in matters of conscience. The text "After Ten Years" shows what this entailed.

VI. The Significance of Ecumenism for Opposition and Resistance

In research on contemporary history, the "national conservative" resistance's plans for a postwar time after Hitler are severely criticized. Too much continuity with old plans for positioning Germany as a superpower — complete with a claim to have colonies — is found, an undiscriminating anticommunism is discovered, and the insight that the state and society need democratization is missed.

Bonhoeffer served the counterintelligence resistance group with his ecumenical connections. He helped to communicate with the incipient Ecumenical Council of Churches in Geneva, with church people abroad, generally speaking, and especially in England, and there most of all with Bishop Bell, who at that time had Gerhard Leibholz, the emigrant, as his advisor. In the churches of England and America, a reorganization of Europe after the war was widely discussed, and Bonhoeffer sometimes took part in this discussion. His views, while of course not typical of the counterintelligence resistance group, may yet be regarded as reflecting the Bonhoeffer-Dohnanyi circle's thoughts. The members of this circle could and had to take up convictions concerning international law and international understanding which they — in many aspects in agreement with Stresemann — had advocated prior to 1933. I will not deal here with the tasks assumed by Bonhoeffer, via the Ecumenical Council of Churches and with parallel efforts via the Vatican, which aimed at obtaining agreements from representatives of England about a peace treaty with a German government after an overthrow of Hitler's regime. Especially Dohnanyi deemed such agreements very important, in order to move the generals to action.

The English ecumenist William Paton had published in 1941 a booklet on *The Church and the New Order*. In Geneva, Visser 't Hooft, the key person in the ecumenical headquarters, together with Bonhoeffer, wrote an English manuscript on "The Church and the New Order in Europe" that was based on a short memoir of Bonhoeffer's reactions to Paton's booklet which he had just read. Visser 't Hooft officially presented his manuscript as reflections of "two Continental Christians from two nations which are on opposite sides in this war." Thus, the combined thoughts of a Dutchman, whose country had to endure the German occupation, and a German were — anonymously — made public.[52]

Bonhoeffer notes in his memoir that every worker-uprising in Germany would definitely be crushed by the SS with bloodshed. Only the military would be able to remove Hitler, but they — like the entirety of the opposition — were hampered by the English radio propaganda which insisted on the unilateral disarmament of Germany and did not take into account the political situation within Germany. This practically meant at that time that the other side was not willing to distinguish between Nazis and other Germans. Hitler's opponents on both sides were agreed that the state's omnipotence would without doubt be broken. In the Anglo-Saxon world, the omnipotence of the state was combated by appealing to the concepts of freedom and human rights; in Germany, it was combated because it effected "the arbitrary dissolution of all true bonds (family, friendship, homeland, people, powers that be, humankind, science, work, and so on)." These different ways of expressing a convergent intention could be explained historically. The concrete conclusions must be "complete removal of the National Socialist system, including, especially, the Gestapo," "reinstatement of the sovereignty of equal rights for all," "a press that serves the truth," and a free church. "The whole question is whether there will be a readiness in England and America to deal with a government that stands on this basis, even if, at first, it does not look democratic in the Anglo-Saxon sense of the word. Such a government could suddenly come into being. Much would depend on whether it could then count on the immediate support of the Allies."[53]

At first, not democratic? But how could a democracy possibly be created right away with a German population, the majority of whom were fascinated with Hitler after his great victories in the West, and recently in the Soviet Union! Democracy without a somewhat democratically in-

---

52. P. 541 in DBW 16, *Konspiration und Haft 1940-1945* (Gütersloh: 1996); the extant parts of Bonhoeffer's German memoir are on pp. 536-41; the English version is on pp. 541-49.
53. Pp. 539-41 in DBW 16.

clined population is, in itself, a contradiction. But the term "at first" [*zunächst*] indicates that, according to the will of those whose speaker Bonhoeffer was, democracy would be a concern in Germany in the long run.

Bonhoeffer also addressed another difficult problem, although the incomplete text fails to provide us with full clarity. Thus we have to complement it by Visser 't Hooft's manuscript. What is problematic are the future relations with the Bolshevik-governed Soviet Union that gave just as little consideration to civil and religious liberties as the Nazis, annexed the neighboring countries, and, in the German view, would become the real future threat after Hitler.

All German attempts to make the rulers in England understand more precisely the specific German problems in a time after Hitler, and to make clear that the resistance had a truly different outlook on peace, and not merely a moderate version of Nazi politics, were frustrated. The reasons cannot be discussed here. But one thing is certain: The forces pushing for Hitler's overthrow had to reach at least a minimal agreement with the Allies if they wanted to succeed, since otherwise the unavoidable collapse of the fronts after Hitler's removal would be seen by the German people as a "stab in the back" and as an irresponsible surrender to the enemies, and a new government would lose all popular support.

The Bonhoeffer-Dohnanyi circle had fundamental visions of a German state after Hitler. They wanted it to be a "secular order" that would keep within the limits of and submit to critique by the Ten Commandments,[54] a constitutional state without discrimination, an order that would not tolerate that "the poor were exploited and robbed, while the strong were enriched and corrupted."[55] There should be no unrestrained exploitation of labor. The contacts with leaders of labor unions and the workers' movement (Leber, Leuschner, Mierendorff, Noske, Ernst von Harnack, among others), mostly made and maintained for the circle by Klaus Bonhoeffer, were not a merely goal-driven alliance, but were based on fundamental convictions that arose, as Dietrich Bonhoeffer wrote, out of having been forced to experience matters in a perspective "from below."[56] How far this circle was in a position to translate its princi-

54. P. 539 in DBW 16.
55. DBWE 6, 140.
56. DBW 8, 38-39 in *"Nach zehn Jahren."*

ples into concrete politics cannot be judged at all, since there are no written "programs" in the sources.

VII. Resistance, Inner Conflicts, and Religious Views in Prison

Members of this circle were arrested in two batches that diverged greatly in time. The first arrests were, on April 5, 1943, those of Hans and Christine von Dohnanyi — Christine was released after some weeks because she skillfully presented herself as a simple housewife — Dietrich Bonhoeffer, who happened to be in Berlin, and Josef Müller, from the counterintelligence office in Munich, with his wife. Müller had engineered the Catholic contacts with England via the Vatican. In the cases of these prisoners, the ambitious and fanatical Senior Military Prosecutor Manfred Roeder, who earlier had substantially participated in bringing the members of the communist resistance group "Red Orchestra" [*Rote Kapelle*] to death, led the juridical inquiry on the charge of high treason and treason against the state.

The other batch of arrests happened after the unsuccessful coup d'état of July 20, 1944. At the beginning of August, Justus Delbrück, active in Canaris' staff since 1940, was arrested; on October 1, 1944, Klaus Bonhoeffer, chief syndic for Lufthansa; on October 3, 1944, Rüdiger Schleicher, as ministry officer, the director of the juridical department of the Reich aviation ministry until the summer of 1939, then honorary professor and director of the Institute for Aviation Law at the University of Berlin. The latter two were sentenced to death by Roland Freisler, president of the central People's Court, on February 2, 1945, and were executed by an SS commando on April 23, immediately before Berlin was captured by the Soviet army; along with them, Friedrich Justus Perels died, who had been arrested in the night of October 4 to 5, 1944, and been imprisoned at 3 Lehrter Street. Eberhard Bethge, who like Perels was a prisoner at 3 Lehrter Street, escaped execution, as did Delbrück, who nevertheless died at the end of October, 1945, as a prisoner of the Soviet army in the camp of Jamlitz. Hans Oster, arrested on July 21, 1944, was, like Dietrich Bonhoeffer, hanged in the Flossenbürg concentration camp on April 9, 1945; on the same day, Hans von Dohnanyi was killed in the Sachsenhausen concentration camp.

The decisive turning point, aside from July 20, 1944, was the discovery of the so-called Zossen files on September 22, 1944, by Gestapo Commissar Sonderegger. In Zossen, parts of Hans von Dohnanyi's documents fell into the hands of the investigation boards, for instance, a memoir from 1939 addressed to the generals and the X Report,[57] material enough to make the whole circle appear absolutely inimical to the Third Reich, a "conspiratorial kinship" [*Verschwörer-Sippschaft*] under the name of Bonhoeffer. By order of General Beck, the files had not been destroyed,[58] because Beck could not do without such prosecution material when an indictment against the criminal regime would be brought in, to prove that the resistance had already planned the overthrow at a time when the whole world still believed in Hitler's military victory.

Detention meant, above all, the continuation of resistance by other means and under completely different conditions. The interrogators tried to instigate the prisoners to incriminate each other. They alleged, for example, that the other prisoner had already confessed to this or that, had "betrayed everything," and that further denial was pointless. Since it was difficult to see through such allegations, especially when they on occasion were corroborated by interrogation protocols with forged signatures, they caused unrest among the accused, and a great deal of suspicion and alienation between their next of kin, whom the accused notified of the alleged facts. The unity within the Bonhoeffer family was not damaged through such manipulations and blackmail, yet contact with friends and informed persons [*Mitwisser*] surely was. Moreover, the interrogators threatened again and again that in case the accused would refuse to confess, measures would be taken against the relatives of the accused. The letter that Constantin von Dietze was able to smuggle out of prison[59] depicts many of the usual methods in the prison on Lehrter Street: the bluffing, the threats, the promise to spare the family in exchange for a confession, the whipping

---

57. This was the title of Joseph Müller's final report on his conversations in the Vatican that he had dictated to Christine von Dohnanyi to type. Cf. Bethge, *Biography*, 673, and in more detail H. C. Deutsch, *Verschwörung gegen den Krieg 1939-1940* (München: 1969), 304-24.

58. Cf. Christine von Dohnanyi's notes on *The Zossen Files* in Bethge, *Biography*, 935-41, especially 937-39.

59. [According to information obtained by E.-A. Scharffenorth from a telephone call with Gottfried von Dietze in Niedermoos on January 25, 1993, this was Constantin von Dietze's first secret message *(Kassiber)*, in stenography, directed "To my wife or my brother, as information for all of our friends and dear relatives," in which he described his prison experiences in detail; accessible in his legacy in the archives of the University of Freiburg.]

of prisoners into unconsciousness from which they were then forcibly awakened with gushes of cold water. The prisoners had, above all, to be careful not to reveal any names, in order to save the possibility of a conspiracy, or at least the lives of friends.

The military justice system, at the time of Dietrich Bonhoeffer and Hans von Dohnanyi's arrests on April 5, 1943, proceeded much more correctly, but the burdens were also extremely heavy. In the beginning, Dohnanyi was mainly depressed by regret that he had dragged his wife and Dietrich Bonhoeffer with him into the matter.[60] Dietrich was able to answer in a letter, "You must know that not one atom of reproach or bitterness is in me about that which has happened to you and me. Such things come from God, and from God alone, and I know myself to be of one mind with you and Christel that before Him there is only submission, perseverance, patience — and thankfulness. With that, all questions of 'why' are silenced, because they have found their answer."[61]

The prisoners' stubborn struggle for their lives and for the freedom of their families and friends cannot be described here. Instead, attention will be paid to some expressions of the faith of those who under the most extreme burden, and sometimes conscious of having to bid farewell, could say words that otherwise would hardly have passed their lips. These concern "religion" and its significance in detention.

Bonhoeffer's letter cited above that speaks of submission to God's will and of thankfulness betrays his conviction to be in God's hands, whatever might happen. Already in the account "After Ten Years" he had written, "I believe that God can and will make arise from everything, even from the worst evil, that which is good. For this, God needs human beings who let all things serve them for the best."[62] Eberhard and Renate Bethge have edited letters written by resistance members from the Bonhoeffer family circle written shortly before death. These letters allow deep insight into the experience, the hopes, the troubles, and the faith of the prisoners. Christine von Dohnanyi wrote on April 25, 1943, to her three almost-grown children, apparently with cheerful irony, about life in a cell, in the "clink," but added simultaneously admonitions and maxims. Then the letter turns completely serious. "Now, I want to say one more thing to you:

60. Letter of April 23, 1943, pp. 47-49 in DBW 8; LPP, 24.
61. Letter of May 5, p. 59 in DBW 8; LPP, 32.
62. P. 30 in DBW 8; LPP, 11. Cf. Romans 8:28.

carry no hatred in your hearts against the power that has done this to us. Do not embitter your young souls; for to do so avenges itself and takes from you the best thing there is, namely trust. We have not spoken much of religious things with each other. It is not given to everyone to speak of these things. But I want to say to you that I am so firmly convinced that all things serve for the best of those who love God, and our whole life has demonstrated this again and again, that I, in all my loneliness and anxiety about you all, never really was in despair even for one moment. You will certainly be surprised that I say this, of whom you surely have believed that I am farther removed from all that. With me, it is such that I must sit in prison, in order to express something like that, and maybe thus to comfort you that I do not suffer as much as you surely imagine. Read the saying that we wrote in your Bible, my little Barbara."[63]

Christine's statements show, in a very characteristic way, a reticent, outwardly reserved, and taciturn Protestantism that has as its support a specific trust in God. God allows all things to serve for the best of those who love him — in "After Ten Years" Dietrich Bonhoeffer wrote almost the same words which his elder sister Christine used. But such a conviction is not shown to the outside, and is expressed, if ever, only in an extreme situation.

Rüdiger Schleicher, who had probably most of all discussed and debated theological matters with the theologian in this circle, told about a worship service he had held on a Sunday in his cell, "indeed, if I may say so, it is God's own doing that one really comes to be perfectly quiet and above all things." Psalms 42 and 43 touched him — probably with the verses, "My soul thirsts after God. When will I come to look upon God's countenance?" and "May God provide justice for me, and lead my cause against the unholy people," and "What grieves you, O my soul, and why are you so unsettled within me?" — along with hymn book songs and words of consolation from Isaiah chapters 40 and following, but not so much the rather "contorted declarations" in the New Testament letters, or "dogmatic" reflections. "That which is solely essential in religion is the 'relationship to God,' if you want to put it that way: prayer and the attitude arising from this."[64]

Klaus Bonhoeffer wrote a long letter to his children on Easter 1945, in the conviction that he had to bid farewell. "The times of horror, destruc-

---

63. Eberhard and Renate Bethge (editors), *Letzte Briefe im Widerstand: Aus dem Kreis der Familie Bonhoeffer* (München: 1984), 67-68.

64. *Letzte Briefe* (previous note), 31-32.

tion, and death, in which you, dear children, grow up, impress the transitory nature of all earthly matters upon humankind; for all of the human being's splendor is as the flower of the grass . . . But here begins all wisdom and piety that turns from the transitory to the eternal. That is the blessing of this time."[65] Finally, he called on his children to make the world of the Bible their own.

On April 23, 1943, a Good Friday, Hans von Dohnanyi wrote from his cell, "I am often reading in the Bible now; it is the only book that does not let my thoughts stray again and again. This morning, Matthew 26–28, Luke 22–24, and Psalms 68 and 70. The strange divergencies of the two Gospels in the Passion story have never before struck me so. How much would I like to talk this over with you."[66]

Justus Delbrück wrote from the prison in Moabit, "If God wills it, he can say more through the death of a person than through his life."[67] Klaus Bonhoeffer thought about death in a similar way, and made friends with death as a "noble comrade," in contrast to the Devil as a stinking opportunist. Delbrück converted to the Catholic church in prison; Protestant ecclesiasticism appeared to be too dry and rational in its arguments. Without a doubt, he was "religious by nature," and immersed himself deeply in religious thoughts.

Friedrich Justus Perels was certainly the "most ecclesiastical" person in this circle, apart from the theologian Dietrich Bonhoeffer. In addition to the Bible, he meditated in prison on Thomas a Kempis' *De Imitatione Christi*, as Bonhoeffer had also done at the end of 1943. Perels' letters are filled with statements from the book, and are orientated toward the Passion and cross of Christ. "The entire life of Christ was a life of the cross and of agony, and you want to have nothing but quiet and joy?" Like other prisoners, he received Holy Communion in deep devotion.[68]

This selection of religious experience and probation in prison indicates, on the one hand, the distinctive individuality of the members of the Bonhoeffer-Dohnanyi circle; the Christian faith here had not taken on the form of a firm ideology, but, as expressed by Klaus Bonhoeffer, had to be made one's personal own. On the other hand, however, it shows that they

---

65. *Letzte Briefe*, 56.
66. P. 49 in DBW 8; LPP, 25.
67. *Letzte Briefe*, 93.
68. Cf. M. Schreiber, *Perels* (above, note 8), 216-19.

did have in common a piety which, while not closely connected to the church, was related to the Bible. This was a typically Protestant group, even up to the deficit in church affiliation, which caused Delbrück to convert. The trust that God will make all things serve those for their best who love God is not the only dominating characteristic; for this can also present itself as a rather secular optimism, as a general basic trust *(Grundvertrauen)* that suppresses the unresolved contradictions of the world and one's conscious advance toward imminent sufferings and death. Therefore the motive of trust must be completed and deepened in faith by the soul's turning from the all-too transitory to the eternal (Klaus Bonhoeffer), by the preparation for death in consciously following the path of Christ (Perels), by the meditation on the Passion story (Dohnanyi), by confirming the notion of the martyr's bearing witness — God "can say more through the death of a person than through their life" (Delbrück). Of course, the situation in a prison is not such that all aspects of faith will unfold, all the more since prisoners, in their written testimonies, had to be silent on many things, or to make matters seem wholly personal, and much has been lost.

In the framework of this study, the question to ask is whether there exists a clear relationship between Christian faith and the path toward joining the resistance, that is, whether and how far religion became a motive for resistance. At first glance, the prisoners appear to have been so occupied with the ordeal of interrogations and detention that only in connection with these did religion come into play, namely, in the process of and as strength for accepting and consenting to one's own fate, which was probably bound for death. The ethical or active aspect of Christian faith that traditionally was prominent in Protestantism, although it had become marginal in the theology of the 1920s, could hardly be called on in prison, unless it was needed in the endurance of threats and tortures so as to keep secret the names of friends and co-conspirators. However, the fact that the Party's and the state's continual violation of justice, the persecution of the churches, the racist ideology, the extermination of human lives (euthanasia, "final solution" to the Jewish question), and the aggressive intention to wage war were definitely stated in the interrogations as reasons for the objection to National Socialist rule,[69] shows that the members of this circle were motivated by a Christian outlook to view these features of National Socialism as contrary to the Ten Commandments, and thus contrary to

69. Cf. note 14 above.

God's will for humankind, as trespasses which made action in accordance with the Christian tradition of the *clausula Petri* necessary: "One must obey God more than man" (Acts 5:29).

During the two years of his imprisonment, Dietrich Bonhoeffer, like all other prisoners, had to wrestle with his personal fate. Until October 8, 1944, when he was taken to the Gestapo cellar on Prince Albrecht Street, his prison conditions in Tegel had been relatively fair. Because of that, he was able for a while to write much and to smuggle letters and papers out of the prison. In 1944, he concentrated on drafting new thoughts that seemingly were detached from the daily problems posed by National Socialism and resistance. Indirectly, however, he introduced his experiences so deeply into the theological fundaments that theology was changed in an astounding and even breathtaking manner. In a time when National Socialism had reached the peak of its barbarous actions of violence and extermination, Bonhoeffer, robbed of freedom and confined to a cell, dealt theologically with the ambivalent yet irreversible coming of age of humankind in the modern world, and asked who Christ can and must be for the human being in this situation. As a prisoner, he saw religious people in their need and weakness flee to God and ask for help. Is the people's need of help the crucial fundament of religion? Bonhoeffer saw that other people who were quite unfamiliar with religion were capable of coping in their own way with "the world" and with their fate. He deemed it inappropriate to "find fault with" [*madig machen*] the strength of people who in this sense were "mature" [*mündig*]. Instead, he asked how Christ addresses and claims human beings in their strength, "in the center" of their lives, human beings who know that they themselves must take their lives into their own hands and are responsible for their behavior. Civil religion tends to remain restricted to mere consolation of the human being who is weak, and teaches resignation to fate. If this aspect of religion is unilaterally developed, the human being will become estranged from feeling responsible, and the proclaimers of such a religion will be intent on exposing, above all, the human being's sinfulness and destitution. As a counterpoint to this, Bonhoeffer emphasized authorization through faith. Christian faith, as Luther had taught it, propels the human being into this-worldly responsibility, provoking and claiming human strength. Then, the human beings' primary concern is not their fate, suffering, or bliss, but what they have to venture in this world. This entails a new way of taking sufferings upon oneself, namely, the sufferings that arise from the mature person's responsible deed. The fact that people in the resistance were impressive examples of this is not mentioned in the prison texts. Counteracting the injustice in the world by struggling for and winning not one's own rights but the rights of others meant, theologically, partaking in God's suffering from the world. God loves justice, and sides with the cause of the poor and oppressed, to whom first of all God's promises are addressed — this is shown in the Sermon on the Mount and in many other biblical sayings, and is taught by the cross of Christ. Faith, as understood by Bonhoeffer now, propels into mature responsibility, and from there into suffering, and so to the side of Christ, and therein has all promise. But this is never experienced if a person does not venture to act responsibly. Whoever freely ventures the responsible deed must know that, in doing it, guilt cannot be avoided. But the doer may trust in God's promise that he wills the deed done for others, and forgives sins.

Bonhoeffer's theological outlines in prison are indeed, as Eberhard Bethge has stated,[70] a "new theology" for the future after Hitler. But they are just as much a precise meditation on the experiences of the resistance to the National Socialist rule of violence. Did Dietrich Bonhoeffer put into words what was intuitively alive in the piety of his friends? In any case, his conception of theology established the Protestant connection of faith and ethics, of desire for redemption and readiness for responsibility in a way that we otherwise hardly encounter in a theological text from the twentieth century. The ever-increasing dissemination of his writings, thoughts, and words in world Christianity suggests that many people, especially in situations of oppression, at least sense that Christian faith here confronts them in a way that deeply affects them.

The prison writings that were published by Eberhard Bethge in the posthumous book *Letters and Papers from Prison* brought to expression an aspect of Christian faith that Bonhoeffer, in prescience, had approached in earlier years without yet arriving at full clarity. The breakthrough required a new and deeper understanding of how God is at work in the world. God does not bring his omnipotence to bear on the world, but rather holds it back, thus giving room to the human being for responsible action. Instead of fascinating through the exhibition of power, God reveals his loving solidarity with the human beings through suffering, and so attracts them to himself. This theological reflection, relevant to the future, arose from pon-

---

70. Bethge, *Biography*, 856.

dering over past experiences in the resistance. Bonhoeffer, in the loneliness of the cell, tried to formulate theologically what had been experienced. The experiences that made this insight possible were those of his circle of family and friends, the common experiences of people who risked their lives in order to live up to their responsibility.

VIII. The Postwar Echo and Its Discords

Whoever believes that after the 1945 collapse the German resistance's being "in the right," as opposed to National Socialism, was acknowledged, is thoroughly mistaken. The resistance heritage was not taken up and developed, neither in the Federal Republic of Germany nor in the German Democratic Republic. On the one hand, the ideological option for the West was too abrupt, too tactical, and too complete to allow visions from the resistance to be put in practice. On the other hand, even the heritage of the left-wing resistance drowned in the antifascist ideology, initially defined by Stalinism. Memorial celebrations usually cover this up. Research that feels all-too-much bound either to Western categories of democracy or to Marxist-Leninist methods has trouble judging the resistance legacy to be potentially realizable. It is rather considered illusory and utopian — which it has indeed become through the postwar development, although it only *became* such.

We shall discuss here a narrower aspect, namely, the great difficulty of appropriately presenting the resistance heritage in the postwar situation. At first glance, the Bonhoeffer-Dohnanyi circle appears to be the least likely instance of such a difficulty. Thanks above all to Eberhard Bethge's work, Dietrich Bonhoeffer's thoughts and fate continue to influence people all over the world, and his person has almost become a symbol of the connection between the Church Struggle and the resistance. However, the friends who were by his side and surrounded him have either been all but forgotten, or else they have been depicted in a defamatory manner. For example, this happened to Hans von Dohnanyi in Count Thun-Hohenstein's book on *Der Verschwörer* (The Conspirator).[71] A considerable portion of

---

71. Romedio G. Graf von Thun-Hohenstein, *Der Verschwörer. General Oster und die Militäropposition* (Berlin: 1982), 247. In the later pocket edition (Deutscher Taschenbuch Verlag, 1984), the author dropped his harsh judgment regarding Dohnanyi.

the guilt of distorting the image of the resistance lies on the German justice system. How did that happen?

After 1945, many people claimed, in wishful thinking, to have fought in the resistance. They produced (self-)descriptions, (hero-)legends, and information. This confused the picture very quickly. Additional confusion was caused by an evil debt incurred in the last years of the Third Reich. Extortionary interrogations that sought to pit one prisoner against another had created suspicions, rebukes, mistrust, and rejection between the relatives of the resistance members who had become victims, and also among the survivors. In the chaotic early postwar years, these strained relations could not be cleared. For example, responsibility for the fact that the incriminating documents, which cost so many people their lives, could have been found in Zossen was, entirely unjustly, imputed to Hans von Dohnanyi. Christine von Dohnanyi tried to set this straight, until in the end she retreated with resigned despair into silence. In addition, only few authentic statements written by resistance members were extant — in a conspiracy, all written material is a great danger to the participants — whereas interrogation protocols from the Nazi justice system and its abettors existed in great quantities. These contain a large number of assertions by which the prisoners tried to protect themselves, which are not easily recognizable as consciously falsified "autobiographies" of those arrested, but, if they are taken as factually true statements, distort the conspirators' image.

The prisoners have mostly not survived, whereas those who had interrogated and sentenced them did survive. In the Federal Republic of Germany, a number of cases concerning the one-time prosecutors and judges were investigated by courts of inquiry without subsequent charge, and some of those persons were put on trial. Depositions of witnesses in these lawsuits are an indispensable but highly questionable basis for present research. Juridical inquiries in Lüneburg against Manfred Roeder, who had led the interrogations of Dohnanyi, Bonhoeffer, and Josef Müller, lasted for years. Fifteen volumes containing records of testimonies and other documents, and a 750-page-long sixteenth volume of files, the prosecutor's "final report" [*Schlußbericht*], accumulated. But then the inquiries against Roeder were ended, without trial in a court, by means of a "decree of closure" [*Abschlußverfügung*]. The sixteenth volume was declared "secret," and not handed over with the other files to the branch of the Lower Saxony [*Niedersachsen*] State Archives in Pattensen near Hanover, but was withheld from the branch for a long time.[72] The prosecutor's tendency to exonerate Roeder apparently struck even the Lower Saxony ministry of justice and the government as being too obvious. It is well known that there is a high degree of continuity between the personnel of the Nazi justice system and the postwar justice system.

The ordering and evaluation of the Dohnanyi literary legacy will make it possible to set straight the defamations. And that is necessary. Often enough a direct path leads from, for instance, Roeder's rebukes against the arrested Hans von Dohnanyi via the files of the postwar justice system to the monographs of historians. Today, more than forty years after the end of the war, the necessary research has not yet been done. This is evident also in the fact that research in neigboring fields, such as resistance research, Church Struggle research, research concerning the persecution of the Jews and anti-Semitism, research concerning National Socialism (including its justice system, and its euthanasia and compulsory sterilization actions), continues to be pursued with little mutual communication. It is thus especially important that in our project all of these fields of research come together, because each of them is indispensable to the study of the Bonhoeffer-Dohnanyi circle.

IX. Concluding Remarks

The Bonhoeffer-Dohnanyi circle cannot be included among the "national conservative" resistance. One might speak best of a republican Protestant group. Neither can the Kreisau group be labeled "national conservative." These two examples make it necessary to treat and characterize the so-called "bourgeois" resistance with more differentiation than has become customary.

Research methods also require critical revision. Structural-historical and socio-historical approaches rightly have their functions, but also have clear limits. Limits become especially apparent when a certain anthropology is linked up to a method. Whoever expects human beings to be essentially directed by power interests, and assumes that these interests will be awakened in them within groups and power elites who, on their part,

72. Only in May of 1987, after the prime minister had intervened, was this volume transferred to the archives. [Tödt had seen to it that this happened.]

struggle above all to retain their influence, will judge the motives for joining the resistance quite differently from a researcher who holds conscience and responsibility, sense of justice, and moral integrity to be real factors that can tip the scales in making decisions. Yet, whoever proceeds from the latter assumption — without negating the former absolutely — must show plausibly how religious, moral, and worldview attitudes took shape and produced effects. In order to be able to do so, a very differentiated analysis of the biographical genesis and the socialization of the concerned persons is necessary, as well as a critical screening of the arguments they give as reasons for or in justification of their behavior. Moral self-knowledge frequently deviates far from actual behavior; social existence is seldom congruous with subjective consciousness. This applies with full force to religious consciousness as well.

The Bonhoeffer-Dohnanyi circle deserves more detailed investigation for the sake of the cause for which they fought. Furthermore, in hardly any other case is as much source material available as for this circle, especially with regard to biographical and subjective issues — several large literary legacies, like those of Bonhoeffer, Dohnanyi, Perels. The archives contain information and documents that have not yet been made use of. And there is the good fortune that experiences were not only documented, but were also theoretically processed. This was done by the expert in political law Gerhard Leibholz — in his writings until 1933 in Germany, and from 1938 on in England — partially by Dohnanyi, Perels, and Klaus Bonhoeffer, and, in a singular manner, in Dietrich Bonhoeffer's theological works and other writings, which encompass more than ten thousand printed pages.

The treatise presented here thus cannot be understood as final, but rather as an introduction into the peculiarity and the significance of the Bonhoeffer-Dohnanyi circle. After the conclusion of the Heidelberg research project it will perhaps be possible to present a more comprehensive and more adequate study.[73]

---

73. [The *Zentralstudie* in which Tödt had planned to do this could not be written. Tödt died in 1991.]

The November Crimes of 1938 and
German Protestantism: Ideological
and Theological Presuppositions
for the Toleration of the Pogrom

1989

Fifty years after this brutal event, the victims must be remembered first. In
the second place, the deeds and those who did them come into view. I will
deal with them only as long as is necessary for the understanding of what
follows. Third, we must look at the group of those whose behavior was one
of the parameters of the pogrom, namely, the German population and the
public in the world at large. I choose from this group the German
Protestant church in 1938. Its role was passive, its attitude was primarily silence. This silence, and the scarcity of recognizable reactions, are the problem. Had a wave of public protests moved through German Protestantism,
had this objection caused others to join in, for instance, the Roman Catholic Church, then, perhaps, the extermination of European Jewry would not
have gone on as we must mourn it today.

I. The Pogrom and its Problems for the Party and the State

A. The Course of Action

On November 10, 1938 — actions began on November 9 around midnight
— ninety-one Jewish citizens were murdered, and many others were injured or ill-treated. One hundred ninety-one synagogues and innumerable
prayer rooms were laid waste, mostly by fire, along with almost all of the
Jewish cemeteries. Seven thousand five hundred shops were destroyed or

partially looted, uncounted apartments were smashed. Around midnight, the radio broadcast the news that the mass actions, arising out of the people's anger, had come to an end.[1]

These actions had been preceded by shots from the revolver of the young Jew Herschel Grünszpan that hit Ernst vom Rath, one of the secretaries at the German embassy in Paris. Although Grünszpan's parents and other Polish Jews had been deprived of any nationality by decisions of the Polish state, they had been chased, together with other comrades in suffering, over the German border and, at first, had not been allowed into the country by the Poles. In Paris, Herschel Grünszpan had received a postcard on which his sister had depicted the despondency of this deportation. Vom Rath died of his injuries on November 9 at 4:30 p.m. In clever stage-management, Hitler was notified of the death in the evening as he, at the traditional meeting with leaders and old guards of the National Socialist German Workers' Party, commemorated the 1923 "sacrificial" march to the Cenotaph in Munich. Hitler left the meeting at about 10:00 p.m., while Goebbels broke the news to the meeting and gave a speech that initiated action. He ordered the newspaper *Völkischer Beobachter* (the people's observer) to announce on November 12 that "The justified and understandable indignation of the German people at the cowardly Jewish assassination of a German diplomat in Paris was extensively vented last night. Actions of retribution against Jewish businesses and buildings happened in numerous cities and towns of the Reich." Goebbels was the only Nazi leader who did not conceal his role as the initiator of the pogrom. Hitler stayed covered up. However, all indications known today suggest that Goebbels acted in agreement with and commissioned by Hitler.

Goebbels' initiative evoked deeds of rivalry and imitation, especially by Göring and Reich Economy Minister Funk, Himmler, and Heydrich. Almost thirty thousand Jews were hauled off to concentration camps, where they had to lead a bare existence for some time under frightful conditions. Those whose emigration was guaranteed were preferentially released. This arrest cost more than one thousand lives, and severe injuries to health. The scope and consequences of this action were worse than those

---

1. Among the many recent treatises are in W. H. Pehle (editor), *Der Judenpogrom 1938. Von der 'Reichskristallnacht' zum Völkermord* (Frankfurt/Main: 1988); W. Benz, *Der Rückfall in die Barbarei. Bericht über den Pogrom*, 13ff.; and U. D. Adam, *Wie spontan war der Pogrom?* 74ff.

of the November pogrom itself, yet it was hardly noticed. On November 12, a special tax (contribution) of one billion Reichsmark was levied on the German Jews. The state confiscated the insurance sums for all damages. Measures were hastened to exclude the Jews from the economy, to take away their possessions, and to declass them socially into bitter poverty. Forced emigration, which was made very difficult, reached a peak. The ousting of the Jews from the public, and also from private social relations went rapidly ahead. The November pogrom was not a single event, but, through the Party organizations' activities in which the mob in the street participated, propelled a process that would also have happened in formally legal paths, only more slowly. In a thoroughness without example, the Jewish citizens were now disfranchised and segregated from the population, and it became still more risky to stay in contact with them.

B. The Legal "Coping" with the Pogrom in the Justice System of the Party and the State

The police and the justice system were completely surprised by the staging of the violent actions in the night of November 9 to 10.[2] Despite their rivalry with Goebbels, the initiator of the pogrom, Himmler and Heydrich, in charge of the German police, felt it necessary to issue a directive to all state police stations after midnight not to act against the destruction of the synagogues, businesses, and apartments, but to protect Jews with foreign citizenship and Aryans. Looters who did not act in the way the state wanted them to should be arrested and registered with the Berlin Gestapo (secret state police) headquarters.

Reich Justice Minister Gürtner first heard of anti-Jewish riots in Berlin after midnight. But soon the officials in the ministry had to realize that this — like the murders on June 30, 1934, on the occasion of the Röhm affair — was a violent and unlawful action initiated and organized in the topmost leadership circle that should appear, contrary to the truth, as a spontaneous reaction of the angered people. A central legal problem was that those who acted mostly under the order of their leaders, and were of the correct opinion that they acted in accord with the Führer's wish, were presumably widely

2. For the following see pp. 484-96 in L. Gruchmann, *Justiz im Dritten Reich 1933-1940. Anpassung und Unterwerfung in der Ära Gürtner* (München: 1988).

unaware of the unlawfulness of their actions. So the ministry, during November 10, issued instructions to the public prosecutors' offices for the treatment of criminal acts. Only plunder, receipt of stolen property, and selfishly motivated deeds should be prosecuted in court, and this only in case the state police approached the Public Prosecutor's Office. Law and justice were rescinded by the Reich ministry of justice, called to be the guardian of the constitutional rule of law. The ministry suffered a further loss of competence in that it now granted what it had up to now tried to avoid, namely, that the Gestapo and Party authorities decided, after their own preliminary inquiry, which cases should be handed to the prosecution at all.

The loss of competence for the state justice system became still greater when Göring, commissioned by Hitler with the regulation of all problems consequential on the actions, after the supreme Party court of the NSDAP and the Führer's deputy Rudolf Hess had intervened, decreed that the Party courts, together with the Gestapo, should decide whether proceedings should be handed to the justice system at all. Gürtner and the secretary of state Roland Freisler tried to explain the powerlessness and loss of competence of the established justice system euphemistically to their subordinates. But of course they could not hinder the sudden rise of the feeling of legal insecurity in the justice system as well as in the population. In the following months, records of the justice system indicated that the population, even in Party circles, condemned the violent actions. Records by diplomats from abroad confirmed this. For the judgment-forming in the churches, this further erosion of the constitutional rule of law was highly influential. Traditionally, the Protestant churches refrained from protest that intervened in affairs of the state. Their silence about the legal discrimination of the Jews through state measures could theologically be based on, and excused by, the strict distinction between spiritual and worldly power — the (neo-Lutheran) two-realms teaching. But they could not simply treat the law as merely a matter of the state. Law had to be understood as being supported and grounded in God's commandments. In this matter, the church had to speak.

C. Reactions from the German Population and from Other Countries

The secret records of the SS security service on the situation say almost nothing about the attitude of the population to the November pogrom.

Instead, they establish an increase of the destitute Jewish proletariat. At the end of the year of 1938, the number of those dependent on relief had by far exceeded the number of Jews who could live on their own means, or were even well-off.[3] Records within the justice system state that the population had scarcely approved of the violent actions, and in part had condemned them.[4] In January of 1939, the prosecuting attorneys general were informed by the Reich ministry of justice that critical remarks should not, as was customary, be prosecuted under the Malicious Practices Act of March 21, 1933, "if made in justified indignation," and not by a notorious slanderer. From some records it could be inferred that there was objection to violent actions, but that "the population would consent to . . . a legal proceeding against the Jews."[5]

The official version that the people's soul had vented its indignation on November 10 was accorded even less credibility abroad than domestically. Diplomatic and foreign records, and also the Sopade records of 1938,[6] report the rejection through the population. But the records do not distinguish between the dislike for violent actions combined with consent to other measures against the Jews, and the clear rejection of any segregation of the Jews from society. To state that "The latest massive resistance against the wielders of power in the Third Reich took place at the end of 1938"[7] is certainly an exaggeration.

The international public was vehemently enraged about the pogrom. But this did not help much. In July of 1938, thirty-two nations had discussed at a conference in Evian the emigration and immigration of German Jews. *The New York Herald Tribune* wrote on July 8, "Six hundred fifty thousand Jewish refugees in Evian rejected by all."[8] Hitler stated triumphantly that no one wanted to have the Jews. This fact could provoke new

---

3. See H. Boberach, *Meldungen aus dem Reich. Die geheimen Lageberichte des Sicherheitsdienstes der SS 1938-1945*, volume 2 (Herrsching: 1984), 21, and 221ff. The SS (*Schutzstaffel*) was the National Socialists' paramilitary organization.

4. See p. 494 in Gruchmann (above, note 2). Jochen Klepper noted similar observations in Berlin in his diary, pp. 674-75 in *Unter dem Schatten Deiner Flügel. Aus den Tagebüchern der Jahre 1932-1942* (pocket book, second edition; München 1983).

5. Gruchmann (above, note 2), 496 and 495 note 39.

6. *Deutschland-Berichte der Sozialdemokratischen Partei Deutschlands* (fifth year), new edition by K. Behnken (seventh edition; Frankfurt/Main: 1989), 1205-11. Sopade is short for So(cial Democratic) Pa(rty) of Germany.

7. Wilfried Mairgünther, *Reichskristallnacht* (Kiel: 1987), 166.

8. P. 31 in Mairgünther (see previous note).

considerations for how to resolve the Jewish question. The power centers of the Third Reich were not in agreement about a concrete solution. Joseph Goebbels' diary entries, beginning on November 12, 1938, mainly oppose, in a cynical and haughty tone, the "raging foreign press" with declarations of his own.[9]

II. The Conduct of the Protestant Church as Seen by the SS Security Service

The secret records of the Security Service strangely qualify today's criticisms and condemnations of the church's attitude toward the November pogrom. The record for 1938 and the record for first three months of 1939 begin with the following rubrics for hostile activities: Freemasonry, Jewry, political churches, (Marxism,) liberalism, and the rights movement.[10] The records report that the two great churches were rather disappointed about the peaceful settlement of the Sudeten crisis in Munich at the end of September. Earlier, in March, the annexation of Austria had given the "regional churches' confessional front" the opportunity "to prove their political trustworthiness." In these churches, the clergy had not gone as far as swearing an unconditional oath of allegiance, but had taken a solemn vow of loyalty "under explicit reference to the vow of ordination." Then the record states, "The radical confessional front, however, could not be moved to take such a step." It also remarks that in the region of Saxony thirty-six members of Martin Niemöller's Pastors' Emergency League had refused to swear the oath, despite being threatened by the German-Christian church leadership with dismissal from the ministry. The "treasonous" prayer liturgy which the Provisional Church Administration, under the leadership of the Confessing Church Councils of Brethren, had issued in the Sudeten crisis had moved the (Lutheran) "Confessing Church bishops" to distance themselves from the radical wing, so that the radical and the moderate confessional front had been separated. But the Lutheran regional bishop Marahrens had afterward corrected the declaration addressed to Church

---

9. The diaries of Goebbels were edited, on behalf of the Institute for Contemporary History and in connection with the Federal Archives, by H. Fröhlich, *Die Tagebücher von Joseph Goebbels. Sämtliche Fragmente* (München et al.: 1987). Part I (1924-1941), volume 3 contains the entries from January 1, 1937, to December 31, 1939.

10. Boberach (above, note 3), 8ff., 216ff. In 1939, the rubric *Marxism* is missing.

Affairs Minister Kerrl that the Provisional Church Administration's attitude was "treasonous to the state." With this correction, he had indicated "anew the spiritual and worldview connectedness between the radical (Provisional Church Administration) and the moderate (Lutheran Council) confessional front."[11] Also, all distancing from Karl Barth — who, in a letter of September 19, 1938, to Hromádka in Prague, had encouraged the Czechs to fight Hitler's troops[12] — was of little use to the German church leaders in the eyes of the Security Service. Barth, the Swiss, was regarded as the founder of the "confessional front." The Security Service was of the opinion that ecumenical world-council Protestantism, in its anti-German activities, closely collaborated with Catholic and Jewish personalities, especially in aid to the "Jews who were pursued by fascism and racism." Measures that had been taken against the churches in school and tax affairs would intensify the churches' needs, but new church activities had arisen in the intelligentsia. There had been little success when the National Socialist Teachers' Alliance had demanded of the teachers, "following the Jew action of November 9, 1938," to drop religious instruction.[13]

The records of the Security Service show how little the Protestant churches had won by all the homage addressed to the Führer, and all the assertions of adjustment and allegiance, and with what disdain these were dismissed. The Security Service presumed that in the fall of 1938 the attitude of all church groupings, the German-Christians excepted, toward the political successes of the National Socialist state was "on the whole negative." It presumed that they were only "outwardly reserved," meaning that at bottom they thought treasonously, and vowed loyalty only tactically. This was a grotesque misconception of the mentality of Protestant church leaders of the middle part of the church and the "confessional front," whose loyalty to the state was naïvely unbroken.

The Security Service now regarded the Jewish question, updated by the November pogrom, as the decisive question with which the churches as well as the Christian teachers of religion had to be confronted. In the record on the first quarter of 1939, the Church Leaders' Consultation in Godesberg on March 24 through 26, 1939, is treated in astounding detail.[14] The Godesberg

---

11. Boberach, 45 and 48.

12. Karl Barth, *Eine Schweizer Stimme 1938-1945* (Zollikon/Zürich: 1945), 58-59.

13. Boberach (above, note 3), 51.

14. See K. Meier, *Der evangelische Kirchenkampf,* volume 3 (Göttingen: 1984), 75ff.

Declaration had established, among other things, that "Christian faith is the unbridgeable opposite of Jewry." There had been plans of joining the Institute for Research into the Jewish Influence on the Religious Life of the German People. The German-Christian leadership of regional churches had already in February and March enacted laws that prohibited "the admission of Jews into the church, and ministerial service to Jews in church rooms and at burials of non-Aryan Protestant Christians." Faced with the "political successes of the Third Reich," "an unmistakable fear of the steadily increasing power of National Socialism could be perceived in the entire clergy." The radical "confessional front" was in financial need. Nevertheless, the prospects of an enforcement of the Godesberg Declaration were small. The following passage is especially informative: "The relations of the confessional front to Jewry were expressed time after time in occasional statements of ministers. For instance, a Protestant pastor admonished the congregation during the worship service 'to pray for the Christian brothers from the house of Israel.' The 'church aid station for non-Aryan Protestants' built up within the church is a further proof of the pro-Jewish position and attitude of the Confessing Church in the racial question. Although the [party newspaper] *Stürmer* [stormer] repeatedly pilloried Protestant ministers because of baptizing Jews, such ministerial services were not discontinued."[15]

These Security Service records establish that only the German-Christian national-church groups, together with some sympathizers represented in Godesberg, severed the bonds of loyalty with Jewry after the Jews had been ousted through the November pogrom. All other groupings in the Protestant churches were regarded by the Security Service as still siding with German Jewry, the victim of the pogrom. This promised a similar fate for "obstinate ones," especially for the "confessional front." Goebbels notes after the pogrom several times that the struggle between the state, the church, and Christianity cannot be avoided. He considered the earlier punishments and repressive measures to oust the churches from the public to be only a prelude.[16] The judgments of the Security Service are astounding

---

15. Boberach (above, note 3), 234-36. A *Hilfswerk für evangelische Juden* (aid for Protestant Jews), *"Büro Grüber,"* was founded in the first months after the November pogroms. H. Ludwig, *Die Opfer unter dem Rad verbinden. Vor- und Entstehungsgeschichte, Arbeit und Mitarbeiter des "Büro Pfarrer Grüber"* (typescript, dissertation B2, Humboldt University, Berlin, 1988).

16. Goebbels' diary entries (above, note 9) of December 3, 1938, and January 31, February 12, December 29, 1939.

because they rather sharply contrast with the picture of the Protestant churches' failure and lack of profile in 1938 that today is drawn by contemporary history including church history. Obviously, the Security Service noticed a colorless middle church less than the high-profile critical statements by preachers and church governing bodies of determined parts of the Confessing Church.

III. The Spectrum of Protestant Reactions to the Pogrom at the End of 1938

A. National-Church Consequences

The national-church attitude of regarding Christian faith as the unbridgeable opposite of Jewry was an old pattern, impressed on the minds anew by Adolf Schlatter in the 1936 brochure "*Wird der Jude über uns siegen*" (will the Jew win the victory over us).[17] Theological and church statements mentioned race in this context only in passing, and not in connection with racial anti-Semitism. It was possible to remain in the tradition of religious anti-Judaism, and yield room to the National Socialist pressure through keeping religious distance from the Jews. This calculation did not work out for baptized Christians of Jewish descent. In the regional churches of Thuringia, Saxony, Mecklenburg, Anhalt, and Lübeck, clear conditions were established by a legislation of segregation. For example, on November 30, 1938, twenty days after the pogrom, the Thuringia regional church council decreed that "ministerial service to non-Aryans naturally is out of the question."[18] This severed every bond of community with Jewish fellow citizens and fellow Christians. The ideological and practical pressure on the churches had achieved its next goal. However, juridical opposition arose in the official gazettes of the Lutheran Council and the German Protestant Church against announcing such laws and decrees as legally valid.

17. Compare, for instance, W. Halfmann, *Die Kirche und der Jude* (21st to 30th thousand printing; Breklum: 1937). Halfmann, who after 1945 became regional bishop of Holstein, was a leading spokesman of the Confessing Church. His 1937 text is even more sharply anti-Judaistic than Schlatter's brochure. On Schlatter, see M. Smid, *Deutscher Protestantismus und Judentum 1932/1933* (München: 1990), especially 256-59.

18. See W. Gerlach, *Als die Zeugen schwiegen* (when the witnesses were silent). *Bekennende Kirche und die Juden* (Berlin: 1987), 298.

Was it the alleged opposition between Jewry and Christianity — that is, Christian anti-Judaism — or simply the anti-Semitic concept of race that was decisive for the national-church statements and measures excluding, from 1939 on, non-Aryan parishioners from the church? In negotiations in 1939 with the Church Leaders' Conference that did not consist of German-Christians, Reich Church Affairs Minister Kerrl tried to push them to ever-sharper formulations — and, in the end, got himself a majority refusal.[19] But the regional church leaders from Hanover, Brunswick, and Hesse-Cassel finally nevertheless assented to Kerrl's so-to-speak two-step formulation — first, racially anti-Semitic, then, religiously anti-Judaistic. "The National Socialist worldview relentlessly combats the political and intellectual influence of the Jewish race on our national life. In obedience to the divine order of creation, the Protestant church affirms the responsibility for maintaining the purity of our nation's way of life. Moreover, there exists no sharper opposition than that between the message of Jesus Christ and the Jewish religion of legalism and expectation of a political messiah."[20] As soon as racial anti-Semitism comes into play, even baptism will not help the Jew to enter the community of the faithful. The National Socialist and national-church conviction was that racial descent was an unavoidable determination. The middle part of the church differered from this conviction. If those belonging to the middle wanted to be loyal to their confession, in spite of all anti-Jewish attitudes, they had to maintain church community with the "racially foreign" Christians, and had to say no to the consequences of racial anti-Semitism (not in the state but) in the church. After baptism, Jewish descent was no longer relevant, and the reference to an opposition between the message of Jesus and the Jewish religion was no longer valid.

19. Kerrl's endeavors reaped disdainful criticism throughout from leading National Socialists, such as Alfred Rosenberg and Joseph Goebbels. Goebbels noted in his diary (p. 544 in Fröhlich, see above, note 9) on December 8, 1938, "Kerrl does nothing but stupid things again. Talks nonsense about a new Protestant synod. He has a rare talent to stir up again things as soon as they have quieted down. The Führer commands him to stop. We will now first of all resolve the Jewish question."

20. P. 37 in K. Meier, *Kirche und Judentum. Die Haltung der evangelischen Kirche zur Judenpolitik des Dritten Reiches* (Göttingen: 1968).

B. Regional Bishop Wurm as a
Representative of the Middle Church

The middle part of the church did nevertheless think and act in anti-Jewish patterns. This appears most forcefully and painfully in the letter written by Bishop Wurm on December 6, 1938, to the same Reich justice minister who had not been in the position to counter the pogrom by means of the public prosecution and the police. Wurm did not send a protest to Gürtner but "some thoughts on the present internal situation in Germany" springing from "a Christian and German conscience's need," submitted to the minister as the one who was "called to be the guardian of the law and of the notion of justice in our fatherland." The concluding request is that all be done which "serves the reestablishment of the authority of the law and the sense of justice." Wurm did not directly intercede for the persecuted Jewish citizens — for whom he felt personal compassion — but petitioned for avoiding unjust methods when anti-Jewish measures were taken. Such methods would mean, according to Wurm, a transgression of God's commandments that was bound to be avenged sooner or later. "In view of our people, we intercessorily, admonishingly, and warningly lift up our hands, even when we know that because of this we are labelled servants of the Jews and threatened with measures similar to those applied to the Jews."[21]

Here, a fear was openly stated that after the pogrom was rampant among Protestants. There was reason for fear, as is evident from the Security Service records. Those who were objective allies of the Jews because they could not completely disassociate themselves from them, were destined to meet a similar fate to that of the Jews. But there was much which, in the bishop's own view, separated him together with a large number of consciously Protestant contemporaries from "the Jews." Wurm explained in his letter to Gürtner, "I do not deny the state with a single word the right to combat Jewry as a dangerous element. From my youth on, I have considered the judgment of men such as Heinrich Treitschke and Adolf Stoecker that Jewry has a disintegrating effect in the religious, moral, literary, economic, and political fields to be true."[22] Wurm regarded Jewry as

21. Pp. 116-18 in G. Schäfer, *Von der Reichskirche zur Evangelischen Kirche in Deutschland 1938-1945*, volume 6 of *Die Evangelische Landeskirche in Württemberg und der Nationalsozialismus. Eine Dokumentation zum Kirchenkampf* (Stuttgart: 1986).

22. P. 116 in Schäfer (above, previous note).

an enemy, as a disintegrating force. Is he, through this enmity to Jews that was widely harbored in the Protestant milieu, a racial anti-Semite as well? In the opinion of Stoecker, whom Wurm adduced as his example, being a Jew came to an end in baptism.[23] An enmity that includes the baptized co-Christian of Jewish descent is impossible here. Precisely this is the point of contention with racial anti-Semitism, and marks the line of separation from it.

In his letter, Wurm does not give anti-Judaistic reasons for the enmity to Jews. That is, he does not refer to the contrast between Christian faith and Jewish religion, although he is also moved by such thoughts. Instead, a third factor comes into play: the alleged disintegrating effect of Jewry "in the religious, moral, literary, economic, and political fields" — and this is crucial. Later, we must look more closely into this third factor besides racial anti-Semitism and Christian anti-Judaism.

Wurm is concerned about justice in Germany and about the state. He fears that God's punishment will visit the nation that transgresses God's commandments. Therefore — not out of solidarity with the Jewish co-citizens — he has to write to the Reich justice minister. My impression is that Wurm speaks representatively for majorities in German Protestantism around 1938[24] — notwithstanding the fact that many individual Protestants rendered help, care, and compassion to many individual Jews. But the individual is not "Jewry," not "the synagogue," and not "the Jew." Individual help could well thrive under the cover of public silence. But the church, except for several courageous preachers, seemed almost silent. Wurm's letter was a nearly private letter, not public, although the fact that the bishop had written a letter to the Reich justice minister was mentioned in the Württemberg church.[25]

A similar or even worse case was Hanns Lilje's report on a trip to America that was meant to be forwarded via Bishop Heckel in the Church Foreign Office to the Reich Church Affairs Minister. The summons to take

23. See W. Jochmann, *Stoecker als nationalkonservativer Politiker und antisemitischer Agitator*, in G. Brakelmann, M. Greschat, and W. Jochmann, *Protestantismus und Politik* (Hamburg: 1982), 123ff., especially 148-61.

24. Compare J. Thierfelder, *"Es lag wie ein Bann über uns." Landesbischof Theophil Wurm und die nationalsozialistische Judenverfolgung*, in *Blätter für württembergische Kirchengeschichte*, volume 88 (1988), 446-64.

25. Circular issued by the Württemberg High Church Council on December 6, 1938, Schäfer (above, note 21), 116.

a stand in patriotic solidarity against Jewish atrocity propaganda abroad, especially in the United States of America, had influenced the statements of Protestant church leaders on the "Jewish question" as early as February and March of 1933. Much of what followed had been predetermined by this start. Lilje continued in this line. In 1938 he, as a virtuoso on the instrument of church political diplomacy, described the stubborn and skillful management of American protest assemblies against the November pogrom by Jewish groups. "The religious question was always pushed into the foreground. They did not want to see the racial question as such." The American Lutheran churches had stayed completely away. For this reticence in the face of the pressure of public opinion, "high personal courage" had been needed.[26]

The religious question in the foreground? Did Hanns Lilje not see that in 1938, for the first time since the beginning of modernity, and moreover throughout the Reich, brutal force had invaded the sphere of the Jewish religion, what had until then been the protected sphere of belief and practice of religious liberty? Two hundred synagogues and perhaps even more cemeteries destroyed!

C. Attitudes in the Radical Confessing Church

Should the radical Confessing Church, under the leadership of the councils of brethren, have spoken publicly on the pogrom? The Security Service records give information as to why this was almost impossible. There were punishments because of the prayer liturgy issued by the Provisional Church Administration, compulsions to maintain a distance from Karl Barth's letter to Hromádka, reproaches of state treason, and splits in the leadership groups under the continuous and almost intolerable pressure. Individuals did speak representatively. Pastor Julius von Jan immediately addressed the events in his *Busstag* (penitence day) sermon, six days after the pogrom. A crime had happened in Paris. The death of the victim was mourned. "But who would have thought that this one crime in Paris

---

26. Pp. 245-46 in Gerlach (above, note 18). Lilje emphasized the Lutheran churches' distanced attitude toward Jewry and said what the Reich church affairs ministry wanted to hear, namely, that the racial question was crucial, and more decisive than the religious question. This was hardly in accordance with his knowledge and conviction.

should result in so many crimes in Germany?" "Passions have been unleashed, God's commandments disregarded, houses of God that were sacred to others have been burned down *unpunished,* the property of strangers has been either stolen or destroyed, men who faithfully served our German nation and consciously fulfilled their duty have been thrown into concentration camps, simply because they belonged to another race!"[27] Nine days later, Julius von Jan was beaten up by a crowd, taken into protective custody, sentenced under the 1933 Malicious Practices Act and section 130a of the penal code to one year and four months imprisonment, and was finally expelled from Württemberg.[28] Bishop Wurm in his memoirs speaks of the depressing preparations for the proclamation of the Word of God on *Busstag,* November 16. "We lived as if under a ban. It was as if one's mouth had been closed by some unseen force." And then, "Pastor von Jan had to undergo penance for a very sharp phrase in his sermon."[29]

A decree by the Württemberg High Church Council in Stuttgart sent to the deans' offices, which, significantly, was titled (not "Acts of Terrorism against Jews" but) "Acts of Terrorism against Parsonages" — such actions also happened after November 9 — stated with regard to the preaching and fate of von Jan, and to the abusive label of "servants to Jews" attached to pastors, that the church, even when faced by this method of defamation, must not refrain from preaching in the sense of Micah 6:8.[30] Nevertheless, "it stands to reason that the servant of the church in thus preaching must avoid everything that amounts to an inadmissible criticism of concrete political processes." "If a pastor, however, in the view of the state or the church, gives occasion to justified complaints, then the boards of prosecution of criminal cases and the controlling body of the church are authorized to call the per-

27. Meier (above, note 20), 108-9.

28. Schäfer (above, note 21), 120ff.

29. Wurm, *Erinnerungen aus meinem Leben* (second edition, Stuttgart: 1953), 150-51. After 1945 Wurm deplored "the frightful excesses," and the fact that "a man of such spiritual greatness as Adolf Stoecker should first have unleashed this movement against Jewry." He also says, "However, justice demands that we also speak of the arrogance which the Jewish literati practiced in the press, and of the devastating effects which Jewish usury has in the country." Thierfelder (above, note 24), 448. In 1943, Wurm very courageously signed alone an intervention by the Church Leaders' Conference to be submitted to the Reich government in view of the "ever more acute campaign against the Jews" (p. 170 in *Erinnerungen*). Bishop Marahrens could not decide on signing along with Wurm.

30. "He has shown you, O man, what is good. And what does the Lord require of you? To act justly, love mercy, and walk humbly with your God."

son concerned to account. The indignation of the church-community against lynch-justice and acts of terrorism, as they were described above, is fully justified."[31] An awkward comment on von Jan's sermon, twenty-five days after the pogrom. And yet it reminds one of Bishop Meiser's warning on September 13, 1935, to the Provisional Church Administration against "guiltily self-made martyrdom."[32] The church board apparently considered the truthful mention of the indisputable facts of November 10 to be an offense against the commandment of obedience to the authorities. One did not dare to question whether those who had plotted the pogrom, or had protected it through the state police, were still the authorities. Was von Jan's suffering really "guiltily self-made martyrdom"? More recent research concludes that it is obsolete to use the category of martyrdom in serious descriptions of the resistance against Hitler.[33]

Not a few pastors preferred the method of encrypted speech after the pogrom. It seemed harmless, but those who had ears heard what was necessary. A model is Helmut Gollwitzer's *Busstag* sermon in Berlin-Dahlem, certainly overheard by the Gestapo.[34] We do not know how many pastors preached in this way with more or less skill, how many of them overcame the traditional dislike of Jewry as they fulfilled the task of proclaiming the Word of God. A resolution of the *Kirchentag* (church assembly) in Berlin-Steglitz on December 10 through 12, 1938, stated that "Others have preached in earnest God's Ten Commandments even in view of the offense against the Jews, and were therefore persecuted." Wilhelm Jannasch tried in vain to make the *Kirchentag* say a clear word to the congregations against the persecution of the Jews.[35] There was a widespread awareness within the Confessing Church of a shared responsibility for the oppressed Jews, and not merely for the Jewish Christians. But then the question arose of whether a Christian who saw through the cynicism of the National Socialist regime of injustice was entitled or obligated to knowingly deliver himself up to the bloodhounds.

This question must be asked today also of those who wonder, re-

---

31. Schäfer (above, note 21), 115-16.

32. W. Niemöller, *Die Evangelische Kirche im Dritten Reich. Handbuch des Kirchenkampfes* (Bielefeld: 1956), 49.

33. See M. Broszat, *Resistenz und Widerstand*, in Broszat et al. (editors), *Bayern in der NS-Zeit. Herrschaft und Gesellschaft im Konflikt*, volume 4 (München: 1981), 693.

34. See *Evangelische Theologie*, volume 11 (1951-1952), 145-51.

35. Gerlach (above, note 18), 246-47.

proachfully, why there was no public protest by Dietrich Bonhoeffer against the pogrom. Such a protest would fit in with the wish to stylize Bonhoeffer into a hero. At the end of 1938, he was the director of so-called collective pastorates, an illegal sequel to the Finkenwalde preachers' seminary that had been closed by the Gestapo in 1937. In addition, he was informed of plans for a coup d'état in the fall of 1938, and as such should on no account attract the attention of the Gestapo. Bonhoeffer's biographer Eberhard Bethge records how the pogrom is referred to in the intimacy of a circular letter to the one-time Finkenwalde candidates.[36] In 1938, he certainly wanted for Germany that the rule of law and Christian obedience to the commandments be renewed. But he wanted more, namely, a reflection in theology and church on the inextricable connection in salvation history between Israel, Jewry, and the church, and he accepted the specific path of Jewry with God. In the *Ethics* manuscript "Heritage and Decay," composed in 1940 and 1941, he stated, "Driving out the Jew(s) from the West must result in driving out Christ with them, for Jesus Christ was a Jew."[37]

After the pogrom, not merely a protest against the persecution of the Jews was called for, but also the overcoming of the fundamental disapproval of Jewry in the Protestant milieu and churches. Karl Barth, who had been on difficult terms with the concrete Jewry in Germany, took a big step forward in his Wipking lecture on December 5, 1938. Barth points out, in a section about anti-Semitism on principle, that what had begun in the pogrom, namely, the physical extermination of the people of Israel, the burning of the synagogues, the deprecation of the Jewish Bible as abhorrent, was an attempt to destroy the church at its roots. "What would we be, what are we without Israel? Whoever rejects and persecutes the Jews, rejects and persecutes him who died for the sins of the Jews, and only then and thereby for our sins as well."[38] These words mark the approach to a new theology on Is-

---

36. Eberhard Bethge, *Biography* (English 2000), 607: "In the Bible that Bonhoeffer used for prayer and meditation he underlined the verse in Psalm 74, 'they burned all the meeting places of God in the land,' and wrote beside it 'November 9, 1938.' . . . In the newsletter sent to the Finkenwaldians a few days later he wrote, 'I have lately been thinking a great deal about Psalm 74, Zachariah 2:8, and Romans 9:4-5 and 11:11-15. That leads us to very earnest prayer.'"

37. DBWE 6, *Ethics* (Minneapolis: Fortress Press, 2005), 105.

38. P. 90 in Barth (above, note 12). The lecture is on pp. 69-107. Barth, who had taught in Germany since 1921, was dismissed in 1935 by the Prussian Minister of Culture, and then taught at the university of Basel.

rael. Protestant tradition preponderantly defined the gospel message in opposition to the legalism and cult statutes characteristic of Jewry. The
Protestant image was emphasized while the connection between Jewry and
ancient Israel was abandoned. Barth and Bonhoeffer resolutely turned away
from this course in 1938. They accepted the tension between the Jewish rejection of Jesus Christ and the christological concentration of their own
biblical theology. In the history of God's election, the community of Israel,
Jewry, and the church, exist in this tension. Bonhoeffer stated concisely in
his *Ethics,* "The Jew keeps open the question of Christ."[39] This was accompanied by Barth's most sharply worded thesis, confirmed by contemporary
research, "National Socialism's living and contriving, however, is absorbed
in anti-Semitism."[40] Barth feared that the Confessing Church had not yet
grasped this, even in view of a sign as unmistakable as the pogrom.

The spectrum of Protestant reactions to the November pogrom is
broad, and the boundaries are not fixed. Radical racial anti-Semitism, with
its violent measures, was decisively rejected by the majority. Reactions var-
ied, also in the different lines of the Confessing Church, regarding the
questions of whether a formally lawful segregation of the Jews on the
grounds of legal regulations could be approved of, and whether aid measures for Jews in their need were a matter of love of one's neighbor in general, or a matter of a special solidarity with Israel in salvation history. The
community with Christians of Jewish descent was the real test for the
scope of racial anti-Semitic thought that could not permit such a community. Even where community with 'baptized Jews' was maintained in principle, the practical realization of it was hindered by certain inhibitions
within the church, which in part can only be explained as arising from a
deep-rooted aversion to Jewry. So it happened, especially after 1938, that
Jewish citizens of Christian faith felt, and had to feel, more deserted than
the non-confessional or the Mosaic Jews, who now were thrown back on
the Jewish community, and found more succor there than the churches
gave to their Jewish members who remained separated from the Jewish
community.[41] It therefore is necessary to comprehend more precisely by
what roots the Protestant disapproval of the Jews was fed.

39. DBWE 6 (above, note 37), 105.
40. P. 90 in Barth (above, note 12). Compare E. Jäckel, *Hitlers Weltanschauung* (second edition, Stuttgart: 1983), 55-78, especially 64.
41. Compare Ludwig (above, note 15).

IV. Ideological Presuppositions of the Church's Behavior

I have defined the terms *anti-Semitic* and *anti-Semitism* in a narrower sense than is customary today. I consciously spoke of 'racial anti-Semitism,' and distinguished it from other conceptions and mentalities of enmity to the Jews. There are good reasons for doing so. Doubtless, it must be clarified whether, for example, the attitudes of bishops Wurm, Meiser, and Marahrens, or of the theologians Asmussen and Künneth, bore the stamp of racial anti-Semitism, and how they were influenced by traditional elements of Christian anti-Judaism. Such attempts at clarification for the sake of contemporary history are not assisted by theological lexicography. The articles on anti-Semitism in TRE[42] and on anti-Judaism and anti-Semitism in EKL[43] simply do not discuss the time from 1935 to 1945. The standard work on basic historical concepts, *Geschichtliche Grundbegriffe*, yields more. Its article on anti-Semitism, for example, records the directive issued by the Reich Propaganda Ministry in 1935 to replace the word *anti-Semitic* in principle with the word *anti-Jewish*[44] so that motivations which were not restricted to racial anti-Semitism could also be mobilized. But even here, no clear categories are found for differentiated research into the whole spectrum of disapproval of Jews in Germany between 1933 and 1945.

My terminological proposal is to distinguish between three categories: 1. racial anti-Semitism, 2. a moral socio-cultural kind of enmity to Jews, and 3. Christian traditional religious anti-Judaism. I do not consider here the problem of anti-Zionism.

42. Short for *Theologische Realenzyklopädie*. The article is in volume III (1978). Section 5 on the time between the two World Wars [*Zwischenkriegszeit*] summarily refers to the path toward the "final solution" [*Endlösung*] of the "Jewish question," and is immediately followed by section 6 on the development since 1945 (p. 161). The argument that National Socialism only adopted the anti-Semitic ideology, without adding to it, is no acceptable explanation for this gap. Nipperdey and Rürup (pp. 150-51 in the article on anti-Semitism in *Geschichtliche Grundbegriffe*, volume I, see below, note 44) rightly establish that Hitler consistently systematized the theory of anti-Semitism, elevated it to the level of an alleged science, and based it solely on a theory of race that required him to focus the "struggle" (Hitler's *Kampf*) not merely on the restriction of Jewish influence but on the elimination of the Jews.

43. Short for *Evangelisches Kirchenlexikon*. The article is on pp. 74-181 in volume I (1986).

44. P. 151 in volume I of *Geschichtliche Grundbegriffe. Historisches Lexikon zur politischen Sprache in Deutschland*, 129-53.

A. Racial Anti-Semitism

Semitism is a term that was coined in the late eighteenth century in the discussion about ancient history and the history of religion. Anti-Semitism, as a concept, existed since 1879, immediately interlocked with racial anti-Semitism, that is, connected with the myth of the high value of the Aryan race, and the low value of the Semitic race, represented by the Jews, that produces disintegration. The prehistory of this ideology begins with the work of Count Gobineau on the inequality and the unequal worth of the races.[45] Gobineau reactionarily opposes modern developments that were set in motion by the ideas of 1789, and puts on the behavior of an antidemocratic aristocrat. By the way, similar ideas of enmity to Jews were harbored by Richard Wagner and the young Nietzsche, and later by Wagner's stepson Houston Stewart Chamberlain.[46] The journalist Wilhelm Marr, the historian Heinrich von Treitschke, in the line of the German-National People's Party, and — despite the anti-Christian connotations of the teaching on race — the court-chaplain Adolf Stoecker, attacked "the Jews" in the 1879-1880 Berlin Anti-Semitism Dispute.[47] Their most important opponent was Theodor Mommsen, a representative of the liberals, whose 1880 text *Auch ein Wort über unser Judentum* (another word on our Jewry) was reprinted three times. The inhuman character of racial anti-Semitism was aggravated when, toward the end of the nineteenth century, social Darwinistic notions of natural selection and the survival of the fittest were added to it. The spokesperson was the French Count Georges Vacher de Lapouge, who published *Les sélections sociales* in 1896. Here, the Jews were regarded as spongers, parasites, and destroyers of the uniquely culturally creative Aryan race. It was said that progressive racial interbreeding

45. J. A. Comte de Gobineau, *Essai sur l'inégalité des races humaines,* 4 volumes (Paris: 1853-1855).

46. Compare J. Schmidt, *Die Geschichte des Geniegedankens in der deutschen Literatur, Philosophie und Politik 1750-1945,* volume 2 (Darmstadt: 1985), 215-37, 141 and following pages. A problem not yet solved is how far and in what sense Nietzsche rose above racial anti-Semitism, in his disdainful pronouncements on anti-Semitism. In any case, ideologies of enmity to Jews preferably referred to Nietzsche. The lexicon article by Rürup and Nipperdey deals with this problem as little as does the valuable book by R. Rürup, *Emanzipation und Antisemitismus. Studien zur Judenfrage der bürgerlichen Gesellschaft* (Frankfurt: 1987).

47. Compare W. Boehlich (editor), *Der Berliner Antisemitismusstreit* (Frankfurt/ Main: 1965). No texts by Stoecker are printed in this volume.

could only be prevented by the extermination of the Jewish race. In complicated ways, these conceptions entered the National Socialist ideology and came to constitute its core. Anti-Semitism, then, is an anti-modernistic ideology, stamped by teachings on race, with a characteristic history of its own and a virulent dynamic, but not — contrary to today's usage of the term — a designation appropriate for all kinds of enmity to Jews.[48]

B. Christian-Religious Anti-Judaism

The history of Christian — and then also Protestant — anti-Judaism is much older. Its roots reach back into the New Testament. The Lutheran Reformation, especially Luther himself, added new motifs.[49] The fate of the Jewish people — its being rejectable and having to suffer — is seen as the consequence of the rejection of Jesus Christ as the Messiah and his execution that was blamed on the Jews. Since the middle of the nineteenth century, historical critical Bible exegesis and history of religion research depict the Jewish religion in the post-prophetic period, or since the appearance of Jesus Christ, as a deformed and rigid religion of legalism, as the sum of everything Jesus is said to have fought. The most militant anti-Judaism comes about when churches and Christians understand themselves to be co-executors in the alleged course of salvation history of God's judgment on the Jewish people, or when they incite the "powers-that-be" against "the Jews," and approve of the state's harsh exceptional regulations against Jews. In the 1920s and early 1930s, Christian anti-Judaism is present as a tradition and mood in the Protestant churches, but hardly aggressive in itself. So it can be understood that Wurm's letter of December, 1938, to

48. Rürup, *Emanzipation* (above, note 46), 81ff., competently analyzes, with methods of social history, the societal and cultural conditions for the rise of (racial) anti-Semitism after one hundred years of continuous, even if in no way completely, successful emancipation of Jews. Significantly, this rise happened after the German founders' crash [*Gründerkrach*] of 1873 and during the worldwide economic depression of that time. Rürup's description is complemented by Jochen Schmidt who treats, with methods of literary history, the ideology of (racial) anti-Semitism in its specific history and dynamic, in volume 2 of *Die Geschichte des Geniegedankens* (see above, note 46), 129ff., 194ff. and 213ff. Boehlich (see above, note 47) presents key texts especially from the two years of 1879 and 1880, in which the catchword *anti-Semitism* was coined and rapidly spread, by Heinrich von Treitschke, Heinrich Graetz, Hermann Cohen, H. Nauhd (alias of H. G. Nordmann), Theodor Mommsen, and others.

49. Compare the article *Antisemitismus* in TRE, volume III (see above, note 42), 145ff.

Reich Justice Minister Gürtner contains no religious anti-Judaistic arguments. People of Jewish descent who have been baptized are regarded even in anti-Judaistic thinking in the churches as being free from the burden of a divine judgment, happening in history, on the Jewish people. This is the decisive distinction from racial anti-Semitism. The latter regards people as being inevitably determined by their racial descent, which no behavior on their part can change. In the 1920s, the churches lived, without much public strife, at a distance from the synagogue that was a religious community fully recognized by the state in the Weimar Republic. Mission among Jews took place in hiddenness. The question only is how far the National Socialists and the German Christians could mobilize the latent religious anti-Judaistic traditions and harness them for their intentions. To those who did not adhere to Christian anti-Judaism, and fully acknowledged the spiritual 'inward' community with Christians of Jewish descent through baptism, a two-realms teaching in neo-Lutheran deformation still offered a way not to practice an "outward" civil community with them, since this was prohibited by the National Socialist regime, and was frequently avenged by sanctions against "friends of the Jews." Then, they gladly pleaded that the church and the Christians must not seize the arm of the secular authorities to hinder their actions. The disdain for the Jewish religion which was seen as "antiquated," "finished," and "disinherited" through Christianity often found its secular continuation in the disdain for the Jews as a minority with stubbornly maintained strange customs and culture, and different social behavior.

C. Moral Socio-cultural Enmity to Jews

In the Protestantism of the 1920s and 1930s, another syndrome, or a third factor, is at work, and stronger than racial anti-Semitism and religious anti-Judaism. It can roughly be termed socio-cultural enmity to Jews. For its characterization, I again quote from Bishop Wurm's letter to Gürtner after the pogrom of November 9 to 10, 1938, the statement about the "disintegrating effect in the religious, moral, literary, economic, and political fields" that Wurm, from his youth on, had considered to be a true judgment by men such as Heinrich Treitschke and Adolf Stoecker.[50]

---

50. Schäfer, 116. Compare the minutes of the conversation with Reich Governor Murr

Religious disintegration — but certainly less through pious synagogue Jews, who kept themselves apart from society as a whole, the decay
of which is mourned here — occurred especially through secularized
modern Jews. For almost a century, numerous Jews were found among
atheists, socialist freethinkers, and other critics of Christianity.

Moral disintegration: If a homogenous Christian morality, averse to
all pluralism, of the German people, or even a Christian state, was presup-
posed, then secularized Jews who did not regard morality marked by
Christianity as an indispensable basis for a people's life and for the existence of a state must appear to be helpers in the dissolution of such bonds.
This stood out in the literary field, in newspapers, films, and in the theater,
where the proportion of people of Jewish descent was especially high.

Economically: Already Marx, and many others after him, had denounced the Jewish spirit as the quintessence of modern capitalistic development. The big Jewish department stores that were ruining the smaller
businesses, and factual and alleged Jewish war and inflation profits, demonstrated to the middle-class citizenry [*Bürgertum*] the decline of old economic conditions, and aroused envy.

Politically: Since the nineteenth century, disproportionately many
and remarkable Jewish personalities were often among the leaders of
socialist-revolutionary and republican-democratic parties. After the Anti-
Semitism Dispute in Berlin in 1879, and after the founding of the Weimar
Republic in 1919, the freethinking progressive party, and later Naumann's
German Democratic Party, was denounced by the political right wing as a
"party of Jews." All of this was bound to be regarded as particularly disintegrating by adherents of a theology of nationalism which Paul Althaus
had programmatically proclaimed at the Königsberg *Kirchentag* in 1927.
This was a theology in which Christian bonds and nationalistic bonds
were closely united,[51] and so effectively, that Karl Barth made the struggle
against natural theology the center of his activity in the 1930s. When German defeats and political misdevelopments were considered to be results
of the disappearance or loosening of tight bonds, a scapegoat could be
pointedly discovered in the modernistic section of Jewry — of course less

on July 31, 1938, according to which Wurm defended the preaching of the Old Testament,
questioned the compatibility of the National Socialist worldview with Christianity, and yet
criticized the process of assimilation of the Jews.

51. See Paul Althaus, *Kirche und Volkstum. Der völkische Wille im Lichte des Evange-
liums* (Gütersloh: 1928).

so in the middle-class conservative section. The latter section included many of the so-called "good" Jews who were assimilated in a German-National sense, who counted themselves predominantly among the Western Jews (the Sephardim), and often enough objected to the immigration of Eastern Jews.

This moral socio-cultural enmity to Jews, which was shared by many theologians and church people who were oriented toward nationalism, appears to be, on closer analysis, the main factor in the disapproval of the Jews, and in their abandonment without protest by the Protestant churches around 1938.

D. The Synergy of the Attitudes of Enmity to Jews

Racial anti-Semitism, Protestant religious anti-Judaism, and socio-cultural enmity to Jews were certainly not unrelated to each other. Even if their motivations differed sharply, and they never became one, an interplay could happen that was especially dangerous after 1933. Wurm showed himself to be neither a racial anti-Semite, nor a fervent religious anti-Judaist, but harbored socio-cultural enmity to Jews. He wished that the Jewish influence be dammed, but, in terror, addressed the Reich justice minister in the letter of 1938 because — as he wrote later — of the "frightful excesses of racial anti-Semitism against the Jewish people, and also against many good German fellow citizens."[52] In 1933, and in the following years, it had obviously not been clear to him that socio-cultural enmity to Jews and religious anti-Judaism would dangerously reduce inhibitions and weaken the resistance to brutal racial anti-Semitism.

All three manners of disapproval of the Jews evidently seek their segregation. But they differ about the means and the severity of it. Racial anti-Semites tend toward the expulsion and extermination of all Jews. Christian anti-Judaists want full community only with those citizens of Jewish descent who accept baptism, and lean toward requiring or approving of harsh measures to be taken by the state against all others. Socio-cultural enmity to Jews strives for the restriction of the strong influence of Jews on nationalhood, politics, economy, culture, morality, and the public, which could not be attained without legal and administrative discrimination.

52. Thierfelder, 448.

To be a German and, at the same time a self-conscious Jew, was rendered impossible by all three attitudes. They led, at least, to a refusal of resolute solidarity with the persecuted Jews, even if, for the sake of justice in Germany, all unjust measures of persecution were rejected. Above all, the wide proliferation of the theology of nationhood, with its anti-Jewish implications, created a climate in which it was impossible for the Protestant churches to oppose the November pogrom and undergo the wrath of Hitler's party and increased repressive measures by the state.

V. Responsibility and Guilt

After the undisguised pogrom of 1938, every Protestant in Germany could become aware of being burdened with guilt through not standing up for the persecuted Jews. Everyone knew Jesus' parable of the good Samaritan, Luke 10:30-37, about the failure of those who are called to be helpers, and the help given by the religiously despised stranger to the victim of the robbers. But many factors hindered the rise of an awareness of guilt. How strong these factors were can be approximately gathered from watching how slowly and with how much difficulty guilt was acknowledged after 1945.[53] Even now, contemporaries of the events, and also many of those who were born afterward, still avoid acknowledging guilt. This makes us see that the church's silence cannot be explained by the fear of the regime's persecution measures alone. Certainly, in 1938, the pressure exerted on all who, in the eyes of the regime, showed themselves to be "servants to Jews" or "treasonous to the state" was great, and in fact endangered life and limb. But when, in 1945, the pressure had disappeared, in no way did an awareness of guilt because of their omission to help arise with elemental impact among Protestants. So we must look into the other factors that continue to have effect.

In 1941, after Hitler's overwhelming victory in France that yielded predominance on the continent, Dietrich Bonhoeffer wrote a confession of the church's guilt that clearly relates to the events of 1938. "The church confesses that it has witnessed the arbitrary use of brutal force, the suffering in body and soul of countless innocent people, that it has witnessed oppression, hatred, and murder, without raising its voice for the victims

53. Compare below, chapter 13.

and without finding ways of rushing to help them. It has become guilty of the lives of the weakest and most defenseless brothers of Jesus Christ"[54] — that is, of the Jews. This is the confession of guilt of a concerned participant who does not overlook his own part in the silence of the church, even when, in 1938, his obligations had made it necessary for him to take upon himself the guilt of non-protest. The background of his confession of guilt is theological recognition of the indissoluble solidarity with Israel and the Jews, as well as the "co-responsibility for the course of history" which cannot be refused.[55]

When research into contemporary history tries to come to terms with the events of 1938, it cannot simply repeat the confession of guilt of a participant, or recommend its direct adoption. The question of the church's responsibility and guilt is posed differently from a temporal distance. We must arrive in a different way at an awareness of guilt which has consequences for those who live today, namely, via historical analysis. Otherwise, if we would affirm at large the guilt of that time's generation, a guilt we only grasp as a cliché, we would think much too lightly.

Might perhaps the analytical differentiation by means of the three categories that I have suggested — socio-cultural enmity to Jews, Christian anti-Judaism, and racial anti-Semitism — not only yield a more precise insight into the motives of the omissions, but make the guilty behavior of the church and the Christians in the situation at that time look harmless? The opposite ought to be the case. When insight into the train of events and into the motives as well as the attitudes of the participants grows, their responsibility and their guilty failure can be grasped more precisely, and the consequences can be seen more clearly.

Where a racial anti-Semitic mentality reigned in the church, that is, among fanatical German Christians and German-National church members, where, correspondingly, community with parishioners of Jewish descent was refused on principle, people excluded themselves from the church of Jesus Christ. Here occurred the irresponsible adoption of a misanthropic ideology, the falsification of church teaching and theology, and the pseudo-religious encouragement of the regime to proceed on its path toward the violent expulsion of the Jewish co-citizens — behavior burdened with guilt.

54. DBWE 6, 139.
55. *Nach zehn Jahren*, 25; LPP 7; Bonhoeffer's account in December of 1942, in DBW 8.

Christian anti-Judaism, as it was effective in the 1930s, believed it was supported by New Testament statements on and against "the Jews," and also by ancient church traditions. This is different from the racial anti-Semites who were strangers to the Bible. The belief that the Jewish people had to bear God's punishment or a curse was hardly interpreted as a warning that concerned the Christians. Instead, this belief favored the society's anti-Judaistic mood, and abolished inhibitions that stood in the way of racial anti-Semitism. To this was added the one-sidedly negative, distorted, and unrealistic perception of the Jewish religion in the nineteenth and twentieth centuries that, through the Christian-Jewish dialogue of the 1920s, with Jews such as Martin Buber, Leo Baeck, or Franz Rosenzweig, should have been outdated. The distorted and distorting one-sidedness of anti-Judaism effective in the 1920s was especially due to the fact that biblical exegesis had neglected or weakened the statements of chapters 9 through 11 of the letter to the Romans, where Paul, in view of the Jews' rejection of Jesus Christ as the Messiah who had come, counters the opinion that "God had repudiated his people" (Romans 11:1) by explaining that, when the full number of the Gentiles had come to find the gospel, then all of Israel would be saved (Romans 11:26). Thereby, a solidarity of both is proclaimed that overarches all opposition between Jews and the church of Christ. This solidarity was pre-established in the person of Paul (Romans 9:3-4), and ought to find its theological place in today's Christology, contrary to all traditional neglect. Here we see a theological deficit at the root of Christian anti-Judaism, a guilty misperception of the reason why Jews and Christians belong together in salvation history. A clearly recognizable feeling of Christian superiority even ruined the earlier Christian-Jewish dialogue, as it was perceived, on the Jewish side, to be a hurting contempt for the powerless people of the Covenant on the part of the allies of the powerful. Under such conditions, the Jewish religion had to put up with being defined from outside by foreign categories, without an adequate chance to express itself in such a way that Christian theologians could fully perceive it. From these presuppositions, the way was not far to the silent abandonment of the Jewish religious institutions destroyed in the pogrom and of the people who belonged there. Guilt in scholarly theology must be contemplated just as much as guilt in the church's behavior.

After 1945, silence, oblivion, and evasion took the place of a frank and mourning look into such failure. Only the 1980 resolution of the synod of the Rhenish regional church on the renewal of the Christian-

Jewish relationship — drafted and adopted after moving conversations with survivors of the Holocaust — has clearly revealed the theological dimension of the question of guilt, together with the outlook on theological consequences, and led to a necessary theological dispute.[56] Judged historically, anti-Judaism in theology and church was a grave obstacle to public expression of trends toward resolute solidarity with the discriminated Jews, trends which existed in the Confessing Church, in official church communiqués. Thus the regime could exacerbate its persecution measures undisturbed.[57]

Even more effective than Christian anti-Judaism and racial anti-Semitism was the socio-cultural enmity to Jews. This disapproval found confirmation again and again in the high percentage of Jewish citizens participating in the progress of modernization that influenced many sections of the population. In Germany, especially strikingly since the founders' crisis of 1873, a reconstruction of living conditions was imperative. For the popular explanation of impending concomitant circumstances of industrialization and modernization, it was a welcome excuse to regard the evil that would befall the people not as a problem of the construction of "free competitive economy," but as the consequence of Jewish machinations.[58] The remarkable contributions of Jewish citizens to German development were suppressed or negatively reinterpreted. The more a Christian-conservative mentality was harbored that was not open to modern developments but fixed on the good old German and Christian conditions and customs, a restoration of which was expected to overcome all predicaments, the stronger was the inclination to regard liberal modern Jewry as being in fact the primary agent in the disintegration of old bonds — a one-sided and distorted perception of the reality of society and of Jewish existence.

The anti-Jewish attitude of the time was promoted in the Protestantism of the 1920s and 1930s by a theology that incorporated nationalistic ideas. Klaus Scholder named it "political theology," and discussed it in a chapter along with the Jewish question in Protestantism.[59] Since it is deci-

---

56. See above, chapter 6, and Wolfgang Huber and Ilse Tödt (editors), *Ethik im Ernstfall. Dietrich Bonhoeffers Stellung zu den Juden und ihre Aktualität* (München: 1982).

57. See M. Smid, *Deutscher Protestantismus und Judentum* (München: 1989).

58. Rürup, *Emanzipation*, 108ff.

59. Scholder, *Die Kirchen und das Dritte Reich*, volume 1 (Frankfurt/Main et al.: 1977), 124-50.

sively characterized by a strict religious bond to the (German) people's traditional nationhood, I prefer the name "theology of nationhood" for this widely held line of thinking in the 1930s. In its opinion, Jews, both in their Jewish peculiarity and in liberal assimilation, cannot but jeopardize nationhood as a binding supreme religious value. What was socio-psychologically declared to have disintegrating effects was now also condemned by reason of Christian-theological standards. This interplay of a one-sided view of societal processes in which Jews had a role, and the nationalistic-theological enhancement of the disapproval of Jews, must appear to us to be a guilty combination of natural theology that conforms to the spirit of the times (Karl Barth), or to predominent current ideas, and a narrowed perception of reality. For people who held this view of reality, the utmost possible effort was to demand that restrictions on and segregation of the Jews should be settled legally and justly. To risk one's own existence by objecting to the discrimination and persecution of Jews was out of the question.

In this perspective, guilt and failure not only occurred where there was no protest and intercession for the Jews out of a certainly not unfounded fear of the regime's repressive measures, and where aid was lacking for the persecuted Jews — including the baptized Jews. Guilt was already incurred where the societal reality was perceived in a prejudiced and narrow way, and where theological traditions were accepted or developed that fostered the reflex action of ousting Jewish fellow citizens. Human beings are not only responsible for living up to accepted or self-imposed ethical standards, but are also responsible for their own view of reality, and for their own theology which determines this view. Faced with that failure and guilt painfully evident in attitudes toward the crimes of November of 1938, we cannot simply distance ourselves morally, or just condemn it. Today's dealing with it will have to contemplate critically and overcome productively that view of reality and that theology which rendered possible what we recognize as guilt, and guilt's fatal consequences.

13 Dealing with Guilt in the Church's Confession and in the Justice System After 1945

1990

I. The Initial Situation After 1945

When the National Socialist regime had collapsed, the curtain was drawn that with astonishing efficiency had concealed the crimes of the wielders of power. The concentration camps and other horror chambers of the Third Reich opened, and they confronted the German population with a shocking reality. Certainly, tens of thousands had fairly well been informed before, and millions had to some degree known of arrests and of casualties in the concentration camps, of the deportation of Jewish fellow citizens to Eastern Europe, of euthanasia murders, and of many other deeds of violence. But they either could not or were not willing to believe that these were no frightful errors, or arbitrariness on the part of individuals or of certain organizations, but belonged to the core and essence of Hitler's regime. Now, the gruesome scene was in view, and almost everyone was faced by the incredible facts and the enormous scope of the crimes. The population of Weimar, for example, was compelled to look at the mountains of starved and mutilated corpses in the Buchenwald concentration camp.

I had spent the five years of the war on the fighting front. This had been a world of its own. All attention was directed toward the opponent, who lay facing us, and our world almost ended only a couple of kilometers back in the base. I knew shamefully little about what happened behind the front. After the capitulation, in the Soviet prison camp at Telschai, where forty thousand of us were packed together on the premises of a school, we were shown documentary films about concentration and extermination camps. Filled with doubt, I asked myself: Is this manipulated Soviet propaganda? Wanting to hear about this with greater certainty, I went from one trustworthy fellow prisoner to the next in order to ask him: Have you seen such things with your own eyes? The horrifying Yes came quickly, from the second or third person I asked. He had had to witness extermination in the area of Riga. But can I be exonerated from guilt because I did not know, for the simple reason that I was on the front? After all, we soldiers waged Hitler's unjust war of aggression — but not even we theologians had learned that one must refuse to participate in an unjust war.

The mass crimes could no longer be denied. But in the need and chaos of postwar times, when more than ten million people had fled from their homes in the eastern regions of Germany and did not know where to stay and how to survive, when hunger and black market reigned, when millions of prisoners of war were deported, when rumors about the Red Army's brutalities, but also about many a misdeed and act of retribution on the part of the Western Allies, were passed on by word of mouth, there was little time and energy left to deal with German guilt. Of course, the occupation forces took up this matter. They wished to de-Nazify, to re-educate the Germans either democratically or socialistically and anti-fascistically, and exorcise the evil spirits from them. However, they failed thoroughly, and with bad consequences. The Germans, caught under this pressure, ever more vehemently made the occupiers accountable for their misdeeds and crimes — the bombardment of the civilian residential areas of large cities, the Soviet mass murders of Polish officers in Katyn and of their own population, the atomic bombs dropped on Hiroshima and Nagasaki. There was enough material to distract from German misdeeds. Much too late did the occupiers realize that only the Germans on their own could really come to recognize and cope with German guilt. It was too late, since under the pressure of Allied measures and blunders the intra-German confrontation of Nazis and Nazi opponents had long been leveled in favor of a solidarity of survival. Common defensive reactions against the occupiers' measures, which were perceived as unjust and absurd, increased ever more. When the Allies had handed over the legal proceedings in the chambers of justice and appeal [*Spruchkammern, Berufungskammern*] to Germans, non-Nazis who participated in the de-Nazification soon found themselves discredited, defamed, and isolated. The Social Democratic Party lost significant sections of its postwar electorate because the despised reputation of being a "party of de-Nazifiers" became attached to it. The attempt by the occupying powers to awaken recognition of guilt from outside and in a top-down fashion, and to hand over the perpetrators to their deserved punishments, ended, on the whole, in miserable failure, and effected exactly the opposite of what had been intended. It had indeed not been realized that guilt, even the major guilt of mass crimes perpetrated among a people, can only be dealt with by this people. I will sketch out, even if briefly, incompletely, and often one-sidedly, the dealing with guilt that nevertheless happened in this bungled situation and in spite of adversities, with regards to two institutions — the Protestant church, and the justice system.

II. The Church's Confession of Guilt and the Counter-Reaction

After the collapse of the National Socialist regime, the churches had a virtually unique advantage. Everyone knew that Hitler and many of his accomplices had been inimical to the churches and had planned their liquidation. Further, what had been not been possible in any other institution — not in the university, not in the army, not in industry and commerce, and not in social establishments — had occurred here: public and even organized protest, which the Party assessed as absolute opposition. Certainly, the Party ascribed to the churches in general what was borne by only a strong minority, namely, the church struggle, or rather the determined struggle of parts of the Confessing Church that was not merely fought for the church's self-preservation, but included the protest against various forms of public injustice. Interrogation, punishment, arrest, confinement in concentration camps, and the death of some clerics in these camps were consequences that had consciously been taken into the bargain. Now, church members could speak freely, and could face the occupiers with some self-assertion. The Confessing Church also seemed predestined to find ways of dealing with the guilt incurred through the now obvious crimes, and ways of dealing with the perpetrators.

Yet the situation was not quite so clear, particularly because it could not be known how far the Confessing Church had the backing of congregations and Protestantism in Germany. There was a stubborn national-Protestant tradition that massively opposed the confession of Germany's guilt for allegedly patriotic reasons. This tradition was well known among the representatives of churches of other nations in the Protestant ecumenical movement. After the First World War, the German representatives in the ecumenical movement had struggled passionately — and, according to what was known at that time, even rightfully — against the article 231 of the 1919 Versailles Treaty that ascribed to Germany the sole guilt for the war.[1] Would the same sort of thing repeat itself?

This had to be settled at the first meeting of a delegation from the Ecumenical Council of Churches with the provisional Council of the Protestant Church in Germany [*Evangelische Kirche in Deutschland*] in Stuttgart, an almost completely destroyed city, on October 18 and 19, 1945. There was considerable anxiety on both sides as to how this would end up.

At this meeting in Stuttgart in the fall of 1945, the pathway toward a new ecumenical community, which also meant increased help for the starving German people, was cleared through the Stuttgart Declaration of Guilt. It was formulated specially for and at this meeting, and was not really addressed to the German public. There, however, the Declaration dropped like a bomb, when the general press, without prior authorization, published it one-and-one-half weeks later under screaming headlines.

The *Kieler Kurier,* for example, chose the headline "Protestant Church Confesses Germany's War Guilt" with a national-Protestant undertone suggesting high treason against the state — and this in a part of Germany where the natives were almost outnumbered by refugees from the eastern parts of Germany, whose minds were still under the horrifying impression of the Red Army's recent invasion.

The most conspicuous statements in the Stuttgart Declaration ran like this: We know "ourselves to be not only within the great community of suffering, but also within a solidarity of guilt with our people. With great pain, we say, Through us, boundless suffering has been brought on many peoples and countries . . . Certainly, we have struggled through long years in the name of Jesus Christ against the spirit that found its frightful expression in the National Socialist regime of violence. But we accuse ourselves that we have not confessed more courageously, have not prayed more faithfully, have not believed more joyfully, and have not loved more

---

1. See Bethge, *Biography* (above, chapter 6, note 24), 144, the statement by Friedrich Siegmund-Schultze, "This war educated our German people to peace, this peace educated it to war."

fervently. Now, a new beginning shall be made in our churches . . . [They] set about . . . cleansing themselves of influences that are foreign to their faith, and giving rules to themselves.[2] . . . We hope to God that, through the common service of the churches, the spirit of violence and retribution that today tries to become powerful anew all over the world, may be warded off, and that the spirit of peace and love come to prevail, in which alone tortured humankind can recover."[3]

After the publication in the press, a storm of indignation arose. A few quotes, mostly from letters to the bishops of regional churches, hint at the nature of this storm. "The resolution effectively plays into the hands of our merciless enemies. They could not wish for better support for their measures of suppression and extermination." "You will understand that a wave of discontent is running through the congregations, since such a confession on the part of the church is throughout met with incomprehension. We are convinced that the declaration was worded differently, and was improperly interpreted. For our nation would surely never forgive our dear Protestant church, or absolve it from its curse, if it had made a confession of this kind and in this form."[4]

What can be concluded from these and other characteristic reactions is, in my opinion, the following. The curtain that had mostly hidden from the population the gruesome National Socialist mass murders and exterminations had indeed been pulled back. Yet Germans were so preoccupied with their own need, with arbitrary and unjust measures of the occupation forces, and with inner compulsions to repress guiltiness, that a large section of the population at best wished to see German guilt measured against foreign guilt. The general tendency was to regard themselves as the poor victims of hostile arbitrariness, without considering who had started the war and the concomitant atrocities, and had extended these beyond all previous limits. Could the bombardments and the internment camps of the occupation forces really be mentioned in the same breath as Auschwitz and Treblinka?

Only a small section of the church membership understood the confession of guilt. Everyone knew that the Confessing Church had fought hard and suffered greatly. There was scarcely anyone among those who

2. In the Third Reich, the National Socialist church policy had come to dominate the church rules [*Kirchenordnung*] to a large extent.

3. Martin Greschat (editor), *Die Schuld der Kirche* (München: 1982), 102. Preliminary drafts, the final text, and reactions to the Stuttgart Declaration are on pp. 100-119.

4. Greschat (see previous note), 117-18.

signed the Stuttgart Declaration who had not experienced prisons, penitentiaries, or concentration camps from within. How was it that precisely these people were now accusing themselves? Was this an unfair trick? After all, the disaster had been caused by fanatical and brutal Nazis. Now the fact was forgotten that the Nazis had had millions of fellow-travelers [*Mitläufer*] and accomplices, and millions of lookers-on, opportunistic, apathetic, or paralyzed by fear, and that the partial cooperation, the toleration, and the silence had rendered possible the misdeeds of the regime. If there was talk of guilt and repentance, then the misdeeds of the others ought to be openly named, as well. But the occupying powers would not allow this.

The lack of comprehension indicated the extent to which major sections of the population were estranged from and opposed to a biblical-prophetic understanding of guilt and repentance. Theologians as popular as Helmut Thielicke articulated this incomprehensibility with propagandistic effectiveness, and thus seemed to legitimize it theologically.[5] A declaration of guilt could be deemed a loathsome and hypocritical gesture of feigned humility, in the intention to purchase the victors' approval, rather than enduring the defeat silently with manly pride.

All these postwar arguments sidetracked the way in which the Confessing Church had dealt with guilt already during the Third Reich. Far from posing as the ostentatiously wiser [*besserwisserisch*] and innocent victims of the Nazi regime, the Provisional Church Administration and like-minded members — men like Martin Niemöller, Dietrich Bonhoeffer, and others — prior to 1945 asked first and foremost what they and the church owed to the faithful. When in September of 1938 an outbreak of war was most probable because of Hitler's political aggression against Czechoslovakia, the Provisional Administration, mindful of the church's conformity with war enthusiasm and perseverance slogans [*Durchhalteparolen*] in the First World War, ventured to draw up, in a quite different tenor, a prayer liturgy for the worship service of congregations on September 30, which spoke of the church members' own guiltiness for a coming war.[6] The consequences of this call to repentance were severe punishment and the reproach

5. See Ernst-Albert Scharffenorth, *Helmut Thielicke. Ein lutherischer Theologe in der Nachkriegszeit*, pp. 145-66 in Wolfgang Huber (editor), *Protestanten in der Demokratie. Positionen und Profile im Nachkriegsdeutschland* (München: 1990).

6. See Kurt Meier, *Der evangelische Kirchenkampf*, volume 3 (Göttingen: 1984), 54-55, and Kurt Scharf, *Widerstehen und Versöhnen. Rückblicke und Ausblicke* (Stuttgart: 1987), 112-13.

of treason against the fatherland. When Hitler stood at the peak of his power and prestige after the triumphant victory in France in 1940, Dietrich Bonhoeffer, in a 1941 manuscript for his planned book on ethics, wrote a confession of the church's guilt that was both detailed and concrete. I will cite but one short passage. "The church confesses that it has witnessed the arbitrary use of brutal force, the suffering in body and soul of countless innocent people, that it has witnessed oppression, hatred, and murder without raising its voice for the victims and without finding ways of rushing to help them. It has become guilty of the lives of the weakest and most defenseless brothers of Jesus Christ"[7] — and here Dietrich Bonhoeffer thought chiefly of the Jews as "brothers of Jesus."

The Stuttgart Declaration thus lines up with the Confessing Church's confessions of guilt, even if it looks rather pale and vague compared with Bonhoeffer's statements. For the church membership and for the German public, however, even such general but truthful Stuttgart statements like "Through us, boundless suffering has been brought on many peoples and countries" were already too much. People did not wish to hear this in the hour of their own need and misery. But was it not true, that precisely now, when a new beginning was at stake, the church owed the people the harsh truth, and had to steer a course to counter the inclination toward self-pity and hardened self-righteousness?

Here we approach the fundamental question of the right and significance of the church's confession of guilt, from which in postwar times churches and church groups often withdrew, with the exception of those who placed themselves in the tradition of the uncompromising Confessing Church. The three examples given — the prayer liturgy in the Sudeten crisis of 1938, Bonhoeffer's 1941 confession of guilt, and the Stuttgart Declaration of 1945 — have traits in common.

1. As the confession is primarily made before God, and subsequently before the people, the Church first expresses its own guilt, and thus gives an impulse to a critical recognition of guilt also by those who are farther removed from the church.
2. The church's confessions speak not only of active offenses, but also of guilt-incurring complicity, in which all get entangled who accept as lookers-on, affirming or silent, the crimes and the injustice that oc-

7. DBWE 6, 139.

cur before their very eyes, or about which they could inquire. Without this mostly silent complicity, the actions of euthanasia and mass extermination, and the preceding deportations, would not have been possible in the Third Reich.

3. The general confession of sin in Sunday worship services aims at also making people aware of concrete guilt, offense, and sin in everyday life, both in the personal and in the public dimension.

4. Almost every one of us feels obstinate inner resistance when it comes to recognizing our own concrete guilt. The drives toward self-justification, especially the subconscious ones, are enormously strong in us. This shows in the public reaction to the Stuttgart Declaration of Guilt just as it shows in our interaction with other people. As a general rule, we are capable of speaking to another human being openly of our own guilt only if the other one, for his part, speaks of his own guilt. Thus, we make our own behavior dependent on the other person's behavior. The fetters of such dependence on mutuality are broken by the church's confession of guilt, in that it begins as a confession before God, and from there goes on to the brother, the sister, the neighbor, and the political community (Matthew 18:21-35).

5. The human being who trusts in forgiveness becomes more free to clearly perceive his own guilt in its depth, concreteness, and scope, and to give up the self-justification that veils this guilt.

6. Forgiveness before God means that the other's admission of guilt is not made a precondition of one's own confession of guilt. In view of God's forgiving, Bonhoeffer wrote, "Confession of guilt happens without a sidelong glance at the others who are also guilty."[8]

7. Recognition and confession of guilt frees from a fixation on the past. Repressed guilt indirectly and unwittingly takes effect, deforms our knowledge of reality, and makes us prone to mis-assess our own position in this reality. It blocks our capability for new community with those to whom we would otherwise be bound by a reciprocal relationship of guilt. Here too, Jesus' saying holds true: "The truth shall make you free" (John 8:32).

In the ecumenical movement, the Stuttgart Declaration of Guilt did have the liberating effect that one could expect from it, but it did not have

8. DBWE 6, 136.

it among the German people. In earlier times, wars, catastrophes, and revolutions have often resulted in major religious revival and renewal movements. After 1945, revivals occurred individually, also in groups, but not on a large scale. Protestantism, by largely objecting to a concrete confession of guilt, locked out the possibility of internal renewal springing from a central dimension of faith, and rejected the gift of justification by grace alone. Thus, to the shame of theology and church, the issue migrated to the secular realm. In 1967, the psychoanalysts Alexander and Margarete Mitscherlich published their moving book, *Die Unfähigkeit zu trauern. Grundlagen kollektiven Verhaltens* (the inability to mourn: foundations of collective behavior). In 1987 appeared the book which in its journalistic form appealed to many, *Die zweite Schuld, oder Von der Last, Deutscher zu sein* (the second guilt, or, on the burden of being a German) by Ralph Giordano.

Nevertheless, there is at least one great breakthrough for the Church — the 1965 *Ostdenkschrift* (memoir on the eastern regions) by the Protestant Church in Germany that treats the topic of expulsion and reconciliation *(Vertreibung und Versöhnung)*. It became an essential precondition for a new policy of understanding with Germany's Eastern neighbors who now owned the territories from which Germans had been expelled. At the center of this memoir stood the hard task of admitting and forgiving guilt.[9]

III. Dealing with Guilt in the Justice System After 1945

One of the very big tasks of the postwar justice system was the creation of conditions of constitutional rule of law *(rechtsstaatlich)*, in accordance with legislation. This could not happen without coping with the guilt and crimes of Nazi times. However, extraordinary difficulties stood in the way. The justice system was deeply entangled with the old ruling system, had

---

9. This was preceded by the November 6, 1961, Tübingen Memoir of a group of Protestant personalities. A noteworthy sentence from the memoir reads, "We cannot acquit any of the political parties of the reproach that they frequently withheld from the people the truth that must be known, and instead said what they thought people would like to hear." See Georg Picht, *Die Verantwortung des Geistes* (Olten/Freiburg: 1965), 411-18. Without one of those who signed this memoir, namely, the jurist Ludwig Raiser, the *Ostdenkschrift* would not have come into being.

actively participated in many a misdeed, and had on the whole not been particularly resistant to the ideological demands of this arbitrary rule. One aspect of this process was therefore that the justice system had to cope with its own past and with guilt in its own ranks. There was a basic internal problem that showed itself especially clearly in 1946.

After the American occupation force had acknowledged the failure of its de-Nazification policy, it proclaimed a so-called Liberation Law.[10] This took effect on March 5, 1946, and soon provoked massive protest on the part of the Protestant churches. They asserted three legal tenets that allegedly had been insufficiently considered. First, the tenet of *nulla poena sine lege,* meaning that a deed should only be punished if it violated a law that had been valid at the time of the deed. Accused jurists defended themselves by maintaining that they had merely adjudicated and acted according to the laws of the Third Reich, and could not be punished on the basis of later laws. Second, the church protest demanded that only unjust deeds be punished, but not dispositions of mind [*Gesinnungen*]. Finally, it was demanded, in accordance with constitutional proceedings, that the Liberation Law must not shift the burden of proof of their innocence to the accused, but that the justice system had to be burdened with the proof of the punishable deed and guilt.[11]

These were three solid principles of positivistic law, asserted in a situation that was extremely unfavorable for their implementation. For if twelve million de-Nazification procedures had to be carried through, if the justice system itself had to exclude from its own ranks or condemn those liable to penalty, how should this be done? For example, in the state superior court district of Bamberg, of 302 judges and prosecutors only seven remained in the late summer of 1945. Only these seven had not been mem-

---

10. More precisely, the Law for Liberation from National Socialism and Militarism. See Gebhardt, *Handbuch der deutschen Geschichte,* volume 22 (Stuttgart: 1980), 115-16. This law introduced a second phase of de-Nazification, with more participation of the various German authorities, especially the prime ministers of the states of Hesse, Bavaria, Württemberg, and Baden.

11. The text of the memorial of the Protestant Church in Germany, signed by Bishop Theophil Wurm, is in Vollnhals, *Entnazifizierung und Selbstreinigung im Urteil der evangelischen Kirche. Dokumente und Reflexionen* (de-Nazification and self-cleansing in the judgment of the Protestant church: documents and reflections) *1945-1949,* 118-23. This protest signaled a significant change in the mood among the church leaders regarding punishment of guilty conduct during the time of the Third Reich.

bers of the National Socialist German Workers' Party.[12] This may be an extreme example, but is nevertheless a characteristic one.

The problems became even more complicated by the fact that members of the National Socialist Party, among them many an "old guard" [*Alter Kämpfer*] of the early years, had often been only nominal party members, and had, partly from the outset, partly from a certain time later, in no way acted in accordance with the regime, or with Nazi ideology. Quite a few of the prosecutors and judges, and quite a few of the defense attorneys had at great personal risk pleaded cases or handed down sentences that brought upon them heavy reproaches and various sanctions by fanatical representatives of the regime. The Confessing Church, especially until 1935, had so often prevailed in the courts against National Socialist-oriented church and state authorities, that the regime deemed it necessary to remove most church procedures from the justice system and have them adjudicated by a *Beschlußstelle* (decision office) within the Reich ministry of the interior.[13] Yet the many partisans, opportunists, careerists, and those servile to the powers that be [*Obrigkeitshörig*], who had helped to make possible the functioning of the National Socialist regime and its misdeeds, were hiding behind such intellectually independent and courageous jurists and civil servants.

The legal tenet of punishing no one who had acted in accordance with valid laws created the biggest problems. The National Socialist regime had created a very opaque legal situation by eroding the constitutional rule of law and a proper state of justice [*Verfassungs- und Rechtsstaat*]. On March 23, 1933, when the German *Reichstag* (the national parliament) passed the so-called Enabling Act [*Ermächtigungsgesetz*], the competence for legislation was surrendered to the government, and thus in practical reality to Hitler. Moreover, on June 30, 1934, Hitler ordered and led an action, in which the allegedly high treasonous leadership group of the SA around Ernst Röhm, and with them, quite a number of those in opposition to Hitler who had nothing to do with Röhm, were murdered without any legal

---

12. See p. 86 of Joachim Perels, *Staatliche Kontinuität nach 1945?* (continuity of the state after 1945?), in M. Bennhold (editor), *Spuren des Unrechts. Recht und Nationalsozialismus. Beiträge zur historischen Kontinuität* (traces of injustice: justice and National Socialism. Contributions to historical continuity; Köln: 1989).

13. By reason of the Reich law dated June 25, 1937, regarding the "decision procedure in legal matters of the Protestant church." Meier, *Der evangelische Kirchenkampf* (see above, note 6), volume 2 (Göttingen: second edition, 1984), 67.

proceeding. Instead of a unanimous protest, the exact opposite arose from the German justice system. Carl Schmitt, the leading and world-famous authority on national law, quickly wrote in the *Deutsche Juristenzeitung* (German jurists' newspaper), on the occasion of the murders, his infamous article, "The Führer Protects the Law" [*Der Führer schützt das Recht*]. Schmitt maintained that Hitler in the hour of danger, by virtue of his leadership, had also been the supreme lord of justice. "The true Führer is always judge as well."[14] The surrender of law and justice system to Hitler's arbitrariness was thereby legitimized.

Alongside the regular justice system, special courts were created, the superior of which was the People's Court [*Volksgerichtshof*], and the special courts were supplemented with the praxis that the police, and especially the secret state police, or Gestapo, which had been subordinated to the Reich Leader SS Heinrich Himmler, could interrogate, arrest, torture, and send people to concentration camps without any legal proceedings. Finally, the Führer's written or oral commands attained virtually the status of legal orders. For example, in the case of the euthanasia murders, a Führer order was the basis on which 100,000 adults and 20,000 children were killed. The so-called drumhead courts-martial [*Standgerichte*], toward the end of the war, killed shoals of people under suspicion of refusing to continue the senselessly destructive war, without even complying with the minimal formal rules that the military penal code provided for this. Thus, Dietrich Bonhoeffer, Hans von Dohnanyi, and many of their friends from the resistance, could in the end, after two-year-long procedures for some of them, simply be hanged or shot as adjudicated by the drumhead court-martial under a veneer of residual legality.[15] After the war, those who had perpetrated these murders under a threadbare veil of legality were not punished.

In the postwar situation, when the dead could no longer speak up for themselves, while the perpetrators could make exact agreements with one another, and reliable witnesses were hard to find, effective prosecution of perpetrators was very difficult. Almost all of them could adduce alleged commands and orders, the origin of which was the Führer, that rendered

14. Quote in Gebhardt (see above, note 10), 97.
15. See Elisabeth Chowaniec, *Der "Fall Dohnanyi" 1943-1945. Widerstand, Militärjustiz, SS-Willkür* (*Schriftenreihe der Vierteljahrshefte für Zeitgeschichte*, volume 62; München: 1991).

their activity legal. The positivistically interpreted legal tenets paralyzed the jurisdiction with regard to these groups of perpetrators. If a sentence was indeed passed, it was mostly due to some incidental infringements and cruelties that had happened by the way and that could for once be proven. What had to be proven was not only that the accused had broken the law, but that law which had been valid at that time had intentionally been broken.

The basic problem that lies herein was recognized early on. For example, Adolf Arndt, a consciously Protestant jurist, racially persecuted in the Third Reich, at first active in Hesse after 1945, and introduced into the Social Democratic Party by Kurt Schumacher, denied that the Enabling Act, the Führer's commands, and the special courts were in general formally legally valid and binding. True, it was correct that, according to the general understanding of the law, a revolution that brought forth a new state would set up a new binding law. But the National Socialist rule, Arndt argued, had not come into being through a revolution, but through "usurpation," forcing its will on the public in ways that were similar to a coup d'état. No new state had been created, whose goals would have had to be legal security and peaceful order, but a criminal regime had usurped the control over state bodies to itself, and had demonstrated its illegal character via a continual chain of lawbreaking.[16] To see this differently would mean to do further injustice to those who had exercised the right to resistance at the cost of their lives. The great Heidelberg jurist Gustav Radbruch, a decided defender of legal positivism until 1933, approached this view somewhat, even though he accepted the notion of natural law which Arndt had rejected, in that he spoke of "legal injustice" — justice that, while formally counting as law, materially offends the law so greatly that it can only be termed legal injustice.[17]

These critical considerations of the legal situation in the Third Reich did not gain ground in the postwar justice system. Thus the possibility of convicting Hitler's "blood judges" was blocked in countless cases. One instance was the procedure against Hans-Joachim Rehse that has been widely known since 1963. As Roland Freisler's judicial assessor [*Beisitzer*]

---

16. Arndt, *Gesammelte juristische Schriften. Ausgewählte Aufsätze und Vorträge 1946-1972* (München: 1976), *Das Verbrechen der Euthanasie* (1947), 269-84, and especially 24-27, as well as *Die Krise des Rechts* (1948), and *Agraphoi nomoi. Widerstand und Aufstand* (1962), 87-97.

17. Radbruch, *Gesetzliches Unrecht und übergesetzliches Recht* (1946) in A. Kaufmann (editor), *Widerstandsrecht* (*Wege der Forschung*, volume CLXXIII; Darmstadt: 1972), 349-61.

in the First Senate of the People's Court from 1942 on, he had signed at least 230 death sentences with his own hand. Rehse was acquitted in 1968. No appeal occurred, since Rehse then died. Only in February, 1985, forty years after the end of Hitler's Reich, did the German Federal Parliament [*Bundestag*] declare all decisions of the People's Court to be null and void.[18] At no time, so it was argued, had the People's Court been a court. It had instead been an instrument of terror for the implementation of arbitrary National Socialist rule. Yet is this not true for almost all of the special courts, and in particular for the Gestapo and the Security Service of the SS? The judgment came thirty-five years too late. On October 21, 1986, the prosecutors' office in Berlin irreversibly closed the case of the People's Court.[19] Apparently these matters now belong in the province of the historians rather than in that of the jurists.

How did the justice system deal with the problem of guilt after 1945? The findings are almost paradoxical. By holding onto indispensable constitutional legal tenets, for the sake of future legal security, the justice system became in many instances incapable of classifying evil deeds perpetrated in Nazi times as legally punishable injustice. In consequence, even jurists from the murderous People's Court could pursue their careers in the Federal Republic unhindered. This had the grotesque result that eventually, when someone was on trial for grave offenses against men of the resistance, not only the accused, but also the prosecutor and the judge or judges could be one another's former Party comrades. One can easily imagine what family members and descendants of those who were persecuted and victimized by the Nazi regime, or of those who were executed as resistance fighters, thought and think about justice, guilt, and atonement in Germany's postwar justice system.

But not only has the outcome of the legal proceedings against National Socialist perpetrators — the many acquittals, or minor punishments for proven incidental crimes, mostly with early release from custody — contributed to the forgetting and suppression of National Socialist injustice. These proceedings also had an evil impact on research into contemporary history [*Zeitgeschichte*], especially regarding the image of members of the resistance. Since most of the important resistance

18. According to Giordano, *Die zweite Schuld* (see above, toward the end of part II; Hamburg/Zürich: 1987), 134.

19. Giordano (see previous note), 160.

activists were no longer alive, their persecutors, when brought to trial, could enter their previously agreed upon versions of what had happened before 1945 into the record, and have witnesses substantiate these versions. Researchers to the present day have to rely on such court documents. An example will illustrate.

Superior War Court Justice Manfred Roeder, after he had hunted down the members of the so-called Red Orchestra [*Rote Kapelle*], conducted the interrogations of Hans von Dohnanyi, Dietrich Bonhoeffer, and Joseph Müller from April of 1943 on, using extortionary threats. Beginning in 1949, the prosecutors' office of the district court in Lüneberg searched for evidence against Roeder. The wide-ranging inquiries filled fifteen volumes. For decades, the ministry of justice of the state of Lower Saxony [*Niedersachsen*] withheld the sixteenth volume, the 750-page-long final report giving the reasons for the resolution to put an end to the prosecutor's inquiry proceedings, from the state archives. The volume was neither included nor registered there until — after a vain petition to the minister of justice for its release — the sixteenth volume was finally handed over to the state archives in May of 1987, thanks to the intervention of the prime minister. The contents of the sixteenth volume, produced by a prosecuting attorney whose National Socialist leaning was proven, is a major source for the untruthful defamation of Hans von Dohnanyi's resistance activity that is found in a small sector of historical research on resistance.[20] This occurrence shows in an especially crass fashion how the echoes of National Socialist influence in the postwar justice system have falsified, with lasting effect, the image of opposition to and resistance against the Hitler regime, by means of a prejudiced production of documents, while authentic sources from the time of the Third Reich were lacking. They may continue to do so, if research is not able to judge and use the documents of judicial inquiries in the postwar justice system most critically.

For me, what is at stake is not primarily accusations against the postwar justice system. Even Carl Schmitt, the ideological trailblazer for Hitler's arbitrary justice system, could continue to assert his wide intellectual influence — albeit after 1945 without a professorship. My concern is the underlying problem. A crucial factor is that liberation from the Nazi regime had to be brought to the Germans from outside, which put them —

20. See Romedio G. Graf von Thun-Hohenstein, *Der Verschwörer* (the conspirator; Berlin: 1982), 241, corrected in a later pocket edition of this book.

at least in the Federal Republic — into a position in which they appeared to be direct successors to the legality [*Rechtsnachfolger*] of the German Reich. Had one of the attempts of the resistance to assassinate Hitler, or the overthrow planned for July 20, 1944, succeeded, perhaps even via the stage of a limited civil war, then the revolutionarily created new German state would have been able to resolutely set up a new legal system, and to declare National Socialist injustice legally to have been injustice — which only began in 1985 with the Federal Parliament's decision regarding the People's Court. On this basis, the lack of retribution, and the suppression of guilt and injustice, would in no way have been possible to the extent that we have come to see in the postwar decades. The great collective of followers and accomplices of the National Socialist system who penetrated all of Germany — especially German elites — surely could not have so quickly, so inconspicuously, and so incomprehensibly become invisible, hide that which had happened from the eyes of the public, and suppress it from their own consciousness.

Surely, we must not forget that many who had supported National Socialism from 1933 to 1945, and who, after 1945, could have been subjected to punishment or retribution, reversed their own thinking and attitude. What was called "cold amnesty," or "the great peace with the Nazi perpetrators," has contributed to a new democratic consciousness that not merely sprang from opportunism, but also from conviction. It is only astounding that there appear to be hardly any literary testimonies as to how this "inner path" was really traveled. In the case of a theologian as renowned as Friedrich Gogarten, those who, especially at the beginning of the Third Reich, experienced his support of the German Christians as a seduction, might perhaps have had a right to an explanation of the great shift from the 1932 proclamation of the "bondage" [*Hörigkeit*] to the state,[21] to the 1953 theses on maturity and secularization in his book on "doom and hope of modern times."[22] Similar cases are influential theologians such as Paul Althaus, Emanuel Hirsch, Werner Elert, and several others.

The opinion held by neo-conservative philosophers, historians, and ideologues that the systematic non-disclosure of guilt perpetrated in the Third Reich was a political necessity in postwar Germany, without which a

---

21. Gogarten, *Politische Ethik. Versuch einer Grundlegung* (Jena: 1932).

22. Gogarten, *Verhängnis und Hoffnung der Neuzeit. Die Säkularisierung als theologisches Problem* (Stuttgart: 1953).

reconstruction would not have succeeded, distorts partially correct facts of the matter [*Sachverhalt*] by generalizing. Indeed, twelve million de-Nazification trials would not have been possible without causing heavy damage to the sense of justice and communal living in a new democratic society. An uncompromising legal prosecution of crimes and blatant offenses, focusing on a relatively small but relevant group of individuals, recruited preponderantly from the ruling and responsible elites, would have corresponded with the public's sense of justice, and would have limited the virulent process of suppression. Since this did not happen, single prosecutions took and take place — attempted far too late, which renders strict proof almost impossible — that are perceived as compensatory acts, with discomfort in many quarters, especially if one considers the consequences for the families, both of the victims and of those belatedly accused after decades.

If that violence, murder, persecution, and discrimination which happened under Hitler's rule is seen as the first and fundamental guilt, then the publicist Ralph Giordano certainly is entitled to speak of a "second guilt," namely, a guilt incurred by suppressing, glossing over, and not coming to terms with this first guilt in the postwar decades. Younger generations cannot be directly implicated in the first guilt. My generation — those who at that time were very young — is still implicated. The liabilities following from the first guilt, however, also burden the younger people. As for the second guilt, matters are different. It is shared by whoever simply accepted, after the war and until today, what happened and what was suppressed, without inquiring into the results of this failure to ward off and to cope with guilt that affect our political community to this very day.

Is this truly still relevant today? Just now, a book is being published on "Peace with the Soviet Union: An unfinished task", to which I, too, have contributed.[23] This was preceded by years of discussion, in which the call for a *Denkschrift* by the Protestant Church of Germany on this subject was repeatedly made and repeatedly rejected. The rejection does not trouble me in one regard. In many memoirs, there is too much compromise. In this book, we can submit our contributions with less compromise, and thereby, perhaps, provoke the great public discussion that is needed. It will

---

23. See Heinz Eduard Tödt, *Gefangenschaftserfahrungen und Versöhnungsbereitschaft*, 331-43 in Dietrich Goldschmidt (editor), *Frieden mit der Sowjetunion — eine unerledigte Aufgabe* (Gütersloh: 1989).

then be seen how highly relevant for today the problems are that must be tackled.

IV. Admission of Guilt and Justice

After all that I have lived through in seven decades of this century, I must say, justice is not the way of the world, not even under a constitutional rule of law. Only rarely can one recognize directly and from the outside how injustice and guilt catch up with the perpetrators. The church and the justice system, both of which are charged with the great responsibility of dealing with guilt, are themselves deeply entangled in the suppression of guilt and the irritation of the sense of justice. I see this especially crassly in research on contemporary history. However, I cannot help but ponder on this in my own life. The five years of participation in Hitler's war of aggression are a truly burdening memory. Perhaps, in my old age, I am beginning to understand Luther's words I learned by heart as a child, "I, a poor, wretched, sinful human being, confess. . . ."[24]

Caught by internal and external bonds, no one is spared the burden of incurring guilt. Accordingly, recognition and confession of guilt are necessary, both for us personally, and for us as participants in public life. But from this assertion, which perhaps at first glance looks like resignation, something else should grow, namely, a passion for the struggle against injustice. It is tied to the former, to the unsparing recognition of injustice in ourselves. What I often experience today is the unsparing exposure of Nazi crimes and of postwar guilt — a journalism of exposure [*Enthüllung*] in research on contemporary history as well, that condemns without mercy, without fantasy, and without distinction. Seduced by this lust for exposure, many people are no longer capable of distinguishing between perpetrators and resisters, and are incapable of recognizing what a seemingly pro-Nazi statement means in a particular situation, whether it is spoken for camouflage, or ironically, or for another important function. Whoever cannot and will not differentiate produces all-inclusive judgments. I see the generation that is young today in danger of lapsing into all-inclusive judgments about people of the Third Reich and the postwar years, seduced by mass-media exposures. My plea is: Grapple earnestly

24. The beginning of the confession of sin in Luther's *Small Catechism*.

with the fatal circumstances I have sketched. But do not let yourselves be deceived and seduced by the many voices speaking with a lust for exposure that plays down the sense of justice and makes judgments shallow and one-sided. Not only suppression, but also this way of dealing with our past deforms our relationship to reality and is part of a "second guilt." Whoever must become clear about and judge the behavior of others will do well to pause frequently and examine themself. Thereby the measures of judgment might become more precise and more just.

14 Suppressed Responsibility: Protestant Church and Theology Forty Years After the Day of the End of the War

1985

The Second World War, with its prelude, its battles, its sufferings, and its results, has transformed the civilization of our planet more thoroughly and suddenly than perhaps any previous historic event. Europe, up to then a political and economic center, had to give up colonial empires, was divided into a Soviet and an American sphere of influence, and from then on in the East-West conflict was reminded of its duty as an independent ally of one side or the other, as a security buffer zone, and as the most sensitive area of confrontation and cooperation. We Germans, misled by a misanthropical and megalomaniacal leadership, have instigated this war, and with it, the downfall of Europe. As the defeated ones, we have realized last of all what has been changed or overthrown in all the world in the postwar decades since September 1, 1939, and May 8, 1945. The British, Dutch, French, Spanish, Portuguese, and Italian colonies were decolonized, the former colonial powers had to seek compensatory earnings in their own lands to make up for the earnings lost from their colonies, and had to develop new relationships with the so-called Third World. But decolonization was executed all too mindlessly, and the decolonialized parts are in a wretched condition.

Since the war, we Germans deal with the loss of the regions to the east of the rivers Oder and Neisse, the division into East and West Germany, the dreaded pressure of the Soviet Union, and the activities of protection and hegemony of the United States of America. Nobody can foresee how long that will last. Only wishful thinking that is blind to political reality can hold that we are safe, secured through the North Atlantic Treaty Organization and the German Federal Army, under the conditions of the new instability of the nuclear system of threat and deterrence. After having sown the wind, we are still reaping the consequences of the tornado which miserably expired forty years ago after it had ripped open the floodgates of mass annihilation that had been unimaginable before. German extermination camps for opponents, for Jews, Russians, Poles, and other Europeans, but also the acts of terrorism of Dresden and Hiroshima, and the archipelago of Soviet death camps, along with Japanese genocide activities, lie in the path cut by this storm of destruction.

Guilt did not remain confined to the instigators of the war. In the letter to the Romans, the Apostle Paul writes, in reference to Psalm 14, "No one is righteous, not a single one. No one is reasonable, no one seeks God in earnest. All have gone astray, they all together have become useless. No one does good, not a single one. Their throats are open graves, their tongues speak deceit."[1] Although the context in the letter is different, I cannot but think of this terrible summing-up when I remember the horrors of the war and its results. But this accusation against all parties does not exonerate us. On the contrary. We were the ones who are guilty of having unleashed the furies.

We? We Germans? In the meantime, most of us were born so late that it can no longer be said that they participated in guiltiness. But all of them have to participate in taking the consequences, that is, in being answerable for that which their folk became guilty of before their birth, unless they dissociate themselves from the land in which they were born, and acquire a new nationality. Whoever realizes this may begin to ponder. Was it really impossible to hinder Hitler's seizure of power, his rapid march through the institutions toward a dictatorial Führer state, his obvious practical and ideological preparations for war? And after the war, what did those do who indeed did not hinder it? These were unrelenting but vain questions, mostly repressed or not asked in order to spare parents or grandparents. But questions that simmer under the covering. This makes the younger generations' perception of the older generations just as uncertain as it is irritated.

At a session in the beginning of November of 1984 in Travemünde, the synod of the Protestant Church in Germany discussed the 1934 Theological Declaration of Barmen and the "Path of Protestant Christianity in

1. Romans 3:10-13.

Germany." Professor Ebert, a member of the synod, born in 1937, asked a personal question, "What has moved me most of all is that the Barmen Declaration seemed to have included no directive for Christians in Germany to object to military service in Hitler's war. The second Barmen thesis clearly speaks of the joyous liberation of God's creatures and the thankful service to them. Despite this, the Christians at that time were not able to withstand the coercion to conform. They not only conformed to and tolerated the regime, but really became killers in Hitler's army. This question haunts me, because I transfer it to our times and question myself, The Barmen confession is valid for us as well. To what do we conform? Where do we collaborate?"[2]

Naturally, Ebert's apparently insensitive and condemning word *killers* provoked enraged admonitions, and the habitual explanation that the professor was of course too young to understand. He himself declared that he regretted the inappropriate expression *killers*. His concern ought to have been worded differently. "I beg your pardon" (275).

The synod member, Colonel Walter von Lossow, answered "as an officer in the German Federal Army, and your Christian brother," avowing that "I cannot conceal from you that I was shaken most deeply that, in this synod, in which we address each other as 'brother' or 'sister,' such a word should be used at all. I will have to explain to my German comrades in the army, and certainly also to my allied comrades, what has happened here, and I will do this as chivalrously as is demanded by my profession" (280).

Why did the synod member feel duty-bound to explain to "allied comrades" a statement which forty years ago the Allies had made about Hitler's army? Did he apply what had been said of Hitler's army to the German Federal Army, which should rather be disconnected from the former? A strange reaction, and perhaps just as indicative as Ebert's unseemly word *killers*. Both utterances together show how explosive the Second World War is as a topic of discussion even today.

Some of the synod members gave an honest account of their service as soldiers in the war. This obviously had a liberating effect on the synod. "Only after the war did it become clear to me that my membership in the Confessing Church had not prevented me from lending a hand (as a

2. P. 272 in *Lübeck-Travemünde 1984. Bericht über die siebte Tagung der sechsten Synode der Evangelischen Kirche in Deutschland vom 4. bis 8. November 1984* (Hannover: 1985). Page numbers of this report are inserted in parentheses in the following text.

Handlanger) to the greatest criminal of all time, as I say occasionally," declared synod member Dr. Siegfried Müller, and he spoke of recognizing his sin and failure (283). After such statements, Colonel von Lossow could more openly speak of his real problems. "You do not believe how incredibly difficult it is to make plain, to a generation that is without any relation to these matters, the narrow path between performing a rightful and guilty duty, and warding off criminal action, thinking, and planning" (287). He asked not to be pulled to and fro between theological and ethical opinions.

Do we hear in these sentences a wish for an unequivocal legitimation by the church of the commission of the German Federal Army within NATO, and thus for relief of the fundamental problems of conscience that inevitably arise when a stand has to be taken on war with weapons of mass destruction? And do we hear in this wish a reproach that the theological and ethical discussion has remained ambiguous and fruitless? The synod's concluding statement suggests that the answer is yes.

But can confusion be avoided when forty years have passed after the end of the war, and only now matters are discussed openly, or when only now — instead of merely postulating the common moral responsibility of Christians for peace — the biographical situation of those who at that time were entangled in guilt is laid open to contemporaries and other generations, for example at a synod session of the Protestant Church in Germany? Why was this not possible up to now, at least in the church all over the country? How does it come to pass that reflecting together on the Barmen Theological Declaration opens up new spaces for free discussion? Does a public comprehension of the entanglement in guilt in this war begin here, at long last?

I myself, born in 1918, was drawn into the events of the war from beginning to end. In 1939, after the two years of compulsory military service, I hoped to take up theology at the university. Instead, I went with the active troops — in one of the best German infantry divisions, as it turned out — into the Polish campaign. Was there an alternative under the then prevailing external conditions of life? Was I aware of an alternative internally, through my knowledge and intentions? At that time, conscientious objection to military service meant a death sentence. Very few Protestant Christians took this path. One of them was Hermann Stöhr, who had a doctorate in politics, was secretary of the German Alliance of Reconciliation, and was a member of the World Alliance for Promoting International Friendship through the Churches. Bonhoeffer was ready for that path. Many of Jehovah's Witnesses consistently objected to military service. Information regarding conscientious objectors was withheld from the public. We actually had no alternative solutions during the entire war. Desertion, or evasion abroad, or the like, was out of the question. The Führer, to whom we had sworn an oath of allegiance, had his hand firmly on us. But not only he. We were tied to "the German fate"[3] internally as well. My Schleswig-Holstein regional church did not teach me the Barmen Theological Declaration. I got to know it only after the war and after five further years of being a prisoner of war in Russia. But my church taught me what Werner Elert had programmatically and pointedly demanded in his widely distributed 1937 brochure on the Christian and the folk's will to defense [Der Christ und der völkische Wehrwille], namely, the unconditional commitment to one's own people [Volk], as a "natural order" [Ordnung] created by God. I was taught that, according to the law of God, I was unconditionally duty-bound to my nation, even up to the sacrifice of my life. Any attempt to reject Elert's false teaching after the war met with apologetic or offended reactions.

In 1939, I did distinguish between the National Socialist regime and Germany. The godless character of the system had provoked in me the wish and resolve to study theology. I thought I had dissociated myself from National Socialism. On September 2, 1944, I explained to two lieutenants in my artillery department — both of them fell in the next weeks — what had long been my outlook. "If Hitler wins, then we Christians, especially the theologians, will be brutally oppressed. If Stalin wins together with the Western Allies, then our fate will be a different and yet comparable subjugation. In both cases, I see no future. What I — as an officer in the reserve — can solely do, is to bring the troops who are entrusted to me through the war with the least possible casualties, and that means full effort in battle in one's own section of the front. Troops that retreat in disorder under pressure will instantly be in danger of being ground down and suffering dreadful losses of men and horses." Our horses — I can hardly make that clear to anyone today — counted emotionally for many of us.

In this impasse, I was still "lending a hand to the greatest criminal of all time." Just four weeks before the conversation with the two lieutenants,

---

3. Compare, for example, the position of Paul Althaus. Aside of the 1934 Ansbach Recommendation, see his books Die Deutsche Stunde der Kirche (the church's German hour; Göttingen: 1933) and Obrigkeit und Führertum. Wandlungen des evangelischen Staatsethos (the powers-that-be and leadership: transformations of the Protestant state ethos; Gütersloh: 1937).

my men, through their full effort in battle, had prevented the collapse of the German northern front. Thereby, however, they had given Hitler and Himmler and their bloodhounds more time to gas hundreds of thousands in the annihilation camps. We received medals for bravery. But behind us, the nameless victims from many European peoples, above all, the Jews, died in the factories of extermination. Even though it seems unbelievable, I came to know this only after the war. Was it my personal guilt to be uninformed? Was it my personal guilt that I did battle for my people's future chances, and was not at all ready to capitulate, or go into captivity, but would rather die — and that I actually lengthened Hitler's murderous rule? Was it my personal guilt that I had won a considerable, but finally insufficient, distance from the opinions of the Lutherans who at that time were famous in theology and the church, Friedrich Gogarten, Emanuel Hirsch, Wilhelm Stapel, Werner Elert, and Paul Althaus? They were the authors of the only theological writings I came across in the nationalistic church [*volkskirchlich*] situation on the Schleswig North Sea coast. Could I have said after the war, in view of the pictures and documents from the concentration camps, that it was not my guilt that I, following these teachers, had fought with unconditional readiness on the front? Could I, on the other hand, unreservedly assent inwardly to the verdict of guilty? After all, I had no alternative, neither externally nor internally. My inner condition or socialization had not opened up, let alone unconditionally commanded, the path of conscientious objection to military service.

It is obviously inadequate to think here only in terms of personal guilt. The mobilization at the end of August of 1939 made me a passenger on a "moving train," and the points of "my" train had already been shifted in the years from 1930 until 1933, long before I in any respect had come of age. Had I been included in a more than personal destiny in history that dictated this role to me and made me guilty? In Romans 5:12-19, Paul speaks of such an inclusion. He himself, who once had "beyond all bounds persecuted God's community, and tried to destroy it,"[4] saw himself included in a train of events, and in need of redemption. With the fall of humankind, sin entered the world, and death invaded all human beings, "because they all have sinned." So there is no possibility for the individual to remain free from sin and guilt. Human beings are not only under external compulsion, but have long internalized their inclusion in the train of sin-

---

4. Galatians 1:13.

ful events, and have adapted to living under circumstances in which guilt is concrete in each case, but not seen through. Guilt is not adequately grasped in terms of the moral failure or moral blamelessness of an individual. Nevertheless the individual, included in the fatal train of events that is connected through guilt, remains morally responsible. It was possible to fight morally blamelessly in the war without personally violating international law. It was possible to reject Hitler and his regime and yet to be included in the fatal connection, knowingly-unknowingly, "lending a hand to the greatest criminal of all time," as the synod member Müller has put it.

Taking this into account, the difficulty we had and still have to bring ourselves to acknowledge our guilt should become understandable. As German soldiers and officers, we waged war at greatest personal risk. We can surely not wish that our many comrades, friends, and brothers fallen in the war are deemed worthy only of being called "killers in Hitler's army." The morale of many of the fallen doubtlessly deserves admiration still today. When the war is discussed in private, one can still hear that "Never again, and nowhere else, have I experienced one standing up for the other as vicariously as was the ethos of the troops on the front." I confirm this judgment. But the horrible truth is that, precisely with this high morale of comradeship and staking one's life, we objectively were instruments in Hitler's designs of genocide, whether we knew or intended this or not. The few who had the possibilities and the means in hand to change that — I mean the top leadership especially of the army — were not able, and above all not in time, to resolve on action against Hitler. And people who tried to bring them to this resolve, such as Hans Oster, Hans von Dohnanyi, and Dietrich Bonhoeffer, had not even the backing of the Confessing Church. That generation was too much under the sway of awe of the powers that be, and lack of courage to act in free responsibility connected with guilt.

Why was no one able to stand up in 1984 and say, "On the question which professor Ebert has raised in light of the Barmen Declaration, we already had an exchange of views in all personal openness at this or that synod twenty-five or fifteen years ago?" Why was the openness with which, for example, church president Hild, an officer of the Second World War, accepted what was legitimate in Ebert's question,[5] still a novelty? Surely the Stuttgart Confession of Guilt of 1945 had been followed by all kinds of church declarations on the question of guilt. But such declarations obvi-

5. Pp. 280-82 in *Lübeck-Travemünde 1984* (above, note 2).

ously met with so many inhibitions and hesitations that it was hard for us to get from generalities down to what is biographically concrete.

There are enough historical explanations for this: for example, the mistaken method of de-Nazification. It was forced upon the Germans from without, and paralyzed the perhaps existing will from within to clarify matters. It rather provoked an exonerating and veiling solidarity with compatriots who were entangled in Nazism, instead of leading to an open acknowledgment of guilt, repentance, and conversion [*Umkehr*].[6] Theology was no exception. Never did the theological teachers, whose influence made me go to war, give an open and theologically reflected account for the path they took during the Third Reich, and for the guilt they incurred by helping to veil the truly fundamental antagonism between the confession of faith in Jesus Christ and the barbaric ideology and religion of National Socialism. Never did they candidly inform the public of the delusions through which they themselves had been misled. Furthermore, their blindness, with its objective function of misleading others, was hardly regarded as a criterion for judging their theology. Their teaching is passed on and interpreted in the standard works of German theology as the classic theology of the preceding generation — as if their attitude vis-à-vis the Third Reich and the war were biographical accidents irrelevant to theology. What perception of theology is this, which can disregard the consequences and presuppositions of theological teaching in life?

In a journal for Protestant ethics,[7] we should ask what would result from the recollection of the Second World War for theological ethics. For me, the most urgent task is to search for criteria that make responsible action possible even within a fatal train of events. If it is correct that in the years 1930 to 1933 the points were nearly irreversibly shifted for Hitler and his war, I am first of all urged to ask, How could it happen that so many were uninterested in, or blind to, the impending barbarism, even though it was exposed in Hitler's widely available book *Mein Kampf*? Nearly all of this can be explained, in the light of the situation at the end of the Weimar Republic, by research into contemporary history, history of ideologies, and socio-psychology, when Hitler's ability to delude people, and his appeal to their wishful thinking, are taken into account. But ethics presupposes and

6. Compare above, chapter 13, part I.

7. The present text was first published (in German) in *Zeitschrift für Evangelische Ethik*, volume 29 (1985), pp. 127-38.

indicates that the course of history, notwithstanding many fatal sequences of events, is not immovably determined, but leaves space for human beings to find orientation and to make their own decisions, which of course must be related to the events.

When examining theological ethics from those years of fate, 1930 to 1933, two things stand out. First, the incongruity of an extremely subtle reflection within the field of theology, and an almost naïve ignorance of what happened in politics and society, and of the dangers included in these events. The theologian Friedrich Gogarten could publish a widely read "Political Ethic" in 1932 that took no notice of any work of political science, and only considered a few pronouncements on political law which favored National Socialism. Theological ethics appeared incapable of studying and using insights and information from critical sciences in order to form a theological judgment. For this reason, theological ethics was helpless, and prone to adapt to National Socialism and its preparations for war. When I see how theological departments — but also the regional churches — lost interest in the teaching of ethics during the last decade, and how many a theological examination neglects or is disoriented in ethics, then I fear comparable results in cases of newer dangers that threaten our civilization.

Second, I notice how little theology opposed specific theological criteria to the trends of *Weltanschauung*, or worldview, in those critical years. Then, like today, statements of Christian ethics were, above all, intended to be "communicable," intelligible to all, or, as it was expressed at that time, "in accord with the people of the nation [*volksgemäß*]." Even within the Confessing Church, the Barmen Theological Declaration was criticized as remaining silent "about proclamation in accord with the people."[8] This tendency prevailed in ethics, while theology claimed for itself an eschatological orientation throughout, fully convinced, looking to the end and judgment that would come from God. In hardly any respect did this eschatological orientation influence ethics so that criteria other than those of the times were used. Ethics was more interested in the religious needs of the nationalistic [*volkskirchlich*] church.

---

8. According to notes taken by Karl Lücking at a meeting in Leipzig on May 22, 1934, this was an objection by Hans Meiser, bishop of the regional church of Bavaria; see p. 92 in Carsten Nicolaisen, *Der Weg nach Barmen. Die Entstehungsgeschichte der theologischen Erklärung von 1934* (Neukirchen-Vluyn: 1985).

It can be demonstrated that some theologians, who in earnest kept to this eschatological orientation also in ethics, nearly "automatically" felt urged to oppose and resist Hitler's regime. I am thinking of Karl Barth and Dietrich Bonhoeffer, in whom I am especially interested because their ethics advance both a critical perception of the reality of our world in the perspective of the gospel, and the development of criteria for orientation and decision making in faith. Bonhoeffer's *Ethics* manuscripts are the only Protestant ethic written in Germany during participation in the resistance against an inhuman regime, which reflects the spiritual conditions of political resistance. We can learn from Bonhoeffer's writings what would have been required in theology and church for opposing National Socialism, and with it, the imminent Second World War. There was little inclination, since the 1950s, to remember the war concretely, and just as little motivation to reflect further and rethink for the own situation an ethic that is pervaded by the experiences of the resistance.

The war from 1939 to 1945 could still be limited to the regions of the industrial nations. Such a war is hardly probable in the future. In the question of war or peace, industrial civilization as a whole is at stake. What torments me, when I remember the Second World War, is whether Protestant ethics today is motivated and alert enough to face the crucial problems more adequately than fifty and forty years ago. Will Christian ethics again fall prey to interest in the national church religion that made it so hard after 1933 to withdraw from the spell of the Hitler regime?

Index